T0392430

Le Théâtre du Soleil

Le Théâtre du Soleil traces the company's history from a group of young, barely trained actors, directors, and designers struggling to match their political commitment to a creative strategy, to their grappling with the concerns of migration, separation and exile in the early decades of the twenty-first century.

Béatrice Picon-Vallin recounts how, in the 55 years since its founding, the Théâtre du Soleil has established itself as one of the foremost names in modern theatre. Ariane Mnouchkine and her collaborators have developed a unique and ever-evolving style that combines a piercing richness of shape, color, and texture with precision choreography, innovative musical accompaniment, and multi-layered, metaphorical dreamscapes. This rich, storied history is illustrated by a wealth of spectacular rehearsal and production photos from the company's own archive and interviews with dozens of past and present members, including Mnouchkine herself.

Judith G. Miller's timely translation of the first comprehensive history and analysis of a remarkable, award-winning company is a compelling read for both students and teachers of Drama and Theatre Studies.

Béatrice Picon-Vallin is the former director of France's research laboratory for the Performing Arts at the National Center for Scientific Research (CNRS) and professor of Theatre History at the National Conservatory of Dramatic Arts (CNSAD) in Paris, France. She is currently Director Emeritus of Research at the CNRS.

Judith G. Miller is professor of French and Francophone Theatre and collegiate professor at NYU, New York, USA and affiliate professor at NYU, Abu Dhabi.

Le Théâtre du Soleil
The First Fifty-Five Years

Béatrice Picon-Vallin

Translated by Judith G. Miller

With Emelyn Lih, Drew Jones,
Amelia Parenteau, and Rachel Watson

Documentation: Franck Pendino and
Béatrice Picon-Vallin

Routledge
Taylor & Francis Group

LONDON AND NEW YORK

First published in English 2021
by Routledge
2 Park Square, Milton Park, Abingdon, Oxon OX14 4RN

and by Routledge
52 Vanderbilt Avenue, New York, NY 10017

*Routledge is an imprint of the Taylor & Francis Group,
an informa business*

First published in French 2014 under the title: *Le Théâtre du
Soleil, les cinquante premières années* by Actes Sud Editions,
18 rue Séguier 75006 Paris and the Théâtre du Soleil

British Library Cataloguing-in-Publication Data
A catalogue record for this book is available from the
British Library

Library of Congress Cataloging-in-Publication Data
Names: Picon-Vallin, Béatrice, author. |
Not enough room for printer logo
Title: Le Théâtre du Soleil: the first fifty-five years / Béatrice
Picon-Vallin; translated by Judith G. Miller.
Other titles: Théâtre du Soleil. English
Description: Abingdon, Oxon; New York: Routledge 2020. |
"First published in English 2020; First published in French
2014 by Actes Sud Editions ... Paris"–Title page verso. |
Includes bibliographical references and index.
Identifiers: LCCN 2020001526 (print) |
LCCN 2020001527 (ebook) | ISBN 9780367141554
(paperback) | ISBN 9780367141547 (hardback) |
ISBN 9780429030611 (ebook)
Subjects: LCSH: Théâtre du Soleil–History.
Classification: LCC PN2639.5.T54 P5313 2020 (print) |
LCC PN2639.5.T54 (ebook) | DDC 792.0944/361–dc23
LC record available at https://lccn.loc.gov/2020001526
LC ebook record available at https://lccn.loc.gov/2020001527

ISBN: 978-0-367-14154-7 (hbk)
ISBN: 978-0-367-14155-4 (pbk)
ISBN: 978-0-429-03061-1 (ebk)

Typeset in Sabon
by Deanta Global Publishing Services, Chennai, India

This book has received support from the École
Universitaire de Recherche Translitterae ("Investissements
d'avenir" program, ANR-10-IDEX-0001-02 PSL* et
ANR-17-EURE-0025).

Contents

A word from the author

Throughout this study, the citations that are not referenced refer to the many interviews I conducted between October 2013 and May 2014 in Paris, at the Cartoucherie/Théâtre du Soleil, in Moscow, and by mail or by phone with Jean-Claude Penchenat, Sophie Moscoso, Joséphine Derenne, Georges Bigot, Gérard Hardy, Lucia Bensasson, Guy Freixe, Liliana Andreone, Étienne Lemasson, Hélène Cixous, Maïtreyi, Erhard Stiefel, Myriam Azencot, Bernard Faivre d'Arcier, Duccio Bellugi-Vannuccini, Mauricio Celedon, and Stéphane Brodt; and in June 2010 at the Cartoucherie with Ariane Mnouchkine, Charles-Henri Bradier, and Jean-Jacques Lemêtre.

Sources for other citations will be found in the notes to each chapter.

Acting and producing credits and program notes can be found at the back of the volume, reproduced as the Théâtre du Soleil imagined them for each production, each set of credits unique. They are a story unto themselves and if read carefully will reveal all kinds of information as well as a certain poetry. They bear witness to all those who have crossed the path or lived the life of the Théâtre du Soleil – some of whom I was unable to cite or mention in the body of my study. As the adventure of the Théâtre du Soleil has lasted a very long time, the names of some of the actors have changed and show up slightly transformed in different program notes. This also explains certain disparities that might be found in the captions of production shots. I have included near the end of the book in "Transverse Perspectives" a section of production photos that illustrate particular themes: they should be consulted as a complement to the iconography in each chapter. If a few photos are a little difficult to read, it is because they have come from personal archives and were not originally destined for reproduction.

I would like to thank the Bibliothèque Nationale de France, and in particular the librarian Corinne Gibello-Bernette. Thanks also to Franck Pendino, with whom I've happily navigated the ocean of images of the Soleil made available to me. These were gathered little by little, many shared by people who have lived the different phases of the Soleil's existence; those from the experience of the first ten years are particularly precious. Thanks to Liliana Andreone, who has been unfailingly supportive. Thanks to Jean-Claude Penchenat, a "living memory" of people and places whose recollections and images from the early years helped me shape the Prologue. Thanks to Georges Bigot for sharing his memories. Thanks also to Marcel Freydefont, Maurice Durozier, Georges Bonnaud, and Jean-François La Bouverie.

Thanks to Sophie Moscoso who gave me ready access to her archives and generously helped me each time I was about to lose my way. Thanks to Charles-Henri Bradier for his indispensable help in pinning down the details and for his friendship and support. Thanks, also, to the photographers, most especially to the Magnum Agency/Martine Franck archives and to Michèle Laurent, and finally to all those who, in the contagious happiness afforded by this project, made the effort to jog their memories and open their archives – and to answer my endless questions.

I have written an additional chapter for the English-language edition of this work, which covers the productions and activities of the Théâtre du Soleil through 2019. I would like to express my deep gratitude to Routledge and particularly to Ben Piggott, who committed themselves to this great editorial adventure, as well as to my research lab. This book has received the generous support of Translitterae (École universitaire de recherche, program "investissements d'avenir" ANR-10-IDEX-0001-02 PSL and ANR-17-EURE-0025). I would also like to acknowledge warmly the translator of this volume, Judith Miller, whose fluency in French and in the work of the Théâtre du Soleil has allowed her and her excellent team to reproduce with competency and enthusiasm my study.

In this changing world in which we live, on both sides of the Atlantic, across the English Channel, or elsewhere, the Théâtre du Soleil opens the way for thinking about the world differently and resisting forces of oppression, for living together in our various cultures and languages with compassion and empathy – and for creating a new theatrical language. The Soleil suggests ways to approach the sources of great theatrical traditions in order to create an art for today. It shows us how with courage and invention the concept of cultural transference can illumine collective practice.

Béatrice Picon-Vallin
2014, 2020

A word from the translator

The story of the Théâtre du Soleil has lived with me ever since I, like the author of this comprehensive and intimate volume, first saw the company's work. In my case, it was 1968, a fabled spring in Paris when the Soleil produced its *Midsummer Night's Dream,* a production that would forever anchor my sense of what acutely consequential theatre could be. I have followed, written about, and taught the Soleil since then, even directing many years ago with students at the University of Wisconsin a version of *1789*, the Soleil's stunning break-through 1971 production. Later, in 2005, at New York University, a colleague at the Tisch School of the Arts directed my translation of Hélène Cixous's last full script for the Soleil, *Drums on the Dam*. Students I have been privileged to interact with have thus lived with the Soleil almost as long as I have.

Trekking out to the Cartoucherie still holds the kind of excitement Béatrice Picon-Vallin describes when she talks about this mythic space. She captures Ariane Mnouchkine's generous welcome and the sense of a communal project. And something of the Soleil's collective ethos has, perhaps unsurprisingly, entered into the work of translating Picon-Vallin's history of the company. The translation team: Emelyn Lih, Drew Jones, Amelia Parenteau, Rachel Watson, and myself have shared and commented on each other's work, ending up, we hope, with a coherent voice that represents us as a fellowship of writers and represents Béatrice Picon-Vallin as the remarkable researcher and critic she is.

Picon-Vallin's study is the only up-to-date history of the Théâtre du Soleil, spanning some 55 years of continuous transformation but also of steady theatrical vision. To make this vast and simultaneously personalized knowledge of the Soleil as accessible as possible to English-language readers, we have on occasion added information or precisions to clarify a reference or historical moment; and we have chosen to move most of the text into the past tense, rather than keeping the "historical present" of Béatrice Picon-Vallin's descriptions, a tense more appropriate for French-language readers. Her expertise

in Russian theatre will be obvious in her several compari-
sons between the story of the French company she so admires
and that of other innovative artists in Russia in the modern
period. Throughout the study, we have also kept a capital "H"
on "History" when spoken of by Ariane Mnouchkine and/or
brought up as a concept to describe the Soleil's commitment to
speaking about contemporary times through metaphorization
and epic human stories. The Soleil itself enters "History," we
feel, as a model of how to make art in and for a community that
values every member. We hope our translation communicates
this spirit of intelligent awareness as well as the company's irrepressible appetite for creative work – a spirit apprehended in
Béatrice Picon-Vallin's ebullient appraisal.

As I write this note, I sit in the "Office" of the Théâtre du
Soleil in the Cartoucherie (a term which both means the ensemble of theatres in Paris's Vincennes woods and designates,
particularly, the Théâtre du Soleil's theatre space). I am surrounded by a wealth of material about the Soleil contained in
multiple files and documents; some of this material now being
moved to France's Bibliothèque Nationale. Much other material is still in the personal archives cited in many chapters of
this study. Franck Pendino, the Soleil's archivist, makes order
and keeps track of this treasure; and it is also his expertise and
knowledge that contributed significantly to locating the photos
and documents for the original volume, as well as the several
photographic additions to the English edition. It has been a joy
to work with him; and I am grateful for our several meetings.

I would also like to thank those people and institutions who
have helped make this translation possible: Routledge and our
editors Ben Piggott and Zoe Forbes; and particularly the production team headed by Stephen Riordan who has worked so
hard to reproduce the invaluable photographic documentation; the Cultural Services of the French Embassy in New York
City; the funding arm of Béatrice Picon-Vallin's research lab
in Paris; The Department of French Literature, Thought and
Culture at New York University, and New York University
Abu Dhabi's research support system. Most of all, the translation team thanks the Théâtre du Soleil and Ariane Mnouchkine
for exploring theatrical form with such wit and ingenuity and
for inspiring so many theatre makers, scholars, and spectators
with their intellectual daring and artistic mettle.

Judith G. Miller
2020

The Last Caravanserai: Odyssey. On tour at Lincoln Center, New York City, July 17–31, 2005. Photo by Étienne Lemasson.

The Survivors of Mad Hope (Dawn). Final tableau: the theatre troupe is like a lighthouse in a storm. "In these dark days, our mission is clear [...] to bring to ships lost in the storm our lighthouse's obstinate illuminations." (From the program/text of the play, 2010). Photo by Michèle Laurent.

Opening
For all those who have worked, or are working, with the Théâtre du Soleil

"I'm convinced that a well-conceived collaborative structure would never diminish the authority of a troupe's director, unless he had the soul of a criminal. [...] It's troupe spirit that counts – that's the greatest asset, and those who have led men confirm it."

Charles Dullin[1]

"Theatre isn't just a building with a box office where you pay money to buy a vision [...] and after that, you leave. It's a place where the world can be seen again, be thought about, and in a certain way transformed – or in any case where I believe that transformative forces can be called upon, shared, and circulated – albeit very modestly, very mysteriously – but unquestionably."

Ariane Mnouchkine[2]

In France and across the globe, the Théâtre du Soleil represents an exceptional theatrical adventure and does so from many different angles: the length of its existence, the quality of its work, its political and social commitment, the permanent self-questioning, its international stature. Nothing quite rivals the Soleil, a company led by a woman, and it is remarkable that France has been able to create and sustain such a theatre company, despite all the difficulties the Soleil has had to face and, indeed, still faces. We might also wonder how such a long trajectory has been possible – a vitality which shows no signs of slowing down.

In the title of one of the more recent productions of the Soleil, *The Survivors of Mad Hope (Dawn)* [*Les Naufragés du Fol Espoir (Aurores)*] (2010), we can discern a revealing self-portrait. The Mad Hope, a 1914 cabaret on the banks of the Seine River, parallels the Soleil of 2010, when the show was created, and even conjures up the present. The play's troupe of silent movie actors, making a film based on Jules Verne's last utopian dream, is none other than the Soleil itself. The story of the many months of making the film, with a director so focused that she works 11 months non-stop, and with actors so passionate that they never lose hope, even when their director starts to question herself, is the story of almost every Soleil production for the last 55 years – from *Ephemera* [*Les Éphémères*] (2008) to *Drums on the Dam* [*Tambours sur la digue*] (1999), and as far back as *The House of Atreus Cycle* [*Les Atrides*] (1990) and even further to *1789* (1970) and *The Golden Age* [*l'Âge d'or*] (1975): openings scheduled, then delayed, sometimes several times. Debts accumulating, despite success. Sleepless nights. Actors lending a hand to technicians and administrators – from restructuring the theatre space, to set construction, to communal meals. Art as work; art as research on how to create afresh and how to live together.

Art as risk-taking too. A troupe always on a tightrope, both financially and emotionally. A troupe that renews itself as a result of the variety of crises it's forced to confront – like every human collective. At the same time, initiating new projects, workshops, encounters – always with that great openness that characterizes the Soleil.

In *Mad Hope*, as well as in its more recent production, *Macbeth* (2014), these actors, and the technicians, as well as the "pillars" of the administration – working in the Cartoucherie in the Vincennes woods on the outskirts of Paris (a wonderland, an incredible land of theatre) – are the true survivors of mad hope. The huge and loyal company incarnates the generous, radical, and radiant utopia that Mnouchkine has always sought to bring into being, incredibly faithful, as is her wont, to the ideals she held as a 20-year-old theatre maker: her dream has always been to make "the most beautiful theatre in the world" for a large and diverse public, for spectators who would also be partners in the adventure.

In *Mad Hope's* closing scene, the troupe is likened to a lighthouse, shining brightly through the dark of a storm: this image precedes the emotionally charged final bows. In this last, unforgettable sequence, we see the company not as exemplars to follow – they are too modest for that – but, rather, as inseparable from their art and their public, inspiring spectators with the hope, even if faint, that they, too, will arrive, no matter where they start out from, at rigor, at precision, at respect for others, at the sense of community the troupe embodies: because "we are nothing without others."[3] That's the secret of performance and of life. To create, we need everyone: those who perform in silence, those who project the dialogues that are silently performed, those who follow their colleagues with spots, those who make the water shimmer, the wind blow, and the marionette of the bird fly (a "seagull" in homage to other great theatre makers)[4], those who make snow dance by shaking bits of paper out of baskets, those who from dry ice create smoke, those who crank the camera, and those, whom we mustn't forget, who produce the music and design the sound. Everyone has a part to play. In *Mad Hope*, we see all of them, one after the other. It's a super-reverberating metaphor of how the Soleil has worked for the last 55 years. We already apprehended this in the staging of Arnold Wesker's *The Kitchen*, whose action takes place during a restaurant's rush hour. Mnouchkine's production highlighted an enduring commitment to the fruitfulness and intensity of collective work.

In *Mad Hope,* the Théâtre du Soleil explores and makes palpable the secrets of theatre, thanks to how the fictional company gives shape to the birth of cinema. It had earlier done so by observing and recreating the theatricality of fairground trestle tables and an imagined Orient. With an approach to theatre making that's artisanal and a little magical – as is everything that depends on human synergy – the Soleil transports us through time and space beyond our individual selves. Having begun as nomads who had no choice but to travel, the Soleil is now rooted in the Vincennes woods; yet it carries actors and spectators away on select voyages, and it willingly leaves the woods to tour in many different parts of the world.

Four generations of theatregoers constitute the Soleil's public; and the old-timers thoroughly enjoy bringing the youngest with them. This is not a repertory theatre, as in what used to be Eastern bloc countries, where a production could live on over many years, reprised and tweaked by a director trained to do just that, a production, then, that could be seen by several generations. The Soleil's process is quite original and very removed from the usual French production system. The company always makes new work, rehearsing and performing for months, even for years, playing in other parts of France and elsewhere in the world: this touring allows them to continue to survive. Nevertheless, each new show carries the memory and markers of productions that preceded it, and from which it emerged – especially from the moment the troupe, with Mnouchkine wielding the camera, began filming its work. This creates a constant dialogue between productions and the public, the older spectators sharing with the younger ones earlier Soleil experiences by remembering them.

* * *

My own travels in this book, to the origins of what I name, without any hesitation, one of the most significant adventures in the history of theatre, have prompted me to use as guide my intuition and my perseverance. The trajectory I've discovered seems, retrospectively, unbelievably rational, even planned. Almost everything was there at the beginning, because for

Mnouchkine and the Soleil it has always been a matter of reinventing a "theatre for our times" – but reinventing from the stage, from what is concrete, from action. And along the way, building on the work of great forerunners and theatrical traditions that have always impacted the troupe's work, without limiting it.

There is so much to say about the life of the Théâtre du Soleil, and the different groups of actors who have succeeded each other in making theatre with Ariane Mnouchkine, that this book can only reflect some of what I've learned. I am indebted to the actors and theatre makers who have accompanied Ariane at various periods in her career, as well as to the "leader" herself, who speaks so lucidly about her work. It would have been, in fact, impossible to take on this fulsome and noisy universe all by myself. I will call on others when necessary, but never enough to account for everything they have said.[5]

In *Nightwatch* [*La Ronde de nuit*] (2013), a production by the Théâtre Aftaab, an Afghan theatre company born of working with actors from the Soleil, a character claims that theatre contains the "world's archives." What is certain is that on her ship docked in the Vincennes woods – which she has almost never deserted to create elsewhere – another unusual facet of the director she is, Mnouchkine takes on the world's greatest problems. History is the Soleil's major focus; the troupe asking again and again how to make history dialogue with the present, and how *not* to confine the world in a Eurocentric vision.

Notes

1 Charles Dullin, "Manifeste du Théâtre de l'Atelier," *Ce sont les dieux qu'il nous faut* (Paris: Gallimard,1922), 31–32.
2 Ariane Mnouchkine, "Changement de décor," radio program dedicated to Patrice Chéreau, France Culture (October 13, 2013).
3 See the Soleil film, *Au Soleil même la nuit* by Eric Darmon and Catherine Vilpoux, AGAT Films & Co, La Septième Art (1997).
4 The Soleil referenced here Chekhov's celebrated seagull at the Moscow Art Theatre's production.
5 Citations that are not referenced in notes refer back to the interviews Béatrice Picon-Vallin conducted between October 2013 and May 2014 – at the Cartoucherie de Vincennes, and, also, in Moscow, over email, or by phone with Jean-Claude Penchenat, Sophie Moscoso, Joséphine Derenne, Georges Bigot, Gérard Hardy, Lucia Bensasson, Guy Freixe, Liliana Andreone, Etienne Lemasson, Hélène Cixous, Maïtreyi, Erhard Stiefel, Myriam Azencot, Bernard Faivre d'Arcier, Duccio Bellugi-Vannuccini, Mauricio Celedon, Stéphane Brodt. Others are the interviews Béatrice Picon-Vallin held in June 2010 at the Cartoucherie with Ariane Mnouchkine, Charles-Henri Bradier, and Jean-Jacques Lemêtre. All of the photos used in this book that come from the personal archives of Soleil actors are now housed either in the archives at the Théâtre du Soleil or in archives housed at the Bibliothèque nationale de France.

The Clowns. The Théâtre du Soleil adopts the allure of a circus. Summer, 1969: stage design for the Avignon Theatre Festival. Photo by Joël Lambert.

Prologue: origins

"The theatre is the art of the other."[1]

Ariane Mnouchkine

The Soleil has grown bigger and bigger as time has passed. It's like no other company in France, and it functions according to rules it established at the beginning, rules that are in operation even now. A company that has its own, very special space, chosen and restored by the Soleil team, with its rituals and methods. A theatre troupe motivated by the necessity of reinventing the theatre and by faith in the notion that "theatre is greater than theatre,"[2] a troupe that's already a legend.

At the crossroads of the world of contemporary theatre, the Soleil is admired from Vienna to Sao Paulo and from Tokyo to Sydney, well known in countries as far away as Afghanistan and Cambodia. But what was it like at the beginning? Ariane Mnouchkine often says that everything was easier in the 1960s than it is today for people who wanted to do theatre together. If we look more closely, however, nothing was really that simple.

"Asia has arrived."[3]

Everything began in 1959, when Martine Franck and Ariane Mnouckine, with other friends (notably Frances Ashley and Pierre Skira)[4] created l'ATEP, the Association for Parisian Theatre Students. The group immediately became the rival of another student association at the Sorbonne that produced classical Greek theatre, a group that had not fully accepted Mnouchkine. But truthfully, things probably started earlier, most likely on the sound stages where Mnouchkine, the daughter of the film producer Alexandre Mnouchkine, who had immigrated from Russia, was a regular – even acting at times (for example, in *Fanfan la Tulipe*, 1952). Moreover, on her mother's side, her British family, especially her aunt and uncle, were immersed in the theatre: their father performing Shakespeare with the Old Vic. Mnouchkine could also boast having the French actor Edwige Feuillère as godmother.

"My childhood dream was to travel." (Ariane Mnouchkine, in *À la recherche du Soleil*, a documentary film by Werner Schroeter, Ziegler film Berlin, 1986.)

L'ATEP had a multi-faceted mission: training actors, learning about different forms of theatre in France and elsewhere, and creating shows. Some who would become theatre legends, such as Jean-Claude Penchenat and Philippe Léotard, joined the association right away. Ariane Mnouchkine headed it, and noted theatre practitioner Roger Planchon accepted the position of honorary president.[5] Mnouchkine was just 20 years old and had recently spent a year in England at Oxford, where she had performed all kinds of tasks with a student theatre company that included Ken Loach, who was to become a celebrated filmmaker. Talking about this time, Mnouchkine remembers a moment of epiphany traveling in one of England's red buses: after a rehearsal of *Coriolanus*, she knew that theatre "would be her life." Working with a film crew on stage also made her think hard about how one can represent life and the world, but she left the crew when the film was finished. Ariane Mnouchkine chose theatre because a theatre troupe never has to separate.

L'ATEP's members came from all kinds of disciplines, and Mnouchkine organized the company according to suggestions sent her by Loach in a very long letter, on her request. She set up evening acting courses, hired two teachers employed by the National Education system, Charles Antonetti and M. Azaria, and added a third teacher, Gérard Lorrin, an actor with the Comédie of Saint-Etienne. The director Sasha Pitoëff and philosopher Jean-Paul Sartre were invited to give lectures. The first show, *Blood Wedding* (1960), by Federico Garcia Lorca, directed by Dominique Serina from Charles Dullin's school, was produced at the American Center on the Boulevard Raspail. Mnouchkine took care of the costumes designed by Jacques Schmidt; and the actors included several people who would launch the Soleil a few years later: Anne Demeyer, Philippe Léotard, Jean-Claude Penchenat, and Françoise Jamet.

In 1961, after a year of preparation, Ariane Mnouchkine directed an eight-night run of her friend's, the poet Henry Bauchau's, *Genghis Khan*. Bauchau sought to explore contemporary conflicts through the legendary Khan and his conquest of China and Persia. Mnouchkine says of this experience: "We had to represent all of China,"[6] and do so in the circular expanse of the open-air Arènes de Lutèce, a Roman arena she fitted out with inclined planes and multiple staircases. At least a dozen nationalities were represented in the casting, including Philippe Léotard, Gérard Hardy, Georges Donzenac, and Jean-Frédéric Brossard.[7] J-B. Maistre, the son of the Director of the Théâtre des Nations, A-M. Julien, designed the set. Jean-Claude Penchenat stage-managed the show. The students took turns guarding set and props throughout the night. Mnouchkine took her inspiration for this production of *Genghis Khan* from the Beijing Opera's *The Jade Bracelet*, a show she had seen in 1958 at the Théâtre des Nations. Her vast cinema culture, notably films by Pudovkin and Mizoguchi, also influenced her directorial choices. Practicing with lead soldiers on a model of the set, she figured out how to choreograph movement, choruses, fights, and cavalcades, all this in the middle of trees and vegetation and the surrounding noise of Parisian traffic. White banners waving to the sound of drums suggested the wind. A student at Arts et Métiers, Françoise Tournafond, served as impromptu costume designer[8] and in just a few days repurposed the American blankets stocked and offered by the Secours Populaire, an aid group. With no budget, she managed to dye and shape them into a multitude of striking costumes. This was Mnouchkine's only directorial work with l'ATEP, which she left at the end of the year, but it was while staging *Genghis Khan* that the idea of starting a professional company took wing.

Major aspects of the Soleil could already be seen, if in outline: theatre for the people, international reach, attraction to the East, self-education for non-professional actors (humanists, or from the Institute of Political Science: J-C. Penchenat), who often went to the theatre and, even more often, to films together. Not one of them, not even G. Hardy who had attended Dullin's school or J-C. Penchenat, who had taken classes with Jacques Lecoq, had really been trained professionally. It was an expansive time for university theatre: Patrice Chéreau started his trajectory at the prestigious high school, Lycée Louis-le-Grand, in the late 1950s; in Nancy in 1963, Jack Lang created an international festival of university theatre.

Mnouchkine next took a job in the film industry as assistant director and editor; she worked with Philippe de Broca, Daniel Boulanger, and Jean-Paul Rappeneau on the script for *The Man from Rio*, released in 1964. But she wanted to leave France, go to the China that had been calling her ever since she was little: no visa, however, was forthcoming. So she went to Japan, where a six-month stay turned into a pilgrimage that lasted almost 15. Part of her voyage was with Martine Franck, who had managed to secure permission to visit China. With Franck, she traveled in Thailand, India, Nepal, Pakistan, Afghanistan, Iran, and Turkey. Just like the great theatre adventurers of the beginning of the twentieth century, Mnouchkine thrilled at the colorful, codified, and sacred forms of Asian art: she saw her first open-air Noh in Kobe at sundown, lit by torches; kabuki in Tokyo at The Asakusa Mokuba-kan Public Theatre; and bunraku with its giant puppets.

Genghis Khan. The first directorial effort by Ariane Mnouchkine with her university theatre company (l'ATEP), outdoors, in the Arènes de Lutèce, 1961. Pictured: H. Melon and P. Léotard. Photo by Martine Franck, Magnum Photos.

Third page of the contract of the Soleil's SCOP (Workers' Cooperative) with the names of the founding members. Archives Théâtre du Soleil.

The pact: the co-op of the Théâtre du Soleil

For Ariane Mnouchkine 1963 was a year of apprenticeships: theatre, cinema, travelling, and discovery. Her comrades continued on their own paths: studies, military service, but also theatre. Philippe Léotard directed Paul Valéry's *My Faust* [*Mon Faust*] and Pierre de Larivey/Albert Camus's *The Spirits* [*Les Esprits*] at the Sorbonne. Léotard also staged Marivaux's *The Pretentious Man Corrected* [*Le Petit Maître Corrigé*], while Penchenat mounted Jean-François Regnard's *The Unforseen Return* [*Le Retour imprévu*], both in the south of France at l'UNEF's student union festival, and after that in Istanbul.[9] The time was ripe to launch the theatre project already imagined in 1961: a cooperative where actors, set designer, costume designer, director, authors and adaptors, photographer, and others could all work in unhindered collaboration, according to very unusual statutes. There would be nothing hierarchical or specialized, an agreement that parallels the founding of Lyubimov's Taganka theatre in Moscow and of the Odin Theatre in Oslo, also created in 1964. Penchenat remembers tears of joy in deciding to finally do what they had planned to do all along. Everyone involved contributed to the general funds: 900 francs per person, and no one was paid anything at the beginning, except for those few who were not part of the workers' cooperative (or SCOP). People worked during the day in order to rehearse or perform at night, from 19:30 until midnight, or even later. Mnouchkine's father, whose company called itself "Les Films Ariane," became a member the day the workers' cooperative was established, on May 29, 1964, and provided in his own locale an office that would remain the administrative hub of the Soleil until it moved into the Cartoucherie de Vincennes.

The founding of a SCOP was a radical act in 1964 and remains so. Of course, company rules no longer insist that everyone participate in all of the work, as at the beginning when everyone was the same age and where all the work, be it administrative, artistic, technical, or even housekeeping, was shared. Mnouchkine explains: "I'm 71 years old now, and Sébastien Bonneau is barely 19. He does a lot more of the grunt work, which is normal." She adds: "The electricians are really electricians now, but when they have an enormous job in front of them, at least five actors will volunteer to lend a hand. Otherwise, we could never do what we do." There are currently three or four different generations of actors in the Soleil; the oldest no longer expecting to carry out the most physically demanding work. Certain specializations have developed. Charles-Henri Bradier, the co-director of the Soleil since 2009, recounts:

> The SCOP report has praised us as exemplary for the length of our existence and our success in maintaining an active workers' cooperative. The most important aspect of our commitment is equal pay, which we still believe in and practice. We do ask sometimes if this is really fair, but we always end up agreeing it is the least bad of any system we could have. It's essential for keeping our sense of balance; it keeps the generations equal by not distinguishing the different points of entry into the company. Earning the same salary establishes a strong sense of responsibility to the older members in those who enter the company later on.[10]

The first productions of the Théâtre du Soleil

> *"We were totally confident. She was an adventurer, with a bohemian side, carefree. We followed her. She was imaginative, already thinking about the future. Everything was possible."*
>
> Jean-Claude Penchenat

Mnouchkine chose as a first production Maxime Gorki's *The Philistines* [*Les Petits Bourgeois*], in an adaptation by Arthur Adamov. It opened in November 1964. This is unquestionably the most Chekhovian of Gorki's works, an unsurprising choice for someone who would incorporate the last scene of *The Cherry Orchard* in her production of Thomas Mann's *Mephisto* or have her actors work on scenes from Chekhov when they got stuck during their improvisations for *Ephemera*. The number of members in the workers' cooperative had grown: Martine Franck, the photographer, had also joined. Performed at the Maison des Jeunes et de la Culture in Montreuil, and a year later in Paris, *The Philistines* was successfully reprised in the Parisian suburbs and in the provinces. The company consequently received its first subsidies. Soon after their success with Gorki, they performed *Captain Fracasse* and then, Wesker's *The Kitchen* [*La Cuisine*], which finally made everyone sit up and take notice.

Their working methods developed in fits and starts, but their one clear direction in a theatrical culture that had always been "textcentric" was to begin rehearsing with concrete stage actions, rather than decoding the text. Reading what other theatre makers had to say and consulting specialists slowly helped them clarify how they would approach each creation. The Soleil kept on learning.

Thus in 1965–1966, while other members held down day jobs, Mnouchkine took, if intermittently, morning courses at the

The Philistines. From left to right: G. Hardy, E. Zetlin, C. Lazarewsky, C. Merlin, P. Giuliano, L. Guertchikoff, N. Carcelli, P. Besset, P. Léotard, C. Solca, J. Sagolce, S. Kachadhourian, C. Ricard. Photo by Martine Franck, Magnum Photos.

Jacques Lecoq school, Lecoq being better known and admired abroad than at home. She had already participated in a workshop he led in London. She would transmit to her actors in the evening what she had learned, and they, in turn, would develop the exercises. She pushed them to delve into choral formation, to find scenic balance, to represent textures and animals, to communicate through gesture, and to develop communal storytelling – in which one actor would start a story and others, called forth by him or her, or stepping in, would pick up the story and run with it. This latter exercise was excellent training for focus and readiness. Mnouchkine took up mask work and discovered how to work with half-masks. She launched into physical, vocal, and acrobatic training. Although she has never really liked the neutral mask, actors remember working with it while they were creating *The Kitchen*, as well as in their first year at the Cartoucherie. That's when she met Erhard Stiefel, today a "maître d'art," who became the Soleil's mask-maker.

The Philistines

Mnouchkine wanted to move the workers' cooperative to rural Ardèche in order to raise sheep as well as make theatre. She explored possibilities for a location with Philippe and Liliane Léotard. Gérard Hardy was meant to spend some time at a shepherd's school in Fontainebleau, but didn't. Energetic and determined, Mnouchkine led and the others followed, her adventurous and risk-taking spirit and her conviction that everything was possible convinced them to leave Paris. They spent five months preparing *The Philistines*, nearly two of those in Saint Maurice d'Ibie, in Ardèche, and three in Paris. In Ardèche, they rented houses or rooms, but they cooked and ate together every evening in the main house, which had been lent by the mayor. An older actor, Martine Deriche, who had performed in Jean Prat's televised *Ivanov* in 1956, was hired to play the role of the Mother. After the Ardèche experience, she left the production and Louba Guertichikoff, who had recently joined the troupe, took her place. (This kind of replacement happened frequently as time went on.)

Readings illuminating Gorki's work were assigned. The daily routine brought the group together. The actors worked not on the text, but, rather, "from the text," that is, with the text as inspiration. Prompted by her reading of Stanislavsky, Mnouchkine was already proposing a system of improvisation, inviting actors to look for the motives and the rationale behind the actions of the characters: why were they so tired of living? It was almost as if the Soleil was being trained Russian-style. Georges Donzenac, one of the original members of the company and a physical education teacher, conducted robust exercises in a field.

Recycled vintage clothing comprised the costumes for the show. The set and lighting design was by Roberto Moscoso, an Italian who had studied at the Rue Blanche School[11] as well as with Raymond Rouleau's theatrical Communauté and at workshops run by the Théâtre des Nations. Recruited by a member of the company to lend a hand, he stayed, becoming part of the "family of friends." For the props, he kept the furniture Mnouchkine had already bought at a flea market: a high boy, a Henri II table and chairs, a sofa, a stuffed parrot. He used fabric and lights to structure the space: a few projectors, lots of lace, macramé, fringed bed covers, and curtains lined with embossed material so they wouldn't be too white. These were hung from booms 2.5 meters in height, whose base was mobile, facilitating set changes. Moscoso also created the suggestion of a window with filtered light. Martine Franck's production photos shimmer with what we might call "Russianness."

"We will build the space and the time for happiness." (Program notes, *Captain Fracasse*, 1966.)

"Think about it as if it were the circus." (Ariane Mnouchkine, in M-L. and D. Bablet, *Le Théâtre du Soleil ou la quête du bonheur*, 1979, 16.)

Captain Fracasse

The next project dated back to l'ATEP and brought to fruition an adaptation of Théophile Gautier's *Captain Fracasse* [*Le Capitaine Fracasse*]. Here, the idea was to recuperate the imaginative heft of outdoor theatre, an ambulatory theatre of trestle tables, of fair actors, of theatre in the theatre, of pleasure in performance, and, especially, in working together. A new kind of work – adapting a novel – meant reading each chapter, then doing improvisations. Twenty-five actors improvised, then discussed what they had created with Mnouchkine; and she and Philippe Léotard structured and signed the text, which would be read again and reworked again by the actors. Donzenac took charge of the fight and slapstick training.

This was an ambitious project, perhaps a little too ambitious, and the first time the Soleil had encountered the figures of the *commedia dell'arte*. For the set, Moscoso started with the idea of a circus and then designed a space that recalled the traveling carts of ambulatory theatre, or Thespis's Wagon: meter-high trestle platforms that could pivot. Moscoso describes this as "a double trestle, closed at the back by a frame from which backdrops could be changed to indicate each new location." Props were rented, the stage was built (one of the actors, P. Besset, was also a carpenter); friends lent whatever else was needed. A 5 × 3-meter tower with a balcony, anchored by pillars, was built for the character Matamore (G. Hardy), the only character to wear a mask throughout the performance. Moscoso painted immense backdrops (15 square meters or more) of picture-postcard environments – a forest, a chateau, an inn, a playing space as seen from off-stage. Through the varying intensities of the color scheme, the backdrops evoked the time of day or inside and outside, without resorting to naturalism. While Moscoso produced an enormous number of backdrops, only five or six were kept. One of them, cut into two, represented the red curtains that often frame the front of the stage: for this production, actors opened them upstage to signal the beginning of the show.

The set could easily be struck and transported. The music included songs and accordion. There were masks designed by Moscoso, cardboard props, candlesticks, folding chairs, recycled costumes, all the paraphernalia of fairground theatre, that *balagan* (or carnival chaos) that Meyerhold so prized at the beginning of the twentieth century and that Jean Renoir embraced for his subject matter in the film *The Golden Coach*. Dreamed up by Moscoso while researching the show, the traveling wagon of *Fracasse* presaged the wagons built for the Soleil's film *Molière* (1976) – and all of the numerous variations on wagons and glides invented and put to use thereafter by the "jesters" of the Théâtre du Soleil. Nicole Félix, a makeup artist for film, took charge of the makeup and soon joined the company. *Fracasse* was created outdoors in 1965 on an athletic field near Montreuil's Maison des Jeunes et de la Culture. When reprised in Paris, notably at the Théâtre Récamier, where actors had no back-stage space, Françoise Tournafond, who had followed rehearsals and sketched all the actors, remade the costumes using more vibrant colors (fuchsias and reds) and with more input from the actors themselves.

Despite a successful opening and positive reviews that probably came a little too late, *Captain Fracasse* never found its public, and the Soleil began accumulating debts, taking out bank loans to keep on going. The company restaged the piece in 1968, but Mnouchkine remained dubious about its worth. It seemed too impromptu, not sure-footed enough – and that was not what she was looking for. She had a sense of what she didn't want, even if she was not yet sure of what she wanted.

The Kitchen

In October 1965, Mnouchkine decided their next production would be *The Kitchen*, written by Arnold Wesker, a young, politicized British playwright who crafted the text from his own experience working in the kitchen of one of Paris's grand restaurants.[12] Martine Franck brought the script back from England and Philippe Léotard translated and adapted it.[13] Mnouchkine says: "If I can speak of a through line in my choice of plays, it would be something like: *The Philistines* shows people who can't stand to live any longer – and *Captain Fracasse* people who want to live no matter what." What interested her in *The Kitchen* was what remains of the desire to live in people whose work has exhausted them, restaurant kitchens having become

Captain Fracasse. From left to right: P Giuliano, seated; J-C. Penchenat here called Thomas Leiclier; M. Robert. Second row: C. Merlin, H. Starck, F. Decaux. (The cast changed frequently.) From a performance at the Théâtre Récamier. Photo by Martine Franck, Magnum Photos.

Captain Fracasse. The actors G. Hardy and C. Solca in front of a backdrop representing a theatre, created by R. Moscoso. Photo by Martine Franck, Magnum Photos.

The Kitchen. Performed in a factory in May 1968. The running characters include: Raymond, pastry chef (F. Herrero) and Ida, waitress (F. Jamet). Photo by Martine Franck, Magnum Photos.

The Kitchen. From left to right: José, hot vegetables (F. Joxe); Anne, coffee (N. Félix); head chef (S. Coursan); Philippe, soups and eggs (R. Patrignani); Max, butcher (P. Forget); Liliana, waitress (F. Jamet); Peter, fish chef (P. Léotard). Photo by Martine Franck, Magnum Photos.

factories devouring their workers. About the play, she adds: "It's a very simple play, in fact, no need for explanations – and that's what popular theatre should be."[14]

The company grew bigger and renewed itself over the course of a year and a half of rehearsals. In the winter of 1966–1967, without any idea of where they would perform, they rehearsed in a hangar and in a freezing parish house on rue Pelleport in Malakoff. Everything about the play might have suggested a realistic staging, but even Wesker indicates that the cooks aren't using real ingredients, that the serving dishes should be empty, and that much of the action should be mimed. For two months at the beginning of the process, the Soleil's actors improvised. They had read the play once; and then they put it aside until the translation/adaptation was finished. Their improvisations helped them work on every character and on what each one's function was in order to understand what a head chef, a fish cook, a pastry chef did. Mnouchkine recounts that the play became a kind of "intensification of what they had originally imagined."[15]

No proscenium theatre wanted to take on the production, so the company continued rehearsing, either at the Medrano Circus[16] or at the Cirque d'hiver when the Medrano was busy.

"There are a lot of reasons to work. But there's one essential and less understood one: seeking happiness." (Program notes, *The Kitchen*, 1967.)

"Skinning a fish that doesn't exist is theatre. Seizing people's despair by the way they beat their eggs is theatrical." (Ariane Mnouchkine, in Fabienne Pascaud, *L'Art du présent: Entretiens avec Ariane Mnouchkine*, 2005, 17.)

The Kitchen. From left to right: Anne, coffee (L. Bensasson); Raphaël, assistant chef (M. Gonzalès); Berta, cold buffet (L. Guertchikoff); Philippe, soup and eggs (R. Patrignani); Max, butcher (P. Forget): José, hot vegetables (J. Weizbluth), Youssef, assistant chef (S. Teskouk); Liliana, waitress (D. La Varenne); Franck, second chef (R. Amstutz.) First Row: Alfredo, grill chef (G. Laroche); Peter, fish chef (P. Léotard). Reprised at the Elysée-Montmartre Theatre, 1969. The cast changed frequently. Photo by Martine Franck, Magnum Photos.

The Kitchen opened at the suburban cultural center of Kremlin-Bicêtre; then the show moved to the Medrano, where it became a smash hit.

Moscoso's stage design was constructed directly from his model and fastened to the floor of the circus ring, which had been enlarged and elevated by 1.2 meters.[17] The stage design opened to the audience on one side only, and consisted of metal frames covered by translucent plastic, through which the audience could see the comings and goings of the various characters, including the dishwasher doing his job. Everyone was, then, always present, even if off stage. Two metal doors, stage right and left, led out to the restaurant's dining area or to the street. The set was again easy to transport and adjust according to the constraints of the theatre in which they were to perform. Kitchen furnishings were varnished and made of light wood; the work tables and stations were covered in tin; and the professional stove boasted working elements, notably a griddle, burners, and grill. There were sinks, serving dishes, silver ware, frying pans, dish rags, bottles, stewpots, dishes, and copper pots lent by the bistro of the Montparnasse railroad station, which was undergoing renovation. There was, however, no food. The actors had improvised how to prepare the hot dishes and the cold entrées; and Nora Kretz from Lecoq's School had stepped in to work through the proper movements with them (all this duly noted in the program). She helped them master how to "create" something sweet, tart, or spicy.

Mnouchkine remembers:

> In the middle of winter when it was –5 degrees outside, we improvised handling hot plates! It was fantastic! We always worked as if for real; and for the warmups, I created relevant exercises. For example, I had a pile of plates I could break, and I'd throw them at the waitresses, yelling: "Hot" or "Cracked, you've just cut yourself." The actors practically became jugglers.[18]

A chef came by to give lessons. Jean-Pierre Tailhade, who played the fish cook, and Penchenat, who played the pastry chef, interned in prestigious restaurants. Moscoso, who was then working in the Enghien casino, spent time in its kitchens. The work became a mixture of observation and transposition, a dialectic between realism and poetry.[19] Critics compared it to Chaplin's *Modern Times* – noting the director's talent, her musical staging with its crescendos, pauses, silent moments, harmonies, and dissonances. Mnouchkine comments: "*The Kitchen* depends on a work rhythm that creates noise that in turn provokes an emotional reaction. The noises keep people from being able to speak; the noises are as important – more, really – than what the actors try to say."[20] To her mind, her work wasn't really musical, but the reason the rhythm seemed so was because it perfectly expressed the situations and relationships of the characters: "When thirty people are in the same, very urgent situation, it ends up looking like a musical score."[21] The score also made room for numerous solos. What the public found impressive, the actors found fascinating, still moved today when they recall the experience. There was abundant praise for the staging. Mnouchkine recognizes retrospectively that: "The work was very technical. I choreographed it on a dime, because I was too afraid it would get away from me."

The Kitchen won three major theatre awards in 1967: the prize from the Association of Spectators, the prize from the Critics' Union, and the Brigadier's Prize. But the Soleil did not win the Young Theatre Competition: Patrice Chéreau took the prize for his staging of Lenz's *The Soldiers*. Ariane remembers this without rancor, recalling the camaraderie of theatre people at the time, and how they had all pitched in together during the competition to get the electrical circuits working: the exhausted Chéreau would sleep in an arm chair after they'd finished.

They performed *The Kitchen* for a very long time, and every evening handed a check to their landlord, Joseph Bouglione, at the Medrano. The actors were finally able to give up their day jobs: Penchenat at the Ministry of the Interior, Hardy at a religious bookstore, Philippe and Liliane Léotard their work as teachers at the Sainte-Barbe high school. In 1968, the troupe reprised *The Kitchen* during the events of May in order to perform in striking factories in Saint-Etienne, in Grenoble, and around Paris (the Citroën plant, the Peugeot plant, and the SNECMA aircraft plant). Given free license, the actors also invented cabaret acts. Everyone would be changed by this contact with the workers.

A Midsummer Night's Dream

Mnouchkine now felt she could propose to the company one of the world's great classic texts, Shakespeare's *A Midsummer Night's Dream* [*Le Songe d'une nuit d'été*]. From the beginning, it was she who proposed and the company who agreed or didn't; most of the time, it did. She had been wanting for some time to stage this sensual, erotic Shakespeare, to explore love's unconscious, the overwhelming feeling that Jan Kott speaks about in *Shakespeare, Our Contemporary* (1962), his psychoanalytic study of the great Elizabethan playwright. Before deciding in 1959 that theatre would be her profession, Mnouchkine had begun psychoanalysis with Henri Bauchau's group: this helped

"I'd like to see a work in which profundity held out its hand to lightness, just as walking does to dancing." (Nietzsche, from the program notes, *A Midsummer Night's Dream*, 1968.)

"I remember spending three nights alone with Roberto in the circus, covering the floor with animal skins to create a brown and magical forest floor; and we could hear the elephants trumpet and the big cats spitting and growling." (Ariane Mnouchkine, in Fabienne Pascaud, *L'Art du présent: Entretiens avec Ariane Mnouchkine*, 2005, 33.)

her orient the troupe toward dream work, rather than working on the physical demands of the job. The program notes capture the approach:

> *A Midsummer Night's Dream* is the most uncivilized, the most violent play one can imagine. It's a fabulous bestiary of what sleeps in the hearts of men, nothing less than "savage Gods." Everything is direct, brutal, and un-trafficked. No fairy tale, no wonderland, but, rather, the fantastic and all that makes the fantastic poisonous, anguishing and terrifying [...]. It's also what is accidental and unforeseen, a rupture in the natural order of things, a transgression of the forbidden.

Mnouchkine was, then, proposing a daring reading of a play that had the reputation of being un-performable in France. She insisted: daring is fundamental to great theatre. But to begin, she needed an image of this fantastical world, and it wasn't coming. She turned first to photos of Africa, looking at animals in the wild. For inspiration, the Soleil watched films based on the play at the Cinémathèque but found them disappointingly sugar-coated.[22]

They settled again on the Medrano circus and again rented the space for rehearsals. Because they thought they might be there a while, they called on René Allio to improve the playing area and the acoustics. They invested in sound and lighting equipment. Philippe Léotard took on the translation and adapted the work to eliminate the feel of fairies and winged elves. Roberto Moscoso started researching what it would take to cover the floor in animal skins, as a way of capturing the fantastical imaginary that would infuse the staging. Mnouchkine remembers she wanted goats' skins and moss. To suggest the vegetal and animal nature of the forest, the circular flooring was covered in brown-spotted, cream-colored goatskins, delimited by a curtain of thin strips of wood shaped to allow an eerie stream of light to pass through. Cutouts of suns and moons were attached to the wooden strips. The actors worked barefooted, rolling about and luxuriating in the softness and the scent of the fur.

Ursula Kübler-Vian and Germinal Casado, two of Maurice Béjart's dancers, were hired to play the roles of Titania and Oberon. René Patrignani played Puck, in this production the god of "Eros," as different as possible from a sweet cupid. Mnouchkine thought about having the actors perform without clothes but changed her mind: "The public won't see characters who are naturally naked, at ease in their nudity; it will register as crass exhibitionism. That kind of daring doesn't interest me."[23]

A Midsummer Night's Dream. The Mechanicals. Center: J-C. Penchenat, P. Léótard, G. Hardy, G. Denizot (the Moon), C. Merlin (the Narrator); right: S. Coursan (the Lion). Photo by Martine Franck, Magnum Photos.

A Midsummer Night's Dream. Titania (U. Kübler) and Puck (R. Patrignani) surrounded by satyrs dressed as crested hoopoes with fantastically long-beaked masks. Photo by Martine Franck, Magnum Photos.

A Midsummer Night's Dream. Titania (U. Kübler), in tights, dances on the fur-covered stage. Archives Sophie Moscoso.

The composer Jacques Lasry, whose compositions had already been used for *Genghis Khan*, wrote the music during rehearsals, basing it on melodies sung by the actors. The entire Lasry family performed the music. Ursula Kübler-Vian choreographed a number of scenes, rehearsing them with actors on the balcony of her apartment in the Cité Veron, near Jacques Prévert's home, whom they visited from time to time. She danced the lullaby that a fairy normally sings to Titania, and made the dance speak of hidden desires. The actors crawled, did somersaults, worked from what became a living, seething ground. The company mixed new approaches with ones they had used before: improvising without text the roles of the mechanicals, using clown makeup, working with masks, having actors and dancers improvise together, working with the music that itself emerged from rehearsals. They didn't stop experimenting. Because the wood and the fur were absorbing the sound, Moscoso introduced directional mikes, a technique he would use later for *1789*. Rehearsals for *A Midsummer Night's Dream* alternated with energizing rehearsals for the reprisal of *The Kitchen*. The Soleil announced the opening for January but pushed it back to February 15. The production had cost a great deal of money; the costumes had to be entirely rethought.

While it was immensely successful, *A Midsummer Night's Dream* fared less well with critics than *The Kitchen*, and there were fewer spectators. The show had to close when the events of May 1968 and the general strike broke out. Guy-Claude François, whom they had met while performing at the Théâtre Récamier and who joined the Soleil at that point to handle the loading in and out and general construction of the sets, encouraged them to build something that could travel. But it didn't get much use. The actors Michel Piccoli and Yves Montand lent them money so they could perform again at the Medrano at the end of June. While they were working on *Midsummer*, they also created a play for children, *The Magic Tree, Jerome, and the Turtle* [*l'Arbre sorcier, Jérôme et la tortue*], in which some Soleil actors performed. Staged by Catherine Dasté, also in a magic forest filled with animal characters,

The Soleil's summer sojourn in the Royal Salt Works of Arc-et-Senans. From left to right: J-F. Labouverie (back to camera), A. Mnouchkine, P. Léotard, L. Léotard, F. Descotils (further back), J-C. Penchenat, M. Donzenac. Photo by Max Douchin.

the play was based this time on children's designs. The Soleil performed *Midsummer*, as well as *The Magic Tree* and *The Kitchen*, again in January 1969, in Grenoble, to make up for having cancelled all performances the spring before. And during this time, the company began rehearsals for *The Clowns* [*Les Clowns*].

"I won't go backwards. I can't. I want to go farther with each production." (Ariane Mnouchkine, "Une Prise de conscience," in *Le Théâtre 1968-1*, Fernando Arrabal, ed. Christian Bourgois, 1968, 124.)

"What the actors accomplished in *The Clowns*, very few French actors are capable of accepting and succeeding in doing." (Lucien Attoun, in *Europe*, 1969.)

The Clowns

The Soleil took advantage of being forced to stop their tour of *Midsummer* to take stock of where they had landed. The company accepted a proposal by the regional government of Doubs[24] to spend summer vacation at the "Saline," the Royal Salt Works at Arc-et-Senans. In the eighteenth century, the visionary architect Nicolas Ledoux had imagined the Salt Works as a utopian community that would house both the workers and the salt plant. In that exceptionally utopian environment, the second Soleil retreat far from Paris, the company would not only re-experience working and living together, but they would also come into close contact with a different kind of audience, not "Parisian" at all.

Almost all of the actors accepted the challenge, and many came with their children. They slept on camp beds. They took turns in the kitchen. They discussed the events of May, and the possible staging of Jules Vallès's novel *Jacques Vingtras*, which Philippe Léotard had adapted, or *Michael Kohlhass* by Heinrich von Kleist, a kind of French Western located in the Cevenol mountains, that Arnaud des Pallières would finally make into a film in 2013, calling it "one of the most fabulous political stories that has ever existed." They discussed the possibility of mounting *Baal*, Brecht's first play. And because of their bucolic existence, they grew closer. The poet and writer Claude Roy, a member of the French Resistance and a politically committed journalist, who spent time with the Soleil in the Salt Works that summer, summed up the experience as: "Neither a phalanstery or a commune, it's more appropriate to think of the Théâtre du Soleil as a workshop on friendship."[25]

What should the next step be? During performances of *The Kitchen* and *Midsummer*, they had worked on *commedia dell'arte*, improvisation, and acrobatics with Mario Radondi, who had a studio not far from the Medrano. Masks, which started to be used during rehearsals for a reprisal of *Captain Fracasse* and *Midsummer* for a festival in Teheran (cancelled like everything else), began to influence creativity. During their stay in Arc-et-Senans, they realized they didn't want a written text, but preferred to be a full-time theatre lab looking for a new aesthetic. Instead of enhancing or accompanying work on a play text or an adaptation, improvisation had shown itself capable of generating a show – even a text. What they learned that summer is that theatre could happen without a text, that their training would benefit from more research into forms of popular theatre, that they should leap and work without a safety net.

Mnouchkine recounts: "At first, we had intended to improvise with all kinds of stock characters – Harlequin, clowns, even the Breton comic figure Bécassine. But little by little, as we moved forward, we saw that the clowns were really modern; they took over. They didn't have the anachronistic feel of a Harlequin. So we were en route with a show solely based on clowns."[26] One evening, lit by candles, the Soleil improvised before a public come to the Salt Works from their nearby homes. The spectators were wildly enthusiastic.

Back in Paris in September after the Venice Biennale, where they had performed *The Kitchen*, they continued rehearsing in various theatre spaces lent by friends: a stage in the cavernous Théâtre National Populaire at Chaillot, under the big top of the cultural center of the Kremlin-Bicêtre, finally at the Théâtre de la Commune d'Aubervilliers, where *The Clowns* eventually premiered in April 1969, cheered on by the Commune's director, Gabriel Garran.

There were more than six months of rehearsals, resulting in a 2-hour and 30-minute production. Penchenat, who like most of the troupe went to bed every night exhausted, remembers a "show that overtaxed us physically." Only the athletic Mario Gonzalès (as Pepe la Moquette) and Max Douchin

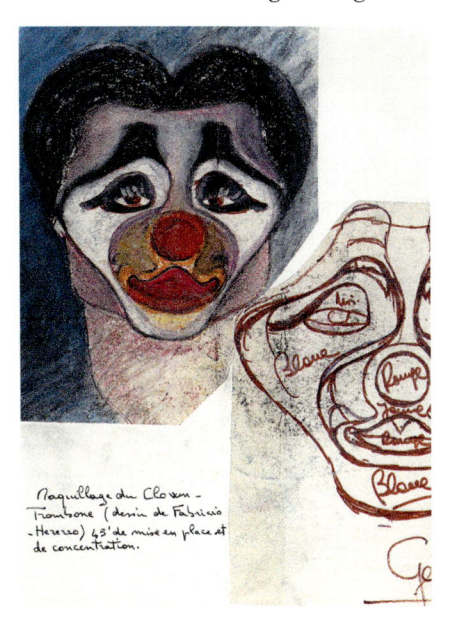

The Clowns. Fabrice Herrero's makeup sketch for the clown-trombone player (Georges Bonnaud). Herrero first designed paper sketches of what he would eventually create on each actor's face. Archives G. Bonnaud.

The Clowns. G. Bonnaud in clown makeup. Archives of Jean-Claude Penchenat.

(as Monsieur Albert) could really handle the physical demands, Douchin himself being responsible for the training. The Soleil's clowns had to learn how to project in all of their different accents, how to dance, jump, fall, pirouette, do back flips, play drums, and never lose the energy of improvising. Mnouchkine

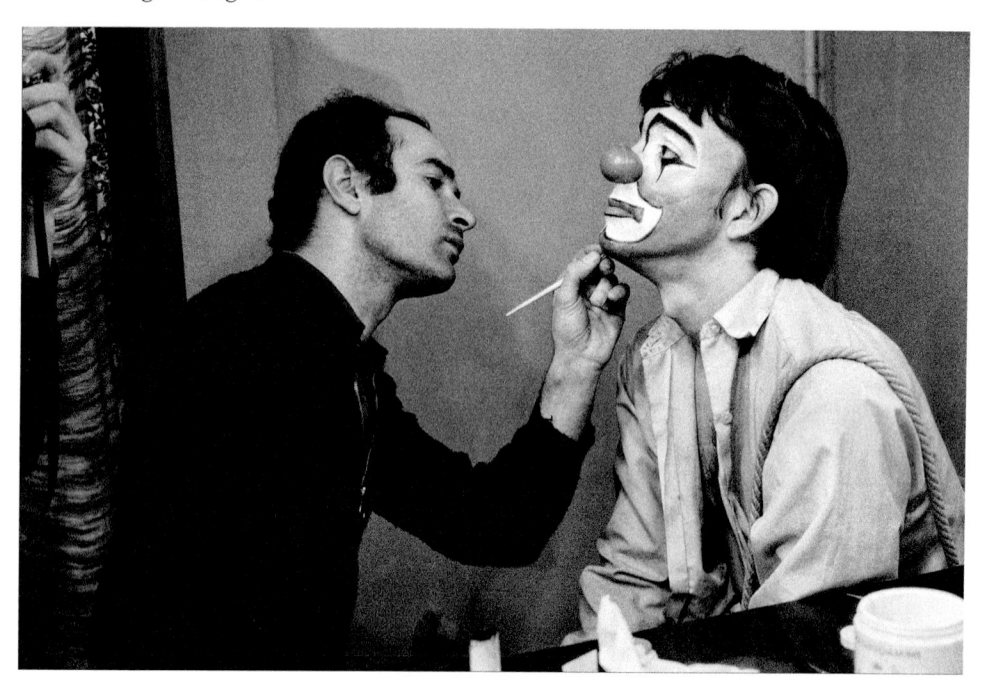

The Clowns. Makeup workshop. Pictured: Fabrice Herrero and Mario Gonzalès. Photo by Martine Franck, Magnum Photos.

The Clowns. Pictured: Anne Demeyer putting on her makeup. Photo by Martine Franck, Magnum Photos.

The "light box" set of *The Clowns*. Pictured: J-C. Penchenat and C. Merlin. Archives Jean-Claude Penchenat.

recognized even then that: "Clowns need to be athletes not just acrobats."[27] Everyone had a red nose, the basic mask of the clown – a celluloid bulb bought at a specialist's shop. But the makeup design came along slowly, developing with the improvisations: Fabrice Herrero began with patches of light, then developed the lines that would transform the actors' faces. In similar style, the costumes that had been bought here and there were taken apart, recombined, designed during the rehearsals so as not to fix the character too early nor to slight the research by creating them too late.

Although clowns are historically performed by men, the Soleil made no distinction in roles: women and men both sought to create their own clown.

The Clowns. Madame Patafiole, the fiancée of M. Laïobule (A. Demeyer). Archives Jean-Claude Penchenat.

Through individual or two-person improvisations, each actor started from scratch to create a character based on who they were and on their own concerns. Schematic plots, improvisations, physical exercises ... a lot of work but also immense

The Clowns. Ariane Mnouchkine, made up as the character Mlle. Scampouzzi, watches the actors improvise. Photo by Martine Franck, Magnum Photos.

The Clowns. Raucous entrance of the actors through the doors of the set. Pictured: J-M. Verselle, M. Gonzalès, M. Douchin. Photo by Martine Franck, Magnum Photos.

freedom. There was no particular point of reference, just some solid input: clown work with Philippe Gaulier at the Lecoq School; the book *Entrées clownesques* by Tristan Rémy; a film about the life of the clown Grock at the Cinémathèque; sessions with the celebrated Achille Zavatta, an acrobatic clown, animal trainer, and musician, whose particular accent and linguistic tics would be heard in the production. The director watched, commented: "The actors show me, and my work is to make sure that what they're finding can be read as easily as possible by the public."[28] As the first spectator, Mnouchkine selected scenes and created an order. Many improvisations were thrown out. Others grew deeper, ending up in a form that would eventually stop changing. This method created a good deal of frustration, as the director and actors saw their initial roles evolving; the former was no longer the director but the guide, the latter were becoming authors or, rather, a group author. In the end, the collective production was more like a collage of individual performances, of stories that more or less picked up on each other.

The themes spoke to the times, and the common thread (somewhat weak, in fact), was the quest for the mandrake, a plant that purportedly permits human beings to realize their most cherished childhood dreams. (They had encountered the theme of the mandrake during their collective reading of German romantic authors, when they had thought to develop a production based on the work of Kleist.) Looking for the mandrake involved the clowns in many basic human situations. The actors worked on what was dearest to them, creating concrete poetry on stage. When the improvisations felt caricatured, they dropped them. Some of the more memorable scenes included: taking refuge on a desert island; turning into a Casanova/Monsieur Laïobule (Claude Merlin), who can't manage to seduce Madame Patafiole (Anne Demeyer); showing up as a chef/Monsieur Appollo (Jean-Claude Penchenat) who dresses like an intellectual; finding Paradise. The men developed sketches about power, about domination and seduction. Josephine Derenne, as Madame Cléopâtre in spangles and a boa, became a flirty housewife, running from the cradles of her five, little, clown-headed children to her bread dough, dough she kneaded as though strangling her children. When interviewed by the *Elle* magazine reporter Mademoiselle Scampoussi (Mireille Franchino), who was dressed in a checkered jacket and playing an accordion, Madame Cléopatre tried on the skates offered to her and fell over and over again – but charmingly – in order to look her best for the photo shoot. The buffoons disappeared into thin air, killed each other, died, and were born again. The gags came back, like a refrain. A spectator remembers that the sketches were actually "terrifying," a qualifier evoking the terms used to characterize *The House of Atreus* project: "superb and terrifying." The clowns, in their

The Clowns. Sketch of the open-air set for the performance of *The Clowns* at the Avignon Theatre Festival. Pictured stage right, the entrance ramp or "flower path" that cuts through the audience as in a kabuki production. Archives Sophie Moscoso.

sophisticated "mask-up"[29] and their brilliant costumes were pointing a way forward. At the end of the show, one of the clowns declared: "I'm going to blow up this joint. Nobody will be left. Just water everywhere. I'll keep a tiny island in the middle of the Pacific and only the best swimmers will find their way. The destiny of the cosmos will land in the hands of the froth of the human race." This strong and ambivalent image would migrate to later productions and be transformed, incarnated again in the finale of their 2010 *Mad Hope*.

At the end of *The Clowns*, Monsieur Appollo holds a ticking bomb. It has been passed around from character to character to end up in the hands of the clown who always succeeds, having, indeed, just been named a Presiding Judge. But it explodes, plunging the audience into darkness – until the lights go up for bows. That's the human condition, as seen in every compelling clown show. But it was also the situation of the Soleil's young actors, searching for a place in the world of theatre that had become their life. Mnouchkine says of the experience: "At that point, politically conscious actors needed to know if they were of real use to the world."[30]

Clowning and kabuki

Six clown-musicians (trombone, tuba, drums, cymbals, piano) accompanied the tragi-comic theatrical clowns. They formed a wild orchestra, and were located stage right, off the main performance area. The piano clown (Rosine Rochette) played music composed by head music clown Teddy Lasry. Lasry's music helped structure the performance and scored the gags and pratfalls.[31]

According to Roberto Moscoso, the stage design was meant to be "the most seductive it could be." Mnouchkine started with the memory of having seen in Bangkok facing Chinese theatres that were working hard to attract each other's public. The first idea was "a fairground stand": Mnouchkine suggested a boulevard lined with carnival shanties. Then they discussed something "boldly showy, full of bling." They finally arrived at "a lighted box that could house any story, in which anything could happen, that wasn't an illustration but was, rather, beautiful – and at the same time simple, made of wrapping paper and fairy lights." They recycled wood from the set for *Midsummer*.[32]

A double door with swinging panels sided with mirrors, and two lateral doors, covered by shimmering beads like the curtains in Noh, were located upstage. A narrow bench ran along the entire length and width of the paper-paneled box. The energetic, athletic entrances and exits took place among the audience on the L-shaped entrance ramp, inspired by the *hanamichi* (or flower path) of kabuki theatre. Everything was designed to foreground the actors' work. The ramp could tilt or be raised and lowered; the set was decorated with many mirrors and garlands of lights, "like a hairdressing salon in the south of France." The floor was painted an explosive yellow. There were fringed circus stools covered in plush rose velvet. A few props graced the set: suitcases, a hammer, a decanter of water, a pistol, etc. When performed at the theatre in Aubervilliers, the circus box filled the stage. The design was simplified for the Avignon theatre festival (metal connectors, collapsible legs), so that *The Clowns* could be performed outdoors in public squares, where barkers would attract an audience.[33] Easily transported, the simplified set allowed the Soleil to tour for a month around Avignon: the company managed 24 shows in sports arenas, school courtyards, and shopping centers. The Avignon festival director, Jean Vilar, thought it was wonderfully funny. One evening, the mistral wind was blowing so hard that technical director Guy-Claude François had to make sure the set wouldn't fly away. This particular moment inspired one of the more striking scenes in the Soleil's 1978 film, *Molière*.

The Clowns would be performed indoors in Milan in November 1969 on the invitation of the Piccolo Teatro.[34] Federico Fellini, whose film *The Clowns* was released in 1971, went to a performance, liked it, but thought there was too much dialogue. The Soleil performed again in Paris in January 1970, alternating *The Clowns* with *The Kitchen*. Joseph Bouglione, miffed by their success, had refused to rent his circus space to them, choosing, instead, to sponsor a beer festival. So the Renaud-Barrault company, and especially Madeleine Renaud, came to the rescue. Having seen *The Kitchen* with all of their own actors, Jean-Louis Barrault and Madeline Renaud helped the Soleil secure the Elysée-Montmartre, where Barrault had earlier staged his *Rabelais*. But success was slow to come.

The requirements of clowning were so demanding, so unforgiving, that they led, at times, to meltdowns. The program cites helter-skelter many actors as the creators, and Mnouchkine is listed among them, not as director. She had, in fact, replaced Mireille Franchino on a moment's notice, substituting a drum for Franchino's accordion. Those who had worked on the show but weren't in it were cited, as were those who did perform. Well-known actors, such as Loleh Bellon and Josette Boulva had begun to work on the piece but hadn't been able to keep up. The work was very hard; communal life was not easy either; people were leaving for personal, political, and artistic reasons. (And, indeed, this would be the case at the end of every one of the Soleil's major cycles.) But this experience proved formative, determining the company's orientation and objectives.

Mnouchkine would say at the end of the tour of *The Clowns*:

> Now it's time to work with more developed themes. We'd like to end up with one great idea, and even at a place where an author would be able to use everything we've invented to construct something brilliant. What we've done resembles the kind of collaboration Brecht asked of his companions and his actors. We need to find our Brecht.[35]

And to find Brecht, the company abandoned Brecht – that is, they abandoned their idea of producing *Baal*, even though it had been cast and Moscoso had designed a transformable set with ramps, and a screen for what would have been the filmed portions. For the moment, the author would be the troupe itself; and after Avignon, the actors continued to work on improvisations, which Mnouchkine considered fundamental. They improvised from fairy tales: *Donkey Skin*, *Beauty and the Beast*, and Nazim Hikmet's *The Legend of Love* that Geneviève Penchenat had translated from Italian. This time their improvisations combined narrative and storytelling with physical work. The result led to a breakthrough: not any story would work. They wanted to tell one kind of story, and, specifically, a story from History. They settled on the story that belongs to all French people, the shared patrimony of French audiences – the Revolution of 1789.

It was Mnouchkine's idea, but the company adopted it wholeheartedly. Emerging out of stage work, from trying out ideas, from practice, and not from an abstract notion, the idea has proven to be immensely fruitful. Mnouchkine admits: "I think that History is, in fact, the real story we want to tell."[36]

At the beginning of 1970, the Soleil had 28 permanent members. Everybody was paid, if poorly. Some 50 people were working together, including many actors who took on administrative and technical roles. Neither the subsidy from the Minister of Culture nor their success had guaranteed financial security and the actors now had families to take care of. The situation was frankly catastrophic. They had spent seven years making theatre within a radically different economic structure, based on the notion that an art form is a craft one learns continuously, without stopping, and that work must be dedicated to a broadly based, popular audience. And they had nothing, no space in which to rehearse or even store their sets.

They were finding this lack of space more and more difficult to manage. Without a space, they couldn't work with the fluidity so necessary to their creations: "We're working as though we were floating; we never know in which neighborhood, which suburb we belong." A permanent space would allow them to deepen what they'd learned, to pursue their research without constantly stopping and starting. Mnouchkine would say: "A space is vital, it's absolutely crucial, or we'll have to go into exile." She thought they might emigrate and head to another francophone country that could give them what they needed.

If it was true that they mostly needed a space, it was also true it couldn't be just any space. "I can no longer imagine working in an Italianate theatre," Mnouchkine proclaimed, as someone who had been radicalized by learning to make theatre in a circus, on a thrust stage with a Japanese style entrance ramp, and in the open air. They considered Les Bouffes du Nord, but it was too small for the way the company functioned, as was a cinema space on the rue de Lyon. Someone suggested the Baltard Pavillon[37] of Les Halles, the central market, where in May 1970 Luca Ronconi had produced his *Orlando furioso*. It wasn't yet clear what would become of the building. "It's a huge space, open, metallic, breezy, a space where we could work, prepare, rehearse, perform, but not only that – because even when we're not rehearsing, we need a space in which to be able to grow." Mnouchkine dreamed of a space for a Soleil school, a Soleil open to other companies: "[We could] bring in international troupes who need big spaces for their productions or who just love the idea of this project."[38]

"Every circus lover will jump for joy in seeing the work of a company that has no equal, neither in the Paris theatre world nor in Barnum and Bailey. Long live Ariane Mnouchkine's red clowns." (Louis Chauvet, in *The Figaro*, 1969.)

The Clowns marked the end of the first period in the Soleil's trajectory. The production brought with it crises and defections, but it led the company to an understanding of what it really wanted: freedom from realism and psychological acting, freedom from the everyday, from naturalism. Rather, something of the spirit of the circus, of the fairground aesthetic, an aesthetic that had already been determinant in how the public experienced *The Kitchen* and *Midsummer*. The actors had also learned what it meant to work in very tough conditions. All the actors interviewed spoke about the cold, the odors, the rats, the nearness to the animals in the two circus spaces[39] that had housed *The Kitchen:* the elephant that swallowed someone's wallet, the panther that made them afraid, the circus world where people might not know how to read, but knew how to count (like Bouglione), and whose social rejects (like Monsieur Berthy, a cinema fanatic), would be welcomed into the company later on,

The Clowns. The clown orchestra located stage left. The stage is covered in hundreds of small party lights. From left to right: M. Gonzalès, S. Coursan, C. Contri; G. Bonnaud standing; T. Lasry on the piano; R. Rochette at the piano. Photo by Martine Franck, Magnum Photos.

when the Medrano closed its doors. This was the beginning of a movement to conceptualize a "new circus"; and the circus ring would provide inspiration for many young artists who wanted a different kind of theatre. But not for the Soleil, who had come near to adopting this approach, but who preferred to stay in theatre – even after opening the way for female clowns, well before Annie Fratellini began to perform. Mnouchkine, nevertheless, understood the family resemblance and many years later would call the artists from the new circus, the Arts Sauts, the Soleil's "close cousins."

After *The Clowns*, the Soleil kept on exploring – exhilarated by circus performing, by having rehearsed at night in the main circus ring of the Cirque d'hiver, where the set had to be stored among wild animals; energized by experiencing through performances of *The Kitchen* the loss of balance jugglers have to contend with, "jumping naked into the performance breach," as Josephine Derenne would say of the actor-clowns. They had learned several things: their approach would demand a special kind of space, as well as rigorous and collaborative work focused on a particular form, and, finally, an interrogation of the place of the text and the role of the author in the theatrical experience. Should they be actor/authors? Should they associate a writer to their company? From 1970 on, Mnouchkine would

The Clowns. Energetic entrance of J. Derenne on the gangway/ramp, her wig flying and her arms covered by a feather boa that makes them look longer. Photo by Martine Franck, Magnum Photos.

see two possible trajectories for the Theatre du Soleil, both belonging to the realm of collective creation:

> I hope our experience will lead us to find a certain language, a kind of efficient communication. Theatre is what actors do best. I'm convinced of how important theatre really is, not in its current shape; for the real place of theatre has to be as a participant in knowledge formation, as a purveyor of information, of enlightenment – and not as an emblem of culture. We have to achieve the greatest clarity in performance, as well as revolutionize habits and style. It's absolutely necessary for architects, directors, authors, and actors to stop once and for all attempting to create a masterpiece. Creation cannot belong to one particular person: I'm convinced that we must take a radical, even violent, position. In fact, that's what pushes us – or me, to be honest – to take some distance from the existing theatrical canon (not all members of the Soleil think this way). What I would like for the Théâtre du Soleil would be playwrights who work full time. Maybe we'll get there one day.[40]

Notes

1 Ariane Mnouchkine, oral interview with Marie-Agnès Sevestre, at the Francophone Festival of Limoges, 2015.
2 Ariane Mnouchkine, "Changement de décor," France Culture. See Meyerhold and his idea that "the theatre is an art and something more than an art."
3 Henry Rabine, *La Croix,* June 1961.
4 Frances Ashley would later marry the playwright André Benedetto.
5 Jean-Claude Penchenat was named the vice president.
6 Ariane Mnouchkine, "Entretien avec Denis Bablet et Marie-Louise Bablet," *Le Théâtre du Soleil ou la quête du bonheur* (Paris: CNRS-SERDDAV, 1979), 8.
7 There was only one professional actor in the show: Jacques Torrens, who played Genghis Khan.
8 She had been working as a costume intern in film.
9 After that, they performed in Paris at the Alliance Française and the Théâtre Mouffetard.
10 There is a different salary structure for interns or for those who are only partially employed by the Théâtre du Soleil. However, for *Mad Hope* there was so much work that everyone was a full-time employee with the same salary.
11 Moscoso arrived in France in 1959 and repeated his first year of school in order to stay there.
12 *The Kitchen* had been performed in Brussels, but it was created in France by the Soleil. Gabriel Monnet had created Wesker's *Roots* in Bourges in 1967. That's where Mnouchkine met him.
13 The text for the celebrated scene of the "launch," in the second half of Act I, was developed during rehearsals.

14 Ariane Mnouchkine, *Les Nouvelles littéraires*, March 30, 1967 and *l'Evénement*, May 1967.

15 Ariane Mnouchkine, *Comme il vous plaira*, *Discorama 70*, television interview by D. Glazer, produced by R. Sanglat (1970).

16 At the end of 1963, the Medrano Circus was bought by the Bouglione family who changed its name to the "Cirque de Montmartre." But it was always called the "Medrano."

17 Joseph Bouglione was renting out the circus for beer festivals or for gala performances, such as those staged by Colette Renard.

18 Ariane Mnouchkine, *Le Théâtre du Soleil ou la quête du bonheur*, 23.

19 Arnold Wester, however, thought the production was not realistic enough.

20 Ariane Mnouchkine, *Comme il vous plaira*.

21 Ibid.

22 From the notebooks in the Archives of Roberto Moscoso.

23 Ariane Mnouchkine, "Une prise de conscience," in *Le Théâtre 1968-1*, ed. Fernando Arrabal (Paris: Christian Bourgois, 1968), 120–121.

24 This was to make up for the cancelled tour.

25 Claude Roy, "Ariane Soleil," *Double Page, Le Théâtre du Soleil: Shakespeare*, no. 21 (1982).

26 Ariane Mnouchkine, "*Les Clowns*: théâtre d'aujourd'hui," documentary program by L. de Guyencourt, produced by J. Brard, ORTF (1969).

27 Ibid.

28 Ibid.

29 Philippe Ivernal coined this expression in French: le "masquillage."

30 Ariane Mnouchkine, "*Les Clowns:* théâtre d'aujourd'hui."

31 Some of the actors who performed also participated in the orchestra.

32 Roberto Moscoso stipulates that recycling cost more that it would have if they had purchased new wood, but that "it was the commitment of the company to recuperate everything they could."

33 *The Magic Tree* was invited with *The Clowns* to the Avignon Festival.

34 After 1968, Paolo Grassi's and Giorgio Strehler's leadership of the Piccolo was challenged. Grassi stayed on and invited Mnouchkine, Chéreau, and Bellocchio. Strehler left and founded a company, Teatro e Azione.

35 Ariane Mnouchkine, "*Les Clowns*, théâtre d'aujourd'hui."

36 Ariane Mnouchkine, *Le Théâtre du Soleil ou la quête du bonheur*.

37 In 1969, Les Halles were transferred to Rungis, outside of the city.

38 Ariane Mnouchkine, *Comme il vous plaira*.

39 When *Midsummer* finally opened in 1968, the wild animals were no longer part of the Medrano Circus.

40 Ariane Mnouchkine, in Jean-Jacques Olivier, "Les tribulations du Théâtre du Soleil. Ariane Mnouchkine: le théâtre doit participer à la connaissance," *Combat*, February 11, 1970.

An inside shot of the Cartoucherie when the Soleil arrived there in 1970. This was where *1789* was rehearsed before opening the production in Milan on the invitation of the Piccolo Theatre. In the photo: B. Coursan and M. Donzenac. (The term "the Cartoucherie" is used both to mean the particular theatre space of the Théâtre du Soleil and to mean the entire complex of the old armaments factory that has been gradually transformed into an arts space, with five separate theatres and an arts school.) Photo by Michel Maingois, Archives Jean-François Labouverie.

Working on the theatre space in 1970 after the opening in Italy of *1789*. On the central scaffolding: J-F. Labouverie and M. Toty. R. Moscoso stands, center. Photo by Michel Maingois, Archives Jean-François Labouverie.

Chapter 1   Destiny

"A popular theatre piece is theatre that's beautiful and easy to read; it speaks to something important, something that's really meaningful to ordinary people."

Ariane Mnouchkine[1]

"We were making art; we were making art for the people; we were happy."

Off-stage voice of the Narrator from
The Survivors of Mad Hope

"We invent theatre, that mysterious continent that theater always is for me, needing always to be redefined; we discover all the time archipelagos and shores on which others have, of course, already landed."

Ariane Mnouchkine[2]

"We pursue the color of our dreams
Risking dashing some of your hopes.
Forgive us, dear Public, but time is short.
We may've forgotten what you remember.

Tomorrow, you may think as we do
That the world's beauty is still on its way.
But tonight you and I seek its taste,
A taste only you can help me find – and share."

Philippe Léotard[3]

At the close of *The Clowns* (1969), Ariane Mnouchkine understood that the celebrated "popular public," a public of workers and laborers, was not who was coming to see their shows, even in the outdoor venues around Avignon. She concluded:

And, in a society like ours, they won't come, no matter what we do. We have to stop pretending [...]. I believe an actor does a play for about the same reasons people go to the theatre: there should be a meeting of minds, an encounter. But it doesn't happen [...]. Theatre should be pleasurable and raise consciousness; it's the opposite of entertainment [...]. You can sense that the theatre will either end up simply expressing the despair and rot in our society and in societies like ours (but more and more elaborately and with more and more talent) – and then it will stop, and say nothing more. Or it will re-find its roots and the ability to say something new.[4]

Her vision was radical: a matter of *encountering a new public* and a matter of seeking *the roots of theatre*.

Artisan-Companions

Such was her assessment at the end of seven years of apprenticeship dedicated to organizing progressively an ever-growing company – with its departures and arrivals – assembled around a solid core of people. At the same time as it was creating its shows, the Soleil was training its actors in a strikingly different manner from any arts conservatory, the arts conservatory being an institution that Mnouchkine had always distrusted. In a conservatory, there would be no space for imagining her constant experimentation with staging, for the different configurations of the technical team with its various ways of collaborating on creating costumes and sets and on organizing daily life. At the Soleil, everything was done in the moment, as each situation evolved, with new participants – the new people often recruited by friends or family – according to what each playing space offered as movement possibilities, and always in opposition to any definition of theatre as practiced at the time, both aesthetically and institutionally. Distanced from conventional theatrical practice, the Soleil also took its distance from any form of ideological brainwashing. Of course the company experienced the shock of May 1968 – with Communists, Maoists, or those close to political movements hoping to indoctrinate others. But the kind of political theatre they practiced, even if Marxism was a central lens for structuring dramatic conflict, was, rather, a festive politics – a more or less solemn festival or celebration built around common dreams and myths, with happiness as a goal. A number of leftist critics, after having praised them to the skies, declared the Soleil not Communist enough. Mnouchkine commented on this in 2011: "People started out by telling me I didn't have my card. Either it was my professional card or the card of my political party. I quickly realized I would never have a card." And she added:

> It would be interesting to figure out how many young companies either dried up because of ideological demands or were destroyed by drugs. There were two enemies at the time: extreme partisanship and marijuana. We were extraordinarily lucky to have eluded both.

The notion of what a popular public was – as articulated by the decentralization movement in French arts – certainly influenced the Soleil's thinking. But there were important nuances: first of all, that a critical assessment of the actual absence of such a public in the theatre was imperative. Second, which began as an intuition before it became a conviction, that the foundation of any theatre must be a theatrical troupe and that a popular theatre would, in fact, necessitate a large permanent company. In addition, that the concept of popular art must include forays into master works of American cinema as well as Eastern, that is Asian, theatre – which Mnouchkine always characterizes as: "sophisticated, poetic, metaphorical, and musical."

The history of the concept of popular theatre in France was having a very bumpy ride at the time, subjected as it was to instrumentalization by various dogmatic tribunals. For example, the influential theatre review *Théâtre Populaire*, chastised the director Jean Dasté for being "guilty of carrying out a deviationist staging of Brecht's *The Caucasian Chalk Circle*."[5] And other theatre people, hungry for power, grabbed onto the label to shore themselves up, forgetting those who had theorized the concept before them.

To best situate the Soleil, we will, in the following, think in terms of two parallel strands, both deeply anchored in the materiality of the daily life of the actors and technicians. On the one hand, the slippery, empirical, and fruitful encounter with theatre history; and on the other, the fitting out, on the outskirts of the city, of the instrument destined to realize their dreams, a "space of theatre," totally invented and constantly evolving – without equivalent in the history of Western theatre – meant to bring together all the arts and crafts of stage work and to permit creations which would serve both actors and public.

The Cartoucherie. Located outside of Paris in the Vincennes woods. It is quite a trip to get there. The City of Paris quickly set up a shuttle bus from the Vincennes metro stop to the theatre. The Soleil finally bought its own bus to facilitate the commute. Archives Théâtre du Soleil.

A genealogy: finding their place slowly in theatre history

The young Soleil was not particularly concerned with finding its place in any greater History. This was not a time for such questions. In France, one wanted to be in tune with the present, the immediate now, able to invent everything that was possible. Nevertheless, certain theatre "families" began, almost imperceptibly, to be perceived within the company. Several actors had been trained first at the École Dullin, known for improvisation and mime work (G. Hardy, A. Demeyer, J-F. Brossard, L. Guertchikoff). J-C. Penchenat had attended the Nice Conservatory, which might have disqualified him from the Soleil, but he had also studied physical theatre with Jacques Lecoq, taking night courses with Monique Godard. The actors learned to sing under the tutelage of Alfred Abondance, one of Dullin's close collaborators who ran their stage music workshop and who had trained the actors in Jean-Louis Barrault's company.[6] The Lecoq connection, a further connection to Lecoq's own teacher Jacques Copeau, loomed large: it was certainly in the classes of Lecoq – that outsider to the French theatre world – that Mnouchkine had been able to intuit a crucial synthesis between what she had observed on her travels in Asia and the corporeal and mask work practiced by the Lecoq school. Studying with Lecoq allowed her to understand that what she had seen during her long travels wasn't uniquely Asian – that Eastern theatre is first of all theatre, before being "exotic," and that the Land of Theatrical Utopia she had in mind was not bounded by any particular borders. And, indeed, international actors started arriving: Mario Gonzalès had been a puppeteer and dancer in Guatemala. Fabrice Herrero came from Argentina, accompanying the great Franco-Spanish actress Maria Casarès, who had spent a year there.

"Creating a Fraternity of Actors ... From the beginning, I recognized that was the true problem." (Jacques Copeau, *Registres I: Appels*, 1974, 187.)

The young troupe kept on learning and growing through the rehearsal process – a real source of theatrical research; through continuous physical training with Mario Radondi who followed them to the Cartoucherie; and through outings to the Cinémathèque, where Mnouchkine, the cinephile, led them. They also attended many productions at the Théâtre des Nations: "With my theatre companions," Mnouchkine explains, "we went to the Théâtre des Nations as though opening an encyclopedia. We went to learn. Sometimes we didn't like what we saw, but we learned. [...] The Théâtre des Nations was incredibly stimulating."[7] These were indeed very heady years for the theatre in general: there was work to be seen by Jorge Lavelli, the Living Theatre, the Bread and Puppet Theatre, Maurice Béjart's ballet; there were performances by Maria Casarès, Peter Brook and (as of 1971) his Center for International Theatre Research,

The Legacy by Marivaux, directed by J-C. Penchenat in 1972. Ariane Mnouchkine performs the role of the Countess, with René Patrignani, the Marquis, as her partner. The show was performed once for the Association of Friends of the Théâtre du Soleil during rehearsals for *1793*. Elements of the set for *1793* can be seen in the photo. Archives Jean-Claude Penchenat.

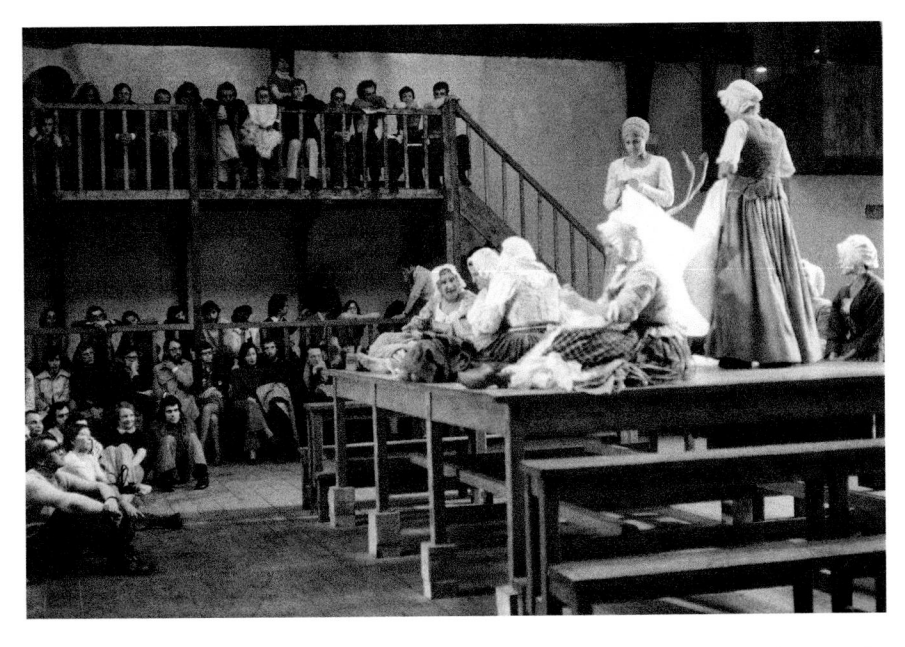

1793: The Revolutionary City is of This World. A scene of the women section members at the communal laundry making surgical bandages. Seated: L. Guertchikoff, G. Penchenat, J. Derenne, A. Demeyer. Standing: M. Donzenac, D. Valentin. Photo by Lesly Hamilton.

Luca Ronconi, Dario Fo, Jerzy Grotowski, whose innovative work one of the Soleil actors, J-P. Tailhade, observed for a short period of time.

Mnouchkine was never an actor and saw herself very quickly in the role of director. But she was always able to step in to replace an actor if needed (replacing, for example, J. Derenne, in *1789*, when Derenne had an accident in London; or M. Azencot as Madame Pernelle in *Tartuffe*). She even performed the role of the Countess in Marivaux's *The Legacy* in 1972, under the direction of J-C. Penchenat; and she worked on the role of Clytemnestra for *The House of Atreus Cycle*.

Although she never worked as assistant to another director, Mnouchkine had, according to her intuition and taste, seen, judged, and analyzed myriad productions. She wasn't satisfied by the static staging of *Marie Tudor*, *The Cid*, or *The Prince of Hamburg* by Jean Vilar. On the other hand, she admired the early work of Roger Planchon, whom she considered "a very great director," and she believed that "when he'd worked with the designer René Allio (as for *Edward II* and *Tartuffe*) he'd taken French theatre to new heights, even equivalent to what was being done at the Berliner Ensemble." She had a very similar appreciation for the work of Roger Blin, whose staging of Genet's *The Screens* may have oriented her own work; and she was so taken and troubled by the work of Giorgio Strehler (*The Servant of Two Masters*, *The Chioggia Scuffles*) and whose *Mountain Giants* she had seen several times, that she almost abandoned the theatre. It was the image of the stage curtain crushing the actors' wagon that profoundly marked her:

> After the production of *The Mountain Giants* at the Théâtre des Nations in 1967, I said to myself, if I want to advance in this work, I have to leave behind the Italianate stage. I was turning in circles. I felt overwhelmed. I thought I should stop doing theatre. Then I realized I had to free myself, start all over again.

This was one of those seminal moments: and the impetus to start afresh heralds the beginning of each new Soleil production.

The idea of the Soleil belonging to a theatrical genealogy, having a "lineage," as Mnouchkine puts is, came slowly into being. First of all there was Jean Vilar, whose writings, if not stagings, Mnouchkine acknowledges as fundamental. Sonia Debeauvais, Vilar's longtime collaborator, who kept alive the happy but weighty responsibility of orally transmitting Vilar's commitment to a popular public, a commitment she transmitted to the Soleil, considered Mnouchkine "the most direct and most faithful descendent of Vilar."[8] The first connection to Vilar took place during Mnouchkine's and Gérard Hardy's initial meeting with Debeauvais in her position as head of the Théâtre National Populaire's outreach to groups and the general public. (Hardy, joined later by Odile Cointepas, had been responsible for the Soleil's outreach since the production of *The Philistines*.) Mnouchkine and Hardy both remember the encounter in 1967 that lasted long after the sun went down, with Debeauvais "telling endless stories about Vilar, about Vilar and administrative matters, about Vilar and relations with the public" and offering them before they left a great deal of advice and many useful contacts. From then on, Hardy began meeting personally with the heads of various associations to speak to them about what it meant to be an actor and about what the Soleil's type of theatre was, so that they could, in turn, discuss this with their own members. And Vilar himself, still hospitalized after a heart attack, extended his support by inviting *The Clowns* to the Avignon Festival – a decision not discussed with anyone else. After Paul Puaux, who succeeded Vilar as director of the Festival, resigned in 1979, it was Mnouchkine who was offered the position. The Soleil had just performed *Mephisto* in Avignon and Mnouchkine was thought to be the only person capable of carrying forward Vilar's vision. She saw the future differently, however, a future intimately connected to her company and to creating work.

If at the beginning of her career Mnouchkine had admired Roger Planchon and invited him to be honorary president of her university theatre association, l'ATEP, she came to see him also as someone who betrayed the ideal of theatre as public service by "hiring movie actors or only mounting his own plays." She found the director Jean Dasté "a man of immense tenderness, of utmost simplicity, with a greatness of soul. [...] He was festive, a raconteur, an easy communicator, his enthusiasm catching." She declared the light in the eyes of Dasté's spectators, as photographed by Ito Josué, wondrous, a light she re-found in the public at Saint Etienne when the Soleil performed *Ephemera* there in 2008. And she was grateful to director Gabriel Garran, who spoke to her as if she were a future colleague, who encouraged her to do theatre with her gang of friends, because "solitude is death," and grateful also to Guy Rétoré, José Valverde, and Gabriel Monnet, who all invited *The Philistines* into their theatres.

In his *Histoire d'une famille théâtrale* [*History of a Theatrical Family*], the director Hubert Gignoux establishes a genealogy that starts with Jacques Copeau, connects to the Comédiens-Routiers and their traveling theatre, and continues on to "the Théâtre du Soleil, the Aquarium, the Campagnol, and the work of Mehmet Ulusoy, André Benedetto, Jean-Louis Hourdin and a few others," those who "show that it's possible to take up a certain [physical and collective] artistic approach" in order to surpass it.[9] Dasté, Gignoux, and Planchon would all perform

Molière or the Life of an Honest Man (1978). Here in this film clip we see part of the Soleil genealogy: Jean Dasté is standing in the middle of this frame, at his side M-F. Audollent and the "young Molière" (F. Ladonne), and other children (S. Bonnaud, P. Cointepas, and S. Ballerini.) Photo by Michèle Laurent.

roles (respectively: Molière's grandfather, a bishop, and the finance minister Colbert) in Mnouchkine's grand filmic epic *Molière* (1976–1977), created after a long cycle of three collective works, *1789, 1793*, and *The Golden Age*. Founding members of the company, many of whom had gone in other directions, came back to work on the film. Together, Dasté, Gignoux, and Planchon would embody the theatrical lineage in which Mnouchkine placed the Théâtre du Soleil. *Molière*, filmed at the Cartoucherie, which had been transformed into a movie studio, and co-produced by Alexandre Mnouchkine, Claude Lelouch, Antenne 2, and the Italian network RAI UNO,[10] celebrated through the story of Molière the idea of popular theatre made viable by a troupe of traveling actors. It concretized the Soleil's anchoring in History.[11]

In fact, Mnouchkine would only truly grasp the Soleil's deep connection with Jacques Copeau in 1974. Here is how Jean-Claude Penchenat remembers her discovery of his importance:

It was Alfred Simon, to whom I was speaking about our research, who brought up Copeau's name. He was reading his correspondence with Roger Martin du Gard. A little while later, Marie-Hélène Dasté, of the Copeau dynasty, sent Ariane the first volume of Copeau's *Registres* [*Theatre Journals*].

Mnouchkine plunged into the first volume, "Appels" [*Solicitations*],[12] which Gallimard had just published, as well as reading Copeau's *Journal de bord des Copiaus* [*The Log Book of the Copiaus company*].[13] In her continual and unfinished quest for true theatre, she grafted Copeau's meditations onto the lineage she'd already imagined of Asian theatrical traditions: "Earlier [before Copeau], I had a whole continent of Asian theatre as my master." But she would discover others, and first among them Copeau, the "master dreamer" as she would call him in the program notes to *The Golden Age*. And she admitted in 2010: "When I read [these mentors], when I feel them next to me, it comforts me, helps me, supports me, makes me gain time."

A little historical parenthesis

The correspondence between Louis Jouvet and Jacques Copeau during the years 1915–1916, when the former was at the front and the latter in the countryside in Limon, reveals their joint dream, even given the extreme conditions of World War I – a dream of a new theatre called "improvised comedy" or "new comedy." The dream takes shape from letter to letter and suggests a direction French theatre might have taken if the two men had continued to get along, and especially if the passion for the central place of text in French theatre hadn't ended up destroying their friendship. Indeed, how could one really expect that Copeau, so tied to the literary milieu of the prestigious journal *La Nouvelle Revue Française*, would really approve and share Jouvet's iconoclastic pronouncements, such as: "We should raise our young artists far from the Comédie Française and the Odéon, far from textual commentaries, maybe far from texts themselves! Rather, they should be plunged solely into the action of each play."[14] Their rapprochement could only happen because of the terrible circumstances that created a kind of parenthesis around actual theatrical life.

In his letters, Jouvet critiques "the influence of school, of classes, and all the commentary that has been laid on classical texts, already literary enough," and that tends to dry them up, embalm, and mummify them. He critiques as well "the deplorable impact of memorization: because the actor forgets about action, loses the scene, and all that's left is the text." He imagines all the research to be done into the genealogy of fools, buffoons, Italian comics, ancestors of the "modern farceurs" he and Copeau would hope to train. He invents exercises in improvisation that he tried out all alone in the ambulance he was driving at the front, and discovers the work of Carlo Gozzi whom he finds transporting. Copeau, for his part, insists: "No reconstitutions, but new creations," and he adds that Jouvet's idea to

> keep children away from texts as long as possible is admirable [...]. The same idea could be applied to improvisational exercises for older people: you'd pull the text out from under them, like a ladder, and see what they'd be able to do.[15]

These ideas – that Copeau developed in his notes on improvisation in January 1916 – would never really be put to the test, not even when his company, the Copiaus, held their famous retreat in Pernand-Vergelesses. There are multiple reasons why they didn't come to fruition: Copeau's excessive authoritarianism, his Jansenism (or theological pessimism and prudery), his utopian all or nothing standards, the fact that he was, after all, more a writer than a director. But in the winter of 1916, Copeau went often to the Medrano Circus, admiring the clowns, "artisans of a living tradition," and the circus ring, "an empty space in which one's imagination can play with constraints."[16] While Copeau was at the circus, his fellow director Charles Dullin, also at the front, did theatre with his fellow soldiers, mounting shortened versions of *Molière*'s plays.

The correspondence between Jacques Copeau and Louis Jouvet ends on a note of regret: "What work we would be able to do if..."[17] As this correspondence was not yet published in the 1960s and 1970s, we might suggest that the spirit of their letters was communicated to Mnouchkine by way of the courses she took with Lecoq. But when, during the performance of *The Golden Age*, she began reading the first volume of Copeau's *Theatre Journals*, she was able to recognize that her path up until then had been pursuing Copeau's unfinished research. The Soleil had, after all, its place in a theatrical lineage. Today, we can surely say that the Théâtre du Soleil has indeed realized Copeau's and Jouvet's joyful dreams of 1915 and 1916, while, at the same time anchoring itself in the reality of the world's politics and social history. Mnouchkine would say of Copeau in 2011 that he was "too dictatorial, but incredibly inspiring." If his theory resulted mainly in unsuccessful attempts at a modern popular comedy based on past theatrical forms, the work of the Soleil produced characters – such as those in *The Golden Age* or later, Félix Courage, the owner of the cabaret in *The Survivors of Mad Hope* (2010) – who proved unquestionably the viability of his dream. The Franco-Ghanaian actor Eve Doe Bruce's Félix Courage emerged directly from her work on the *commedia Harlequin*.

Nonetheless, even those who introduced Mnouchkine to Copeau and who admired her work, such as Alfred Simon, would continue to tell her that the company needed a poet, that it had to have texts to move forward. Such was the opinion of critic Jean-Jacques Gautier, of *The Figaro*, who declared after *The Clowns*: "What is it that we look for in theatre, no matter what anyone says? A text, right?" Or Jean Dutour who snapped: "Without an author, theatre doesn't exist."[18] This was the kind of cutting remark heard frequently in certain later reviews from the 1970s of *1789* and *1793*. No wonder Mnouchkine, as head of a company, became so radicalized in her attempt to escape the tyranny of literature and the advice of so many theoreticians, philosophers, or so-called playwrights who were set to push her experimental work – based in freedom, pragmatism, and exploration – off track. She did know, of course, that texts are necessary; and her stagings of essential authors, such as Shakespeare and Molière (whom Copeau also appreciated) and to whom she would add the Greek classic playwrights, periodically marked a kind of "return to school," after a phase of collective creation. All the same, she would forever maintain: "I believe absolutely in improvisation, in perpetual self-questioning, in examining our motives."

Its French lineage, as the Soleil was constructing it, began to integrate itself into a larger theatre history, that of "authentic theatrical forms," as Vsevolod Meyerhold, whose practice the company would encounter during *The Golden Age*, expressed it, and of "pure forms," as Mnouchkine herself put it. The company would inscribe itself slowly, production after production, discovery after discovery, in a long and vast history of theatre, without ever copying, directly borrowing, or cleverly manipulating through deconstruction or hybridization the work of others. Instead, others' work and thought would serve as inspiration, elements to foster creativity and to free the imagination, starting points for discussion, but always within specific artistic parameters and spatial and temporal dimensions. For the Soleil, creation could not be dissociated from the life of the company and the organization of work; and thus it would also be connected to the world of contemporary men and women – but always through the eternal world of theatre.

Theatre as workshop, theatre as great house, a space of all possibilities

Nomadic up to this point, the Soleil now needed to find a stable space, somewhere where the company could work continuously, according to the rules it had set for itself, as they had done while experimenting in Ardèche or Arc-et-Senans. And Mnouchkine proclaimed:

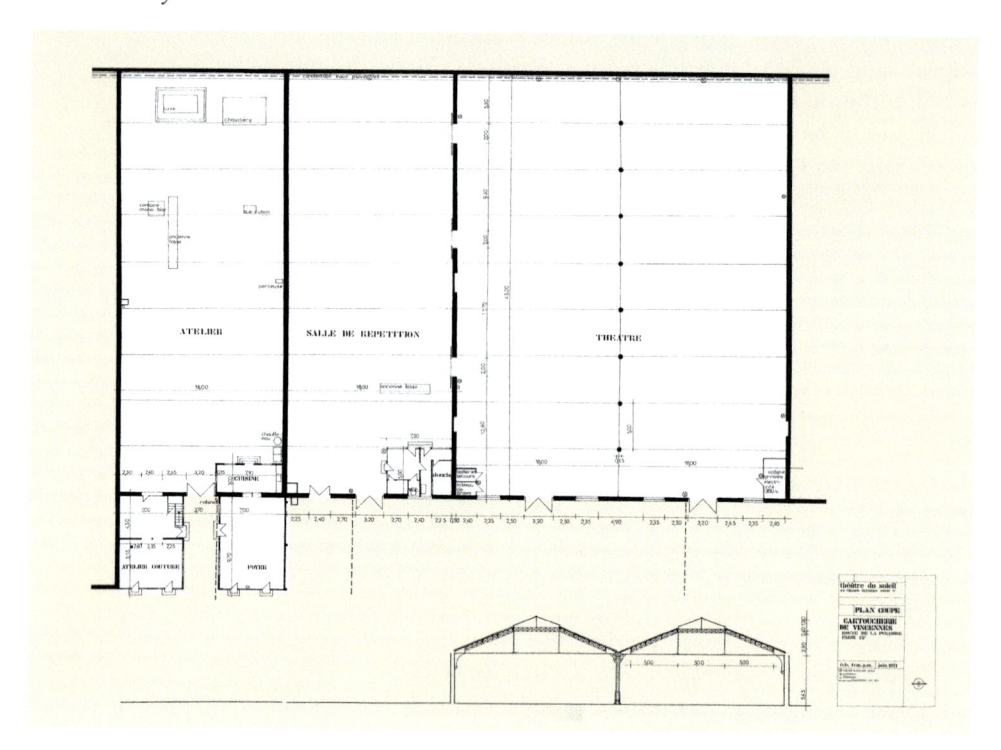

"Blueprint" for the Théâtre du Soleil at the Cartoucherie in 1970. Archives Théâtre du Soleil.

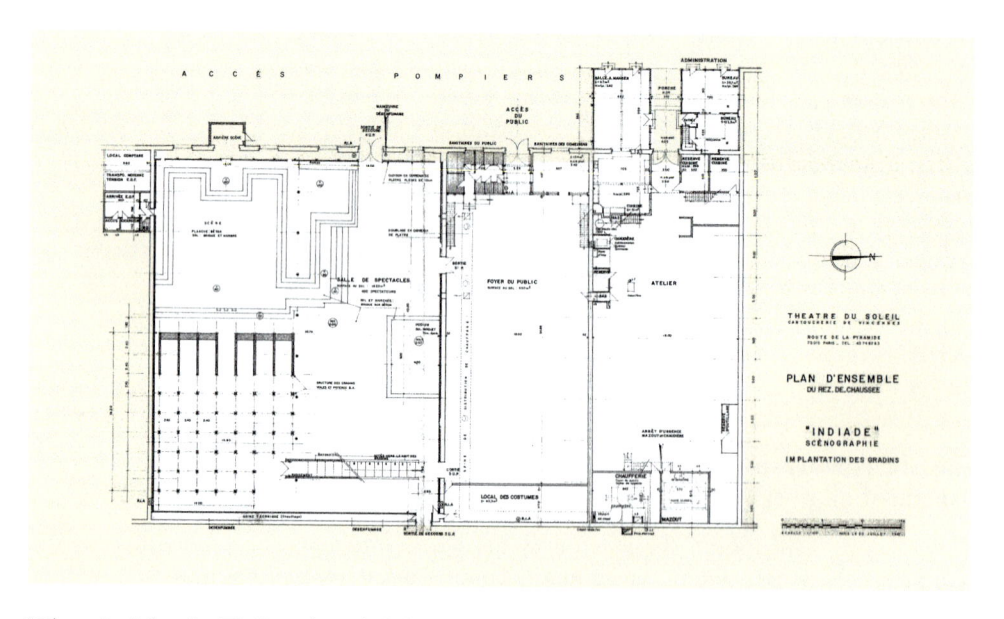

"Blueprint" for the Théâtre du Soleil during the production of *The Indiad* (1987). The changes made from 1970 to 1987 are easy to see. The stage is in the same area as today's stage. Archives Théâtre du Soleil.

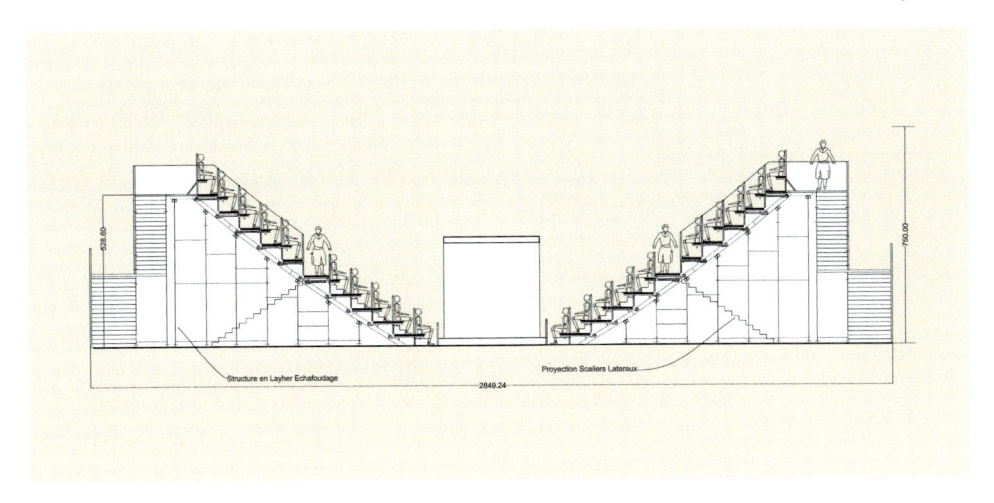

Canto de Montserrat's stage design for *Ephemera* (2006). A bi-frontal design, which had already been used in 1980 for the political action piece, *The Prague Trial*, was installed in one of the naves of the hangar. Archives Théâtre du Soleil.

The Golden Age: First Draft (1974). There was a very long period of rehearsals and restructuring of the space. Hills and valleys were created on the floor of the theatre space. Here we see how piles of earth were shaped and covered, ready for a light concrete coating and coconut matting. Photo by Martine Franck, Magnum Photos.

The drama of actors, in general, is that when they aren't acting, they aren't working. They have nowhere to work. It's as if a pianist couldn't practice scales if he or she didn't have a concert. That's the situation of most of the actors in this country. It's one of the first things we're going to try to remedy.

This space could not be, as we have seen, an Italianate theatre, that "living room scaled for the city," as Guy-Claude François put it. It had to offer vast volumes where one could circulate easily between set and costume workshops, the playing area, the administrative offices, and the space for welcoming the public. During their work on *The Clowns*, with their office on the Champs-Elysées, rehearsals either at Kremlin-Bicêtre or Malakoff, and workshops in Aubervilliers, the Soleil had seen how disruptive to the organic nature of creation a dispersed organization could be. Everything was, instead, meant to evolve together. So with the dream of the Baltard Pavillion up in smoke (Les Halles had been demolished), the sought-for space would turn out to be the Cartoucherie de Vincennes.[19]

"The Italianate theatre is a performance all by itself. It's a show through which you have to pass in order to see the other show." (Ariane Mnouchkine, 2011.)

"[The Cartoucherie] is an absolutely splendid place that's humble at the same time." (Ariane Mnouchkine, in Jean Chollet, *Construire pour le temps d'un regard: Guy-Claude François scénographe*, 2009, 80.)

It was the young architect and editor of the journal *l'Architecture d'aujourd'hui*, Christian Dupavillon, who discovered an ancient military warehouse in the course of his investigation of new spaces for theatre work. He didn't mention the Cartoucherie in the article he produced about new spaces, because it was way too dilapidated, but he contacted the Soleil.[20] Roberto Moscoso describes it this way: "We got the key. The building was abandoned. It was very romantic, very beautiful. Some trees had begun to grow inside the walls, leaning towards the broken glass canopy. It was summer." The Soleil squatted and then rented the space from the city of Paris in 1970 while they finished rehearsing *1789*. In the shape it was then in, nothing would have suggested that the Cartoucherie could become a theatre: it was far from any public transportation; it could only be a rehearsal space. But, back in France from their Italian triumph with the opening of *1789*,[21] and without a space to perform in, the men and women of the Soleil rolled up their sleeves, and in a crazy bet cleaned it up enough in three weeks to be able to perform in it. They invited Christian Dupavillon to join them in the work and he did.

Everyone under the same roof. Everything could circulate. The three naves of their Cartoucherie hangar would permit the Soleil to realize their dream of creating everything

Guy-Claude François on the theatre's bulldozer, the "Derruppé," named for the equipment company. Archives Théâtre du Soleil.

In spring 1971, during the run of *1789*, the company became very attentive to cleaning up the outside area surrounding the theatre space. They installed garlands of fairy lights, a red carpet, and a huge rectangular table under the trees. The welcome was festive and warm. Archives Théâtre du Soleil.

In 1972, the title of *1793* was painted on the wooden entrance doors. Following *1793*, all other titles would be affixed to the red brick outside wall of the foyer that abuts the Welcome Area of the theatre space. For *Mad Hope*, the title was complemented by slogans from the beginning of the 20th century painted on the façade of the theatre, as well as by the name of the cabaret, "The Mad Hope," a name shared with the name of the production. Photo by Martine Franck, Magnum Photos.

themselves, achieving the very highest standards. It was a living dream of a micro-society in which each person would teach the others and learn from them, where all the different theatre disciplines would intersect and inspire each other, where different nationalities would be in dialogue. From 1970 on, other companies started moving out to the Cartoucherie, occupying other hangars: the Tempête, the Aquarium, the Epée de Bois, and the Chaudron would transform a wasteland into a theatre village and an armaments factory into a cultural space.[22]

The Soleil introduced a minimum of partitions into this vast hangar, itself a striking example of nineteenth-century steel architecture, with its tall pillars whose capitals supported the roof beams, and which boasted in one spot a glass canopy all made of one piece.[23] The use of only a few partitions was meant to transform the space into a "theatre-shelter" as Copeau had imagined it, rather than a "theatre-building," which the director Antoine Vitez contrasts with Copeau's idea. In other terms, it was like the Russian "theatre-house" or a space where all work, whether domestic, manual, intellectual, technical,

The Golden Age. An outdoor training session on practice mats with Mario Radondi, professor of acrobatics. From left to right: M. Radondi, O. Cointepas, B. Bauchau, G. Bonnaud, P. Hottier, P. Caubère, C. Massart, H. Cinque, and in the center, J. Sutton. Archives Jean-Claude Penchenat.

Ariane Mnouchkine playing with the children of the Théâtre du Soleil. Photo by Lesly Hamilton.

culinary, creative, or musical, would be shared, where life could become a celebration, where the interior would spill out to the exterior, encountering nature and even spring roses, and where the public space would be the largest and most welcoming of all. Indeed, the public space would be called "The Welcome Area," and the theatre "foyer" would designate the small dining room near the kitchen where the actors, after a day of cleaning up the space, would gather to eat at long tables. The Welcome Area took up the entire first nave or hall, half of the surface of the hangar. In 1981, a rehearsal space would be equipped in a near-by building, adjoining a workshop for costumes and one for the masks and sculptures created by Erhard Stiefel.

The organization of space was integrally connected to the theatre work. As important as the men and women who conceived it and helped it evolve, the space could not be separated from the experience. To understand the experimentation in theatre writing and in performance styles, the specificities of spatial organization have to be grasped. It is the only way to apprehend fully what the Soleil managed to accomplish by refusing to conform to the usual institutional formatting. The gesture to make over the Cartoucherie for *1789* reveals a powerful desire for theatre, an irrepressible need, ever so much more revealing than asking for subsidies.

So the Soleil set itself up outside of Paris in the woods. Did it totally lose its nomadic spirit? In truth, from *1793* forward, the company, led by Guy-Claude François, the former technical director who replaced Roberto Moscoso as chief set designer, would never stop transforming its space. For each new creation, the Soleil imagined new trajectories and itineraries. François, whose imagination was more technical, geometric, and graphic than Moscoso's, the latter known for his beautifully colored and expressive designs, produced truly architectural spaces. For *The Golden Age*, for example, he used concrete, helped in this effort by the Portuguese mason, Antonio Ferreira, who arrived in 1971 and was for thirty years one of the mainstays of the Théâtre du Soleil. The entire theatre space would be changed according to the needs of each production, materially rebuilt and reorganized; and if each change was ephemeral, there was always some trace of it left in the building. Of this Mnouchkine remarks:

> We transform the space for every show, but we never start from zero. We don't destroy everything to start again. [...] One day, while we were building *The Last Caravanserai*, we cut into the floor of the stage with a bulldozer and

we realized that underneath were layers of *The House of Atreus Cycle*, *The Indiad* [*l'Indiade ou l'Inde de leurs rêves*], *Sihanouk* [*l'Histoire terrible mais inachevée de Norodom Sihanouk, roi du Cambodge*], and other shows. It was very emotional: all our history was there, inscribed in the building itself. Everyone in the company who has the opportunity of staying on for a while has their own trajectory: we're on a path towards something, we don't just do a show; you aren't simply in the present when you're with the Théâtre du Soleil. You're doing ongoing research. [...] We don't sterilize the space. We don't make a *tabula rasa*. Even if we start each time by turning a new page, that page is still vibrating with everything that happened before.[24]

Thus a dialectical movement between displacement and stratification, between renovation and memory, would take place across the three naves of the hangar housing the Théâtre du Soleil: an apt materialization of one way of looking at the history of the company. Nothing would be considered definitive. And if a sense of vastness and emptiness took pride of place, there would also be something outsized and grandiose in the conception of that vastness, something precious and rare in the choice of materials that created it. In the simplicity, clarity, even universality of these "spaces that beckoned," spaces that Mnouchkine insisted on for the Soleil's creations, we can certainly see some of Jouvet's and Copeau's research on "bare trestle tables" and fair theatre. But there was none of the latter's austerity.

Nomadic adventures

We can speak of a first nomadic phase within the space of the Cartoucherie itself: a phase, as mentioned, where the location of the stage, the dressing rooms, the tiered seating areas, would evolve as the years rolled on. Every single production necessitated a total or partial re-structuring of the playing and welcome areas. For the company was inviting the public not only to a play, but also to a moment of shared life and art, where spectators were meant to relax before and after the performance, all in being somewhat shaken each time by something of the unfamiliar. As of *1793*, the Welcome Area was customized, with the walls painted white and graced by a large screen, on which the public could watch slides of the troupe working, as well as engravings from the eighteenth century. The company would start serving meals there when *1789* and *1793* were performed

"Our way of functioning was never determined by any special concept or precept. Our approach has always been extremely pragmatic." (Guy-Claude François, Interview with Béatrice Picon-Vallin, wwwtheatre-du-soleil.fr.)

the same day, one almost right after the other. To the delight of the public, the technicians had to rearrange the complicated sets and seating areas in less than two hours – a miraculous feat duly celebrated.

When *The Golden Age* was performed in 1975, the Welcome Area was festooned with festive banners; actors in costume and make-up served meals behind a long bar; and Arlequin appeared on a raised trestle table to announce the beginning of the show and to lead everyone – to the sound of sirens and boats docking in the port of Naples – onto the hills and into the valleys (all covered in coconut matting) that comprised both playing and audience areas. In order to create that particular playing area, Guy-Claude François operated the bulldozer the company had managed to secure to mound hills and valleys out of 630 truckloads of dirt he'd recuperated from the building site of IRCAM, the experimental music center located near the Beaubourg/Pompidou Museum. Having earlier built a model, he realized the full design by refashioning two entire naves. As for their filmic super-production, *Molière*, the Soleil exploded outwards into the area surrounding their hangar, creating sets on the lawn and in the streets adjacent to the Cartoucherie. Filming happened inside and outside; meals were taken in a huge tent; and a great many scenes were also filmed in the French provinces.

In 1981, G-C. François would construct the stage for the Shakespeare project exactly in the space where today we find the entry ramp behind the tiered seating area for the public, a space where once stood the most important dune of *The Golden Age*. This stage measured 18 × 20 meters, like almost all of the playing spaces that followed it. The two main entrances were located stage right. The dressing rooms were located also to the right of the metal bleachers constructed for a public of 500–600 spectators.

In 1985, the naves were rethought, a configuration kept for all future productions: the playing area was pushed further from the main entrance deeper into the hangar. Thus the third nave housed the raised wooden flooring for *Sihanouk*, which would form the basic structure on which all other masonry stages up until the present have been constructed. In order to execute the design for

E. Stiefel and É. Lemasson are fixing onto the wall over the entrance doors the Republican motto: "Liberty, Equality, Fraternity," January 23, 1998. Photo by Liliana Andreone.

Sihanouk, the Soleil succeeded in having reopened the ovens of a Beauvais brick factory that would be able to manufacture 400 small Roman bricks: these were as close as possible to the ideal Asian material imagined for the production. This production also saw the creation of the meter-wide entrance and exit corridor, a double-skin facade, behind the main stage and out of sight of the public, which connected with the terraced second nave. Stage left, the side stage built for Jean-Jacques Lemêtre and his musical equipment also flowed into the second nave. This musical space grew even bigger for the productions that followed *Sihanouk*.

The masonry bleachers that still constitute the audience's seating area were built in 1987 for *The Indiad*. And for *The Indiad*, as well, a marble flooring would cover the stage space created for *Sihanouk*, some of whose set remained intact. It was also in 1987 that the dressing rooms, which had always been in full view of the audience, either in the Welcome Area or in the nave in which the production occurred, were moved under the bleachers. Hélène Cixous calls this "The House Underneath." For *And Suddenly, Sleepless Nights* [*Et Soudain des Nuits d'éveil*] (1997), hundreds of Buddhas, painted by a seven-person team, covered the walls of the second nave; and today continue to watch over the Soleil.[25] This "Buddha nave" has remained in plain view of the public, located stage-left where the musicians work and where the actors effect any quick costume changes. At one point, for *The House of Atreus Cycle*, the floor of the second nave was excavated in order to create what appeared to be an open burial site for a life-sized terracotta army, swallowed up but emerging from the earth. Spectators could wander past the serried rows before and after the performance.

With the creation of *The Last Caravanserai* [*Le Dernier Caravansérail*] (2003), the concrete floor of the stage was raised to 1 meter 20 centimeters from the ground, and the built-out masonry platform stage left in the "Buddha nave" was enlarged to 7 meters 50 centimeters, leading up to a large door. The enormity of *The Last Caravanserai* necessitated building some extensions: a masonry slab (15 × 10 meters and tented) abutting the outside wall of the hangar. Attached to the back of the stage, this extension functioned as wings and as storage for sets. For *The Survivors of Mad Hope* (2010), an extension to the stage (that would later be removed) was built across the width of the "Buddha nave." Two other productions would be performed elsewhere than on the permanent masonry stage: *Drums on the Dam* (1999) took place within the frame of a puppet theatre, while *Ephemera* (2006) was staged bi-frontally. Both were built within the first, or entrance nave, of the hangar.[26] The huge workshop, open to all, where the Soleil has been able to realize

Preparation of the Welcome Area for *The Terrible but Unfinished Story of Norodom Sihanouk, King of Cambodia* (1986). The fresco on the rear wall, facing the entrance doors, is by Roberto Moscoso. Photo by Liliana Andreone.

Most of the time it is Ariane Mnouchkine herself who collects tickets and welcomes the public at the entrance to the theatre. Facing her in this photo is Baudouin Bauchau, who was for almost 30 years the Soleil's doorman, a huge presence and unforgettable silhouette for thousands of spectators. Photo by Liliana Andreone.

its most unbelievable set and costume dreams, can still be found next to the Welcome Area.

Ever since the production of *Drums on the Dam* (1999), the Soleil has transformed its theatre on several occasions into a temporary film studio, disguising various entrances and exits, dismantling the bleachers, building out the playing spaces, reconnecting the stage with the space for the audience, etc. It's fair to say that the Cartoucherie hangar, rather than being a polyvalent space, is a constantly evolving one, always the same and always different, adapting to whatever needs arise. This what truly marks it as exceptional. The image of the theatrical wagon that inspired Roberto Moscoso's design for *Captain Fracasse* continues to nourish the way we might map the Soleil's trajectory. The actors, thanks to their frequent touring, have been enriched by a nomadic life of encounters with new places. And what is more striking, various swiftly moving wagons, glides, and platforms, rolling across the masonry stage, have become the fundamental scenic units of the Soleil's twenty-first-century productions.

With the exception of certain scenic elements, there is nothing luxurious about the Soleil. Their kitchen, for example, was only redone in 2014, thanks to money from the City of Paris, the Ministry of Culture, and the regional Ile-de-France government. Mnouchkine is adamant that the only luxury owed to actors is time, enough time to learn and discover. And whatever the cost – and openings are frequently postponed – time is always taken. The Welcome Area, nevertheless, gets a great deal of attention, being rethought and repainted for each show. There were genealogical frescoes of Greek gods and heroes for *The House of Atreus Cycle*, an immense map of India for *The Indiad*, one of Patagonia for *Mad Hope*, an atlas of countries enflamed by war for *The Last Caravanserai*, replicas of cinema and theatre posters for *Mad Hope* and for *Macbeth* (2014). For the latter, a giant portrait of Shakespeare, superimposed on maps of the world and the universe, graced the wall facing the double, wooden entrance doors to the theatre's Welcome Area. The Soleil opens its doors an hour before every show. Once inside, spectators can wander at their ease. Like the actors, they prepare to experience the production and to enjoy, not just an evening, but a significant moment in their lives.

Already in 1968 Mnouchkine would say:

> I think of theatre as food. I want theatre to give strength to those who make it, including the public. Theatre's social function seems obvious to me, because at the end of a great show, you either leave with your opinions reinforced or opened to possibilities you'd barely grasped before experiencing the work.

A meal during rehearsals for *1789* (1970). From left to right: N. Félix, A. Demeyer, R. Moscoso; back to the camera, G-C. François. Photo by Martine Franck, Magnum Photos.

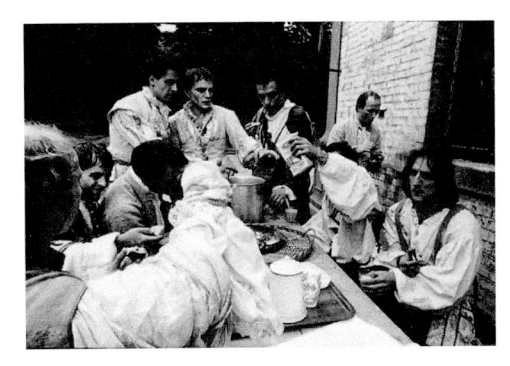

An outdoor meal during rehearsals for *Richard II* in the spring of 1981. From left to right: P. Hottier, J-P. Marry, J. Maurel, P. Fatus, G. Bigot, J-B. Aubertin, P. Carbonneaux, M. Durozier, P. Blancher. Photo by Lesly Hamilton.

A meal around the long table in the actors' foyer during *The Shakespeare Cycle* (1981). Among others, one can recognize L. Andreone, J-P. Hénin, A. Demeyer, J. Maurel, J-P. Marry, P. Hottier. Photo by Lesly Hamilton.

In the foyer, spring 1980, actors eating before Bernard Sobel films *Mephisto*, adapted from the theatre production. Around the table: C. Forget, his wife, L. Aucouturier, J. Pibarot, N. Journo, J-C. Bourbault, N. Félix, J. Derenne, A. Mnouchkine, and Pounchiki, the dog. Photo by Françoise Saur.

Real food has always accompanied this ideal of intellectual and emotional nourishment. The Soleil not only has a kitchen but also cooks to feed the actors while they're creating, as well as the spectators who come to see their shows. The menu offered to the public changes from production to production and is established at the culmination of the rehearsal process. The history of these menus tells an interesting tale all by itself – starting with Mnouchkine's memorable fit when she realized that the ingredients for the sandwiches served during *1789* had not been properly refrigerated, and continuing on to the special menus of Asian delicacies for *Sihanouk* and the addition of African-inspired ginger refreshments after the Soleil sheltered Malian immigrants (1996).

Welcoming means knowing how to receive guests with what is beautiful and good – with what pleases the senses. Thus there is the spacious bar where the actors themselves, over many years, served the public. There are also impressive bouquets of flowers, bought at the major flower market at Rungis, whose scent mixes with the plumes of smoke from the floating candles placed on the round or sometimes rectangular tables where diners gather. There is music, and a book display – richly furnished and also renewed with each production. Hanging lamps or table lanterns encourage the perusal of documentation used in the preparation of every work. This peaceful but also intensely concentrated ambience, inspired by but less commercial than what precedes Asian and especially Japanese kabuki performances, prepares the performance that follows. In winter, braziers warm the entrance. During warm weather, outdoor tables, benches, and garlands of colored lights welcome visitors who meet casually or in order to celebrate a special occasion.

What we might call external nomadism accompanies the Soleil's internal movement – national and international touring being essential for the financial health of the company. But there are also study trips, international internships, private travel for personal enrichment – to Asia and especially to India, and also to South America. This travel is fundamental to how the company lives and functions. The earliest tours were often marked by performances in enormous tents, recalling the first productions of the Soleil.[27] From the year 2000, one could see piled up in the "Buddha nave" giant trunks with the word "Soleil" stamped on them. Whoever was responsible for the set design at the time would also imagine the touring conditions. One of the most incredible tours placed the actors and sets of *Drums on the Dam* on a cargo ship that traveled across three different oceans. The tour of *The Survivors of Mad Hope* crisscrossed France with an exact copy of the Cartoucherie lay-out, so that the production could be installed in Lyon's Palais des sports. In Sao Paulo and in Taipei, *Ephemera* and *Mad Hope* were performed under a fabulous rectangular tent, its cloth imprinted with images from the productions. Extravagant thinking never held back a tour, but rather pushed even farther the ship usually moored at the Cartoucherie.

The sacred

The red and gold that help create the ritual aspect of Italianate theatres can't be found in the naves of the Cartoucherie hangar. Other rituals, however, are enacted or invented. First, there are the rituals connected to the work itself: the distribution of scripts (when there are scripts) at the beginning of the rehearsal process – to everyone, actors, technicians, and administrators.

There is the arrival of the masks in the rehearsal space or on the stage, carried in cases especially made for them and delicately placed on a table backed by a mirror, not far from the music. There is the passage from the rehearsal space to the stage, with a parade through the park outside the theatre and an examination of the stage – itself prepared over a period of several months by the technicians. There are the meetings before each performance with Mnouchkine or Hélène Cixous.

There are also rituals connected to the public. Mnouchkine, the "general," sounds the "*trois coups*," or three percussive strikes on the floor, before solemnly opening the doors to every performance, after having warned all the members of the company that she is about to do so. Most often it is she, herself, who greets the spectators at the doors and takes their tickets. And then there is the feeling of a theatrical ceremony, of a festive coming together that emanates from the luminous shadows of the Welcome Area, with actors mysteriously readying themselves in silence behind translucent curtains, observed by spectators in an attentive and respectful way. There is, moreover, the extraordinary size of the space, its simplicity, its functionality, but also its intriguing decorations. As G-C. François affirmed: "The Cartoucherie is much more than a theatre." Is this because it is full of so many lives of people who have worked so hard together, who have left so many traces? Is that why we feel in this theatrical home, in this Palace of Marvels, a kind of reservoir of strength?[28] Indeed, one of the abandoned (because too expensive) design projects for *1793* would have transformed the space into a decommissioned church, with a stone floor – a "sacred" space that would have served as meeting hall for the revolutionary section members.

Something of the sacred, close to the spiritual and not the religious, can be sensed here – unless we understand "religious" in the original sense of *re-ligere* or "the realigning, or gathering of emotions."[29] To which we can add that other key word from the Soleil's vocabulary, "worksite," with its intimation of hard and off-putting tasks that, nevertheless, find their source in the sacred. This sense of the sacred means a community of people working together and implies Mnouchkine's original decision, which she calls "fateful," to choose theatre as the site of an existence based on duration and the kind of hospitality that comes with a truly creative community. It goes hand in hand with Asia and the "gods of theatre" discovered during her voyage of initiation and, indeed, reinforced during all the travels that have inspired her way of receiving spectators as guests. It goes hand in hand with her rapport with the public and with the corresponding sense that she is "responsible for their souls." It also goes hand in hand with the length of so many of her productions that are also cycles that can require a full day of

"We go to your theatre as if taking refuge under the perfect vaulted ceilings of certain churches, in order to finally feel happy and at peace. In order to be elsewhere and oneself at the same time, outside of time and resituated within eternity." (Letter from a member of the audience, Archives Sophie Moscoso, 1982.)

Dressing rooms during a tour of *The Last Caravanserai (Odysseys)* (Jahrhunderthalle Ruhrtriennale, Bochum, June 2004). From *1789* on, the dressing rooms have been reinvented for each touring space, so as always to be visible to the spectators. Photo by Étienne Lemasson.

The Soleil on tour. The Cartoucherie layout was recreated exactly as it had been for a production of *The Survivors of Mad Hope* in January 2011 at the Palais des sports-Lyon Gerland. On tour in Asia and Latin America, a whole Cartoucherie village (15 containers) was installed in 2011 in the HSBC Arena in Rio de Janeiro. In the photo, we see the pile of traveling trunks stamped with the Soleil's name that figured in every installation of the production. In Porto Alegre, the Soleil installed the entire set in a gaucho village. Photo by Étienne Lemasson.

A huge party organized in the Welcome Area of the theatre during the run of *1789*. Many generations of spectators are already present around the tables. Photo by Martine Franck, Magnum Photos.

And Suddenly, Sleepless Nights (1997). A typical evening at the Cartoucherie: the Welcome Area where one can order something to eat and drink from the bar, where the public gathers an hour before the performance. To the right, lit by candles, lecterns where one can consult documents used to create the show. To the rear, a fresco by Didier Martin representing the Himalaya Mountains in Tibet. Photo by Michèle Laurent.

The Welcome Area for *The Survivors of Mad Hope*. On the wall, posters of silent films as frescoes. Photo by Everest Canto de Montserrat.

The Welcome Area for *Macbeth* (2014): frescoes on the walls, reproductions of posters, and a giant portrait of Shakespeare. Photo by Michèle Laurent.

theatre, punctuated by intermissions in which, as in kabuki or Noh, one can eat, drink, walk, wander, chat – a time not stolen from daily life but rather dedicated to Theatre.

A "sacred" theatre also connects to extreme rigor, to the risks and responsibilities of the actor entering on stage. Mnouchkine warned students at one of her workshops: "The stage in front of you is a formidable place, not because it can do you harm, but because it is, to put it simply, holy."[30] Sacredness has something to do, as well, with the Buddhas painted on the walls of the second nave in the late 1990s and that no one has been able to remove. Mnouchkine explains:

> Guy-Claude was much more radical than me and wanted to paint over them, as we had done for every show. But I couldn't do it. I can't be a Chinese soldier. And, besides, I believe that those Buddhas have a kind of power.[31]

In 2001, visiting monks from Tibet, specialists in Cham dancing, felt an energetic current emanating from them. And Mnouchkine again recognized a sense of sacredness when, upon the death of Guy-Claude François, at the beginning of rehearsals for *Macbeth* in February 2014, she had his body placed upon the stage for a last goodbye to the company. "He consecrated the stage of *Macbeth*," she murmured.

Finally, this sacredness is linked to a celebration of the lives of contemporary men and women. Hélène Cixous expresses it this way:

> Theatre must give us our true dimensions, our depths, our heights, our internal Indias. It's where we have the chance of encountering the gods. The air of theatre is full of them. Which gods? I mean that which is bigger than us, that which takes us over, that which we blindly call forth. I mean our own part of the divine.[32]

Little by little, all of this has made of an old and once devastated military warehouse the magnetic theatrical space it is today, a "temple without dogma or doctrine, but not without many many gods," as Cixous writes in her prefatory remarks to *The Indiad*.[33] Now we must delve into how – with what torment, which debates, what enthusiasm, which passions and difficulties, what kind of success – the Soleil managed to become what it has become. How, with the help of Mnouchkine's tenacity and unshakeable faith, did it develop what the original members had put in place, evolving and yet staying true through each successive generation to the idea of a great common work – no matter which nation company members hailed from?

The Cartoucherie (winter 2010). Braziers have been lit to welcome the public. Photo by Michèle Laurent.

An open-air ball, dancing taking place on a wooden floor (June 2010). Festive moments abound: birthdays, visits, presentations of the next production to the public, holidays, such as The Festival of St. John, or Iranian and Brazilian festivals brought to the company by actors who keep alive traditions that France has forgotten. Photo by Franck Pendino.

The Survivors of Mad Hope (Dawn). Since *The Indiad*, the dressing rooms at the Cartoucherie have been located underneath the bleachers or tiered seating area. Lightweight translucent curtains protect the actors' intimacy before the beginning of the performance but don't prevent the audience members from coming by to look. After the performance, the curtains are opened and the public can speak to the actors. High up on the right, we can see a detail reproduced from the cover of the Jules Verne book which inspired the production, stenciled on a wall by M. Lefebvre and E. Gülgonen. Photo by Michèle Laurent.

Notes

1 Ariane Mnouchkine, excerpt from a conversation about *1789* in *Théâtre et Histoire*, documentary film by Nat Lilenstein, *Théâtre aujourd'hui*, INA, 1971. All undocumented quotations from actors, friends of the Soleil, or from Ariane Mnouchkine in this chapter are taken from interviews Béatrice Picon-Vallin conducted and recorded from 2010 to 2014.
2 Ariane Mnouchkine, in Guy Freixe, *La Filiation: Copeau, Lecoq, Mnouchkine* (Paris: l'Entretemps, 2014).
3 Excerpt of a song from Théophile Gautier's *Captain Fracasse*, adapted by Philippe Léotard.
4 Ariane Mnouchkine, "*The Clowns*: théâtre d'aujourd'hui," documentary program by L. de Guyencourt, produced by J. Brard, ORTF (1969).
5 In Hubert Gignoux, *Histoire d'une famille théâtrale* (Paris: l'Aire théâtrale/Anrat, 1984), 344.
6 The training was for Barrault's *La Vie parisienne*, produced in 1958 at the same time as his production of Claudel's *Soulier de satin*, and reprised in 1962, 1963, and 1965.
7 Ariane Mnouchkine, *Revue d'histoire du théâtre*, vol. 4 (2009), 366.

8 Sonia Debeauvais, in an interview with Catherine Vilpoux for the film *Ariane Mnouchkine: l'Aventure du Théâtre du Soleil*, AGAT films and Co./ARTE France (2009).

9 Hubert Gignoux, *Histoire d'une famille théâtrale*, 121. Mehmet Ulusoy's work was indeed invited to the Théâtre du Soleil: in 1974 after the Avignon festival, *Le Cercle de craie caucasien* was performed in the Welcome Area and in 1976, he rehearsed his staging of *Dans les eaux glacées du calcul égoïste* at the Cartoucherie.

10 The *Molière* project was in competition for funds with a Goldoni project, proposed by Strehler. Thanks to the support of Paolo Grassi, the *Molière* project won.

11 Although roundly critiqued at its release, the film *Molière* has become a classic.

12 Jacques Copeau, *Registres I: Appels* (Paris: Gallimard, 1974), 187.

13 Jacques Copeau, *Le Journal de bord des Copiaux (1924–1929)*, ed. Denis Gontard (Paris: Seghers, 1974). For more on Mnouchkine and Copeau, see Alfred Simon, "Un rêve vécu de théâtre populaire" and "Ariane c'est une grande chose qui commence: une table ronde," *Esprit*, no. 5, June 1975.

14 *Jacques Copeau-Louis Jouvet: Correspondance (1911–1949)* (Paris: Editions O. Rony/Les Cahiers de la NRF/Gallimard, 2013), 232.

15 Ibid., 236.

16 Ibid., 655.

17 Ibid., 237.

18 See *Le Figaro*, May 5, 1969; *Le Figaro*, May 19, 1972; *Le Journal du dimanche*, May 21, 1972.

19 In 1970, Les Halles were classified as an urban development zone. In 1973, all but two of the pavilions were destroyed.

20 Noël Napo, technical director of the Théâtre du Chaillot, put Dupavillon and the Soleil in touch. Napo was very involved in the development of theatre at that point and he suggested numerous films to the Soleil to help their research. Dupavillon had seen *The Kitchen* and *The Clowns*.

21 See Chapter Two on the staging of *1789*.

22 See for more information Joël Crasmenil, *La Cartoucherie: une aventure théâtrale* (Paris: l'Amandier, 2004).

23 Other theatre companies who moved later into different hangars of the Cartoucherie made very different choices in the restructuring and organization of their spaces.

24 Ariane Mnouchkine, in Jean Chollet, *Construire pour le temps d'un regard: Guy-Claude François scénographe* (Paris: Fage éditions, 2009), 82.

25 Danièle Heusslein-Gire headed the team of painters, composed of Didier Martin, Kristos Konstantellos, Pedro Guimaraes, Yael Haber, Maria-Adelia Cardoso-Ferreira, and Jean-Charles Sankara.

26 I am grateful to Étienne Lemasson who kindly supplied all these details.

27 *1789* was performed at the Roundhouse in London, an immense, round, railroad-engine shed that has become an arts center.

28 Mnouchkine has here transformed Meyerhold's expression from a City of Marvels (*Pays des Merveilles*) to a Palace of Marvels (*Palais des Merveilles*).

29 See Hélène Cixous, "Le Lieu du Crime, le lieu du Pardon," in *l'Indiade ou l'Inde de leurs rêves et quelques écrits sur le théâtre* (Paris: Théâtre du Soleil, 1987), 258.

30 Ariane Mnouchkine, in Béatrice Picon-Vallin, *Ariane Mnouchkine* (Paris: Actes Sud, 2009), 94.

31 Ariane Mnouchkine, interviewed by Béatrice Picon-Vallin, wwwtheatre-du-soleil.fr.

32 Hélène Cixous, preface to *La Prise de l'école de Madhubaï, Avant-scène Théâtre*, no.745 (1984), 4.

33 Hélène Cixous, "Le lieu du Crime, le lieu du Pardon," 258.

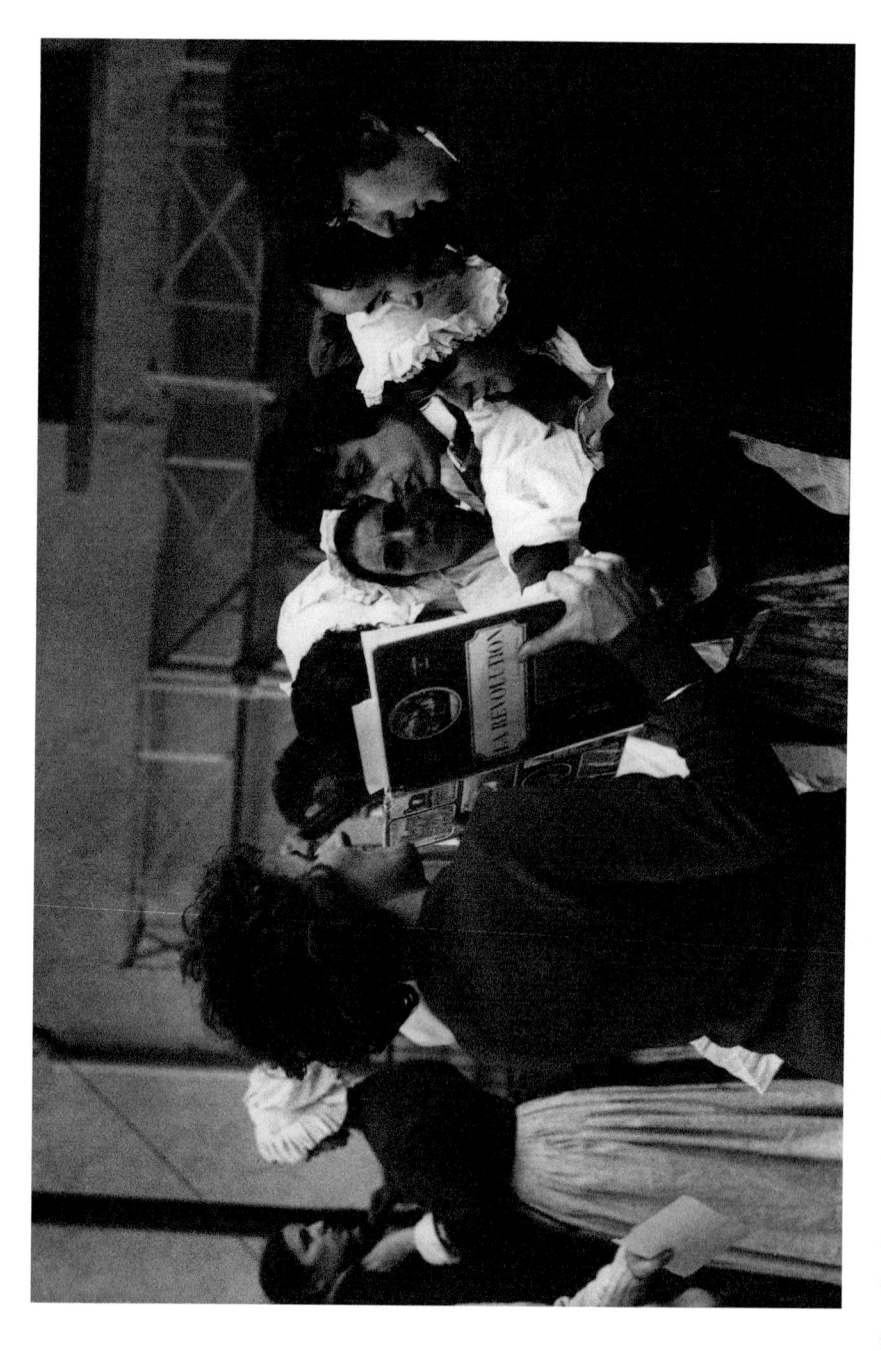

The Soleil's collective creations about the French Revolution took their inspiration from significant documentary sources. Here, Mnouchkine shows documents to the actors who comment on them. From left to right, partially costumed: G. Penchenat, M. Gonzalès, F. Jamet. Photo by Martine Franck, Magnum Photos.

Chapter 2 Collective creation (second try, first draft)

"When I start to improvise, I know that either everything will come from me or from the people I'm going to perform with – or nothing will come at all."

Philippe Caubère[1]

"[The] revelatory force [of the mask] is to prevent the public and the actor from setting up a stereotypical identification from the outset, but, on the contrary, to provide the means to perceive through the character an entire swath of humanity in which one can see oneself [...]. Through its intensity and its wondrousness, the mask in performance creates a magical force in the space of theatre that invites the public, at last, into a real conversation."

Erhard Stiefel[2]

Let's get back to our story and the collective creation, *1789*. The *Baal* project, dreamed up in 1968, did not work out, except for a few readings in a parish hall on rue Vercingétorix. And this was the case despite Mnouchkine having obtained rights to the play, as well as access to five different versions of it, having had *Baal* translated, and having engaged actors, including Roland Amstutz – who would eventually, with others taken on at that point, perform a reprise of *The Kitchen* and then *1789*. Mnouchkine turned fairly quickly away from the project; and Philippe Léotard, who had been scheduled to perform the main character Baal, left the company, unhappy with her decision. Was Baal too ambiguous? In fact, the priority of the company no longer leaned toward embodying individual struggle or representing a poet's life. In addition, Mnouchkine and set designer Roberto Moscoso had probably spent too much time working on the project ahead of time, planning a space where there would be no frontal performance, thinking about passageways, inventing an on-stage screen, placing the dramatic action on several different stages. Moreover, another way of doing theatre, the notion of a collective author, was beginning to emerge in 1969 as central to the Soleil's overall vision. In mid-July1970, having been refused authorization to rehearse *1789* in one of the pavilions of Les Halles, even if completely empty at that point, the Soleil rented the Palais des sports (under renovation and painted a brilliant red), while continuing to petition the Ministry of Culture for subsidies.

1970: a turbulent year, a decisive year, a bet, a challenge

The Soleil kept on working, rehearsing next at the Cartoucherie, which it had rented from the City of Paris at the end of August 1970. But *1789* would open in Milan, invited by Paolo Grassi, director of the Piccolo Teatro.[3] At the Piccolo, the Soleil would work in tandem with Patrice Chéreau, another exile from the French system, who was producing a Pablo Neruda piece. The Soleil had left a strong impression on Italy, the Piccolo having already produced *The Clowns*, and it would later produce *The Golden Age: First Draft*.[4] *1789* opened in November at the Palasporte, a sports center, very close to the Piccolo theatre itself.

Despite the enormous success of the production in Italy, and despite the fact that the set was designed to fit into any normal-sized basketball court (which could be found everywhere and which, more important, made possible a performance in which everyone would be connected visually to every moment of the work), no engagements were forthcoming once the company returned to France. As a consequence, everyone set to cleaning up the Cartoucherie, calling on their friends, repainting, installing toilets and light and sound baffles, and attempting to conform to the minimum standards of security for a theatre venue. An outrageous and very risky solution. The day of the opening, December 26, 1970, Ariane Mnouchkine and Christian Dupavillon, hiding in one of the small wooden cabins then littering the lawn around the theatre, waited, their hearts in their mouths. Watching the public arrive, they realized they had won. The cold, the snow, and the mud of the Vincennes woods had not stopped people from coming. Helped by a contagious word of mouth, *1789* played to sold-out houses for six months.

This time, marking a major difference with *The Clowns*, the Soleil hadn't started work on the production without equipping itself. It embarked on major research, both collective and individual: reading some of the key historians of the French Revolution (Michelet, Jean Jaurès, Albert Soboul,[5] Georges Lefebvre, Patrick Kessel, whose *The Night of August 4th* [*La Nuit du 4 août*] had just been published by Arthaud.) There were lectures by Elizabeth Brisson, whom the theatre program credits as consultant; visits to Jean Massin, who spoke to the actors in his sitting room of Michelet and Robespierre, inflaming their imaginations; meetings with Mary Meerson, the companion of Henri Langlois, who received them at the Cinémathèque with armfuls of films to watch: D.W. Griffith's *Orphans in the Storm*, 1921; Abel Gance's *Napoleon Bonaparte*, 1935 and his *Cyrano and d'Artagnan*, 1964; Conway and Leonard's *A Tale of Two Cities*, 1935; and Harold Young's *The Scarlet Pimpernel*, 1934.

The big question was how to handle this story, whose great moments were known by everyone. The Soleil had to choose an approach, show the Revolution not through the story of its great men, but through the eyes of the people who had made it happen, who had been manipulated and betrayed. Thus, the troupe would rehabilitate Marat, the standard bearer of the oppressed, he who wanted to "teach people their rights," to the detriment of a Mirabeau or a Lafayette. To a new point of view would be added a new form, an acting style that would exclude the kind of realism Mnouchkine had been attempting to eliminate in all ways possible. That resulted in having the actors establish a playful distance from the characters: the actors would, therefore, have the chance of judging the characters they played. The Revolution would thus be performed by "fairground performers" at a "fairground theatre." This kind of *mise en abyme*, with actors playing popular entertainers of the eighteenth century, recalls what Russian director Evgeni Vakhtangov chose to do when he mounted *Princess Turandot* in Moscow in 1922. It's also the kind of dramaturgical choice directly in line with the type of popular entertainment that had already characterized work done by the Soleil. But this time, the Soleil was attacking the "carnival trestles of History."[6]

Exploratory sketch by Roberto Moscoso: for *Baal*, where the set includes a film screen. An early design for *The Golden Age* also included a screen, which would be jettisoned. Roberto Moscoso, Archives Sophie Moscoso.

A sketch by Roberto Moscoso for *1789*, with walkways connected by platforms, an idea that would not be kept. Roberto Moscoso, Archives of Sophie Moscoso.

After two months of rehearsals, it became clear that it would be impossible to treat all of the Revolution in one go. Thus, the company decided to create a two-part piece: the first would end in 1791, at the massacre of civilians on the Champ-de-Mars. The production would show how the bourgeoisie had stolen the Revolution, but would end with the hopeful injunction of Gracchus Babeuf: "Let's concentrate on the goal of creating society, let's concentrate on our common happiness, and let us, after 1,000 years, transform these vulgar and harmful laws."[7]

1789: the Revolution must only stop at the perfection of happiness (Saint Just)

Combined with increased documentary and historical research, the work of collective creation became more complicated but very joyful: there was abundant material and many possible roles to play. The characters who emerged were tried out, vetted, abandoned, and turned inside out. The actors improvised in groups of four or five, sometimes more, working on different historical situations, such as, for example, the taking of the Bastille; or a debate at the National Assembly; the proclamation of Martial Law; the King and Queen's flight to Varennes; the huge farce of the night of August 4, when nobles divested themselves of their privileges; or the Declaration of the Rights of Man. They worked on themes and characters: the salt tax, Madame Veto, the official Lists of Grievances, the peasant women's panic, the French baker and the scarcity of bread, war, the people's lament: "We have nothing to write with," Lafayette and the National Guard, and also on puppeteers and puppets.[8]

Several groups worked on the same themes: the actors presented, proposed, compared, critiqued, reworked, confronted; they added or subtracted, built out, built more. Everybody was completely involved in these forms of collective work and they produced hundreds of improvisations. It was less frustrating than the work on *The Clowns*, where improvisations were more personal and individual. The selection of what to keep, discussed by everyone who had also seen everything, was more obvious, "evident," as they would say.

The staging confirmed Mnouchkine's particular role; she would act as "conductor of collective creation." She was, at once, the attentive spectator, the helpful critic, the person who selected from the mass of documents many of the elements fundamental to the improvisations. She took on the responsibility of validating the correctness of the interpretation, and she had most of the responsibility for the final ordering and articulation of the scenes.

Into this creative mix, a new position emerged: that of the "guarantor of memory." Sophie Lemasson, a Nanterre

University student who had seen *The Kitchen* and *The Clowns* and was writing her master's thesis on the Soleil, had been introduced to the company. She was authorized to watch rehearsals and record them from the last rows of the bleachers at the Palais des sports, where the troupe was rehearsing. When Mnouchkine needed a nudge to remember what had been done, Lemasson would climb down and offer what she had. When the company left to rehearse in the Cartoucherie, she followed, abandoning her thesis, and kept up the work of recording and taking notes for Mnouchkine on the emerging dialogue. The actors, as well, took notes on what they had done and said. Once at the Cartoucherie, she would also help with costumes, with ironing, with whatever was needed: "I was integrated into the Soleil's work; I was there where it was useful to be; it was blissful." Officially named the "guarantor of memory" for *1789* and *1793*, Sophie Lemasson[9] had to learn how to be Mnouchkine's assistant. But it took until *The Shakespeare Cycle* for her to think of herself truly in this role, because at that point she was able to develop a system of recording, by hand, the rehearsal process. She became the mediating interface between the director and the actors, never interfering, however, in how they were coached. Outside of the rehearsal space, the actors also worked on their improvisations and met at each other's homes to discuss what they'd been reading, or to find solutions for realizing in their work such abstract concepts as "The General Will." They worked on clarifying, finding the essential, striking the public's imagination, creating the right stage metaphor for abstract concepts. In the case of "The General Will," the metaphor turned out to be a woman giving birth.

The clear and colorful narration of events was carried out by "storytellers," who handed over the story to "fairground actors" who, themselves, played many different characters in as many different acting styles or performative modes: that of the prestigious Théâtre Français, or official state theatre; of marionettes, both string and giant effigies; of official proclamations of degrees; of parades and processions; shadow theatre; pantomime; or dance. Different attitudes toward the characters, sometimes joyful, sometimes drunken or ironic, were displayed: there was no identification, but a great deal of variation in the distance taken, made possible by the actors' own inventiveness and by how the space was organized.

In his preliminary sketches for the set, Roberto Moscoso imagined a wide-open space where different fairground stands would compete with each other: it would be the kind of all-englobing space conjured up by Antonin Artaud, where the stage and the audience would be intermixed, and where the public would be placed in the middle of the action. At that time in the development of experimental theatre, one might

1789 or The Revolution Must Only Stop at the Perfection of Happiness. Above and opposite: created in a sports arena, Milan's Palasporte, this production was a powerful rejoinder from France to the theatrical proposal advanced by Luca Ronconi with his *Orlando Furioso.* Photo by Danka Semenowicz, Archives Sophie Moscoso.

1789. Rehearsal in the deliquescent space of the Cartoucherie: Madame de Polignac (J. Derenne); Marie-Antoinette (R. Rochette); Madame de Lamballe (M. Donzenac). In the background, actors are putting together their costumes. Photo by Béatrice Heyligers, Archives Jean-Claude Penchenat.

1789. Improvisations with R. Patrignani, J-C. Penchenat, and M. Toty. Photo by Martine Franck, Magnum Photos.

1789. On their trestle table, the Bourgeoisie applauds Martial Law that puts an end to the Revolution. We can see a stage curtain attached to the back of the table. Photo by Martine Franck, Magnum Photos.

1789. "*All the Nobility and the highest dignitaries of the Church, in the face of the People's despair, began to love the People and divested themselves of all their privileges. And thus we have the Night of August 4th.*" Pictured from left to right: M. Gonzalès, J-C. Penchenat, A. Salomon. Photo by Gérard Taubman.

have encountered similar spatial conceptions at The Bread and Puppet Theatre Company, or at the Living Theatre, and especially in the immersive and ambulatory design of Ariosto's *Orlando furioso*, as staged by Luca Ronconi – that the actors had indeed seen in 1970 when it was performed in the Baltard Pavilion of Les Halles. In this Théâtre des Nations production, knights perched high "on horseback" on rolling platforms, moving between spectators, fought each other to the death. The Soleil didn't mention Artaud in their text-program for *1789*,[10] but, rather, quoted Diderot from *The Natural Son* about what theatre must be:

> That's when one will tremble when going to the theatre and one won't be able not to. That's when, instead of those quaint fleeting emotions or that faint applause [...], the theatre will shatter our minds, filling our souls with unease and horror [...]. [That means] knowing how to combine pantomime with dialogue, intercutting spoken text with silent scenes, and making art from bringing all this together.

Another vision of a necessary and cruel theatre!

In the temporary workshop installed in the Palais des sports,[11] actual-size models of the trestle tables for the set were created out of plywood. That way the actors were able to work immediately on the imagined set, grasping its dimensions – the height, the width, the number of individualized playing spaces. A team of six technicians, including the designer and the technical director, eventually constructed five permanent elevated trestle tables, set up in a rectangle, not all the same height, with each wooden table connected by a passageway to another, and each table pegged together, not nailed, as were eighteenth-century fair tables. In the center was a large area in which spectators could stand and move about; bleachers placed on the outside of the rectangle also provided seating. Moscoso speaks of the trestle table as "a kind of stage wagon to which could be affixed on poles located on the back of the wagon a curtain or other elements." But these wagons would not move; instead the public and the actors would run from one table to the next. *1789* was created little by little in a supple and constantly evolving process – despite the limitations of not having a theatre – in which various dramaturgical solutions were found at the same time as the playing space took shape.

We might turn to Françoise Tournafond, who ran the costume shop at the time, in order to understand the degree of collaboration, the willingness of everyone to dig into the work. At that point, the Soleil had a huge stock of theatre and film costumes, those from earlier shows and also those given to the company from a production house (which had produced

1789. Marat, the feverish defender of the People (R. Patrignani) speaks into the microphone. Behind him, the Bourgeoisie participates in the sale of the Church's goods (N. Félix and M. Toty). Photo by Danka Semenowicz, Archives Sophie Moscoso.

the films *Lucrecia Borgia, Madame du Barry,* and *The Grand Maneuver*).[12] Tournafond had also bought a selection of costumes from the Comédie Française that she would use for the scene of "The Night of August 4."

Voice of Françoise Tournafond

> *"I was there for all the rehearsals. For a show performed by 'poor fairground actors,' we obviously couldn't make anything that looked new. The actors rifled through what we had, tried things on, combined things. The role of the costume designer was to help orient, find a unifying style, to eliminate anything that didn't speak to who the character was. [...] I took all the costumes apart, then rebuilt them on dummies, grouping them by two or three. [...] I saved everything I could, lace, beads, jewels. Everything was rebuilt, dyed. The more material I had in hand, the more I could see what the costumes should be, the more my imagination was sparked. It was a constant back and forth between the staging, the actors, their performance, and me. [...] Not being alone in one's corner – creating – but, rather, having living material around is fantastic for the imagination."*[13]

One of the fair actors grabbed Captain Fracasse's costume, just as later Georges Bigot for *Richard II* (1981) would put on the vest worn by Philippe Caubère in the film *Molière*, a vest that would be restructured to work for him. This process of artistic recycling, both pragmatic and symbolic, created costumes that became, in fact, layers of memory. The memory-costumes themselves, imagined by and for each actor, were sketched by the costumer during rehearsals; and the paper sketches helped them, in turn, develop their characters without ever impacting negatively their acting. Mnouchkine explains: "We used our theatrical references, just like we used our memories of what we'd learned at school – those images and engravings stuck in our memories – as a base to rework and subvert by putting things together differently." And, indeed, in *1789* there was no historical reconstitution. For "The Taking of the Bastille" no guns, no canon smoke, but, rather, the representation of a major historical moment through what inspired it: the progressive gathering together of individual stories morphing into a "vocal explosion" and collective gesture, capable of "taking down the old fortress."[14] This image is also the principle of collective creation, in rehearsal as well as in performance. The life of the Soleil, as a theatrical collective, gave life to the Revolution.

The final montage of the improvisations followed the chronology of the Revolution, but the principle of construction was

based on contrasts. There would be two
hours of performance without a break in
an open space, without wings, where the
actors, seated around a giant table, would
do their makeup before the show in front
of a fascinated public, and during the show,
change costumes and redo makeup behind
the trestles. The Soleil would never go back
to closed and isolated dressing rooms after
that experience.

In the first tableau, two actors, followed
by the storyteller who named the places
traversed by the characters, evoked "The
Flight to Varennes." The first movement
of Mahler's *Titan* symphony played while
the "King" and "Queen" moved from trestle table to trestle table. "Let us pass," bel-
lowed the storyteller, speaking for Louis
XVI; and the standing public opened up a
path for the Royals. Seated in the bleachers, the other public watched this mixing of
roles. Called into performance, the standing
public became the popular Assembly. And
then, suddenly, a brutal change: a peasant
woman (Geneviève Penchenat), birthing a
baby, had her pail of clean water torn away
by an aristocrat, a feudal lord: he demanded
payment of his tax. Her cry of despair in
response seared the air. There would follow a series of short sketches, others longer.
There would be dialogued scenes, mimes,
and choral sequences, sometimes on one
trestle table or sometimes on all five at once.

The "Taking of the Bastille" scene was one
of the most overwhelming. It was based on
an anonymous and historically documented
account of an individual who recounted the
day as he'd lived it. This story was magnified
and multiplied by the actors who composed
their own story, with help from Michelet's
history. Actors located everywhere in the
playing area and on the bleachers told the
story to the rhythm of music that helped
them move forward together. They started
by whispering, so that the public would
approach and listen as though being pri-
vately told. Then the whispers began to
grow in waves, the scansions carefully
orchestrated as if a musical partition, until

Some costume sketches by Françoise
Tournafond for *1789*. One of the
marketplace women (for Daïna La
Varenne). Françoise Tournafond,
Archives Guy-Luc Boyaval.

1789. Costume sketch for the fairground
actor (for J-C. Penchenat). F. Tournafond,
Archives Jean-Claude Penchenat.

1789. Possible costume for Louis XVI
(with indications of the color scheme).
F. Tournafond, Archives Guy-Luc Boyaval.

the explosive announcement of the "people's victory."[15] A celebration then ensued under brilliant spots and against vibrant and naïve backdrops made from used materials and hung from the poles on the trestle tables. The fair performers acted out key episodes of the Revolution on their respective tables, sometimes simultaneously: there were jugglers, wrestlers, acrobats with flaming torches, a wheel of fortune, and flag-waving in a general ambiance of joyous carnival, accompanied by circus music. A "trained bear," led by his handler, paraded through the public.[16]

Next would be parodies, such as "The Count d'Artois Emigrates." Actors and spectators ran from trestle table to trestle table, applauding. But a blue and rose-colored Lafayette suddenly showed up and called a halt to the festivities; no more public demonstrations. He would be booed from many places, but nothing stopped him from proclaiming: "The Revolution is over." Thus, the National Guard broke up the crowd, a crowd of spectators that had become the people of 1789. Following that moment, Marat would take in his arms from the people an allegory of "The Sick Nation"; and the aristocrats, in an expressionistic pantomime, would give away, on the night of August 4, their privileges and rights in the form of clothing (only to grab jackets, plumes, and scarves back from the standing public when their declaration was read aloud on a facing table).

Among other outsized sketches, the public witnessed the results of the Declaration of the Rights of Man in a sardonic sketch about Santo Domingo, dominated by huge umbrellas and plumed fans to keep those (still) in power cool. There would be "The Procession of the Women of Paris," dressed in white, waving laurel branches, who "went to Versailles" to look for the Queen and King; and they would "bring them back to Paris" through the standing public in the form of 3-meter-high giant marionettes. Just before this, smaller marionettes representing the banker Jacques Necker, the Clergy, and the Nobility met in a parody of the meeting of the Estates-General. And, again, a stop was put to the excitement; this time by the proclamation of Martial Law and the waving of a black banner demanding "Order." A feverish Marat would try to keep the revolutionary spirit in motion: "Citizens, wake up!" But he would be threatened by the Deputies to the National Assembly – the Guardians of Order – who advanced into the playing area, holding high their black banner.

In all of these ways, the public's attention would be constantly solicited. Standing spectators had to move, come closer, get out of the way when the actors entered, often, into their spaces. In such an immersive design, the public had to stay alert, look in all directions. Spectators were often surprised about where the action was happening next. Sometimes a spectator might fixate on one actor, such as Nicole Félix, as she played the flute and sang. But most of the time, the spectators had to choose where to look; and they would never be on their own, rather always in the middle of other spectators and actors. Having a constantly changing perspective, as in the movies, the spectator had to be mobile, as in all forms of popular outdoor entertainment. Emotions were mobile as well: from the euphoria of the constantly moving victory celebration to the critical distance called on during the satirical sketches of power: spectators found themselves laughing and judging. Through their improvisations, the Soleil sought to "construct the emotional voyage" of its public; and the musical score, never illustrative but always present, intensified these emotions, whether it was by Lully, Rameau, Handel, or Bach, or structured by snare drums and other percussive instruments. Certain of these *1789* evenings have entered into the growing mythology of the Théâtre du Soleil, such as the night of July 14, 1971, when the overflow of audience members, kept out of the theatre, began to dance outside the doors. As it was sweltering inside, the performance stopped at the "Taking of the Bastille" scene, and everybody left the theatre to participate in an improvised ball – the first of many at the Théâtre du Soleil.

1789 wasn't conceived for the Cartoucherie, but it found its place there. The title, *1789*, was affixed in large numbers over the double doors of the entrance. The actors were as much at home there as in their own dwellings. Taken from the last 15 performances, the film that Mnouchkine made of the show captures some of this life: audience members seem to be integral to the troupe. Mnouchkine decided quickly to make the film, acquiescing to those who couldn't bear to see the historic production disappear without a visual trace. Made over the course of 13 days, the film, *1789* – almost like a sporting event – mimics the multiplicity of perspectives created in the play. The next production, *1793*, on the other hand, being built in the Cartoucherie on the heels of *1789*, would portray a specific and unchanging historical space in a much more sober fashion. After the spectacular, even allegorical images in *1789*, *1793* would tell the epic tale of the anonymous *sans-culottes*, those working-class people who had contributed so importantly to the Revolution.

1793: the Revolutionary city is part of this world

For *1793*, the proposed acting style and performance ethos would be entirely different: centered, not volatile, and not in constant transformation. If the production began with a parade where a carnival barker called forth hyperbolic images from the world depicted in *1789*, the tone would change quickly. From their prancing about, caricaturizing power to Berlioz's *Funereal*

"Nobody wants to create a Brechtian-style didactic show." (Actors of the Soleil, interviewed by Claude Morand, *ATAC Informations,* April 1972, 4.)

and Triumphal Symphony, the actors transformed themselves into "Section Members" of the Mauconseil Assembly, a Revolutionary section, or popular assembly, from the neighborhood of Les Halles. These "people," who distinguished themselves during the aftermath of 1789 by the quality of their debates, by having been the first to vote for the dethronement of Louis XVI and the first to denounce the Girondin Party, would, then, tell their story: a story that followed them from the destitution of the king to the interdiction of section meetings by the Committee of Public Safety. Thus, the end of one of France's most poignant forms of direct democracy would be highlighted.

Voice of Sophie Lemasson Moscoso, January 17, 1972

"In October 1971, we were performing in London, and we'd started improvising again with commedia dell-arte *masks, as we did for* The Clowns. *We were working out a method and readapting ourselves to collective creation. After some 200 performances of* 1789 *and given the overall fatigue of the actors, we needed to start training again. In November 1971, we went to Lyons to perform, and while there, we had lessons from a history professor on the period between 1789 and 1795 – two hours every morning. We trained in the afternoons and performed at night. In December, after a week's vacation, we reconfigured the Cartoucherie, kept on having history lessons, and began the first improvisations for* 1793.

It was a pretty tough moment, full of difficult discussions: nothing was clear and everybody had a different idea. Still embodying the fairground style of 1789, *the actors weren't able to find the same powerful, even mythic, images in the events of* 1793. *They decided to abandon their roles as fairground actors to take on the roles of section members from 1793. But in order to imagine the daily life of those* sans-culottes, *they knew they had to dig into political and historical interpretations – and that personal research would also have to be connected to finding or inventing a new acting style. That kind of research hadn't taken place for* 1789. *So, every day the actors presented collective exposés on specific situations from the revolutionary period: on war, the Church, the conservative Feuillants, the moderate Brissotins-Girondins, the King, foreign interventions, the colonial situation, and so on. They took on the full complexity of the period from 1789 to 1795."* And Sophie Moscoso would add, speaking on February 22, 1972: *"1793 marks an evolution, brings a different excitement to our company. We're aware that we're changing profoundly. This is a show based on research and*

1793. Exploratory sketch by Roberto Moscoso for the set. He was imagining a decommissioned church, with a stone-tiled floor, occupied by the Section Members as a place to hold their revolutionary assemblies. Roberto Moscoso, Archives Sophie Moscoso.

1793. The public is seated on the ground, or standing, or seated in the surrounding galleries, their legs hanging over the edge of the ledge. The actors move from one table to the other, often on the same level as the public. Sometimes the table is a stage; sometimes the table is a convivial gathering place. Photo by Martine Franck, Magnum Photos.

1793: Final sketch for the set by Roberto Moscoso. Three large tables in wood (the largest measuring 6×2.7 meters), grouped to form a triangle. The tables, the benches, the galleries, and the lighting (300 florescent tubes, 40 watts each, with shades to cover the skylight) required research and workshops in order to work through the technical difficulties. Denis Bablet would say: "It's the scenography that organizes how the spectator sees." (*Travail Théâtral*, February 1976). Roberto Moscoso, Archives Sophie Moscoso.

1793. "*August 23, 1793, conscription for all is declared; and the revolutionary Section organizes a civic banquet.*" Pictured, on the table: G. Hardy and N. Félix. Archives Sophie Moscoso.

*we don't know yet, of course, where it will take us. It's the
unknown: but at the same time we've never felt our responsibilities so clearly. As much as 1789 was born in joy, 1793
is being born in pain.*"[17]

In that same period, Mnouchkine explained things this way:

> We want to expose what's been hidden in the way the his-
> tory of France has been taught. Tell how much the people
> of Paris, in their various neighborhood assemblies, thought
> outside the box, how far they went in imagining what
> power could be, what it would mean to enact the sover-
> eignty that they'd won [...]. If we succeed with *1793*, there
> will be moments when it feels like science fiction. [*1793*]
> is meant to be a contemporary piece, speaking to us of the
> beginnings of our society.[18]

The work would directly connect to the research already
mentioned, and also plunge into the several volumes of *The
Parliamentary History of the French Revolution* [*l'Histoire
parlementaire de la révolution française*].[19] Moreover, myriad
engravings of revolutionary events, of meetings of revolutionary
clubs and section meetings, with their radicalized *sans-culottes*
(laborers and artisans) would help form the images.

Philippe Caubère, Maxime Lombard, and Jean-Claude
Bourbault, coming from Marseilles and an experimental theatre company based in Aix-en-Provence, were integrated into
the company as though they were "Section Members" who had
arrived from the south in 1793. Two of them would, in fact,

1793: Costume designs by Françoise Tournafond for the hyperbolic fancy characters of the
parade that launches the evening. F. Tournafond, Archives Guy-Luc Boyaval.

perform the roles of *Fédérés* from Marseilles, or citizen-soldiers in the National Guard. Just as the *sans-culottes* took over desacralized spaces for their neighborhood meetings, the members of the Théâtre du Soleil took over their Cartoucherie space and rethought and reworked it – from a fairly wasteland state – for their show. Roberto Moscoso enjoyed saying that it wasn't a matter of creating a set, or designing a playing area, but really of taking over the run-down space and turning it into a meeting place not only for the "Section Members" but also for the Soleil itself. This was a process that reflected both the past of France and the present of the company. And the "Section Members'" debates on equality and power echoed the real political debates taking place within the company. "In olden days, the words 'Liberty Equality, Fraternity' really meant something. They gave people the shivers," said Sophie Moscoso in 1972. But, we might ask, aren't those words from the eighteenth century the same words being queried in 1972, after the political protests and revolutionary events of 1968? Furthermore, didn't the Soleil's 2012 production, *The Survivors of Mad Hope*, by miming and inscribing those words on stage, also attempt to give new energy to the founding concepts of the French Republic?

It was through the stories told by those popular figures who'd been forgotten by History that the events of 1793 were presented. "Section Members" told of their struggles and their dreams: they represented the popular avant-garde of the Revolution. In addition to improvising discussion, the actors also had to define their characters. Twenty-three actors (of the 48 people then in the company) sought the *sans-culotte* they would perform: they would locate them from within diverse professions: ironer, kitchen worker, embroiderer, engraver, baker, blacksmith, carpenter, newspaper vendor, clerk, and more. Given the show's conceit, it wasn't possible to stage anyone from the more bourgeois Girondin circles, so the Girondins would appear in how they were contested by the "Section Members." Each "Section Member" would take on a name, a past, a profession, beliefs, and some education. The troupe's aim was to show both individuals and the strength of the collective these individuals had been able to create. Improvisations were complex, first free form, then directed, with 10 to 12 actors, sometimes as many as 30 participating in one improvisation when the Soleil wanted to make felt the force of the group and the interdependency of the actors. They improvised sometimes for ten hours at a time, in states of extreme concentration.

The actors divided up into two groups: it was the men who would lead the fight, both taking action and building the arguments for the kind of revolution they craved. The women would show through staging it daily life during the Revolution: its misery, cold, and hunger. They quarreled with shopkeepers who had become speculators; they broke the ice on the enormous tub of the public washhouse; they queued up for what scarce bread remained. The chorus of women, protesting and working, corresponded to the chorus of men, all members of the same revolutionary section, growing closer and closer as the show progressed. Both choruses met up in the key scene of the Civic Banquet of August 27, 1793: they sang revolutionary songs, recited the Declaration of the Rights of Man, and shared a meal – and all of this solidarity preceded mass conscription of the men into the French military.

Characters emerged as a function of discussions and documentation: each actor presented their character to the entire company – noting their origins, their political stance, their particular way of moving, their way of speaking, their accent, their vocabulary.[20] Actors also improvised outside of the context of the section meetings; they worked on clowns, which was particularly useful to the women who needed to find a mood of ferociousness in order to confront "shady shopkeepers." They worked on the kind of stylization that allowed them to eliminate naturalism, moving from narrating in the third person to narrating in the first person. They looked for the tragic dimensions of simple people who were meant to have the grandeur and gravitas of "real princes and real kings." They would make their characters heroes, heroes whose daily life would take on a strangeness, a distance. When the improvisations bogged down, the actors worked on scenes from Sophocles' *King Oedipus* and *Antigone*, or on Euripides' *Alcestis*. Mnouchkine tried to film the improvisations instead of relying on notation, but gave up, finding that filming encouraged the actors' narcissism.

The approach to the costuming was very different from what had been done for *1789*: historical constraints in this case being obvious. Françoise Tournafond created a series of models that evolved as the work evolved: the idea was to find an appropriate costume for each type of work. Nevertheless, she didn't follow exactly the mock-ups and images she'd located in historical museums, but used old fabric, whose long use gave to the costumes a particular sheen.

The play began in the second nave of the theatre, with the great parade representing "The Fight of the Powerful against the People." The Royal family, foreign kings and queens, aristocratic generals, important clergy – whose extravagant costumes had come from the Folies Bergères – strutted across a long walkway (15 × 4 meters), in front of a red curtain painted by R. Moscoso and brightly lit by four spots and footlights. The public was led into the third nave, where actors rolled in staircases that allowed them to reach the stages, while audience members took their places on the floor (seated or standing), on the stairs to the stages, or in the galleries that surrounded the playing space. Once the red curtain was closed, the Mauconseil Section, as seen in engravings, came to life, with, in addition to the enclosed galleries on two sides, three huge and very tall tables (the stages), set up as a triangle, with benches on all sides.[21] These tables were, of course, the basic furniture necessary for the meetings of "Section Members," but they were also where the actors of the Soleil ate, argued, dreamed, and worked. Tables could become a tribunal or the washhouse where the overtaxed women beat their clothes – their gestures conjuring up the water and the tub.

The lighting was exceptional: the designers recreated the daylight normally diffused vertically in the third nave through the glass skylight. It was blue, almost white, and felt almost surreal during the evening performances. R. Moscoso, G-C. François, and Jean-Noël Cordier had imagined the effect while *1789* was still running. Florescent tubes with dimmers were hidden outside of the skylight. The dimmers allowed the Soleil to suggest passing time, as well as winter, summer, dawns, and dusks. The simplicity of the lighting contrasted with the highly theatricalized lighting of the opening parade and lit the spectators, as well as the actors. Being able to see the public lent a certain tension to the performance.

Voice of Guy-Claude François, 2004

> "*Ariane wanted to light the theatre as though it were daytime, the kind of light you see at the beginning of the day when you've spent the night remaking the world. It was a lot of work, especially technically, as the electrical equipment (hundreds of florescent tubes) and the light boards that could make them work weren't meant to be used in a theatre. We had to invent a system, which Jean-Noël Cordier, the lighting designer at the time, did. Since then, we've used this lighting ritualistically at the Soleil. A lot of lighting specialists came to see how it worked, including Nestor Almendros, François Truffaut's cinematographer. He was the first one to use our innovation in film.*"[22]

1793, termed a "visionary show" and the story of a "political fiction,"[23] ended with each *sans-culotte* recounting his fate: either conscripted into the army that would fight for France or executed. The clerk read a text by Emmanuel Kant on the exemplary greatness of what had been accomplished, a commentary also on the workings of the Soleil, whose members, too, wanted to be part of a society of equals. There was no direct policy suggested, no recognizable party slogan. *1793* was a show about how citizens might think together after the events of May 1968: freely, autonomously, and self-directed. Some of the actors, notably Georges Bonnaud and Gérard Hardy, would also demonstrate actively in various political movements during this period; for example, during the first festival of the Communist Lutte Ouvrière in 1971, with a marionette play called *The Commune as Told to Children* [*La Commune racontée aux enfants*], or with the GIP, a prison reform group.

Voice of Georges Bonnaud

"It's our habit to create, while we're performing a show, a cabaret performance – something just for us, that can help with training, or be performed at a party we'll throw at some point. This kind of intimate entertainment takes us a month or two of work and we perform it for ourselves and sometimes some friends for one night only. In the context of this kind of parallel project, which had really only been internal until then, some of the members of the Soleil staged two political pieces: one on the Commune *(1971) and the other on* Vietnam *(1973). The work consisted in developing a theme proposed by one of us, without the whole troupe necessarily participating. [The show on* Vietnam*] was performed at the Mutualité and twice at the Cartoucherie, also at La Maison des Jeunes et de la Culture in the town of Drancy, and at the Thomson factory – twice, over lunchtime, on the request of their cultural committee."*[24]

During the six months of rehearsals, working under extreme financial constraints, not everyone advanced at the same pace. Some actors left. The women, in great solidarity with each other, made room for the women actors who were not finding their characters, expecting they'd have more success in a later production. The company stayed alert and welcoming to debates on world events, inviting, for example, the Czech director Otomar Krejca and his Za Branu Theatre to mount an exhibition of their work, as their theatre had been closed by authorities during the events of the Prague Spring. Working with other companies at the Cartoucherie, the Soleil sponsored debates and exhibitions on the Vietnam War, on the peasant opposition to nuclear power plants in Larzac; and, in 1973 – working with the opposition, on the repressive political power structure in Portugal. Company members welcomed supporters of the Chilean government and a Women's Fair – one of the first activities of a revived feminist movement in France.

1793 divided France's critical establishment. Those on the right, given their penchant for literary theatre and their ideology, complained about the mediocre message, the failed and disappointing form, the "Boy Scout leftism." "Not a play, nothing like a text, no thought, negligent form." "A naïve evening

The Commune as Told to Children, a show created by members of the Soleil for the first festival of the Communist group, Lutte Ouvrière, on the wooded grounds of the Château de Bellevue, in Presle, Val-d'Oise, May 30, 1971. We can see an allegory of the Commune (L. Bensasson) in a long white dress with a necklace of flowers. To her right, C. Bousquet and A. Salomon. Photo by Gérard Taubman.

Funeral Procession of May 13, 1973. A tract for a demonstration against the Minister of Cultural Affairs, Maurice Druon. A pair of horses would pull a carriage that symbolized the death of Culture. This was a joint protest by the Soleil, the Vincent-Jourdheuil Company, the Aquarium, the Ensemble de Gennevilliers, the Théâtre de la Tempête, and Action pour le Jeune Théâtre. Archives Théâtre du Soleil.

The second festival of Lutte Ouvrière, May 22, 1972. The Soleil performs a short agit-prop skit: *Steal bread and go to prison. Steal millions and go to a palace* (or the Palais-Bourbon, where the French National Assembly meets.) This slogan would be echoed from cell to cell in French prisons. Left, seated, Ariane Mnouchkine; right, seated, Michel Foucault. Photo by Gérard Taubman.

Vietnam. A show produced at the Cartoucherie in 1972 by the actors of the Soleil, in collaboration with former members of the Bread and Puppet Theatre, lodged at the Théâtre de la Tempête and then at the workshop of the Chaudron at the Cartoucherie. Here we see a giant puppet of Mother America. Photo by Gilles Hattenberger, Archives Georges Bonnaud.

lecture." "A shipwreck that bears witness to the limits of a theatre that wants to be at the same time popular, political, and collective."[25] Gilles Sandier, coming from the left, responded: "Such [negative] views are short-sighted and small-minded." He praised the rigor of the work, the interiorization of revolutionary sensibilities in "a multi-layered show of political force and subtle visual beauty, especially the kind of shy tenderness that elicits, at moments, our tears."[26]

Others from the left were not so positive: some union activists loudly left the theatre during the scene where certain "Section Members" called into question how well they could actually be represented by delegates. Bernard Dort, an unorthodox Brechtian in his theatre tastes, corrected:

> This show, which might appear to be simple and direct, is far more than a celebration or a demonstration of shared emotions. It's the opportunity to reflect – a theatre no longer of illusion but of knowledge. And it is *knowledge in action*, evolving, experienced through the show itself, but that shouldn't end with the end of the production.[27]

He would say rightly that with *1789* and *1793*, the Théâtre du Soleil had become the center of gravity of French theatre. *1793* would, however, only tour to Mantes-la-Joly, where J-C. Penchenat remembers "very beautiful performances under a huge tent, the parade happening outdoors, in the verdant landscape."

"The most beautiful possible emptiness is the best place to perform everything." (Ariane Mnouchkine, in Fabienne Pascaud, *L'Art du Présent*, 2005, 170.)

The Golden Age: First Draft

> We want a theatre that speaks directly to our socio-political reality, that isn't just a simple illustration, but rather an encouragement to change the conditions in which we live. We want to tell our story in order to effect improvements in it – if such can be theatre's role.[28]

This was how Mnouchkine defined the goals of *The Golden Age*. Having confronted the events of the Revolution and the founding myths of progressive thought, "the beginnings of our society," in *1793*, the Soleil found itself needing to come to grips with how to represent the present – even if, in 1971, Mnouchkine was still in doubt about how to do such a thing: "Theatre implies a distance; I don't much believe in its ability to show us contemporary moments."[29] She was well aware of how much preparation such a production would entail; and indeed, this was the case.

During the double bill of *1789* and *1793*, performed on alternate nights, and later during the long phase of unemployment that started in June 1973, the troupe went to work on preparing to "tell the story of our time," as Copeau would have called it.[30] The Soleil would improvise to find the subjects and the characters that speak for today. This was a new economic and artistic adventure that would feed many rumors about what Copeau would have also called "a brotherhood of actors." It was a way of complicating the lives of the members, the rumors ran, who could have mounted another show to pull in the money, instead of opting to keep on learning their craft.

Prolonged by the length of compulsory unemployment benefits, the rehearsal period lasted 18 months, from October 1, 1973 and the company's return from Martinique, where it performed *1789*, to March 4, 1975, when *The Golden Age* opened. In the meantime, company members took on teaching jobs, film gigs, and earned their living in the spaces between rehearsals. The "Friends of the Théâtre du Soleil," an association created early in the 1970s, and Martine Franck organized an auction of art works to benefit the actors at the Delpire Gallery in May 1974. Alexander Calder and Roberto Matta contributed works.

Calder

EXPOSITION - VENTE
d'oeuvres d'ARTISTES
au profit du
THEATRE ᴅᴜ SOLEIL

Galerie Dalpine *13 rue de l'*ABBAYE 6ᵉ
MARDI 14 *au* 18 MAI 1974

This poster was created by Alexander Calder to advertise the sale of artists' works in support of the Soleil. Archives Théâtre du Soleil.

As always, the company was obsessed with finding the right form to tell their story about reality. This time, the masks of *commedia dell'arte* came to their aid. And it was about time! Gérard Hardy, with Monique Godard from Jacques Lecoq's School, had already tried to make masks out of cardboard and cloth for *Genghis Khan*.[31] Masks had been part of the unsuccessful reprise of *Captain Fracasse* in Arc-et-Senans. *Commedia dell'arte* masks had been used by actors who wanted to gift the immigrant children, who came to see them under their tent in Villeurbanne while on tour with *1789*, with a little play (1970). And for *The Golden Age*, the Soleil would finally have as a companion, Erhard Stiefel, who had up to that point only collaborated from time to time: supplying working masks while the actors rehearsed *The Kitchen*, creating masks for *A Midsummer Night's Dream*. For *The Golden Age*, he would be there at all the rehearsals; he, too, on a quest. He'd traveled through Japan, studied with Lecoq, where he'd discovered the masks of Amleto Sartori who had worked with the director Giorgio Strehler as he sought the best way to mount Goldoni's *The Servant of Two Masters*. Working with the Soleil allowed Stiefel to continue his research.

The Golden Age provided, then, another laboratory for experimenting with performance, inaugurating a new collective experience with masks. This was not at all a return to what had been done: the Soleil never wanted to reproduce past forms. Indeed, already in 1971, the company pondered how the productions of the Berliner Ensemble[32] had become such unavoidable theatrical models – Brecht having been turned into a kind of Bible for decentralized theatres in France. For the Soleil, it was always a matter of *taking off* from past greatness.[33]

In 1974, the actors of the Soleil were reading simultaneously the meditations on theatre of Jacques Copeau and the first volumes of Vsevolod Meyerhold's theatre writings (1894–1917). In the latter, the Russian Meyerhold, wanting to create a theatre for the future, went back to a double source: *commedia dell'*arte and Asian forms. Meyerhold had prepared his innovations from his studio on Borodine Street in Saint Petersburg by plunging into the study of what he considered to be "authentic theatrical epochs." The Soleil's readings put into conversation an astonishing meeting between these two great masters of the theatre: Copeau and Meyerhold, speaking to each other from one end of Europe to the other at the beginning of the twentieth century – the first a dreamer; the second, a practitioner. We see their impact in the many citations taken from both Copeau's first *Theatre Journal* [*Registre*] and Meyerhold's *Writing on Theatre* [*Ecrits sur le théâtre*] that fill the special theatre program for *The Golden Age* which includes the text of the play.

The Golden Age: First Draft. The arrival of immigrant worker Abdallah (P. Caubère) in Marseilles and his meeting with the docker La Ficelle (P. Hottier). Photo by Martine Franck, Magnum Photos.

A third figure came into the conversation, and that was the poet Henri Michaux, who in his *A Barbarian in Asia* evoked how powerfully the Asian actor's performance could communicate by suggestion. And then there were the dialogues between Steifel and the actors, between what the actors learned with the ancient Italian masks and with masks from other traditions. In all of these ways, the Soleil revitalized the history of theatre, rather than mummifying it.

In addition to masks, and to what the Soleil calls "Chinese improv" – which means working with costume elements and makeup that recall Asia – the working tool for *The Golden Age* was the document. The Soleil gathered information and articles on important news items: such as the Thévenin Affair, which garnered huge press attention and which the actors wanted to treat (while avoiding pathos), because of its political implications and the tragedy of the situation.[34] The theatre program details the chronology of the events from 1973–1974 that nourished improvisations and helped build the show (for example, Larzac, the LIP Factory, the fire at the CES Pailleron, foyers for immigrant workers, illegal abortions),[35] as well as news items not only from France, but also from Portugal, Italy, and Colombia. Creating the necessary distance between performance and news story was negotiated in a complex dialectic between political engagement, immediacy, and artistic form, which included adding in the actors' own experiences. The Soleil settled on the term "transposition" as being a better way to translate its process than the Brechtian concepts of "distance" and "distanciation."

The Soleil worked to deepen, with help from the masks, that principle of *balagan* (or fair theatre, popular entertainment) evoked by both Copeau and Meyerhold – a form that would exclude a psychological approach to character and any illusionism or naturalism – and that would demote the text as central to the work. But, in a change from *1789* and *1793*, the actors would find themselves quite alone in a new form of improvisation. There would no longer be the choral work of *1793*; but just the actor, with a mask and the character and environment he or she would create. Attempting to work some on clowning, as a boost to the improvisations, turned out to be a mistake.

In mask work, one has to show and not hide anything: the public must understand immediately, recognize the stakes. The actor has to abandon excessive movement, frenetic gesturing, and the kind of energy that leads to confusion. One can't perform two things at the same time. But the actor has to know how to walk, know how to enter, how to mark a stop, how to sculpt in space the body and the mask. Normal time has to be transformed into theatrical time. We can find

The Golden Age. Abdallah (P. Caubère), stuffed into overalls that are too small in the foyer where North-African workers are packed in like sardines, manages to catch a few winks of sleep. Photo by Martine Franck, Magnum Photos.

in what Philippe Caubère[36] has to say about his experience in creating *The Golden Age* analogies to what Meyerhold discovered working in his Petersburg Studio. In Meyerhold's 1914 article "The Fair Stand," there are also analogies to Evgeni Vakhtangov's work on Gozzi's *Princess Turandot*: we learn that the form created must be nourished by the state or condition of the character – being cold, being hungry, knowing joy, being afraid, being unhappy – and by contact with the public. Indeed, this combination constitutes the form's very condition of existence. In theatre work, the actor's freedom, the joy of creating, and the liberty to imagine and invent must be preconditions. These are the laws of theatre the Soleil was discovering – more and more clearly – every day in developing *The Golden Age*; and yet these are also the laws that would have to be *rediscovered* every day with every future production. Thanks to these discoveries, the Soleil had begun to develop a vocabulary for its process.

The character, then, is built from situations, from *lazzi*, from little stories that must be developed through a principle of contradiction. Each character should attempt to be as expressive as the portraits done by great painters; details should become signs; gestures should be clean, clear, not anecdotal. Astonishment and naivety are absolutely necessary. Words are what come last; but rhythm is central, an essential element. The Soleil would, then, work with recorded music or sounds to establish entrances, to create processions, to build particular scenes – such as the amazing scene of "The Worksite." The actors improvised with old masks and looked for modern characters by using masks Erhard Stiefel proposed. And Stiefel would personalize the masks as they were developed, first in papier-mâché, then in leather.

Voice of Erhard Stiefel

> "*I couldn't let the masks be governed by recipes. I figured things out myself, using my intuition, with almost a total lack of direction. Sometimes the results were fruitful; sometimes certain masks, in the rehearsal hall, stayed in the same place on the same table, without the actors being able to give them life. So I took them back, sculpted other ones, and proposed them as possibilities.*"[37]

There would be a lot of improvisations, many characters found but not performed (the list of all of them figures on the original theatre program.) There would be actors who could never conquer the difficulties of a masked performance style. But it was, indeed, the actors who gave birth to the contemporary characters, during rehearsals and in performance. There

The Golden Age. Two Pantalones (in *commedia* masks): Aimé Lheureux, a used-clothes salesman (J-C. Penchenat); and Mahmoud Ali (N. Serreau), owner of a hotel for North African immigrant workers. In the straw chest behind them will be found the overalls that Lheureux sells at an exorbitant price to Abdallah. Archives Monique and Daniel Cordin.

were the Pantalones (sometimes masked, sometimes not): Pantalon Magnifico, an arriviste and money-grubber (Marcel Pantalon, performed by Mario Gonzalès – in whom one could see the image of the wealthy aeronautics entrepreneur Marcel Dassault – and also Aimé Lheureux, played by J-C. Penchenat). There was the Pantalon Bisognoso, little and mean (La Ficelle, the construction boss, played by Philippe Hottier). There was a Pulcinella (M. Gueulette, performed also by Hottier). There were Dottores and Brighellas and, of course, several Harlequins, the most productive mask of them all – thus Abdallah, the North African immigrant worker created by Philippe Caubère; M'Boro, a Senegalese Harlequin created by Josephine Derenne; Max, another boss, an immigration officer, and a Harlequin mixed with Truffaldino – all created by Jonathan Sutton.

There was also the character Salouha, a woman expecting her seventh child, whom Lucia Bensasson finally found after a long gestation period. She would be a combination of Zerbina, a traditionally unmasked character in *commedia dell'arte*, but here masked in a creation proposed by Steifel, and inflected by the work Bensasson did with a mask of Pulcinella and her impressions of Mediterranean women encountered in the souks of Tunisia. Bensasson explains that her character took its final shape by improvising in front of an audience: "My image of Salouha was enhanced and completed by the image that others gave me of her."[38]

The actors used the motor energies of the old *commedia* masks (ruse, hunger, greed, pranks) to give their new masks more vitality. But the work went through many ups and downs, and phases of both exaltation and despair, as well as long fallow periods when ideas didn't come. The Soleil turned to scenes from *King Lear*, and Molière's *The Bourgeois Gentleman*, *The Impostures of Scapin*, *The Imaginary Invalid*, *The Miser*, and Marivaux's *Game of Love and Chance*. The company met up with other artists, including the stand-in for the famous Italian "Arlequino," Feruccio Soleri, who couldn't help and didn't really understand what they were doing. Peter Brook came to the Cartoucherie in one of those moments when the actors were unsure about which improvisations to choose. They saw shows that resembled the grotesque farce they thought they were looking for, such as Dario Fo's *Misterio Buffo* at the Théâtre National Populaire (and Fo would come see them at the Cartoucherie.) They experienced a Latin Carnival with its wild batucadas and sambas; and they encountered in March 1974, thanks to Christian Dupavillon, a troupe of Balinese dancers, led by one of the greatest dancers of Bali, Nyoman Pugra.

This extra-European encounter was capital for the development of the Soleil's own work. The two groups with their different traditions met up at the Théâtre de la Gaïté lyrique, where the Balinese company, invited by the Théâtre de Chaillot, was presenting *The Sorcerer of Diran*.[39] Nyoman Pugra first performed with his companions and then chose, from the masks brought by Stiefel, that of Pantalone. He transformed his costume and began to dance. Stiefel describes the effect this way:

> All of his movements, all of his stops, were so true, so right, that we found them fascinating, needing no explanation. A real lesson! We were completely subjugated by the brotherhood formed by the two sorts of masks, from such different traditions.[40]

It was a magical moment, an historic one. Mnouchkine gave the Pantalone mask to Pugra; and the Balinese *topeng* masks that the Soleil had seen in action, in a show mixing children, marionettes, clowns, masks, and gamelan music, entered the Soleil's imaginary. The masks would appear later on in *The Shakespeare Cycle* (1981); and Stiefel would incorporate the deep eyeholes and red cheeks of the masks he saw into the mask he made for the character Max in *The Golden Age*.

The last test would be meeting up with the public. In November 1974, when formal difficulties had collided with the choice of themes and when the Soleil had had just about enough, the company left Paris for the south of France. In Lussan, in the region of the Gard, they organized evening performances on outdoor squares for the villagers who lived nearby and for the miners of Alès. Returning to Paris, they continued their improvisations in front of audiences in festival halls, or for the employees of Kodak, for retired people, for immigrants, and for military conscripts. The spectators would suggest, propose, react, watch, correct, add information, and unblock the creative process.

The Soleil recorded the improvisations. They kept 18 scenes as possibilities; these had to be further scaled down or the show would have lasted nine hours. The selected scenes were transcribed so that actors would remember the broad strokes, or as Mnouchkine clarified, the "*dramatic* broad strokes." It was not so much the text that was targeted in this exercise, but rather the corporeal language. And a degree of freedom, of nightly improvisation, was left to the actors.

What would be the space of this theatre of masks? Trestle tables? No, but, according to Mnouchkine, "a utopian space," what Guy-Claude François would call "an architecture." Something all in curves and hills. A large golden expanse, composed of four dunes, covered by coconut matting forming valleys and hills and covering the floor of one of the naves. A gigantic and jubilant playing field. To create it, the Soleil had to bring in and spread out 2,500 cubic meters of earth, which they laced with concrete in order to keep it stable under the matting. It was a grandiose empty space, with four arenas, like a Barnum circus. However, contrary to the original plan, the arenas wouldn't be used simultaneously by the actors, but, rather, consecutively; and the audience would sit around each arena, on a hillside. As finally structured, storytellers would introduce and comment each scene and lead the audience from dune to dune. From the ceiling, 1,600 square meters of mirror slabs, interlaced with copper, would be lit by a multitude of garlands of fairy lights of variable intensity. This would diffuse a warm and golden light. On the ground, moveable footlight panels would light the eyes of the masked characters.

A contemporary fable, somewhere in the future, would play out under the eyes of the spectators: *The Golden Age* told a story about social class, about hierarchy, about power and profit, and did so in terms of increasing immigration and the scandalous behavior of grifter-promoters. The show opened to the music of Monteverdi's *Orfeo* with a vignette of the changing of the guard between the old Harlequin (Jonathan Sutton), witness to the Naples plague of 1720, and the new, naive

The Golden Age. Rehearsals in front of a future public. Seated around Mnouchkine and the actors (who have pushed their masks up onto their foreheads) are factory workers from cultural committees. They will propose themes for improvisations to the actors. Photo by Martine Franck, Magnum Photos.

The Golden Age. Performing in the middle of the audience, which is seated on the "hills" of the dunes covered in coconut matting. Left, standing: L. Bensasson. Seated: D. Valentin, who has raised her mask. M. Donzenac, P. Caubère, and J. Derenne have become spectators. The cables are those of the footlights that the actors themselves repositioned. This is a performance for a special audience. Archives Monique and Daniel Cordin.

The Golden Age. A rehearsal on the coconut matting-covered valleys of the Cartoucherie. Standing: J. Vilmont, A. Salomon, F. Jamet. Farther away: J. Sutton. Next to Ariane Mnouchkine: M-F. Duverger, M. Donzenac, L. Bensasson, P. Hottier. Photo by Martine Franck, Magnum Photos.

Harlequin (Abdallah- Philippe Caubère), recently arrived in Marseilles – masked, in a djellabah, and full of illusions. (The 1973 Neapolitan panic, due to a cholera outbreak recalling the plague of 1720, provided the material for a month of improvisations that launched the work.)

Lazzis, those remarkable physical comedy numbers, punctuated the narration and the scenes, engendering for instance: Abdallah in traffic he didn't understand; Abdallah and pesky seagulls; Abdallah exchanging his djellabah for work overalls that didn't fit him. There was also the much celebrated *lazzi* in the immigrant lodging, when Abdallah, lacking enough room, slept while doing a headstand, perched on his arms with his feet in the air. Or the great moment in "The Worksite" scene when Abdallah was forced to climb to the top of a crane, despite the wind that was blowing in terrifying gusts. For this moment, Caubère created a tragic "mistral *lazzi*," fighting like Marcel Marceau against the wind and dizziness, his white overalls shuddering under the impact. The terrible sound of the wind was provided by the storytellers and a few instruments, while Caubère's leg and arm movements made his costume tremble. In the end, Abdallah fell, crushed on the golden matting, to the "Dies irae" of Verdi's *Requiem*. All the future sequences from the Soleil's collective creations in the twenty-first century, in which actors face terrible tempests, their silhouettes knocked about by raging storms, owe something to this first chilling "Worksite" scene.

The show ended at the beginning of a workers' revolt, signaled by the music. A storyteller warned Pantalon: "The workers are coming, Monsieur Pantalon." The sounds grew louder and louder (a recording of Latin American peasants in a slum). "You can't run away!" All the "masters," the Pantalone and Dottori figures, climbed up the walls of the Cartoucherie, but were stopped at the top, pinned like insects. The comedy of social interactions in 1975 was thus demonstrated. And if members of a Maoist group linked to philosopher-activist Alain Badiou complained one night about the over-simplification of the representation of the working class and the lameness of the political critique, another group of about 50 workers, also attending the performance that night, told them archly they were wrong. The Soleil didn't have to intervene; it only had to enjoy the debate. *The Golden Age* was immensely successful: the richness of the acting stayed in memories and minds for a much longer time than a poorly performed theatre text would have – no matter how good.

Meyerhold's words: "The actor has awoken" were cited in the theatre program. Later, Philippe Caubère would reinforce this notion: the actor "had become for the first time in a long time a total creator."[41] *The Golden Age* told the tale of the present from a future vantage point and turned it into a legend: it was a time

The Golden Age. Lovers on the beach (J. Sutton and C. Massart). Naked, they embrace under the stars, suggested by the immense illuminated vault of the ceiling of two naves of the Cartoucherie. They will be chased from there by speculators. Photo by Martine Franck, Magnum Photos.

The Golden Age. Abdallah, fallen off the crane, lies dying on the ground. A workers' revolt is beginning. The master figures, the Pantalones and Dottoris, try to flee by climbing the walls. Photo by Jean-Claude Bourbault.

that could yet be – a time of two young lovers on the beach holding each other on a sand dune facing the sea – before speculators could chase them away. A fleeting moment that illuminated the show. But it was also a time to hope for a new kind of actor, an actor-poet, with a world to transform. The utopian title spoke to theatre as well as to society. In 2008, Mnouchkine would say that in the daring adventure of *The Golden Age* she "learned more than in almost all of her other productions."[42]

The Golden Age. Some of the masked characters from the numerous quick sketches done by Françoise Tournafond. "A Balzacienne," according to J. Gillibert, Tournafond loved details without overwhelming a design. Excellent with scissors, she always knew how to add a little something a bit mad. Her costumes helped realize the design the actors themselves found. Here, Max the Customs officer (performed by Jonathan Sutton). Françoise Tournafond, Archives Guy-Luc Boyaval.

The Golden Age. A Pantalone (performed by Maxime Lombard). Françoise Tournafond, Archives Guy-Luc Boyaval.

The Golden Age. Monsieur Raspi. Françoise Tournafond, Archives Guy-Luc Boyaval.

The Golden Age. Lou la Grosse (D. Valentin). The same mask would be used for the masculine character Monsieur Dussouille (A. Salomon). Françoise Tournafond, Archives Guy-Luc Boyaval.

The Golden Age was performed at the Venice Biennale in September 1975, out of doors on the Campo San Trovaso, where actors from a *commedia dell'arte* troupe had doubtlessly also performed a hundred or so years ago. Guy-Claude François invented a few technical tricks to capture the reflection of the moon bouncing off the waters of the canal onto the façades of the buildings on the Campo. The show returned to the Cartoucherie for three more months and then toured, under a tent, on a sand floor, to Milan, Louvain, and Tours. In Warsaw, it played in a circus building.

During the touring, Mnouchkine started to write the film about Molière that she'd proposed to the actors. She read Bulgakov's *Life of Monsieur de Molière* and her scenario would be developed as a homage to the theatre troupe that she'd been able to create – but that was beginning to disintegrate. For at the end of the long triptyque of collective creation, because of how difficult it had been but also because of what many had learned, *The Golden Age* had become what came to be known in the Soleil's vocabulary as a "sieve," just as *The Clowns* had been earlier and as *The House of Atreus Cycle* would also become. That is the moment when a crisis occurs and the ties among the company members start to loosen. Moreover, the show was fragile; and during the touring, without Mnouchkine's presence, some scenes started swelling in proportion to certain egos, perhaps tormented by the question many were asking: who would be cast as Molière?

Molière or the Life of an Honest Man. Philippe Caubère as the young Molière during the Carnival scene in Orleans. Photo by Michèle Laurent.

While *The Golden Age* was being performed, for example, a central member of the company, Jean-Claude Penchenat had already begun to feel the need to spread his wings. He'd staged Marivaux's *Triumph of Love* in the neighboring theatre, the Aquarium, and would run over to see how the young actors he'd drafted out of a Soleil workshop were doing.[43] Later on tour, he announced he was leaving the company, and would not perform in the upcoming *Mephisto* project [*Méphisto ou le roman d'une carrière*], although he'd already been cast. He would, nevertheless, return to play Louis XIV in *Molière* and even cast the extras. (Penchenat founded his own company, La Campagnol, in 1975 but created in 1977 at the Soleil and with their support an adaptation of *David Copperfield*.)[44] Another very central figure, Philippe Caubère, would be cast in the role of Molière, but he would also, and as agreed upon by Mnouchkine, mount his own production of *Dom Juan* at the Cartoucherie. After that, he, too, would head off. He went on to produce his very successful one-man shows in which the spirit of the Soleil, despite his parody of the company, would shine forth, thanks to his talent and thanks to what he had learned, living in its midst.[45]

1793. A. Mnouchkine, M. Derouin, M. Franck, G. Hardy, J. Derenne, L-B. Samier, J-C. Penchenat, and C. Bousquet look at rehearsal images for *1793*. The experience of filming rehearsals would be abandoned, to be picked back up several years later. Archives Jean-Claude Penchenat.

Molière. Filming the adventure of the man who flies (with wings and in the air: G-C. François). Photo by Michèle Laurent.

Still, the utopian thrust of the Théâtre du Soleil would be palpable in the film *Molière,* both through the past story of Molière's own company and through a metaphorization of the Soleil's future. Mnouchkine took deep pleasure in working with the many children in the film and with Bernard Zitzermann, her chief cameraman and director of photography. Zitzermann would become her faithful partner for all the "theatre films" to come, when it finally became obvious that the Soleil needed to leave a trace and figure out how to do so.

Presented at the Cannes film festival, *Molière* was excoriated by the critics. But as soon as it was released in cinemas, it found a fervent and loyal public. The creation of the film – six months of filming and two years of editing – didn't resolve any of the big questions of the company. But in addition to being a hymn to a theatre company and its work, the film also showed how an author might emerge from the midst of a community of actors. Perhaps that would be the answer to all those critics who lambasted the Soleil for the lack of strong texts in their collective creations? Of course Mnouchkine had already envisaged this possibility after *The Clowns*: it was one of the paths of creation available to them.

Notes

1 From the text-program of *l'Âge d'or* [*The Golden Age: First Draft*], edited by nine members of the Théâtre du Soleil and published by Stock, in its collection "Théâtre ouvert," 1975, 40. In this chapter, any undocumented quotes of Soleil members or of Ariane Mnouchkine come from one of the several interviews Béatrice Picon-Vallin conducted with them from 2010 to 2014.

2 Ibid., 51–53.

3 For more information on the Italian connection, see the Opening to this study.

4 As another example of Italy's interest in the Soleil's work, we might cite Vittorio de Sica's visit to Paris to see the production of *The Kitchen*.

5 See Albert Soboul, *Les Sans-culottes parisiens en l'an II: mouvement populaire et gouvernement révolutionnaire: 1793–1794* (Paris: Le Seuil, 1968).

6 We borrow this expression from Denis Bablet, in *Le Théâtre du Soleil ou la quête du bonheur* (Paris: CNRS-SERDDAV, 1979).

7 From the program, with text, of *1789*, eds. Sophie Moscoso and Jean-Claude Penchenat (Paris: Stock, 1971), 77.

8 We cite here improvisations re-transcribed by hand by Jean-François Labouverie, Ariane Mnouchkine, or Sophie Moscoso, in Chatou or Paris in the evening, some typed, some in several different versions, assembled in six unbound notebooks, Archives J-F. Labouverie.

9 In 1972, she would marry Roberto Moscoso and become Sophie Moscoso.

10 The three productions from this cycle of work have all been published by Lucien Attoun in his "Théâtre ouvert" series, with images, documentation of the work, and interviews with actors.

11 The tools and machines purchased to build the set of *The Clowns* were moved to the Palais des sports.

12 The first two films are by Christian Jacque, starring Martine Carol. The last film is by René Clair.

13 From an interview with Denis Bablet in *Le Théâtre du Soleil ou la quête du bonheur*, 48–49.

14 See Jacques Delcuvellerie, "Sur la limite, vers la fin/Groupov," *Alternatives théâtrales*, 2012, 379.

15 In Milan, the actors had translated their text into Italian, but kept the mounting collective rhythm established by the original French text.

16 This bear anticipated but was surpassed by the creature realized by Erhard Stiefel for *The Indiad*.

17 Sophie Moscoso, interviewed by Claude Morand, *ATAC Informations*, no. 40, April 1972, 4–5.

18 Ariane Mnouchkine, in the text-program of *1793*, 135 and 138.

19 *L'Histoire parlementaire* was written by J-B. Buchez and C. Roux-Lavergne in the 1930s and published by Paulin. See also: Jean Massin, *Robespierre et Marat* (Paris: Club Français du livre, 1956, 1960); Daniel Guérin, *La lutte des classes sous la Première République (1793–1797)* (Paris: Gallimard, 1946) and his re-edited *Bourgeois et bras-nu* (Paris: Éditions Libertalia, 2012).

20 See the two articles by Catherine Mounier in *Les Voies de la Création Théâtrale*, vol. V (Paris: CNRS Éditions, 1977).

21 The largest of these tables measured 3 × 6 meters.

22 Guy-Claude François, in an interview with Béatrice Picon-Vallin, www.theatre-du-soleil.fr.

23 Ariane Mnouchkine, *ATAC Informations*, no. 42, June 1972, 5.

24 George Bonnaud, in "Chronique de l'illusion efficace (1968–1980)," *Le Théâtre d'intervention depuis 1968*, vol. 1 (Paris: l'Âge d'homme, 1983), 36–37. For more on the shows with the GIP, see Chapter Four and Chapter Six of this study.

25 Jean-Jacques Gautier, *Le Figaro*, May 19, 1972; followed by Pierre Marcabru, *Le Journal du dimanche*, May 21, 1972.

26 Gilles Sandier, *La Quinzaine Littéraire*, June 16, 1972.

27 Bernard Dort, "l'Histoire jouée," *l'Avant-Scène*, no. 526/527, 1973, 9. Emphasis ours.

28 Ariane Mnouchkine, theatre program for *The Golden Age*.

29 See Anne Neuschäfer, *De l'improvisation au rite, l'épopée de notre temps: le Théâtre du Soleil au Carrefour des genres* (Bern: Peter Lang, 2002).

30 Jacques Copeau, *Registres I: Appels* (Paris: Gallimard, 1974), 187.

31 The characters Le Roi d'Or and Tangout, performed by Gérard Hardy, wore masks in *Genghis Khan* (1961).

32 The Berliner Ensemble was invited to the Théâtre de la Commune d'Aubervilliers with three productions, including *The Mother*, in 1951.

33 This is the same approach, in the same words, as that taken by Meyerhold and his Studio between 1913 and 1916.

34 A young welder died suspiciously in a police commissariat in Chambéry, France, in December 1968. While police were accused, the charges ended up being dismissed. See Denis Langlois, *Les Dossiers Noirs de la police française* (Paris: Le Seuil, 1973).

35 These various episodes in the history of France were hot spots for discussions about the role of the State, the relationship between workers and management, and the rights of women and immigrants. In Larzac, peasants staged a ten-year, non-violent fight

to keep the military from establishing a base on their lands. In Besançon, workers in the Lip factory became worker-managers after a strike, when management threatened to close down the plant. In Paris, a fire set by angry students in the school, CES Pailleron, killed 20 people and prompted an investigation of the inept construction of the building and the State's responsibility. There were a series of exposés about the shoddy quality of housing for immigrant workers; and women were actively demonstrating for the right to control their own bodies; abortion finally becoming legal in 1975.

36 Philippe Caubère, "À nous la liberté," text-program of *l'Âge d'or* [*The Golden Age*], 28–47.
37 From an unedited manuscript, Archives Sophie Moscoso.
38 From the text-program of *l'Âge d'or*, 61.
39 Thanks to Christian Dupavillon, who had "discovered" the company and its choreographer/director Sardano in 1972, they were invited to the Festival of Nancy in 1973, where they made a deep impression.
40 From an unedited manuscript, Archives Sophie Moscoso.
41 Philippe Caubère, text-program of *l'Âge d'or*, 27 and 38.
42 Ariane Mnouchkine, in J. Chollet, *Construire pour le temps d'un regard: Guy-Claude François scénographe* (Paris: Fage editions, 2009), 79.
43 The play had premiered at the École Normale Supérieure, rue d'Ulm, in January 1974, and then moved to the Théâtre de l'Aquarium, right next to the Théâtre du Soleil within the Cartoucherie complex.
44 Penchenat's staging of Jean-Claude Grumberg's *En r'venant d'expo* would also be performed at the Soleil in 1979.
45 In 1981, Caubère performed *La danse du diable* at the Avignon Festival; in 1986, he commenced his project *Le Roman d'un acteur*, consisting of 11 episodes, the first of which was called *Ariane ou l'Âge d'or*. At the same time that Caubère left, Mario Gonzalès, Maxime Lombard, and Clémence Massart also left the company

Henry IV. The Soleil orchestrated a rediscovery of Shakespeare in a space that was at once sober (the sand-colored coconut matting, striped with black velour, which covered the naked stage) and sumptuous (the gilded backdrops, whose color suggested the character of each scene). The theatrical space was also created by the music, which mixed Western and Eastern tonalities. Depicted here is the arrangement of one of the backdrops (with S. Moscoso in the middle). Photo by Martine Franck, Magnum Photos.

Chapter 3 The Shakespeare Cycle

"One day, I entered a Kabuki theatre. This wasn't Shakespeare, but I saw Shakespeare in it."

Ariane Mnouchkine[1]

"This trip [to Asia] was, and remains, my treasure. I think it difficult to imagine the shock this was – to see in the theatre something completely different, and yet completely universal at the same time. I told myself while watching these performances: I don't understand anything; this isn't for me. But it was as if I was seeing molten gold. I saw the genius of the metaphor."

Ariane Mnouchkine[2]

"Where is the theatre company capable of overcoming insurmountable barriers? Where does tragedy have the ability, in its staging, to change habits, morals and ideas that have been deeply entrenched for centuries?"

Vsevolod Meyerhold[3]

The late 1970s saw the Soleil depict two theatrical artists confronting a monumental power structure, first in a film and then in a theatrical performance. We're speaking, of course, of *Molière* and *Mephisto* (1979). Both would be "a Mnouchkine production" – with Mnouchkine, in the first case, as creator of script and dialogue, and in the second as adapter – not to mention director of both. She was to become the sole guiding hand in the writing of texts during this period of the company's transition, which stretched from 1976 to 1980. All this in a France where the echoes of 1968 had gotten stuck in the defeat of the progressive *Programme commun* of 1974 – the energy of the Left both ebbing and flowing – and where the European elections of 1979 bore witness to the resurgence of neo-fascist elements in French society.

"Be resolved to no longer serve, and you will be free." (La Boétie, epigraph to *Mephisto*, Ariane Mnouchkine's adaptation of the novel by Klaus Mann, Solin, 1979.)

Mephisto

If, with *Molière*, a filmic study of how theatre works, Mnouchkine marked the end of the first ten years of the Théâtre du Soleil, with *Mephisto* she looked at the recent history of Germany and Europe and cast an eye on the sociopolitical mechanisms at stake. Also, more personally, she turned to the story of her own family, which had experienced exile and internment in Nazi camps. She would, in fact, revisit the years that stretched from 1936 to 1945 on several occasions: she had already done so between the productions of *1793* and *The Golden Age*, during which time she briefly proposed to the actors a reflection on the events of the war and Occupation within the framework of a large ballroom in France – for which G-C. François had sketched out a possible set. Then, on a second occasion, accompanied by Hélène Cixous, right after the launch of *The Indiad*, she spent July to September 1988 interviewing members of the French Resistance and gathering documents, with the goal of mounting a production about Resistance fighters.[4] That production never saw the light of day. She would, however, finally return to the subject matter a last time, during the production of *Ephemera* (2008), when her personal narrative would at last be realized through the improvisations of a new generation of actors. But in 1979, *Mephisto* beckoned.

The 1936 Klaus Mann novel, published during his exile in Amsterdam, was banned in Germany when it was published there in 1960 (to appear only in 1981). It describes the rise of Nazism in the Weimar Republic between 1923 and 1933, and draws the portrait of Hendrik Höfgen, a career actor who sold his soul and sold out his Communist and Jewish actor friends in order to rise to the post of director of the Hamburg Theatre. Mann relied for this story on the biography of Gustaf Gründgens, ex-husband of his own sister – one of the greatest actors of his generation, who played Mephisto in Goethe's *Faust* – and who concluded, in real life, his own collaborationist pact with the devil. Mann's cry throughout his novel must certainly have spoken to Mnouchkine: "We are waiting for something like an echo, even if it remains vague and distant. When we have made such a strong call, there must be, at the very least, a small echo."

Mnouchkine's echo – her adaptation – was written while keeping in mind which actor might play each role (the cast having been predetermined). The adaptation was precise and well structured, patterned after a close study of people and characters that Mann had known or invented. It was, nonetheless, also put to the test in rehearsal, and, in accordance with the improvisations of the actors, modified and rewritten when necessary. Thus, Mnouchkine returned to earlier experiences of writing with Philippe Léotard, made richer through collective creation, and tried an approach different from that used in the creation of *The Golden Age* in a renewed attempt to create the "comedy of our time." There was a distance of 50 years between the events of the story and the moment of adaptation, with a further distancing from the everyday due to the fact that the characters, if strongly inspired by reality, were highly stylized, and what's more were actors themselves.

The adaptation produced a doubling of the theatre-in-the-theatre effect, in that the story unfolded in two theatres – on the "official State-sponsored" stage, and on that of a "revolutionary little cabaret." Called the "Storm Bird," this cabaret allowed the character Otto Ulrich, (J-C. Bourbault), a friend of Höfgen (G. Hardy), to look for the "theatre of the future" and to nourish the power to laugh at evil. The plaster work and adornments of the bourgeois theatre, with its gaudily painted scenery, were in stark opposition to the lightness and naïve scenery of the little cabaret – where farcical sketches, inspired both by Karl Valentin and the Soleil's work on clowns from ten years earlier, were performed.

Mephisto provided a survey of all possible styles of acting, from naturalistic to expressionistic,[5] passing in review, as well,

During a break from filming *Mephisto* at the Soleil, under the banner of the title: B. Sobel directed the film, based on the original staging. From left to right: J. Sutton, J. Pibarot, G. Sciama, M-F. Audollent, G. Forget, C. Colin, R. Amstutz, J. Maurel, N. Journo. Photo by Françoise Saur.

masks and clowns. Attention was paid to the danger of fall-ing into a psychologizing style, something the Soleil strongly resisted. The company returned to the centrality of a non-mobile set, in spite of the mobility of the spectators, who were actively encouraged to participate.

The originality of G-C. François's bi-frontal stage design was to place the public in the center of two "theatres," each facing the other, on benches with rotating backs that allowed the spec-tators to pivot to see one or the other stage. The coconut matting from *The Golden Age* that covered the ground was dyed red. Everything was tightly grouped together in a single nave, inside high metal grates evoking incarceration, and through which, at the end of the show, while Höfgen collapsed and moaned, and while night overtook the space, one saw projected on the large wall of the neighboring nave the grey images of the death camps where so many German artists had died. The names of those to whom *Mephisto* was dedicated, characters from Mann's *roman à clef*, streamed by slowly with the date and the place of their assassination or suicide, while the *Song of the Martyrs*[6] surged forth – a song that had rung out in Buchenwald. It was a power-ful finale that would, on occasion, leave the spectators simply unable to applaud.

This was the period in which Mnouchkine helped cre-ate l'AIDA – an International Association for the Defense of Artists who were victims of repression anywhere in the world. Along with organizers Claude Lelouch, Patrice Chéreau, Yves Montand, Simone Signoret, and Joris Ivens, Mnouchkine declared its mission to help artists in totalitarian countries, and more precisely at that time to help support the Aleph Theatre of Chile, a victim of Pinochet's brutal regime. In a more gen-eral way, the production of *Mephisto* asked the public and the artists whether it was better to participate in state-subsidized, official theatre, or to work from the margins.

Important archival and other documentary tools accompa-nied the creation of this production.[7] The actors received musi-cal training from Jean-Jacques Lemêtre, who taught them to play the various instruments that would be heard during the performance. The arrival of Lemêtre marked the beginning of a new period for the Soleil. He quickly became a primary point of contact between Mnouchkine and the actors, and would remain so for the next 35 years.

Touring took *Mephisto* from Avignon to Rome, to Berlin and Munich, its somber and disquieting colors contrasting stunningly with all past productions. Created in May 1979, the show would tour until July 1980. Mnouchkine seemed not entirely satisfied with the adaptation, into which she had intro-duced passages from Chekov's *The Cherry Orchard*.[8] However, a specialist in German culture, Jean-Michel Palmier (who along

In the foyer, a new arrival – the musician J-J. Lemêtre. For *Mephisto*, he led actors in the rehearsal of various instruments. From left to right: L. Bensasson, P. Fatus, C. Colin, L. Andreone, M. Albaiceta, M. Donzenac, and G. Hardy. Photo by Françoise Saur.

with Lionel Richard was one of the consultants for *Mephisto*), maintained that the difficult undertaking was an "admirable success" and very contemporary.[9] In fact, Mnouchkine recognized above all else that

> this (was) a moment when so much attention was given to the set that it had a profound effect on the functioning of the company, sidelining the actors by the enormous budget that was sunk into it, by the time involved, because of the swelling in importance of the technical aspects; all of a sudden, I realized I'd fallen into a trap. We'd made a kind of 'official theatre' that was very beautiful, but that was supposedly in the service of *denouncing* official theatre.[10]

For the next production, Mnouchkine would begin by looking for something even more contemporary. The recent bloody history of Cambodia had opened Mnouchkine up to the possibility of writing on genocide and the disappearance of an Asian people. She imagined a story that would revolve around the minority tribes in the mountains of Cambodia and Laos. But the project got lost there. Faced with the difficulty of moving away from documents and didacticism and into fiction, she gave up. Instead, she plunged into reading Shakespeare, which was one way of answering her need for a true writer. To start her Shakespeare project, she proposed to the actors a grand plan, consisting of eight history plays and three comedies (and even an opera).[11] "Ariane wanted to produce one Shakespeare

Mephisto's double-sided stage: Here, the "official theatre" in red and gold. Photo by Michèle Laurent.

Mephisto. A scene played out in the "official theatre." Theresa von Herzfeld (M-F. Audollent) and Otto Ulrich (J-C. Bourbault). In profile, Hans Josthinkel (G. Bonnaud). Photo by Michèle Laurent.

Mephisto. The revolutionary cabaret, the "Storm Bird." An actor (C. Colin) is depicted wearing a Hitler mask made by E. Stiefel. Photo by Michèle Laurent.

Mephisto. "The Storm Bird," a sketch with two clowns: Madame Grogneboum, the pro-Nazi concierge (J. Derenne); and Madame Linamuque (A. Demeyer). Archives Joséphine Derenne.

play per month for a year. We ended up presenting three in three years," clarified G-C. François.[12]

By the end of 1981, there were still six plays in the running for this project: *Richard II*, the two parts of *Henry IV*, *Henry V*, and two comedies: *Twelfth Night* and *Love's Labour's Lost*. *The Shakespeare Cycle* would, however, end up as a trilogy: *Richard II* opening on December 10, 1981 at the Cartoucherie, *Twelfth Night* opening on July 10, 1982 in the *Cour d'honneur* of the Papal Palace in Avignon, and *Henry IV, Part I* opening on January 18, 1984 at the Cartoucherie. The creative effort had lasted from January 1981 to January 1984 – exactly three years of work, with a sole guide, Shakespeare – the bard's energy demanding urgently that the Soleil "find a way to make the work come alive through acting on a stage, and nowhere else."[13] These plays had seldom been performed in France before; and of her contemporaries only Patrice Chéreau had put on *Richard II* (1970). For Mnouchkine, her choices linked her, interestingly, to the "lineage" she had already acknowledged: Copeau having directed *Twelfth Night* in 1914, Vilar – *Richard II* in Avignon in 1947, and Planchon – *Henry IV* in 1957.

The arrival of a new generation of actors

It was time for renewal – a renewal that meant working on great texts to regain strength, starting over from scratch, knitting together a new troupe in which the actor-authors would seek out solutions in tandem with the director. This was not, under any circumstance, a return to text-based theatre such as was practiced traditionally in France. The return to written plays would not negate collective creation – the past could only lead to a new inflection.

During the performances of *The Golden Age*, the troupe had worked simultaneously on refining that show and on *King Lear* – for which they had used Chhau masks (from Bengali ritual theatre), left by a group passing through the neighboring Théâtre de la Tempête. For *Lear*, as in all that Mnouchkine does, improvisation had been the founding principle, the essential tool. Collective creation, fed by improvisation, had always underpinned the working world unique and specific to the Soleil – it was and is their distinguishing feature. So even if, during this new phase of work, her role as stage director/company director seemed all powerful, because it represented at the same time the center and the spinal column of the renewed group, the Soleil wouldn't move away from improvisation – with or without a text. It would, instead, continue to promote a theatre that could "write itself," collectively and directly on stage.

In the fall of 1979, the Soleil organized a free workshop on masked performance, which was interrupted by the dramatic suicide of René Patrignani,[14] who had been a member of the troupe since *The Kitchen*. The workshop soldiered on as a small group working under Erhard Stiefel, although Mnouchkine's departure was disruptive to the exercise. At the end of this workshop – in which Georges Bigot, an eventual key member of the company, encountered Balinese masks for the first time – an attempt was made, supported by Mnouchkine, to form a new, young company.[15] They had planned to rehearse in the nave with the earthen floor that would finally become, in April 1981, the rehearsal hall for the Shakespeare trilogy. This first reorganization did not succeed. However, a long workshop-audition at the start of 1981 permitted the recruitment of a new generation of actors, among whom were Georges Bigot, Maurice Durozier, Myriam Azencot, Clémentine Yelnik, and Cyrille Bosc. Durozier came from a traveling theatre company based in the Midi; Bigot was a "surreptitious auditor" of Antoine Vitez at the Paris Conservatory for dramatic arts. Others arrived a little later, like Guy Freixe, who came from the Lecoq School. Philippe Hottier came back after an absence of three years.

Richard II (Avignon). Act I: scene I: A gold-and-blood colored silk backdrop shimmers against the stage wall of the Papal Palace. We see the arrival of Richard II (G. Bigot), leaping from a walkway, stage right, accompanied by his court: the Duke of Lancaster (J. Arnold), the Duke of Aumerle (P. Blancher), and other nobles: Bolingbroke (C. Bosc) and Mowbray (M. Durozier). After this entrance, they make a complete turn around the stage and align themselves parallel to the apron. Then, still running, Richard inspects the nobles who bow, one after the other, in front of him. The king then mounts the throne (the central bench, one of the few scenic elements) and begins to speak. Photo by Michèle Laurent.

Some were very young; there were some who wanted internships; several had been fascinated by *The Golden Age*, which they had seen and which, they proclaimed, had given them the "strength to live."

Some older members of the troupe, actors and actresses such as Louba Guertchikoff or Gérard Hardy, who no longer enjoyed performing, found their places elsewhere, in different working groups. The cohabitation of the newer members and the older ones was thus organized, not always an easy task, in an atmosphere which linked the dynamism of the period – launched by the election to the French presidency of François Mittérand when state support to the Soleil doubled[16] – to the necessity of transforming the Cartoucherie so that the Soleil could produce Shakespeare there. On the solid basis of the "beehive" established by the pact of 1964, in which each member would have their own responsibilities, a new micro-society had begun to form, with new arrivals contributing their own special energy.

Voice of Georges Bigot, March 1, 2014

"*I entered the Soleil at the beginning of the Shakespeare trilogy. I remember that when I was accepted into the troupe, on the walk from the metro to the Cartoucherie, I had a sort of feeling of freedom – that was it – a breath of freedom and confidence. Freedom and confidence were finally mine, as well as a great sense of pleasure – not only the pleasure of performing, but also in the life of the Soleil, all of it: cleaning toilets, making meals, painting walls collectively, driving the Derruppé tractor,[17] all the enormous construction projects to accomplish, in complete freedom, with our own abilities. It was marvelous to have the surfaces of giant walls to paint, and fantastic to make concrete! Real work sites, with so much passion and pleasure. The Soleil was not just rehearsals – it was all this collective work where we laid the groundwork for theatre, where we prepared for the spectators. We invented a world to offer up, as if we were preparing an enormous gift, like children – a great gift for theatregoers. It was magnificent for such young people as us. I remember when I arrived at my apprenticeship and saw Julien Maurel and Pierre Fatus outside – dressed like clownish punks, juggling and playing the trumpet – I felt I was finally entering my own place of liberty, of magic, of creativity. There was music, the theatre, the Vincennes woods, nature – life itself. Finally I could breathe; in 1981, the future really was possible. It was that hope that brought us to life – with Mnouchkine and with friends. It was terrific to work with Maurice Durozier, with Philippe Hottier, Clémentine [Yelnik], Myriam [Azencot],*

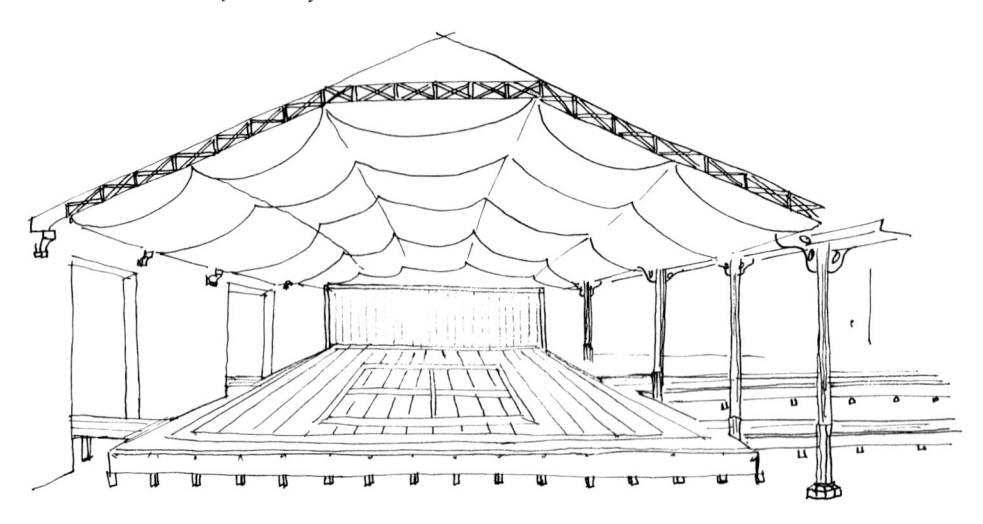

Drawing by G-C. François of the stage for the Shakespeare plays. This is in draft form. The design had already evolved through several stages, including the concept of a small wooden theatre over water. Archives Guy-Claude François.

> *with Joséphine Derenne (a giant of the Soleil), with eve-ryone, with the technicians, the administrators Jean-Pierre Hénin and Liliana Andreone. We were together, there was a fusing together; we were all seeking this gift that we were in the process of making for others, that we were making for ourselves as well."*

Translating Shakespeare, a new writing "strategy"

It's always difficult to give an account of the Soleil's work, as it is multidirectional, made up of so many trials, queries, and encounters, so much chance and intuition. In it, the process of searching is also a sort of training. It's particularly difficult to speak about the Shakespeare trilogy, because, on the one hand, the rehearsals integrated new apprentice actors, taken from the workshop, who would at some point be invited to work side-by-side with the actors of the troupe, then retained in the company – and on the other, because the Soleil was working on all the plays together from February to June 1981. The first table reading of *Richard II*, in a translation by Pierre Leyris, occurred on February 17, that of *Henry IV, Part I*, in the Yves Bonnefoy translation, on March 3.

The Shakespeare Cycle was presented to the troupe as though it were an entire college education. It would require total immersion in the world of the author. A basic premise: the history plays have more male roles; and as the number of women exceeded the number of men in the Soleil in the early 1980s; in

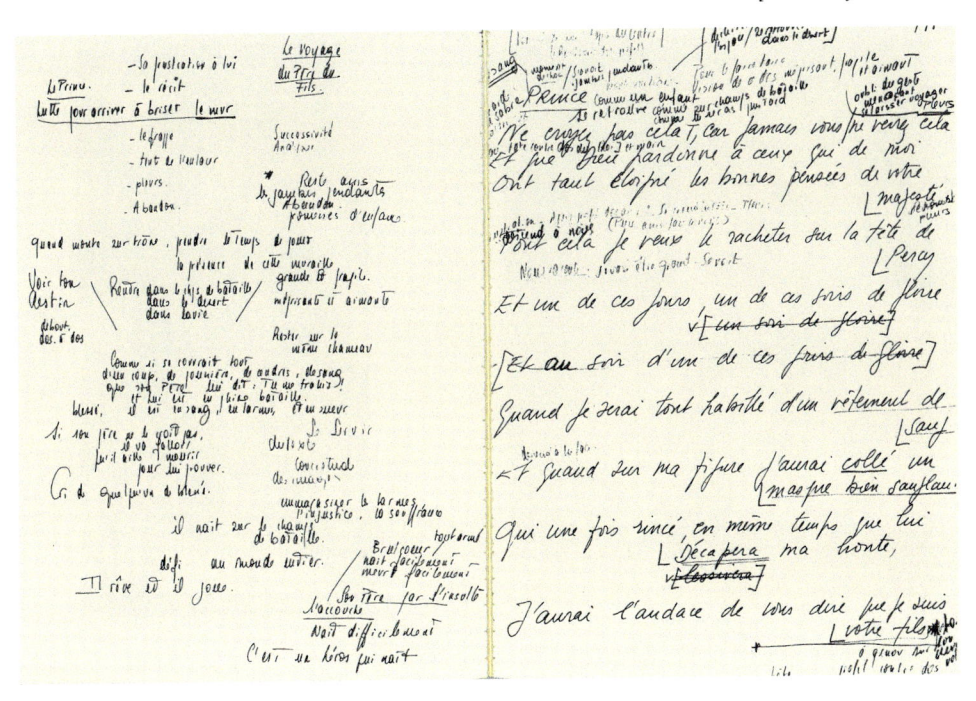

Henry IV. Pages of working notes of Sophie Moscoso: At left, rehearsal notes collected by Moscoso. At right, *Henry IV*. Act II: scene I. Shakespeare's text, translated by Mnouchkine and delivered in manuscript form to the actors, with her corrections; annotations by Moscoso. Archives Sophie Moscoso.

the comedies *Love's Labour's Lost* and *Twelfth Night*, all the roles would be played by women.

Mnouchkine asked Jean-Michel Déprats, who had the previous year translated *Love's Labour's Lost* for the director Jean-Pierre Vincent and his students at the Théâtre National de Strasbourg (performed for the 1980 Avignon festival),[18] to translate the entire group of eleven works the Soleil was considering. As he prudently accepted to translate only the two parts of *Henry IV*, Mnouchkine herself began to translate *Richard II*, which she gave to the actors in a draft translation, called a "word-for-word," on March 30. Given how successful the show turned out to be, she decided to undertake the other translations as well. Her desire for writing was thus transformed into the necessity of translating. She would translate in the theatre every morning, sitting in the foyer and filling decorated pages with her large, clear writing, round and slanted. These very readable pages would be photocopied for the rehearsals in the afternoon. (Soleil actors remember having rehearsed with various translations, and then with these manuscript pages coming to them in dribs and drabs.)

From this point on, all authors' works performed from 1981 to 1998, before the introduction of computers to the company,

Selections from the extensive photo dossiers of rehearsals compiled by Moscoso. *Henry IV, Part II* (not produced) – above: travelers' scene: P. Hottier and H. Cinque; below: H. Cinque, G. Bigot and J. Arnold. The orange curtains are those of the rehearsal room. BnF Fonds Théâtre du Soleil/Archives Sophie Moscoso, 4 COL-153 (931) and NAF-28080–II.

Henry IV, Part II (not produced). Prince Hal (G. Bigot), Falstaff (P. Hottier), Peto (H. Cinque) and Poins (J. Arnold). The actors portray patrons of the tavern, who seem at once drawn and painted. The makeup was meant to finish the work of defining the characters. BnF Fonds Théâtre du Soleil/Archives Sophie Moscoso, 4 COL-153 (931) and NAF-28080-II.

would be given to the actors in this fashion – in manuscript pages, written or recopied in Mnouchkine's hand, brought to the actors, then, by her intervention. This was a new strategy for relating to the theatrical text: the intermediary of a translation that became more intimate, more personalized, and more directly addressed to the troupe about to perform it – as if the text had just been written, in an eternal present. However – and the dialectic is impressive – Mnouchkine insisted that translating meant "accepting and maintaining as much distance as possible": distance between French and English, distance between Shakespeare's language and modern language. She also emphasized not over-complicating, not commentating, not weighing down the translation with unnecessary explanations: "People who don't have contact with the reality of theatre and its actors certainly seek to create translations that are sufficient in-and-of themselves, forgetting that acting is what communicates the text."[19] Mnouchkine gave her actors networks of strong images: direct, strange, motivating, and sweeping: "The construction of sentences was for me more musical than grammatical, like Shakespeare who had at his disposal a language not dependent

Henry IV, rehearsals: Maurice Durozier rehearses Douglas (top left and bottom); George Bigot rehearses Blunt – a character that would later be played by P. Blancher. BnF Fonds Théâtre du Soleil/Archives Sophie Moscoso, 4 COL-153 (931) and NAF-28080-II.

Henry IV. Four shots in a series of close-ups of G. Bigot (Prince Hal) in the rehearsal room, with manuscript in hand. Here we see the versatility of the expressions of the actor. Archives Sophie Moscoso.

(a)

(b)

(c)

(d)

a/b/c/d *Henry IV*. J. Derenne tries out the role of Mistress Quickly, which will end up being played by O. Cointepas. The facial expressions are similar to those of silent cinema. These photos were destined for Mnouchkine, to assist in her direction of the actors. They were not shown to the actors. Archives Sophie Moscoso.

on sentences. English isn't a language of sentences. It's a language of words."[20] More important than the words spoken were the material images the actors had to capture and convey to the spectators. While appropriating the text with a view to production, Mnouchkine was obviously searching above all for rhythm and clarity.

The goal was a "de-literarization" of the play that would escape from the printed word and the set nature of the text – as one could cross out, replace, emend it without worry, unless Mnouchkine herself had already proposed possible variations. This was an appropriation of the work by the director who, in translating, imagined possible further scenic elaborations of all that she transmitted directly to the actors – on behalf of Shakespeare: the "great poet, great metaphysician, great historian."[21]

This "return to the classroom" was accompanied by a return to the "splendid void" that had characterized the creation of *The Golden Age*, and which constituted a space of freedom for the actors, who would, once again, use masks. It was in that blank space that the actors, manuscript pages in hand, learned to "eat the words well," in the recollection of G. Bigot, without learning them by heart, going from one translation to the next and from one role to another. Working with text in hand was not a handicap, especially as the actors were juggling translations: they would not memorize the text until the very end of rehearsals. This relationship to the text, present in its materiality, a text that would fall to the ground and be picked up or be stuffed into costumes, was fundamental. Mnouchkine would repeat: "Take the time to read and to see what you're saying." This reading of what could be called "relay pages" would not prevent physicalization: the pages would inspire the stage action, but the end result would be as far as possible from a textcentric focus. The manuscript pages were, then, a tool to be overcome. And as a concrete medium between director and author, they accompanied the body-in-play of the actors as closely as possible.

The organization of work

Analyzing the relationship of the Soleil to the text can't be undertaken without taking into account the para-theatrical work – the physical work and manual labor demanded of every member of the Soleil from the founding of the company. Everyone participated in these "worksites." For *The Shakespeare Cycle*, at 9 a.m. each day the work was divided according to individual choice: some would work on making concrete for the construction of the new stage;[22] some would work on frames

"At the same time, we created plays and the space, not on paper, but with our hands, our arms, our sweat. And, after creating this space, we went looking for characters far back in History, and brought them here, as Mnouchkine would say. Here, in front of the spectators, but in a place we'd constructed beforehand, giving to the word *construct* all the weight it deserves." (Marc Dumétier, *Fruits*, 1984, 93.)

and wooden supports; some would prepare meals; some would organize the storehouse, etc. The artistic adventure was a total experience that engaged body and mind, just as in daily life, except that here the engagement was collective. This process produced an entirely different approach to the stage.

The worksites were, from this point on, managed by technical staff – masters in their areas whom the actors helped immensely and from whom they learned a great deal. The worksite headed by G. Hardy, "painting, patina, and gilding," was not, however, the work of a specialist, but rather – thanks to the suggestion of G-C. François – of an actor who found pleasure in the work and who discovered his abilities in the preparation of the silk murals that served as backdrops for the shows. Rehearsing another actor, sharing their experience, could also be considered a type of "worksite."

The director was the "inspirer," the guide for the "explorers," the actors on the path to discovery, those in search of what would appear "evident" (a keyword at the Soleil), which could sometimes be deceptive. While it is true that every group of actors called forth something maternal, with this new generation of actors at the Soleil, and the age difference between them and Mnouchkine, her maternal role could no longer be denied.[23] She indeed would start speaking of the birth of actors, and confided: "The day that I'm no longer moved to tears at the birth of an actor, I will stop, because that will mean I'm no longer capable of giving birth, of letting the birth happen."[24] G. Bigot has even said in this vein: "She gave birth to me."

Mnouchkine's assistant, Sophie Moscoso, left abundant traces of these three years of work: large binders, simple to peruse, where she made written notes, on notebook-sized cards, day after day, of what happened during rehearsals – who played which role, who tried on which mask, and the numerous remarks made by Mnouchkine, always targeted and precise, concrete yet poetic, opening up the imagination of the actors. Other notebooks indicate the attempts by different actors to play a specific part, and their eventual shedding of these roles. To these detailed handwritten notes were added photos Moscoso took with a Rolleiflex camera, in black and white and in color, without moving from the spot where she sat next to Mnouchkine. These were grouped in albums, often in series of three, to be consulted by the director. "In the photos, there was silence and forgetting. One must forget in order to find something again," says Moscoso today. Mnouchkine rarely consulted the notes, but Moscoso would furnish her with a synopsis of what was said during rehearsals.

Having worked on documentation for the Soleil productions for a long time, Moscoso suggested for *The Shakespeare Cycle*

Twelfth Night: An entrance on a walkway. From left to right: P. Hottier, C. Yelnik, O. Cointepas, J. Derenne, G. Bigot. Photo by Martine Franck, Magnum Photos.

that the actors look at illustrated books on Asian theater and read some works of history (for example, Georges Dumézil). There was, however, not much research done for this production. She brought the director excerpts of inspirational texts (Brecht, Borgès). The actors, as always, watched films, including *Throne of Blood*, *Dersu Uzala*, *The Seven Samurai*, and *Kagemusha* by Kurosawa, as well as Shakespearean performances by Orson Welles and Laurence Olivier. To prepare for *Henry IV*, they watched *Ivan the Terrible* by Eisenstein. From her rehearsal notes, Moscoso prepared the texts for the theatre programs. She acted as liaison with the various workshops, and remained vigilant so that, for example, in the costume workshop work would not continue on costumes for roles that had been cut. She informed the concerned parties of temporary difficulties the actors were having, so that all might help, or so that actors wouldn't be disturbed during moments of intense creation. She created an indispensable bond between all members of the company.

The costume shop consisted of ten people, headed by Jean-Claude Barriera, a member of the Soleil since 1789,[25] and Nathalie Thomas, a seamstress who had worked on *Molière*. (She had also had a woodworking internship for *Mephisto*.) Marie-Hélène Bouvet joined the team for *Twelfth Night*. These last two costume designers are still there today. And then there was the music: Jean-Jacques Lemêtre, of Roma origin – musician-composer-improviser (free jazz), chef, and great traveler – began collecting musical instruments. He located and introduced 75 for *Richard II*, 100 for *Twelfth Night*, and 310 for *Henry IV*. These instruments came from 37 countries – from Asia, Africa, and Europe – and from different time periods. Mnouchkine allocated specific funds for this research. For *Richard II*, Lemêtre eschewed modern percussion in favor of traditional percussive instruments. He procured, made, or invented instruments according to the given tone or timbre required for each scene, requirements suggested by Mnouchkine or by what the actors brought to their roles. The musician's workshop was located on stage and Lemêtre was present at every rehearsal. At the beginning, actors helped him with the music.[26]

> "We never want to muddy the waters to make them deeper." (Ariane Mnouchkine, Théâtre du Soleil/ Sophie Moscoso Archives, BnF, 4-COL 153 [120].)

Learning in the workshop of a master

> "We have the tendency to say that *Richard II* is a play about power; however, Shakespeare, even if he ended up writing a play about power, first wrote a play that was called the '*History of Richard II*.' And we *must* enact the history of Richard II. And it is up to the public to register at which level they receive the play: as one about Richard II, as one about power, or as one about thievery." (Ariane Mnouchkine, *Fruits*, 1984, 218.)

One must enter the universe of Shakespeare, as it says in the theatre program for *Richard II*, "in order to learn how to perform the world on stage." Entering Shakespeare, the program continues, "prepares us to tell, in one of our next productions, a story of today. [Thus] we consult Shakespeare, the expert who knows all the right tools, the ones that are the best adapted to a tale of passion and to the destiny of mankind." Indeed, in Shakespeare (and above all in *Henry IV*) nobles and *kyogen* both appear. Mnouchkine gave the Japanese name, *kyogen*, which comes from the eponymous genre that forms an intermezzo in Noh drama, to Shakespeare's comic characters. These, she felt, were closer to the common people and were, like them, the carriers of History. They are also, as she puts it: "eternal refugees in their home countries."

To learn how to perform this world on stage, it was first necessary to trim the fat, to clean things up. So everyone tried out each of the roles, and the pell-mell exploration of Shakespeare continued well after April 25, the opening day of the newly completed rehearsal hall. A first casting was done in June, when *Richard II* and the two parts of *Henry IV* began "regular" rehearsals – before turning all attention to *Richard II*. Rehearsals for *Richard II* transferred to the main stage on October 20. Additional short internship-auditions would take place for *Henry IV* in May and June of 1983. *Love's Labour's Lost*, which went into rehearsal twice (May 29–July 21, 1981, then in March and April 1983), bore witness to the fact that the intertwining of Shakespearean plays continued. Mnouchkine said during rehearsals for this latter play: "This is a great workshop and necessary in order to prepare *Henry IV*,"[27] but she questioned the universality of the play and the reason to perform it: "There's not enough human and poetic material to spend months and months on it."[28] *Love's Labour's Lost* would, therefore, be dropped.

One of the problems that arose was that the male roles in Shakespeare's comedies – meant to be played by the women of the troupe, as we have mentioned – were taken back by the men. Women shared them only for a time. For *Twelfth Night*, one exception was the male role of Sir Andrew Aguecheek, which would be played by Clementine Yelnik.[29] This casting presented itself as a "necessity" in the work process, but the actresses who found themselves without roles quit the Soleil.

The particular nature of Shakespeare is his total sympathy for his characters. Through their passions, he expresses his knowledge of the nature of mankind. From this, Mnouchkine took a primary and essential image and gave it to the players: they must hold on to the "miniscule island," the "blessed plot of land" (in the words of John of Gaunt) upon which men, a tribe of adventurous barbarians, at the dawn of the Renaissance, built a society, a small universe. Shakespeare's island was meant to be for the Soleil a metaphor for the world. The "goddess of fuming war" had pride of place in it, near the king. Thus in Mnouchkine's production of *Richard II*, each of the characters concerned looked at each other and analyzed one another's position. With each word, they displayed a "vivisection of the soul."[30] The characters thus became the storytellers of their own inner landscapes.

Attentive to spoken words, the actors had to see what the characters were seeing in order to show it under the theatre's lights. Mnouchkine conceived of the actors as sent by the spectators to look for human passions, and to return as messengers to tell the public, who had vested them with this sacred mission, what they had seen on their journey. *Show*, but not judge.

This search for passions was never a question of introspection in the psychological sense. In that light, the working vocabulary of the Soleil, then and now, includes the word "autopsy," adopted from the Littré definition. The definition suggests the following approach:

> the autopsy of man, this long-cursed operation, [is] like that of the art of the actor (and like him, sacrilegious). [Its] name first meant "inspection, attentive examination performed by oneself," but also, "the state in which the ancient pagans believed they had intimate contact with the gods and a sort of participation in their all-mighty nature."[31]

Above all, for those characters the actors became closest to, it was a question of identifying a "vision," "a state of being."

The "vision" had to be clear, luminous, an image in the present, born of the force of "imagination's muscle," which was being continuously trained. The "state of being" meant no psychology, no sentimentality, but something physiological and primal, such as fear, hunger, fatigue, surprise, anger, drunkenness, laughter, hysterical laughter, hatred, ferociousness, fury, detachment, or pain. P. Hottier speaks of "the particular electricity of a character," at a given moment. He reminds us that the "state" is linked to the work with the mask. The basis of the Harlequin's mask – its flicker, its curiosity, its attention to everything – could be modified by secondary states, like aggressiveness or joy.[32]

Mnouchkine has clarified further:

> What we call the "state" is the primary passion that captivates the actor. When the actor is angry, they must draw the outline of this anger, must act it out. The actor must translate the passions felt by the Shakespearian characters. There's an alchemy to it.

She links this translation to the act of drawing: "The actor produces writing in the air; actors write with the body; actors are writers of space." She adds: "A state is never something tepid. [...] If one wants to show tepidness, the tepidness must be extreme."[33] However,

> the actor cannot – indeed must not – play more than one state at a time, even if it's played for a quarter-second and in the following quarter-second there's another state. In Shakespeare, this happens all the time. Shakespeare is made up of an intense versatility of passions; in half a line of poetry, there can be furious rage, in the next half, celestial euphoria.[34]

How were the actors to find the visions – the dreams, the nightmares – the states? The passions of the characters expressed in Shakespeare were, instructed Mnouchkine, to be taken "literally," while respecting ruptures. One was not to look for gradation or psychological nuance. One must observe others, opening oneself up to them, receiving them, being "concave." Receiving before giving. Mnouchkine insisted that "one must prepare a hollowed-out space to receive the state."[35] She also insisted on the concrete dialectic of a concave/convex listening – a listening that makes up part of the acting vocabulary that was being put into place at the time of *The Shakespeare Cycle*, including the term "versatility." "Versatility" would signify a "rapid passage from one state to another that could be its opposite."[36] Finally, the state would be signaled by "symptoms."

Ceilings of traditional Asian theatres, here, that of the Grand Kabuki in Tokyo. Photo by Béatrice Picon-Vallin.

Ceiling of a Tibetan lhamô, which inspired that of the Soleil. Archives Théâtre du Soleil.

Twelfth Night at the Cartoucherie (the premiere had been in Avignon): From left to right: C. Bosc, H. Cinque, J. Maurel, J. Arnold, G. Bigot, J. Derenne, O. Cointepas, C. Yelnik, P. Hottier, J-P. Marry, M. Durozier, P. Blancher. Photo by Michèle Laurent.

Applied to very specific cases, these notions become clearer when the ambiguous word-tools that cover them are repeated. But they always keep a bit of mystery and magic, thereby creating a "delight of complicity and shared secrets" among the members of the company. These notions are the "gear shifters" that help direct Soleil actors – little lanterns lighting the way. One could add to the list the "premonition of the body," which knows what is what, before the actor or the character does. Or "childhood," with its naivety, its faith and its belief; or "pleasure," that is, the joy of being there, of transforming oneself, of dressing, of being loved, of playing, of knowing that for four hours one will be responding to a need; and, above all, the word "drawing." To draw is to make each gesture into a spectacle, almost a dance; it is to "decompose" one's movements, "not expound, jam words together, or overact." It is to transpose the step, walk while acting; it is also never to forget the gaze of the spectator. To be a visionary does not mean confusing a psychological interiority with the interiority of the imagination; it means being available, always ready and thus present. Mnouchkine cautioned from the beginning of the rehearsals that "this would be a great show for actors, with the goal of attaining what the Japanese call *yugen* (the flower)."[37]

Masks and "mask-up"

Ariane Mnouchkine holds that

> the mask is our basic discipline, as it is a form, and all forms hold one to a discipline. [...] Theatre is a perpetual coming and going between what exists in the deepest part of us, in the most unknown places, and its projection, its maximal exteriorizing toward the spectators. Masks require precisely this maximized interiorization and exteriorization.[38]

Behind the yellow curtain of the rehearsal hall, the masks for *The Shakespeare Cycle* would be placed on shelves, easily accessible – almost as if they were watching the actors.

Masks were present during all the rehearsal work on *The Shakespeare Cycle* – masks of the *commedia dell'arte*, Balinese masks (like *Pandapa* and *Rajisan* – named by the actors, and *Punta* – its real name), and masks created by Stiefel. They were there on their own table, ritually and respectfully placed next to the table where appropriate books were laid out. Red clown noses were added to the other masks used in rehearsals. But few masks would remain in the three shows, and even those would be invented: Stiefel sculpted masks of old people, loosely based on Noh theatre masks. These were wooden, goateed, and allowed the actors to see out of their enlarged eyeholes. They

Richard II. The mask of the Duke of York (P. Hottier). Sculpted by E. Stiefel, pictured as a work in progress in his studio. Archives Sophie Moscoso.

Richard II. Mnouchkine speaks with the actress who plays the Duchess of Gloucester (L. Bensasson). Her face is covered with an articulated mask, her head topped with a shogun coiffure, with a Renaissance ruff as a collar. Photo by Michèle Laurent.

had a moving part, a joint hidden by the moustache that permitted the actors to speak. They resembled each other; but age identified itself in subtle nuances.

In *Richard II*, the Duke of York (P. Hottier), John of Gaunt (John Arnold), the Count of Salisbury (J. Arnold), and the Bishop of Carlyle (G. Freixe) were masked; in *Henry IV*, the King (J. Arnold), the Count of Westmoreland and the Count of Worcester (G. Freixe) were also masked. These "tragic masks," as Stiefel called them, helped young actors play old men and women, allowing them to play suffering and death without delving into their personal biography. The Duchess of Gloucester (Lucia Bensasson) wore a mask as well. Stiefel also made a mask for Falstaff, based on a bearded Orson Welles, but this mask wasn't kept.

Each actor trained with masks, used them to clear out preconceptions, even if afterwards the role was played without a mask. P. Hottier rehearsed the role of the gardener in *Richard II* with an old man's mask, but played him dressed as a clown. The actor who performed next to a masked actor had to adopt the same style of acting. G. Bigot, whose three roles in the Shakespeare plays, Richard II, Duke Orsino, and Prince Hal, were played without a mask, worked very hard

Twelfth Night. The reunion of Viola (J. Derenne) and Sebastian (J-P. Marry). Behind them: Feste the fool (J. Maurel), Orsino (G. Bigot), Olivia (O. Cointepas), Antonio (M. Durozier), and Maria (H. Cinque). Photo by Michèle Laurent.

in rehearsal on Pantalone and then on Harlequin *commedia* figures. Thick white makeup, drawn and painted on actors' faces, sculpting the facial architecture and accentuating the cheekbones, was the equivalent of a personal mask that certain actors perfected gradually. Mnouchkine repeated: "Masks are the school of the essential," and emphasized that even blackened teeth in a mouth that opened into a smile – victory over misery – constituted a mask. She noted: "No mask-scribbling. Find the poetry. Make your face a work of art, not just another mug."[39]

Mnouchkine from rehearsal notes
of Sophie Moscoso

"*If the actor feels a very strong emotion and doesn't find a way to translate it through the transformation of their body, there's no story, no poetry, no metaphor. If, on the other hand, they produce multiple signs that aren't the expression of a single interior truth, with no baring of the soul, then we are witness to a deployment of forms empty of content, to a contortion, a lie, and to the artifice of acting and not to art. Form dies, the character can't be born; we learn nothing about a human being motivated by an infinite number of passions; the mask becomes an object on the face. It goes without saying that the rules of the game are the same for actors who work on a character without a mask; and makeup can also be a mask. [...] The mask that's common to John of Gaunt and Henry IV, sculpted and created by E. Stiefel, has a voice, imposes bodily states; and the actor gives the mask their flesh, breathes life into the mask, infusing it with their blood and their emotional imagination; they must also listen to the mask, thereby creating within themselves the void necessary to hear and to receive delicately. Otherwise, the mask, poorly treated, will fight back! Whence the importance of a certain preparatory ritual for each day of rehearsal, when, after physical warm-ups, the actors prepare together to work on a scene, a double activity which, in our work vocabulary, we call 'the concave and the convex' This is a starting point, an image with which to receive the character: a situation and a state. It's an emptiness, the possibility of starting out on an adventure towards the discovery of an unknown human being, traveling in their soul, their heart, their lungs, their belly; and welcoming someone else inside one's own body. What's an angry king or a drunken prince, a queen who's the victim of an 'evil without name' or a rebel drunk on blood – what's going on within them?*"[40]

Richard II. Entrance of the Queen (O. Cointepas) and Richard (G. Bigot). The fluid folds of the heavy costumes accentuate the energy of the movements. At left: G. Freixe, J-B. Aubertin; behind the Queen: H. Cinque. At right: A. Del Pin and J. Maurel. Photo by Martine Franck, Magnum Photos.

Richard II. The staging is inspired by a Pieta. On the knees of Bolingbroke (C. Bosc), rests the lifeless body of Richard (G. Bigot). At left: Richard's assassin, Sir Pierce of Exton (J. Arnold). On the Asian bench rests a "cube." Outfitted with handles, the wooden cubes were of different sizes. The actors could use them to make themselves taller by standing on them. Behind the bench, a black sabre. Photo by Michèle Laurent.

The invention of a great epic form for Shakespeare

"The fact that we've decided to put on *The Shakespeare Cycle* doesn't mean at all that we've abandoned our project of inventing our shows," affirmed Mnouchkine.[41] To the strategy of new translation was added the tactics of rehearsal. For Mnouchkine, Elizabethan theatre produced great texts, but no great theatrical form. So one had to find the form.

Among the "brush cutters" of the first stages of *The Shakespeare Cycle*, Georges Bigot[42] recalls: "I rehearsed other roles as much as I did Richard II – the Queen, Bolingbroke ... I invented a little musician who followed Orsino for *Twelfth Night*; I rehearsed one of the shopkeepers robbed by Falstaff in *Henry IV*." Bigot describes rehearsals on the strips of coconut fiber matting, "a blank slate to reinvent the world" (but one that weighed a lot and took some time to learn how to roll out properly). He dwells on the process of perpetual invention.

Voice of Georges Bigot on the costume for King Richard

"*A photo of Noh theatre shown to me by Ariane in an issue on Japan of* Double Page *spoke to me: a white face with black strokes, a kimono. Among the costumes, there were no more pants in my size. At the back of the workshop, in shambles, was a wooden wagon with costumes from* Molière *piled up in it. I took out three petticoats and Molière's doublet. Gaiters would be the sleeves of the doublet held on by pins. A petticoat thrown over my shoulder would serve as a kimono sleeve. That part I kept for my final costume, which would be made from these disparate elements. I made my face up in white with the makeup of the clowns from* Mephisto, *and wore a headdress, again from* Molière. *I found what I needed to make a belt with pearls. In our rehearsal costumes, with our large petticoats, our doublet sleeves slipped on as pants, our kneepads, and everything knotted and trussed up, we were very sculpted, like warriors. We prepared for combat as if we were entering an arena. Everything was immense.*"

It was thus on the basis of an image and a theatrical collage, by improvising and drawing from old trunks, or on the costumes that in the past other members of the troupe had made, that the Shakespearean character was born in the Soleil. "Carried by Shakespeare's work, we invented a form that didn't exist before," affirms Bigot.[43] The result was an imaginary kabuki production, a form invented by the Soleil that helped create, starting with *Richard II*, a stunningly theatrical universe – gleaming and leaping. The audience was staggered, jubilant, and taken aback.

Of course in Tokyo in 1963, Mnouchkine had already recognized Shakespeare in kabuki; and in 1980, she brought her vision of theatrical Japan into rehearsals. But there was no study, no analysis nor theorization, no imitation, just transposition. Her knowledge didn't come from books; it was made up of her impressions as a spectator and traveler faced with theatres that knew how to keep their "pure form." Such a form was necessary to communicate the force of the Shakespearean text. Mnouchkine worked from her memories, from her own personal shock at what she had seen, and proposed to the actors strong images from the universe of Asian theatrical traditions: kabuki and Noh. These provided antidotes to the clichéd imagery of feudalism and knights. The only direct borrowings were the high hairstyles of the shogun-like characters that increased their height, and the kimono sleeves – but most often only one per costume! The rest was inspiration, active dreaming, and work – very long collective work.

Improvisation, the invention of characters, roles worked on by many actors; sometimes in one single day the same character being masked and barefaced; the simultaneous approach to all the plays – these elements, combined with or added to the visions and propositions of each actor, exploded the notion of a direction imposed by a lone creator. What's more, this "imaginary Japan," born of concrete stage work with elements of kabuki, Noh and *kyogen*, surpassed any specific reference to Japan. Through the discipline imposed by the masks and formal precision, the Soleil rediscovered forgotten but universal theatrical laws. An imaginary Japan was the tool that rendered Shakespeare "strange," at once far away and near. Shakespearean samurais, as the critics called them, were, above all, theatrical creatures, based on "extreme truth and extreme artifice," a principle that permitted the creation of a "hyper-realistic performance."[44]

"At the theatre, one is always abroad."[45]

Twentieth-century European stages had already felt the influence of Asian theatrical styles. This, Mnouchkine knew well – quoting Brecht, Meyerhold, or Artaud. But the Soleil's exploration was a little different. Thus, to the Japanese references in *Richard II* and *Henry IV* would be added those of India, less present in the history of Western theatre. For *Twelfth Night*, Mnouchkine's Illyria would indeed become "an imaginary India," with kathakali eye rolling, movements from bharata natyam folk dancing, gigantic colored parasols, and costumes with vivacious and contrasting colors.

Henry IV. Entry of the rebels: from left to right, Douglas (M. Durozier); a parasol carrier (C. Bosc); Henry Percy, called Hotspur (J. Maurel) pictured midair in a spectacular jump; and Worcester (G. Freixe). Douglas wears a half-shoulder armor – a Japanese military accessory – in leather, gilded by hand with gold leaf by the actors. Photo by Martine Franck, Magnum Photos.

Henry IV. After having killed several stand-ins for the king, Douglas meets the real Henry IV (J. Arnold). Just as he is about to kill him, Henry's son, Prince Hal, surges forth, armed with a wooden Japanese training sabre. (Carpets brought by the black guards define the scenic space: for the tavern: a patchwork of coarse linen; for the exterior scenes – encampments or battle scenes – silky patchworks). Photo by Michèle Laurent.

Henry IV. Douglas, the Scottish rebel, battles Blunt (P. Blancher) – Henry IV's battle double. The scene is at once comic and cruel. Photo by Michèle Laurent.

Henry IV. King Henry IV wears a second, blood-covered mask, specially created by E. Stiefel. The blood that escapes from the mouths of the wounded is dyed cotton. Photo by Michèle Laurent.

Acrobatic leaps of the Soleil actors: *The Golden Age*. Abdallah (P. Caubère) leaps onto the stage. We are in Marseilles. Archives Monique and Daniel Cordin.

Henry IV. Falstaff's stoutness does not prevent P. Hottier from leaping. Photo by Martine Franck, Magnum Photos.

Henry IV. Prince Hal (G. Bigot) appears to fly. Photo by Martine Franck, Magnum Photos.

Twelfth Night. One of the magnificent jumps of Feste the fool (J. Maurel). Photo by Martine Franck, Magnum Photos.

Henry IV: On the battlefield, the Earl of Douglas (M. Durozier) flees. Photo by Martine Franck, Magnum Photos.

J-J. Lemêtre among his instruments, which numbered more than 300 for *The Shakespeare Cycle*, and which came from, or were inspired by those of 37 countries – from the Indian tanpura to the epinette des Vosges, from the African balafon to the sitar or psalterium. Photo by Michèle Laurent.

When the actors had already advanced in their work, they would watch, in addition to the films of Shakespeare's works, documentaries on Asian forms: on kabuki, Noh, and bunraku (July 1981), on kathakali at the Mandapa Center (April 1982), rounded out by the films of the great Indian director Satyagit Ray. *The Shakespeare Cycle* constructed itself as a sort of "*bricolage*," in Levi-Strauss's sense of the term—intercultural, born from images and from the work on stage, reinforced by filmed pieces on theatre. Asia was vast – a space of voracious imagination.

The influences of Asian theatre were, nevertheless, mixed with those of *commedia dell'arte* (especially for *Twelfth Night*); and elements of Western visual culture were laid on top of that – for example, references in rehearsal to Italian painting (the battle scenes of Paolo Uccello). Some scenes in *Richard II* were based on motifs from Christian paintings (the crucifixion of Richard in his prison, a Pieta when Bolingbroke held the corpse of the King in his arms). To all this was added the influence of classical ballet, from which emerged the jumps performed by certain actors on stage. These different elements, displaced and mixed in the crucible of the work and present in the costume-collages (ruff collars and kimonos) – as well as in the space and acting techniques – combined to give new life to Shakespeare.

It was with these combined methods that the story (and History itself) was told to the audience. *To the audience* – this was one of the guiding principles of the performance, an audience faced head-on. The characters, Mnouchkine relayed in rehearsal, were to "tell their pain to the public. Take the public in their arms and tell them."[46] One of the many salient features of her direction was the positioning of the characters to face the audience, their dialogue communicated in direct address to the public. The performance space was thereby wide open; there was no possibility of imagining a fourth wall.

A common space for all the plays

The images for the space of the action that Mnouchkine sent to the actors included an island, the dawn, the void or "a grand space with stars above";[47] – and the first vision for the stage design was an island with terracing on the water and references to the film *Kagemusha*. Starting from these proposals evoking Japanese theatre and the necessity for a "pure space" (one that would only contain what was indispensable to the actor), G-C. François began "by drawing a big sun – and that worked right away. The consecutive lowering of the backdrops, as well, was inspired by Japanese theatre."[48] François placed on the masonry floor covered with a wood veneer, a flat expanse of beige coconut matting whose strips were connected by rubber joints covered with black velour – which gave greater depth to the stage.

This brush-carpet, this coconut fiber, common to all the plays, would be installed in the rehearsal hall before being put on the stage. But at first, rehearsals would occur on the dyed-red coconut mat of *Mephisto*. The architecture of the stage for *The Shakespeare Cycle* would borrow from kabuki its *hanamichi*, but would lay it out laterally, like the short walkway of Noh theatre, and would double it, making two long, parallel paths. G-C. Francois thus brought into being another architectural organization of the naves of the Cartoucherie.

There were also immense silk panels, backdrops that covered the entirety of the rear wall, which were painted according to drawings conceived by François. They evolved, and some were rejected during the rehearsal process. The final product wouldn't be ready until the very night of the opening. They were covered with gold leaf, the metal weighing down the silk a little; but they still quivered and undulated at the least breath of air. Held in place with electromagnets, each panel cascaded like water when dropped to the floor, allowing a different one behind it to appear. There were around 15 silk panels per production: golden colored with red, black, and white elements for the history plays; pastel colors for *Twelfth Night* – all created to convey the atmosphere of the scenes, with the time of day indicated by motifs of the moon or the sun. In *Henry IV*, seven panels were dropped in quick succession.[49] Actors removed them. These were the servants, roles that evolved over the course of the three plays – simple "servants" becoming "servants of the scene" then "black guards" – transpositions of the *koken* function in kabuki. They were responsible for lifting the backdrops with poles, shaking them, or putting them away after their fall, and also for handing over spears, and for helping *Richard II* remove his royal adornments upon his dethronement.

Dark blue velour curtains permitted a view of the dressing rooms under the tiered seating. On the theatre's ceiling, under the metal structural support, a number of small bright canopies were attached, reminiscent of the roof of the Grand Kabuki theatre of Tokyo, or of the pagodas where the Tibetan *lhamô* is performed. Through them was diffused the lighting that animated and brightened the stage. An ever-changing sky thus hovered over the heads of the actors. Small follow spots, which shone their lights on the rich cloth of the costumes, gave the impression that the light was coming from the actors themselves. Footlights bordered the set, installed on metal rods. With the lighting, Jean-Noël Cordier deepened the volume of the stage. There was a simplicity, a beauty, and a luminosity in the choice of materials. The rustling of the luxurious and refined silk backdrops contrasted, when they were released, with the barbarity of the combat scenes. It was, indeed, an empty space, immense and augmented.

The actors' entrances

The actors reached the stage by lateral walkways, which gave them time to compose themselves, find the required state and draw their characters in the air. This extension of the space of the entryway onto the stage, a major theatrical moment – which is usually fleeting and rapid when one has only to cross the backstage area to enter – was, in effect, a transposition of the *hanamichi* and the *hashigakari* of Japanese Noh theatre. Placed sideways, these walkways allowed the public to see actors arrive from afar, entering to the rhythm of the percussions – veritable retinues of characters running or prancing, adding individual details to their impetuous stampedes. Mnouchkine recounts:

> In kabuki, there are solemn entries, but these entries are very slow, with just one character, with a pause on the walkway. For Richard's first entry on stage, I wanted to begin in the heart of the action, in the maelstrom of the struggle. The king enters, surrounded by hornets that don't touch him yet, but who await their moment.[50]

The court of Richard II was a swarm, or a mob, with group entrances giving off streams of hatred, boiling – the entrances

Henry IV. Staging and performance in a reduced space: a grouping on a carpet. From left to right: Peto (H. Cinque), Bardolph (F. Gargiulo), Poins (J. Arnold), Prince Hal (G. Bigot), and Falstaff (P. Hottier), who leans on a cube. His corpulence is made apparent by a giant Japanese breastplate designed to protect his fat belly: his cowardice is thus depicted in his costume. Photo by Michèle Laurent.

showed the seeds of the civil war, as well as demonstrating the hierarchy that was still accorded to rank. The costumes flew, and, at the very moment of stepping onto the stage, some actors would throw themselves against the wall for support and then bounce off of it, the fabric of their vast costumes redrawing and inflating the forms of the bodies in motion. In *Twelfth Night*, Orsino used the walkway in a more "Japanese" fashion, walking nonchalantly along it.

Training

For *Richard II*, it was P. Hottier who took charge of warming up the actors, one hour before each rehearsal and performance. Some did kickboxing (forbidden after a broken nose); others did karate. They entertained themselves with martial arts during the breaks. The whole troupe, including the technicians, practiced tai chi during a certain period of time. Some were real athletes, capable of jumping very high, like Julien Maurel. No one skirted physical exertion, and all were constantly surpassing their limits.

It was for *Twelfth Night* that Mnouchkine brought in Maïtreyi, a bharata natyam dancer whom she had seen perform – because this Indian dance, of sacred origin, requires the skills of an actor. From then on, Maïtreyi would take on the regular training of the actors.

Voice of Maïtreyi

> "*Starting from the technique of bharata natyam, we looked for a plan that would allow the actors to feel as if they were elsewhere, in an imaginary India. My role was to give them a class on Indian dancing in the morning, as well as instructions about style, during rehearsals or just after. Instructions which, in and of themselves had nothing to do with dance – they were of a practical variety – how to sit on the ground and to get up while wearing baggy pants. [...] I taught them the first position, demi-plié, knees turned outward, crouched as low as possible, which would allow for extremely quick movements. This way, one can maintain a very close relationship to the center of gravity and the ground, and eliminate the vertical lengthening of walking upright. The center of gravity is pushed towards the horizontal axis. This allows one to go very quickly and to accomplish a maximum displacement with a minimal range of motion in the legs.*"[51]

But only some actors made their characters dance on stage (Maria, played by H. Cinque and Feste played by J. Maurel).

The physical preparation was all the more important in that the precision of the actors' movements, the virtuosity of the actors bounding through the air or along a long central bench (one of the only scenic elements in the empty space) had to take into account the weight of the extremely heavy costumes, such as they were in their final form, which turned the actors' jumps into true achievements. Dresses with multiple petticoats, fabrics in preciously accumulated layers, belts and bands that harnessed the actors, could not prevent them from becoming centaurs – man and horse simultaneously, galloping in place with, for their only accessory, a riding crop which beat the air, flinching and shuddering to evoke a horse's movements. These centaurs thus drew the public into vast imagined spaces, traversed by a vision of power – or into the violence of a tournament where men crossed swords and fought like ferocious dogs, within an arena designated by a tight, mobile cord. The costumes themselves became masks from which only hands were visible, hands with bandaged forearms and fingerless gloves. Theatrical life gushed forth from the physical work of the masked body, which took on the "grand" second position of classical ballet to signal combat, with the knees spread far apart, with arched legs, hands on thighs, a codified position of deified man, positioned so as to make heroic the Soleil's Shakespearean characters, "who," said Mnouchkine, "have the arrogance of wanting to live even if they are delirious and greedy."

"For me, the music is as important as the text." (Ariane Mnouchkine, Interview with Béatrice Picon-Vallin, 2004, www .theatre-du-soleil.fr.)

The Music

The Soleil, as we have seen, has always used music, recorded or live – an orchestra being present for *The Clowns* and for *Mephisto*. In *The Golden Age*, music played during the intervals between each sequence. For *The Shakespeare Cycle*, the work of the actors in rehearsal happened in the presence of the musician, and no longer to recorded soundtracks as in *The Golden Age*. "There was, from the beginning, simultaneous invention and mutual influence between performance and music."[52] Different sorts of theatrical music, as Jean-Jacques Lemêtre developed the scores, were articulated across the three plays. More rhythmic for *Richard II*, the music especially accompanied the entrances and transcribed the sounds and rhythms particular to each character. The music was more melodic for *Twelfth Night*, where there were different musical motifs for each of the characters, motifs that also announced their entry on stage. For *Henry IV*, the music evoked places and times and had similarities to that of *Richard II*. Even if he sang sometimes, Lemêtre was never a soloist; he was in sync with the actors, matching the tempo of their gait, or the speed of their discourse. Neither Japanese, nor Indian, nor Balinese (even if Lemêtre used Balinese drums for the scene of Richard in his prison), the music was first of all alive to the present, as in Asian theatre. As a connoisseur of Asian music, Lemêtre could treat it in a free and imaginative manner. The theatre orchestra was placed in a space just below the stage, in front of the first walkway for *Richard II*, as well as for *Twelfth Night*. It was enlarged from two to three musicians, and occupied the space between the two walkways for *Henry IV*.

In the final analysis, the Shakespearean text became a musical source text, the translation of which was worked on as if poetry. One had to evacuate realistic diction, accentuate consonants, work with the rhythm, in long and short tempos. The meter of the performance was found in working with the music. The voice was to "sing" but never scream.[53] "I had the impression I was part of a rock group playing before its own generation," commented Georges Bigot.

> "Through delving into these traditions, I know today that I was looking for the freeing corset. The corset that would keep me upright but allow me to fly." (Ariane Mnouchkine, Interview with Béatrice Picon-Vallin, 2004, www.theatre-du-soleil.fr.)

Twenty years old

The great constraints imposed by form did no harm to the joyous sensation of freedom of all those Soleil actors keen on inventing. They were, at once, animated and supported, propelled and restrained. The story was more complicated for those who never pinned down a role. It was, without a doubt, the departures from the company that ensued that prevented the Soleil from continuing its work on the Shakespeare plays, notably Part II of *Henri IV*, which had started rehearsals, as well as the filming of *Richard II*. But the work was there, in its fullness: a tragedy, a comedy, and a tragicomedy by Shakespeare. What's more, invited twice by Bernard Faivre d'Arcier to Avignon, Mnouchkine triumphed in 1982 with *Richard II* and *Twelfth Night*, a triumph that repeated itself in 1984 with *Henry IV* in the courtyard of the Papal Palace – with its grandiose dimensions and with the silk backdrops quivering in the mistral breeze against the stage wall.[54] In Los Angeles, at the Olympic Arts Festival, in a Hollywood studio set up as a duplicate of the Cartoucherie, the public was dazzled by these Shakespearian plays in French! In the workshop that he directed afterwards in Los Angeles, G. Bigot met Simon Abkarian. He brought him to the workshop that the Soleil organized at the end of 1984. And Abkarian would remain for the following productions.

By 1984, the Soleil had received the Grand Prize of France's theatre critics for *Richard II*.[55] They had performed it to sold-out crowds at the Avignon theatre festival in 1982 twice in a row one evening because of a rained-out performance; and the movement of the 2,500 spectators, who, at 2 a.m. replaced the 2,500 who were leaving after the first showing, remains part of the fabled history of the festival. The company again

Richard II in rehearsal. The assassination of Richard in prison by Exton (J. Arnold), surrounded by his two acolytes: at left, P. Fatus, on the right, J. Maurel. Photo by Martine Franck, Magnum Photos.

Henry IV. On the ground, Sir Walter Blunt (P. Blancher); in the air, Hotspur (J. Maurel). P. Blancher has put down his beribboned lance. M. Durozier remembers that with J. Maurel, they tried to create moments of frozen motion in mid-air, as in Bruce Lee movies. Photo by Michèle Laurent.

Twelfth Night. Viola (J. Derenne), Duke Orsino (G. Bigot), and Feste (J. Maurel) on his "flying carpet" – so dubbed by Mnouchkine, who also underscored for this play about desire and amorous passion: "It's not because the water is limpid and transparent that the bottom is less deep, or the world we see in it less mysterious." She insisted: "Look for the small, the minute, in order to find what is grand." Photo by Michèle Laurent.

made its mark on the history of the Avignon Theatre Festival by performing *Henri IV* in the courtyard of the Papal Palace, refurbished by G-C. François at the request of festival director Faivre d'Arcier. Opening the Festival in 1984, they had even come back from Los Angeles to close it, while their American tour was replayed on a giant screen on Avignon's Île Piot.

At 20 years old, the Soleil and its rays shone brightly in the world of theatre. "I believe a theatre company isn't made to last forever. When one thinks that we're celebrating the 20th anniversary of the Soleil this year, I find that truly extraordinary. There are few theatre companies that hold together for as long," noted, in awe, the administrator J-P. Hénin. L. Guertchikoff added: "One truly wonders how [we] will continue [our] trajectory at this high a level."[56]

Notes

1 Ariane Mnouchkine, in Fabienne Pascaud, *L'Art du présent: Entretiens avec Ariane Mnouchkine* (Paris: Plon, 2005), 49.
2 Ariane Mnouchkine, *La Revue d'histoire du théâtre*, vol. 4 (2009), 366.
3 Quoted by Ariane Mnouchkine, "Il nous aide à poser les bonnes questions," *Le Monde*, March 4, 1976.
4 Mnouchkine and Cixous met with Resistance members Hervé Montjaret, Yvette Farnoux, Pierre Bichet, Marcel Degliame, Serge Ravanel, Daniel Mayer, Raymond and Lucie Aubrac. They also met with Daniel Cordier, who was Jean Moulin's secretary.
5 Two wooden comic masks made by E. Stiefel were used in this show.
6 The song was recorded by M. Rouvières, who was responsible for the vocal training of the actors.
7 Documentation was collected by Sophie Moscoso and Lorenz Knauer. See the long, detailed chronology and the bibliography in *Méphisto, le roman d'une carrière (Paris: Solin, 1979)*. Many German films were shown to the actors (Fritz Lang, Murnau, Karl Valentin, etc.), curated by N. Napo.
8 Théâtre du Soleil, *Méphisto* (Paris: Solin, 1979), scene VII. The production would be toured from 1980 to 1986 to different countries: Finland, Sweden, England, Uruguay, and Germany. Bernard Sobel made a film of the production, commissioned by German television.
9 See "Ariane Mnouchkine, *Méphisto* et le diable nazi," *Les Nouvelles littéraires*, no. 2688 (1979). Kurt Trepke, an old actor from Piscator's Theatre, exiled during Nazi rule, and after the war living in East Berlin, met the actors on the evening of the premiere and shared his memories with them. This was one of the first opportunities the troupe had had to have a face-to-face meeting with one of the characters they were performing or with one of their representatives.
10 Ariane Mnouchkine, "En plein Soleil," *Fruits*, no. 2–3, June 1984, 212.
11 *Les Boréades* by Jean-Philippe Rameau, a proposal that would be quickly abandoned, but which gave rise to epic singing classes each morning at the actors' various worksites.

12 In this chapter, unattributed quotes by Soleil members and by Ariane Mnouchkine come from one of the several interviews Béatrice Picon-Vallin conducted with them from 2010 to 2014.

13 Sophie Moscoso, "Avant-propos," *Double Page*, no. 32, 1984, 1.

14 He played Théophile Sarder in *Mephisto* and would be replaced by Bruno Sermonne.

15 As witnessed by Georges Bigot, who participated in it.

16 Robert Abirached was then Director of Theatre and Performance, while Jack Lang was Minister of Culture (1981–1986).

17 A brand of French earthmovers, bought by Poclain in 1974. This tractor was used until *The Last Caravanserai* and finally scrapped in 2013.

18 The script was published by the National Theatre of Strasbourg. The Soleil rehearsed *Love's Labour's Lost* with this translation.

19 Ariane Mnouchkine, "Le besoin d'une forme," *Théâtre/Public*, 1982, no. 46–47, 11.

20 Ariane Mnouchkine, *Fruits*, 212.

21 Ariane Mnouchkine, *Théâtre/Public*, 10.

22 For more on construction, see Chapter One: "Nomadic Adventures."

23 See *Fruits*, 219.

24 Ariane Mnouchkine, *Fruits*, 218. The manuscript of the translation of the first part of *Henry IV* ends with: "With love from William and me too," Théâtre du Soleil/S. Moscoso Archives, BnF, 4-COL 153 un-numbered red spiral bound notebook.

25 He had been "seduced" into the company by *The Clowns* in Avignon.

26 See notes of Sophie Moscoso, Archives Sophie Moscoso.

27 Ariane Mnouchkine, rehearsal notes from the Shakespeare comedies, Théâtre du Soleil/S. Moscoso Archives, BnF, 4-COL 153 (898).

28 Ibid.

29 Curio in *Twelfth Night* would be played by Hélène Cinque.

30 From the program of *Richard II*.

31 Ibid.

32 Philippe Hottier, *Théâtre/Public*, 12. The term "state" appeared during the rehearsals of *The Golden Age*.

33 Ariane Mnouchkine, *Théâtre/Public*, 10.

34 Ariane Mnouchkine, *Fruits*, 204.

35 Ariane Mnouchkine, rehearsal remarks, Théâtre du Soleil/S. Moscoso Archives, BnF, 4-COL 153 (920).

36 Ariane Mnouchkine, rehearsal remarks, Théâtre du Soleil/S. Moscoso Archives, BnF, 4-COL 153 (907–911).

37 Notebook of Sophie Moscoso, April 21, 1981, Sophie Moscoso Archives.

38 Ariane Mnouchkine, in Odette Aslan, ed., *Le Corps en jeu* (Paris: CNRS Publications, 1993), 233.

39 Ariane Mnouchkine, rehearsal remarks, Théâtre du Soleil/S. Moscoso Archives, BnF, 4-COL 153 (898), then (922).

40 Ariane Mnouchkine, synthesis of notes taken by Sophie Moscoso during rehearsals, *Double Page*, no. 32, 1984.

41 Ariane Mnouchkine, in Alfred Simon, "Les Dieux qu'il nous faut. Entretien avec Ariane Mnouchkine," *Acteurs*, no. 2, February 1982, 20.

42 Bigot would stay 11.5 years at the Soleil.

43 Georges Bigot, *Théâtre/Public*, 13.

44 From the program of *Richard II*.

45 Ariane Mnouchkine, rehearsal notes for *Love's Labour's Lost*, March 23, 1983, Théâtre du Soleil/S. Moscoso Archives, BnF, 4-COL 153 (898).

46 Ariane Mnouchkine, rehearsal notes for *Henry IV*, June 1, 1981, Théâtre du Soleil/S. Moscoso Archives, BnF, 4-COL 153 (921).

47 Ariane Mnouchkine, rehearsal notes for Shakespeare, Théâtre du Soleil/S. Moscoso Archives, BnF, 4-COL 153 (920).

48 Ariane Mnouchkine, *Fruits*, 60.

49 For *Henry IV*, there were 20 silk backdrops in all.

50 Ariane Mnouchkine, *Théâtre/Public*, 10.

51 Maïtreyi, in Odette Aslan, *Le Corps en jeu*, 347.

52 Georges Bigot, *Théâtre/Public*, 14.

53 Jean-Jacques Lemêtre, *Fruits*, 190.

54 Some of the backdrops were painted on the spot in the Grande Audience room of the Papal Palace in Avignon.

55 They had already received this award for *The Kitchen* in 1967.

56 Hénin and Guertchikoff, *Fruits*, 32 and 149.

The Terrible but Unfinished Story of Norodom Sihanouk, King of Cambodia. Hélène Cixous, who wrote this play for the Soleil, was inspired by Shakespeare, and like him brings the dead back to life on stage. The ghost of Norodom Suramarit, father of Sihanouk (G. Freixe), appears several times to speak to the living. Photo by Michèle Laurent.

Chapter 4 A new way of writing: creating the great Asian epics

"Might the difficulty of translating contemporary Western figures to the theatre (as opposed to American cinema) be a result of skepticism or prudence vis-à-vis a certain type of ethics or moral philosophy? If not a total rejection of the notions of Good and Evil?"

Ariane Mnouchkine[1]

The year 1985 saw the writer Hélène Cixous join the core group of creators at the Soleil, a group that included the set designer, the musician-composer, costume designers, and technicians – a more stable configuration than that of the actors. We might say that Cixous was a product of the Soleil itself, or at least greatly influenced by her regular attendance at their performances. Her official arrival had been anticipated for a while. During *The Shakespeare Cycle*, Mnouchkine had proposed that Cixous write for the Soleil: however, her writing, whether poetic fiction or theatre, seemed to be quite distant from what was being performed at the time. But this would be an initial attempt, whose result would have to be submitted to the troupe for approval. Mnouchkine was confident. She felt that she, herself, was only a scriptwriter, and "what was needed was a true writer."[2]

Starting with *1789*, which had filled her with wonder (and which she had seen as a neighbor, as she was teaching at the nearby University of Vincennes), Cixous regularly attended performances and grew very familiar with the work of the Soleil. In 1972, she came to Mnouchkine with Michel Foucault to propose a collaboration with the GIP (a prison information group) for their work in French prisons. This produced *Steal Some Bread and Go to Prison, Steal A Million and Go to A Palace* [*Qui vole un pain va en prison, qui vole des millions va au Palais-Bourbon*], the second half an allusion to people elected to the National Assembly. Cixous considers this four-minute-long play to be their first collaboration – she laughs as she tells the story – even though she never saw it. This is because the police came so quickly that the actors couldn't even set up the stage. This first involvement with the Soleil combined ethics, engagement, acting, and activism. Cixous also participated in the Soleil as an active observer, even to the extent of occasional oversight of the actors at the "Shakespeare Workshop." And it would be the students in her seminar who would take charge of the combined Volume 2/3 (1984) of the review *Fruits*, devoted to the Soleil, examining in detail the working methods of the company during *The Shakespeare Cycle*.

Mnouchkine's proposal was for Cixous to write on the Cambodian genocide, which she had wanted to treat at the beginning of 1981, indignant at the horrors perpetuated by Pol Pot and at the complicity of radical left-wing ideologues in disseminating disinformation. The guiding principal was to depict the big picture through small details, a Brechtian principal that the director had never forsaken. Faced with the enormity of dealing with the genocide head-on, Cixous started with the more modest project of writing a few scenes centered on the Jarai people, a small ethnic group crushed by both the Vietnamese and the Cambodians. But this was not the right scale. "At the Soleil," said Cixous, "one must find the gigantic at the microscopic level."[3] William Shawcross' book *Sideshow: Kissinger, Nixon and the Destruction of Cambodia*[4] opened the way; both Cixous and Mnouchkine read him. The son of a judge of the

Sihanouk. In rehearsal. Work on the text happened on stage. The director is seated to the left; Cixous is at the director's table. Next to her is Sophie Moscoso, Mnouchkine's assistant. Photo by Martine Franck, Magnum Photos.

Nuremburg trials, Shawcross helped them understand through his grasp of the events that Prince Norodom Sihanouk was the metaphor they'd been looking for.[5] He *was* Cambodia. The "kingdom" that Mnouchkine wanted the Soleil to represent was his: larger, but, at the same time, as the King would say in the play "a speck of dust in your eye." A Cambodia which, with the sweetness of its smile, had seduced Mnouchkine thoroughly at the time of her trip in 1963. Would it be a kingdom that could hold its own with that of Shakespeare's England?

After the fantastical Asia that had given epic shape to the works of Shakespeare, it was time for the Soleil to penetrate the history of the postcolonial Asian continent, where the present moment was profoundly mixed with the past. King Sihanouk was the vessel that carried the ancient Khmer civilization; and, ten years after the massacres committed by the Khmer Rouge, the Soleil would recount a tragedy of our time, taking place between 1955 and 1979. In *The Terrible but Unfinished Story of Norodom Sihanouk, King of Cambodia*, they would find a necessary distance for performance by abandoning Eurocentric subjects.

Writing the tragedy of Cambodia: an epic fresco, a historical chronicle of two eras

Voice of Hélène Cixous

"*In the theatre, one can and one must hear the most discreet of voices. Even the voiceless speak. One speaks with one's eyes, one's body, one's feet. One listens also with one's eyes; the illiterate understand all the words because they've been given flesh. The very well educated see the intelligence of what happens beyond the words. In the theatre, we accept that everyone possesses the same innocence. Otherwise, it's not worth the trouble of going.*

For its part, theatre has the duty to bring us into the realm of legends. What can no longer happen in the world-machine still happens in the theatre. A curtain, a stage, a caravan, the high plateaus. What happens: destinies. Destinies?! We who only have our existences left ... and, while waiting for retirement forget that we have the right to a destiny. But theatre can and must remind us that in becoming "Indians" once again, we can again lay claim to our own personal kingdoms, to our individual treasures, to our chances to be the heroes of our own stories.

And, rather than making our way, heads down, toward death, we can go forth to adventure, eyes wide open.

The theatre exists in the present, must always be in the present. That is its good fortune. At every moment, the

"[We seek] a way of writing what characters are feeling, without imposing an ideology on them." (Ariane Mnouchkine, *Théâtre/Public*, no. 46–7, 1982, 11.)

present bursts forth. The present is a brilliant black. We go forward with our hearts beating fast, not knowing what awaits us. And the unknown that makes us hold our breath, picks us up, transports us up and above ourselves – this is life itself. In the theatre, the public doesn't know anything more than the character does about themselves. No one sets a precedent. Together, we fail to understand. Together we hesitate. This creates among us all an obscure, quivering, archaic complicity.[6]

Hélène Cixous, who is, as she says, "African" (born in Oran, Algeria), discovered "Asia," and her approach to it was that of putting difference in motion. Let us remember, in the theatre we are always abroad. Cixous is not only a writer, but also a historian and a researcher. She documented her work and hunted through archives in France and America, consulted specialists on Southeast Asia at INALCO, the National Institute of Oriental Languages and Civilizations in Paris. To get "into the interior of this silent world," she needed to learn its history, but also the geopolitical breeding ground that surrounded it, as well as its geography, ethnology, botany, and Cambodian folk tales. She gathered an enormous amount of documentary evidence, organized a singular writing laboratory for herself, because she had to construct a history that was not yet finished before she could transform it into theatrical words. She worked on written traces, on images, and on eyewitness accounts. She met with members of the Cambodian refugee community living in France, before embarking on what she calls the process of "poetic metabolizing," which allowed her to unburden herself of a scientific approach and let the characters emerge. She wrote and wrote:

> In writing for the theatre, one must get some distance from oneself, leave, travel a long time through obscurity, to the point of no longer knowing where you are, who you are – it's very difficult. One must travel to the point of feeling that space around you has become a completely foreign land, to the point of becoming afraid, until one arrives, lost, in a region that one doesn't recognize, until one wakes up, transformed into someone one has never met – such as a beggar, or a naïve divinity, or a wise old man.[7]

Up to this point, Cixous had written plays with four or five characters – and now she had to carry dozens of them. The discussions between director and author to find the way forward gave way to dialogues with the characters, with interior voices. What names to give them? Mnouchkine insisted

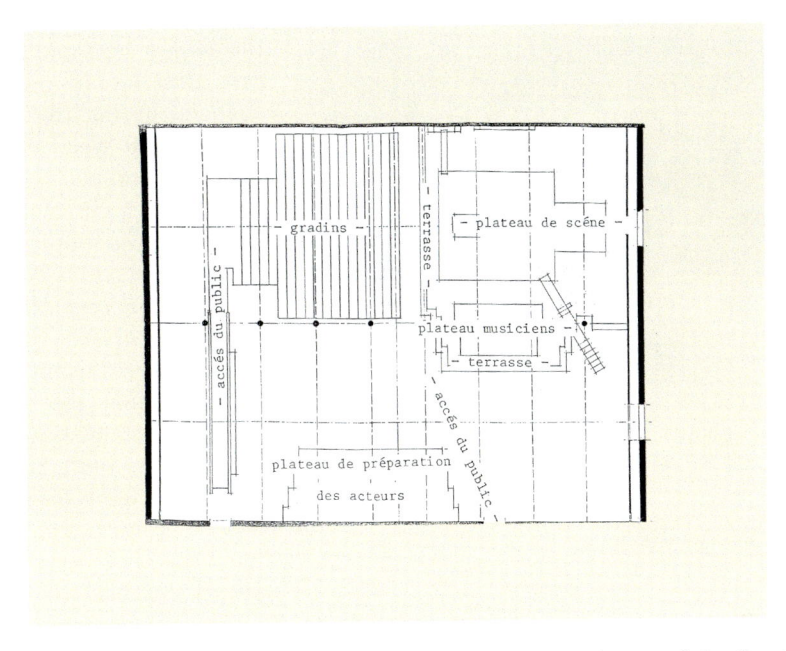

Layout of the stage, the musicians' area, the passageways, the bleachers, and the dressing-room areas for *Sihanouk*. The materials used for the staging evoke the architecture of a Khmer temple. A variety of places can be indicated thanks to different entrances and the addition of some props. Archives Théâtre du Soleil.

Sihanouk. The staging in Brussels, at the Halles de Schaerbeek, during the 1986 tour. Archives Théâtre du Soleil.

One of the photos taken by Mnouchkine in the Cambodian refugee camps on the Thai border, where she met, along with Cixous, Father Ceyrac, a legendary figure for the Soleil. Photo by Ariane Mnouchkine, Archives Sophie Moscoso.

the names be kept secret, in case they would have to be changed during the rehearsal process. But they would end up being retained.

The research would continue in Cambodia,[8] where Mnouchkine and Cixous went on a scouting mission in 1984. Mnouchkine went first, while Cixous was finishing up her work, writing the first part of the play, and beginning to write the second. She feared that the weighty reality of the refugee camps might crush her text. The two of them gained entrance to pro- and anti-Sihanouk camps on the Thai border, at Khao-I-Dang, Tatum, and Kampur, where they enjoyed richly human encounters. They were guided by Father Ceyrac, a Jesuit priest who was passionate about India, a country that would remain dear to the Soleil. Cixous and Mnouchkine entered on a truck with a day-pass to meet groups of smiling children that Mnouchkine photographed. They also met Ok and Mon, former dancers in the Cambodian Royal Ballet, who had organized a dance school for children[9] in a bamboo hut with a straw roof. They met charming, dignified adults who lived delicately and with beauty in devastated areas. The two women heard "true, trembling voices."[10] They gathered horror stories that would nourish their theatrical work on all levels. They succeeded in leaving the camps with a young Cambodian, Ly Nissay, and his family. Nissay would then emigrate to France with refugee status and stay the rest of his life with the Soleil. The writing process continued upon their return to Paris. The play, whose "poetico-diplomatic" structure had been found, was further enriched with new characters.

Rehearsing a play without a title

Voice of Hélène Cixous

> "*To the people of the Soleil, to the people rising up to the tender light*
> *from which this story has sprouted.*
> *My very dear friends, so sweet, my scouts of eternal Theatre*

– I could only write this text while tossed upon the great
waters of dreams
by the Ariane Breeze. And because you exist. It comes
from you all, and it lives only for you and toward you and
by you.
It is truly your work and your child.
This is why I owe you a debt of gratitude – to you who
have
pushed me to make much more than I
without you could have dared help emerge.
(I will add that it is still emerging.
It falls to you, to all of us together, to make a beautiful,
living thing.)
– What's left is work!" [11]

The text that Cixous proposed to the troupe was, indeed, an enormous worksite – first of all, due to the simple fact that the play was only 75 percent complete at the start of rehearsals. There were 57 characters, clustered in groups, as in Shakespeare. Among them: the royal house, friends and those faithful to the king, enemies of the king, and the Khmer Rouge. The action took place across the globe, in multiple locales, from Phnom Penh to Beijing, from Moscow to Paris, from the United States to Vietnam. Unlike in *1789* and *1793*, great historical figures did not disappear in favor of the common man – the play presented the great, analyzed their relationships in terms of violence and justice. It also gave physical shape to the world of the dead by making the ghost of King Suramarit (Sihanouk's father) appear, though this was a theatrical apparition, as he was still alive at the time of the events of the story.

The play, in two "eras," each of which has five acts, sets in motion a polyvocality of positions. The events span the 24 years from 1955 to 1979, across 50 scenes. In the first part of this epic fresco, we witness the abdication of Sihanouk, who enters politics and chooses for the country the camp of non-aligned countries. This first era ends with the alliance among Sihanouk, the Khmer Rouge, and China after the failure of the military *coup d'état* orchestrated by Lon Nol. In the second era, we see Sihanouk, exiled in Beijing, resigned to forming an alliance with his former enemies, again the Khmer Rouge, dominated by Maoist ideas and guerilla tactics, and allied with Vietnamese forces. We also see how in 1975, just after his return to Phnom Penh, the Khmer Rouge empties the city in three days. The genocide begins. Sihanouk is locked up in his palace, his family assassinated. The play ends with the victorious offensive of the Vietnamese, who put an end to Pol Pot's regime, and send Sihanouk into exile once again.

Sihanouk. Above: the statuettes (or dolls) made of wood and clothed, representing the Khmer people, photographed from stage left. In the center: the large saffron curtain, the metaphorical "color of Cambodia," that shimmered and opened for the entrances and apparitions of characters. Pictured: M. Azencot, C. Yelnik, F. Gargiulo. Photo by Michèle Laurent.

The memorial dolls in Amsterdam in front of the Tropenmuseum to welcome the play to the Holland Festival in June 1986. Photo by Liliana Andreone.

A collaborative process

Mnouchkine gave the first part of the script to the troupe for the ritual first reading in the foyer of their theatre on January 15, 1985. The next day, without waiting, everyone was on stage. Entirely copied by hand, the manuscript was preceded, as we've seen, by an intimate letter to the actors in Cixous' handwriting that acknowledged the work that was only just beginning. The availability and the flexibility of the author, her method of working on request, can be understood by the contrapuntal existence of her other writing projects, over which she has total mastery and total control. This manuscript text, which "raves with madness," as she is wont to say, was capacious, and presented itself as a working draft: Sophie Moscoso kept the act by act iteration in five bound notebooks; the manuscript ended with the evocative send off, "to be continued."[12]

Examining the edited manuscript displays many corrections: changes in speakers for the dialogues, elimination and addition of words, entire scenes crossed out, pages attached with paperclips that contain entirely new scenes. The text itself has variants to choose from; and occasionally one sees a second version of a scene replaced with one entitled "second correction." The manuscript became a true worksite of "applied sewing," according to Cixous; it was necessary to adjust, to cut, to move text. This applied to dialogue that proved difficult to enunciate and had to be rewritten, to lines that were cut and replaced by actors' movements, and to scenes to be combined or placed at a different moment in the text. Mnouchkine's fluid method of assigning actors to parts also necessitated the evolution of the text – as a function of who was eventually assigned to which role.

In the great test performed by enacting the text, sheets of paper would arrive on stage, manuscripts in Cixous' fine handwriting, or transposed by that of Mnouchkine. One can truly speak of collective creation, of a text written on the stage, with all the frustrations that such a process can encompass (as much for the author as for the actors). Scenes were tried out, then cut or reduced; some beautiful scenes were replaced by the simple recounting by a messenger. "Did you receive a letter?" the actors asked, when coming on stage for rehearsal. Such a question meant that a scene had been cut, and that an actor would become a messenger. Cixous sometimes changed the dialogue on the spot during rehearsals because lines were difficult to enunciate, or too literary.[13] Some characters became essential, thus "an unnamed character called 'servant' would morph from a useful character to an appealing one to one that was indispensable. So, with haste, the character found a place in the story."[14]

(a)   (b)

a and b *Sihanouk*. The first page of the manuscript of the play by Cixous; and the hand-made copy, destined for the actors, by Mnouchkine. BnF Fonds Théâtre du Soleil/Archives Sophie Moscoso, 4 COL-153 (931).

Cixous compared this constant work of adjustment among author, actors, director, and musicians to the journey of "navigators who tell themselves, 'there must be a passage there,'" and sometimes there is, other times there isn't." In the Soleil, writing "defines itself by a certain alteration of the self"[15] in a collaborative, collective process. And this gestation-journey of the text continued until the last minute.

How to perform after *Shakespeare*? "Diaphanously!"

Some questions needed to be addressed in the rehearsal process: how to perform men and women of today, Cambodians in Cambodia, or students in Paris, diplomats of all nationalities who evolve on the international stage? How to move from the heavy brocade costumes of the Shakespeare plays to the contemporary three-piece suit? How to find the theatrical in the small temporal distance that separated the actors from the subject of the play? To help with this last question, certainly, there was the royal house and Cambodian culture, whose "realistic" portrayal would still create a kind of strangeness for actors and spectators alike.

Sihanouk. First energetic entrance of Sihanouk (G. Bigot) on stage, through the curtain held open by two servants dressed in white (C. Dupont and M. Chiapuzzo). He is followed by members of the Cambodian political, military, and diplomatic universe. In front are Prince Sirik Matak (B. Martin), the American General Taber (M. Dumétier), General Lon Nol (G. Freixe). Behind is General Van Tien Dung (J-F. Dusigne). To the right of Sihanouk are U.S. Ambassador McClintock (F. Gargiulo) and Penn Nouth (M. Durozier). Photo by Michèle Laurent.

Sihanouk. Sihanouk enters, laughing, followed by commoners. Present are Madame Khieu Samnol, the vegetable seller (M. Azencot), and two peasant farmers (S. Abkarian and Z. Soualem), come to ask for an audience with "Monseigneur Papa" (G. Bigot). Also present are the counselor Penn Nouth (M. Durozier), carrying a black umbrella, a parasol porter (G. Hardy), and other servants (among whom are actors M. Chiapuzzo, P. Golub, and L. Nissay), who hold the throne. Photo by Michèle Laurent.

There was also the question of what to do about historical figures, such as Henry Kissinger, Zhou Enlai, and Alexei Kosygin. Should one attempt a realistic portrayal? The initial, elliptical rehearsal notes indicate that actors should, at first, "go looking afar," that is, in depth, "in the nudity and crudeness of passions."[16] Another note regarding Sihanouk simply says: "Eyes. Like Harlequin. A compact intelligence, like a bouillon cube."[17] Passions and masks ... One can also read that it's important "to make us understand how normal people can become monsters" (January 18, 1985). And the following: "Autopsy: open up the entrails" (March 22, 1985).[18] And finally, the all-important "Act before launching into words," which means there should always be a pre-performance preparation; the actors must be in action before beginning to speak.

The Soleil's creative journey of more than seven months of rehearsals was not simple. First of all, the complex machinery of History had to be understood with the help of talks and encounters with witnesses, who were, in a sense, "living archives." This was a true adventure, telling the tale of History in the making: the actors would attend the real-life funeral of one of the characters, Lon Nol, whom they had the impression of knowing much better than some others who attended the ceremony. They tried out many approaches from the very first months of rehearsals. There were as many as five actors interpreting the same character. There were not only improvisations but also manual labor, as for the Shakespeare plays, with actors participating in maintaining the "house of theatre" and preparing the new stage for *Sihanouk*. Physical work and work on acting and presenting the play were thus intimately mingled in "high quality collective work."[19]

Masks would help the actors rise above the everyday aspect of the contemporary subject. All the masks were in play: those of the *commedia dell'arte*, Balinese masks, and those from the Shakespeare plays. Thus, Prince Sihanouk, who made others address him as "Monseigneur Papa," and who was completely fluent in French, was rehearsed sometimes with Harlequin's mask. Georges Bigot[20] remembers that he took up this mask when his body felt blocked. His final makeup and his hair, which was tinted grey, had the effect of making his eyes appear as if they were emerging from brown shadows: he made his own face into a mask. The acting required by the role of Sihanouk was that of someone masked , without a real mask but with a fake belly, thus a kind of corporeal "mask" that gave the actor a certain corpulence. Bigot used gestures from *commedia dell'arte*, voluble yet controlled, marked by stopping points. The starting point was the image of a clown that the real Prince Sihanouk used for himself, an image taken literally onto the stage.

Only two masks would remain in the show – one for an old servant, a copy of a Balinese mask; the other for Suramarit, the deceased king (Guy Freixe), which was a "near replica of a Balinese mask," as Erhard Stiefel put it. To create these new masks, Stiefel was inspired by documentation and examples of an ancient *topeng* mask, one linked to old age, piousness, and death (or the *topeng tua* mask). This was an imposing half-mask made of wood, which left the mouth unobstructed, and which allowed the actor to speak, but robbed him of his ability to communicate with his eyes: the eyes of the mask were those of a ghost.[21] The presence of the *tua* mask imposed a new non-realistic element on the acting. The requirements of a "state of burning" are a constant in rehearsal notes for the production. The acting was addressed to the public, with politicians or third parties bearing witness to conversations between Suramarit (returned from the dead) and his son, who asked his advice – with both simply seated at the edge of the stage.

Resemblances of characters to the real people they represented were created by makeup, with actors' skin tone darkened or lightened, their hair made grey; sometimes they would wear prosthetics, or darken their teeth. Actors practiced the body movements, the grace, the physical positions seen everywhere in Cambodian culture. Cambodians' supple movements of the waist were achieved through torso exercises and by practicing the traditional *sampeah* greeting, which is respectful, and which indicates listening, hands together, bowing. These positions were introduced, corrected, and refined by Ly Nissay or by the scholar, Marie Martin, who, in her role as advisor on the history of Cambodia, clarified pronunciations and comportment. The Indian dancer and company member Maïtreyi helped the actors discover ways to prevent their long scarves from slipping. Hand gestures from dances by the Royal Cambodian Ballet were used on occasion to better design the bodies on stage. The actors needed tremendous endurance, because each part of the play lasted four and a half hours; and, with intermissions, the play when performed in its entirety would last for eleven.

Mnouchkine insisted that the actors not illustrate their lines: they would be helped by the music. The music would render their behavior strange, would create an artistic transposition, making each movement into a sort of dance, different for each actor and actress – small scampering steps for the Cambodian women in their tight skirts, hammering steps for military men. The music would accompany the entrances and exits of the characters and would flow into everyone's way of walking – walking which the music supported as though a flying carpet. The music would also accent the "great entrances" and "great exits" of politicians who swarmed onto or left the stage with their flocks of advisors.

Sihanouk. Sihanouk is pictured in the grips of the torment of decision-making. He is caught between the public and his interlocutors: the Prime Minister of North Vietnam, his minister-counselor, and members of the Khmer Rouge: Ieng Sary (E. Rey), Pham Van Dong (S. Poncelet), Penn Nouth (M. Durozier), Khieu Samphan (A. Pérez), Hou Youn (J-F. Dusigne). Behind and surrounding him, the multitude of dolls representing the presence of the Cambodian people. Photo by Martine Franck, Magnum Photos.

According to his needs for accompanying scenes or characters, Jean-Jacques Lemêtre invented instruments, or had them modified through small transformations. They were made either by him, by luthiers, or by members of the company; and his collection of instruments grew. He looked for the proper timbre for each character, as with the Japanese koto (or stringed instrument), which he fitted into a Filipino mask and played: he aimed for theatrical music, not necessarily Cambodian music.

Voice of Jean-Jacques Lemêtre

"In the performance, there were only eight true Cambodian instruments among the 250 we had on stage. First of all because the Khmer Rouge had destroyed everything, and it was difficult at the time to find any. Second, because, as I was working on transposition and shifting, I didn't want to have many instruments from that country in order to avoid an attempt at being "realistic," or traditional, or folkloric – this

was an ever-present danger. [...] For the war scenes, we'd built a percuphone (an immense hurdy-gurdy with an aluminum wheel and with secondary, tertiary and quaternary wheels), which gave us all the sounds of war (B-52s, bombs, mines, artillery shots, helicopters, automatic weapons, etc.) [...] [There were also]aesthetic considerations about the space we were to perform in. Music was, as always, improvised during the rehearsal process, but then would become fixed, as my work was to find the 'turning points,' that is the changes in the text and in the performance – changes of states of being, of place, of emotion, of time, of space, etc. Thus, at every turning point there was a change of timbre (and therefore of instrument) and my assistant would pass me the instruments one after the other. There was improvisation only in the number of notes that I would play, which was a function of the speed of the actors, and which changed with each performance."[22]

"A whole people entered our lives …"

"A whole people entered our lives," wrote Cixous in the theatre program for *Sihanouk*. It was for this group that G-C. François conceived a new empty space covered with small pinkish bricks, surrounded by low walls. In the center was positioned a large stage of light-colored wood, with two small passageways linking it to the low walls, on which actors could walk. Stage left, there was a space reserved for the music, which was performed

Sihanouk. On the musicians' platform, J-J. Lemêtre, P. Launay, and V. Gargiulo. Seated in front of them: Mme. Khieu Samnol (M. Azencot), surrounded by two peasants (S. Abkarian and Z. Soualem). Archives Monique and Daniel Cordin.

on the stage as in Asian theatre. At the back, detached from the wall, a high curtain, from *topeng* and kathakali traditions, was suspended. It shimmered with the saffron color of the robes of Tibetan Buddhist monks. The curtain was in two panels that the stagehands, here "servants of the scene," parted for the numerous entrances and exits. One of the first projects of G-C. François was to paint on the back wall a sketch of the immense eyes of the Buddha. These eyes would finally be fully completed in 1997 for *And Suddenly, Sleepless Nights.*

The scenic space was as empty as it had been for the Shakespeare plays. Before opening, the saffron curtain would quiver upon the arrival of the characters, as in Noh theatre. Entrances were one-by-one, or in groups (e.g. politicians and diplomats, the king with his household and servants). They were dynamic entrances, visually enhanced by large parasols and heightened by the music. Some furniture appeared on stage – only what was strictly necessary: easy chairs, or benches for an encounter at a summit.

In his ceremonial clothing, Suramarit was not the only one to come back from the dead. Six-hundred small dolls made of wood were lined up, one against another, fitted out and elevated all along the walls of the nave, clearly visible. They represented the Cambodian people, the victims of the Khmer Rouge, some 2,500,000 people. They were the souls of the dead watching the living. The inspiration for this homage came from the rites of the inhabitants of Sulawesi, in Indonesia, who sculpt their ancestors in this way after burning their bodies, and place the figures in steep cemeteries on the slopes of cliffs facing the sea. The dolls, hands extended, costumed, watched the spectators and actors. These dolls were crafted by Stiefel, and were finished by the actors – in a ritual which allowed them, before performing, to pass through a sort of reenactment of an ancient funeral rite. It was between these two presences of the hereafter – the dead king given voice and the silent multitudes – that the play was performed, enhanced by the political and human circumstances of a past massacre and an alarming present moment.

The theatre: maker of History and source of engagement

For Mnouchkine, the only truly grand theatre is historical in nature. J-M. Filippi, a specialist on Cambodia[23] attested that "the theatre turn[ed] out to be a powerful tool for representing reality." Sometimes, for example, a line of dialogue from the play proved to be more on target than an interview would have been. Filippi underscored how the theatre completed the truth through verisimilitude and highlighting. There would even be moments of fiction in the play, independent of any

Sihanouk. The ghost of Norodom Suramarit, father of Sihanouk (G. Freixe) speaks to his son. He wears a mask inspired by Balinese masks. Photo by Michèle Laurent.

Sihanouk. Sihanouk (G. Bigot) and Zhou Enlai (A. Pérez) surrounded by servants. Pictured from left to right: P. Guimaraes, M. Chiapuzzo, C. Dupont, L. Nissay. Photo by Michèle Laurent.

Sihanouk. Close-up of the dolls representing the people of Cambodia. Archives Sophie Moscoso.

Sihanouk. Another spectacular entrance by Sihanouk, stage right, in the margin of the stage, surrounded by numerous servants of the royal household, who are bowing respectfully. Photo by Martine Franck, Magnum Photos.

documentation whatsoever, which would be confirmed as truthful by later documentation or witnesses at the time of the performances.

Theatre has the ability to discover what really happened by an alchemical process of the work of writing combined with the truthful circumstances of the action on stage. In other plays by the Soleil, scenes imagined by the actors have been confirmed by historical accounts, or, on the other hand, contested by witnesses who would then see the show, only to discover that these theatricalized accounts revealed themselves to be, in fact, true. It was the witnesses who had been wrong. Mnouchkine sees in these cases that her actors are, in a way, mediums – conduits of truth.

When they had been on the Thai border in 1984, Cixous and Mnouchkine had found themselves "at the brutal tipping point of events."[24] It is to this sense of urgency that they wanted to bear witness, in the stretched time of theatrical performance. The troupe would learn how to make itself hospitable, and welcome truly as well as metaphorically a people in danger.

The events of the play led up to January 6, 1979, when Vietnam, supported by the U.S.S.R., invaded the Democratic Kampuchea of Pol Pot and sent him packing back into the brush with his partisans. Khmer Cambodia then came under the control of its Vietnamese neighbors (a country with ten times the population), and a new tragedy began. Mnouchkine had determined that President Pompidou's France was unwilling to recognize how much Sihanouk was attached to his country's independence; she was appalled that France did nothing to help him. In 1985, when the play opened, Vietnam still occupied a crushed Cambodia. When, in May 1986, President François Mitterrand came with Robert Badinter to see a performance, Mnouchkine hoped that, as a result, he would give renewed attention to the case of Cambodia. Another arrival (prepared by numerous emissaries), that of Norodom Sihanouk himself to the Cartoucherie, was also a great event. Mnouchkine would say – laughing – that even if Shakespeare had played in front of Queen Anne, "He never performed for Henry IV or Henry V. But we did!"[25] The real King Sihanouk would finally return to a country still in turmoil.

And the life of *The Terrible but Unfinished Story of Norodom*

"If one can only weigh in in favor of Cambodia with the weight of a fly's wing, then let's weigh in with the weight of a fly's wing and avoid the irreparable." (Ariane Mnouchkine, in the film *A la recherche du Soleil*, 1986.)

"Our role is to say to the average French person: Cambodia is your history." (Ariane Mnouchkine, *Le Soir*, June 16, 1986.)

A historic meeting in France: King Norodom Sihanouk and the actor who played him, G. Bigot, in a restaurant near the Alma Bridge, where the King had invited the troupe for lunch (1985). Photo by Liliana Andreone.

Sihanouk, King of Cambodia [*L'Histoire terrible mais inachevée de Norodom Sihanouk, roi du Cambodge*] didn't end with the last performance. It would have a second life starting in 2007, through the commitment of part of the troupe, this time in Cambodia itself.

The Indiad, or India of Their Dreams [L'Indiade ou l'Inde de leurs rêves]

Voice of Hélène Cixous to the Actors

> *"Ariane says that this play has been the fruit of a whole year of my existence. Truly, this has been a year of combat, of fear, and of admiration for the knights of the twentieth century. No, not a year, this is a whole existence, the life that a certain India gave me in order to give it to you, and every day you give it back to me. Thus goes theatre, from life to life, through death, which is nothing but a new entrance. And, of course, straight ahead, to the stars. What luck that the Soleil exists! It is so brilliant that one could easily get used to it and take it for granted. But it is human beings that make up the Soleil.*
>
> *Your Hélène"*[26]

In the Soleil, projects are prepared for years, and can be developed during the performances of the preceding productions. The company needs patience for the work of gestation and maturation: this might suggest to what extent this theatre directed by a woman is "feminine." Without claims to feminism other than those of its artistry, the Soleil is an enterprise conscious of the amount of time required to grow and carry out a project.

In October 1984, after the assassination of Indira Gandhi, it seemed to Mnouchkine that she had found her next contemporary subject, vast enough to be worked on for many months. But Cixous, when asked again to participate, thought that the subject was beyond her reach: India was simply too colossal in scope. Nevertheless, she plunged into historical research. A voyage of two months in India enlightened the two of them tp the error in their choice of subject matter. Indira Gandhi was not yet far enough removed in time, no doubt, and, above all, she had something of a toneless personality, difficult to bring to the stage. So, the entryway for treatment of contemporary India and the continuation of the cycle of Asian epics would find itself in the preceding generation, that of Mahatma Gandhi, of Nehru, of Abdul Ghaffar Khan, and of Muhammad Ali Jinnah, the founder of Pakistan.

The process of approaching the subject matter would stay the same – at first, a blurred focus, sharpened in fits and starts

The Indiad. A documentary source for *The Indiad.* One of the numerous photographs that the actors used, ordered from the Roger-Viollet agency or pulled from newspapers and magazines. Pictured here: J. Nehru and Mahatma Gandhi. Archives Théâtre du Soleil.

The Indiad. Gandhi (A. Pérez) next to his dead wife, Kastourbaï Gandhi (C. Yelnik), a ghost returned to earth. Photo by Michèle Laurent.

by "debates" between the author and the director. There would be a lengthy study of history and documentary sources. Just as for Cambodia, Cixous realized when she was at the Nehru Memorial in Delhi, that history in India does not have the same meaning as in the West. She realized that History consists of different modes of writing history, and above all, that Indian history is far from being entirely written. Significant work on memory remains to be done on a history contested from both sides of the Indian-Pakistani border; subaltern studies are still coming to grips with the impact of British colonization.

The Indiad, or India of Their Dreams presents the dreams of those who, having fought for Indian independence, saw the partition of their country decreed on the eve of the long-awaited day of independence, in August 1947. The tale told by the play begins with the regional elections of 1937, won in most districts by the Congress Party, at a time when the United Kingdom had begun the process of according India the status of dominion. The play depicts the events, massacres, and debates that bring this political party to accept partition as the only means of avoiding a civil war on a grand scale between Hindus and Muslims. Viscerally opposed to this partition, Gandhi, devastated, finally gives his consent, which was necessary for the partition to go into effect, given the great respect that he inspired. He would then be assassinated (the following year, in actual fact). Underlying the historical subject (11 years of fratricide and decolonization) is hidden a more intimate subject: this partition is also a metaphor of *separation*, one of the great scourges of our times.

The play only covers 11 years, but there are almost as many characters as in *Sihanouk*. In addition to England, the play takes us traveling to a number of Indian provinces. The majority of the characters are Indian –Hindu or Muslim – and the anonymous figures of the people of this great subcontinent are numerous. These characters were the most difficult to find, and Cixous said she could only get a hold on them by immersing herself in India on a second journey, with "(her) ear to the chest of the Indian people." As with *Sihanouk*, there is again a character who returns from beyond the grave (the dead wife of Mahatma Gandhi, Kasturbaï). And there are "border crossers," characters independent of any house or faction, in particular a bear tamer with his bear, Moona Baloo. The play required of the actors an immersion in Indian culture. Roles were tried out and exchanged – which, as we have seen, is the standard practice of the Soleil. For a long while the character of Gandhi was rehearsed by two actors, Georges Bigot and Andrés Pérez Araya. Finally, it was Bigot, who was as "evident" in the role of Nehru as in that of Gandhi, who would end up playing the Pandit: Pérez Araya would be Gandhi.

The Indiad. The empty white space conceived by G-C. François. At the center, a large marble surface that evokes the Taj Mahal. This layout and its surroundings would be filled with numerous characters representing the common people, more than for *Sihanouk*. Archives Guy-Claude François.

The Indiad. A group of women, a living reproduction of a documentary photograph. This scene of striking realism was succeeded by a playful scene in which the bear Moona Baloo talks to Gandhi on his low bed. Archives Monique and Daniel Cordin.

The Indiad. In New Delhi, Inder, a rickshaw driver and untouchable (M. Celedon), pulls Sarojini Naïdu (M. Azencot) across the stage. Archives Monique and Daniel Cordin.

The Indiad. The Congress Party celebrates. In the center: Nehru (G. Bigot) and Sarojini Naïdu (M. Azencot). Photo by Michèle Laurent.

The Indiad would be presented in the same space as *Sihanouk*, tying them closely to each other. In the center of the stage, however, a large marble plaque of a brilliant white color was embedded in the rose bricks already there, upon which actors placed brightly colored rugs, or mattresses with white bolsters. A rickshaw, charpoys (traditional woven beds), and easy chairs were brought in and taken away. The entrances were made through small doorways traversing the rear wall, with curtains in front of them. From the canopies covering the skylight fell a celestial light.

It was no longer a question of stylization, as in *Twelfth Night*; and this time the class on bharata natyam, as well as on other Indian art forms, would bring the bodies of the actors closer to the bodies of Indians. From the very start of rehearsals, however, these exercises stopped: they were no longer needed as the significant number of Asians in the troupe already showed a great ease in the "sitting-downs" and "getting-ups" (as Mnouchkine dubbed them), necessitated by how often the actors were seated "cross-legged" on stage.

Photographic documentation held an important role in the work the actors performed in writing with their bodies. Mnouchkine took numerous photos at the Gandhi Museum in Mumbai, photos that became a part of the documentation for the performance. In *dhoti*, in saris, with veils, turbans or caps, a multitude of characters squeezed onto the stage, in a flight of light fabrics, in black and in white. At times it seemed that the Cartoucherie had been transported to India. The play opened with a scene depicting the jubilation of the crowds after the elections of 1937. During intermission, the food at the bar was Indian, and the marble on stage was washed by a cloud of kneeling servants. The "mask-ups" were chosen with verisimilitude in mind, a resemblance that would permit the transformation of the actors into Indians.

An exotic "faraway" was bound up with a theatrical "faraway," the progress of the Soleil's performance research tending toward closing the gap with the faraway geographical reality, which, in any case, represents an elsewhere necessary to the actors and the public in a theatrical performance. It is in this elsewhere that spectators can recognize, above and beyond the problems of a distant India, those concerns closest to them.

The only material mask in *The Indiad* was that of the bear, enormous and magnificent, the brown Moona Baloo, designed by Stiefel. It was a "total mask," inhabited by Catherine Schaub, an actor/dancer trained in kathakali. Moona Baloo was strikingly realistic and surprising agile. She wandered among the characters, escaping from her master, and even had scenes alone with Gandhi. At the start, she seemed like a circus animal, but her games and familiarity with the human race transformed her into a fully realized character, who provided the spectators a necessary focal point from childhood's imaginary realm. In the play, she died in the crossfire of men killing each other, assassinated by mistake at the hands of her master, who thought she'd become dangerous – a parable of the situation of an India in which friends could no longer recognize each other as friends.

The geographic makeup of the Soleil had become even more international since *Sihanouk* had been staged. The origins of the actors were increasingly varied, reflecting an image of the variety of peoples of the Indian subcontinent, with their different languages and religions. Among the new arrivals were Chileans (among them Mauricio Celedon) who came to join his compatriot Andrés Pérez Araya, a street theatre performer from Santiago. Nirupama Nityanandan, trained in bharata natyam, came from Madras. There were other Indians, Cambodians, Italians, Armenians, Brazilians, Tunisians, Iranians, Germans, and more. The troupe was a tower of Babel where languages and accents intersected, just as with the Indian crowds rumbling on the stage. A new position was created in the company, occupied by Françoise Berge, responsible for "phonetic and linguistic training," so that this richness would not detract from the French of the play. During the run of the show, Ariane Mnouchkine, for her work with the Soleil, would become the first artist to receive the prestigious European Theatre Prize, awarded in 1987 by an international jury headed by Irene Papas.

"By choosing India as a subject, as an example, and by working on the partition of India, we were working on all the partitions that followed it, up to Kosovo: all the eruptions and all the national/nationalistic reconfigurations. At the moment of the conflict in the former Yugoslavia, we were asked, 'Will you do something on Yugoslavia?' But we'd just done it. It was *The Indiad*," declared Cixous.[27]

So the play was finished, but the activism implicit in it would continue to have repercussions. Thus, in July 1995, at the Avignon Theatre Festival, where the Soleil was performing *Tartuffe*, Mnouchkine made herself the spokeswoman of the Avignon Declaration, a movement orchestrated by the Radeau Theatre Company with the goal of opposing the lack of European intervention in the Bosnian conflict. After the Srebrenica massacre, she organized a hunger strike at the Cartoucherie, with François Tanguy, Maguy Marin, Olivier Py, Emmanuel de Véricourt (and later, Roland Bourgeois)[28] – supported by a large network of artists. In August, the Soleil became a Mecca for debate, at the heart of contemporary politics. After the intervention by NATO in Krajina, the 29-day long strike was ended, but only after the intervention of the Bosnian president Alija Izetbegović, who personally called for the strike to stop. Mnouchkine then called for the creation of a committee of observers to watch over the Bosnian situation.

The Terrible but Unfinished Story of Norodom Sihanouk, King of Cambodia: 2013

The re-creation of *Sihanouk* in Cambodia with the Phare Ponleu Selpak School of Arts, an NGO based in Battambang, bespoke of a long educational and social project based on artistic creation. The project was encouraged and promoted by Ashley Thompson, a former student of Cixous who had been bowled over by the 1985 staging and who had become fascinated by Khmer culture. She left for Cambodia after seeing the show and became a student and subsequently a professor of Southeast Asian cultures at the University of Leeds and at SOAS. Soleil actors Georges Bigot and Maurice Durozier inaugurated a potential staging in Battambang in 2007, followed by a workshop directed by Mnouchkine in 2008, in which Delphine Cottu[29] participated. The final steps toward a fully realized production were accomplished by Bigot and Cottu, a pair that united two generations of the Soleil. Mnouchkine remembers her workshop with the Cambodians: they were children, some of them orphans; some had to learn to read first in order to perform their own history.

"As soon as one is having fun, as soon as one is happy, one receives things. I think that in Cambodia, in the present moment: we need theatre." (Voice of a Cambodian actor during the colloquium "Histoire et théâtre: autour de Sihanouk," October 25, 2013.)

In 2013, during the Festival d'Automne in Paris, the young Cambodian actors representing the Khmer people entered on stage at the Soleil, emerging from under the bleachers and passing in front of the spectators, one after the other. It was as if, suddenly, the long rows of Erhard Stiefel's dolls had come to life. This movement of resurrection – dreamlike but powerful, made real beneath the eyes of some of the sculpted dolls preserved as a reminder of the original staging – concretized the transmission from the original staging to the current one. After the sounding of the gong by the musician, it was as if a whole people were entering the stage, greeting us, and smiling.

By its power and its innovation, the 1985 production had been written into the history of theatre. Through the memorable, "dizzying" encounter between the two Sihanouks – the politician and the actor portraying him on stage – the Soleil had inserted itself into History. But by the gift of the Cambodian actors, the Soleil's own history was prolonged. As for the Khmer actors trained by the Soleil, and especially trained by the actor who had originally played the role of Sihanouk, they were finally in touch with their own history, which was yet to be written. Cixous' text, shortened with her blessing, translated into Khmer as closely as possible to the original, could be read in French supertitles, to the beat of the Khmer meter, raucous and rhythmical. The acting, simple and virtuosic at the same time, linked the actors to that piece of childhood they kept within themselves, and which was particularly tuned to theatrical narrative. The roles of Sihanouk and of Pol Pot were performed by two young women, visionaries in their own way (San Marady and Chea Ravy).

This performance struck the public as necessary and right, and gave to the objectives of 1985, 30 years later, both historical validity and a rare artistic vitality. We might say that the production of 1985 in all its elements – script, acting, music, stage design – became a theatrical text. These elements formed the basis of a new production that wasn't, however, a copy. From 2007–2013 – including a first French staging in 2011 done at the Célestins Theatre in Lyons for the *Sens Interdits* festival – this long and arduous project was embraced with a great deal of courage. Produced on a shoestring budget, with the participation of academics, militants, and theatre professionals, the final result proved the originality, the power, and the durability of the working methods of the Soleil. On the Soleil's internet site, we can still see a corner of Roberto Moscoso's blue poster for *The Terrible but Unfinished Story of Norodom Sihanouk, King of Cambodia* – a symbol of this enduring work.

Sihanouk. Rehearsal at the Phare Ponleu Selpak school in Battambang, Cambodia, August 2010. The Khmer actors took control of their history through the Soleil's play. Here, Sihanouk (S. Marady) prepares to publicly stomp on a Western magazine (*Newsweek*). Photo by Everest Canto de Montserrat.

Notes

1 Ariane Mnouchkine, from the prompt book of Sophie Moscoso, Shakespeare rehearsals, February 14, 1981 (Archives Sophie Moscoso).
2 Ariane Mnouchkine, in *À la recherche du Soleil*, a documentary film by Werner Schroeter, Ziegler film Berlin, 1986.
3 Hélène Cixous, from an unpublished interview with Béatrice Picon-Vallin, March 2007, for the film *Ariane Mnouchkine: L'Aventure du Théâtre du Soleil*, de C. Vilpoux, AGAT archives Films/Arte, 2009.
4 William Shawcross, *Sideshow, Kissinger, Nixon, and the Destruction of Cambodia* (New York: Simon and Schuster, 1979); (Paris: Balland, 1979 for the French Edition: *Une Tragédie sans importance*).
5 Ariane Mnouchkine, during the colloquium "Histoire et théâtre: autour de Sihanouk," October 25, 2013, at the Cartoucherie.
6 Hélène Cixous, excerpt from the preface to *La Prise de l'école de Madhubaï*, *L'Avant-scène Théâtre*, no. 745, 1984.
7 Ibid., 4.
8 The costumer J-C. Barriera would also make this trip.
9 These two people would give birth to the character Mom Savay.
10 Hélène Cixous, talk given at the colloquium "Histoire et théâtre: autour de Sihanouk."
11 Letter to the actors by H. Cixous at the start of *Sihanouk*, first draft, first part, manuscript recopied by hand by Mnouchkine with annotations by S. Moscoso. Provisional titles of play: *Une Éternelle histoire* or *Le Roi Lépreux*, among others. See first page, red spiral notebook, Théâtre du Soleil/Sophie Moscoso Archives, BnF, 4-COL 153, non-paginated.
12 Ibid. Any unattributed quotes in this chapter will have come from interviews Béatrice Picon-Vallin conducted with Ariane Mnouchkine and actors and friends of the Soleil from 2010 to 2014.
13 This information was told to Béatrice Picon-Vallin by G. Bigot, M. Azencot, and J-F. Dusigne, February 2012.
14 Preface to *l'Histoire terrible mais inachevée de Norodom Sihanouk, roi du Cambodge* (Paris: Théâtre du Soleil/Eds. Théâtrales, 2010), 13.
15 Hélène Cixous, interview for *Ariane Mnouchkine: l'Aventure du Théâtre du Soleil*.
16 Ariane Mnouchkine, rehearsal notes, January 22, 1985, Archives Sophie Moscoso.
17 Ariane Mnouchkine, rehearsal notes, Théâtre du Soleil/S. Moscoso Archives, BnF, 4-COL 153, un-numbered first notebook.
18 Rehearsal notes, http://sihanouk-archives-inachevees.org.
19 Georges Bigot, in *À la recherche du Soleil*.
20 Bigot would receive the Union of French Critic's prize for Best Actor for this role in 1986.
21 The actor rehearsed with a provisional cardboard mask. It was with this mask that the Cambodian actor in the re-creation of 2013 would perform. Peter Brook used Balinese masks in *La Conférence des oiseaux* in 1979. At the Soleil, the Balinese masks on stage were always copies.
22 Jean-Jacques Lemêtre, interview with Marie-Laure Basuyaux, http://sihanouk-archives-inachevees.org.
23 Jean-Michel Filippi, "De la scène de l'histoire à l'histoire sur la scène," site Internet du Kampotmuseum (http://www.kampotmuseum.org/).

24 Hélène Cixous, "Le théâtre se tenant responsable," May 2010, www.theatre-du-soleil.fr.

25 Ariane Mnouchkine, in Fabienne Pascaud, *L'Art du présent* (Paris: Plon, 2005).

26 Manuscript letter from Hélène Cixous to the actors, at the front of the manuscript of *L'Indiade ou l'Inde de leurs rêves*, first version, recopied by hand by Mnouchkine, Théâtre du Soleil/S. Moscoso Archives, BnF, 4-COL-153, un-numbered.

27 Hélène Cixous, interview with Eric Prenowitz, November 2001, www.theatre-du-soleil.fr.

28 François Verret and Jean-François Matignon were the spokespeople for the Déclaration d'Avignon.

29 As with Georges Bigot, Delphine Cottu stayed 11 years at the Soleil.

The House of Atreus Cycle. As the actors of the Soleil tried their hand at another form of theatre, the spectators were greeted with a surprising new arrangement of the halls. In the new layout, which was used for the entire cycle, the audience followed the same path for all four plays: from the Welcome Area to the tiered seats, across pits dug into the ground acting as tombs where tall statues of men and horses stood, made of plaster covered with clay and painted (by Erhard Stiefel). In this way, the audience was made to feel the journey toward the dawn of time that the discovery of the sources of Western theatre entailed. Photo by Michèle Laurent.

Chapter 5   *The House of Atreus Cycle* or the archaeology of passions

"The stage is the vacant lot of the sublime."
Ariane Mnouchkine[1]

"Containment without shrinkage," says Ariane to the actors – but here that mission is impossible. A book's elasticity is limited. At this point in the story, I'm paralyzed by anxiety, submerged by the multitudes that have entered the Soleil: continents, crowds, people. So many new nationalities have already crossed the Soleil's threshold. And the influx of new voices will continue. How shall I give an account of all the encounters and intersections in this most theatrical of theatres, which is in fact precisely the product of the lives and work of all its members, a great caravanserai? For this next cycle, in which Mnouchkine takes on Greek tragedy, thus beginning a journey to the lost origins of Western theatre, I will let the voices of the Soleil speak for themselves.

Ghosts

To fulfill my duties as scrupulous scribe, I must first, however, speak of the "ghosts" of those performances after *The Indiad* that never took place and that nonetheless inhabit the history of the Soleil. The first of these was a creation on the French Resistance[2] which would have been called *Those who Don't Surrender* [*Ceux qui ne se rendent pas…*], or *The French Speak to the French* [*Les Français parlent aux Français*], or even *The France of Their Dreams* [*La France de leurs rêves*][3] in reference to the subtitle of *The Indiad*. The play was to have been centered on French Resistance hero Jean Moulin. Rehearsals were scheduled for February 1989, but never took place. The unrealized project continues to haunt the halls and actors of that period, as it must still haunt Mnouchkine, who didn't find the images she would have needed, nor the right light to bring the members of the Resistance – those creatures of shadow – into full view. In 2010, she admitted she could only imagine the project as a film. It also haunts Hélène Cixous, who had begun writing several scenes in the mid-1980s and who speaks of "eternal regrets."

Another "ghost" is a play written by Cixous for an actress outside the Soleil who ended up turning it down, as she was disappointed to find several major female roles instead of one starring role for herself. The Soleil decided to put it on instead, probably because it was about resistance: that of the great women mourners of Russian literature who fought the Stalinist regime with the help of memory and poetry. The play included only women characters, most importantly Anna Akmatova, Nadezhda Mandelstam, and Lydia Chukovskaya. But soon the Soleil began to lack actresses for this project, since the *House of Atreus Cycle* [*Les Atrides*], already taking shape, required them all. The play was called *Black Sail White Sail* [*Voile noire, voile blanche*] and was dedicated to Ariane's father, Alexandre Mnouchkine, who served as consultant on its Russian context. There must have been some regret when rehearsals ended, especially for Catherine Schaub, Myriam Azencot, and Georges Bigot (who had also been rehearsing with the female cast).[4]

But another problem was looming. In 1989 the Soleil's debts were catastrophic, amounting to 6,500,000 francs. Questions arose: how to put on a new play? Should they enter into a coproduction agreement? Apply for grants from abroad? Form an association with another company? The important thing was to "remain pioneers."[5] In this context, the Soleil was happy to accept a proposition made by Bernard Faivre d'Arcier, who was in charge of celebrations for the 200th anniversary of the French National Assembly: he asked them to produce a film on the French Revolution and the *Declaration of the Rights of Man*. The result was *The Miraculous Night* [*La Nuit miraculeuse*], screenplay by Ariane Mnouchkine and Hélène Cixous, dialogues by Hélène Cixous. The Soleil rehearsed a kind of epic Christmas tale as they would have a play: it was filmed in the "crypt of the National Assembly" created at the Cartoucherie by Guy-Claude François. Erhard Stiefel fashioned dozens of life-size human dolls in the image of Soleil actors playing Representatives to the Assembly, who sat frozen, but came to life through the touch of a child seated at their side in the Assembly chambers.[6] Other scenes were

A portrait of Jean Moulin carried by high school students. Louis Joinet, a fellow traveler of the Soleil from 1972 onward, walks ahead; on the left, Sylvie Papandréou; on the right, Serge Nicolaï. The French Resistance haunted the Soleil for years, in a way still visible in its participation (in theatrical form) in commemorative activities in 2010. Photo by Charles-Henri Bradier.

filmed at the National Assembly itself and on the Place de la Concorde, with characters representing many figures who over the course of history have fought for human rights.[7]

A new cycle, four plays, four choruses

According to some members of the troupe, the Soleil's entire trajectory up until then had been leading inevitably to a performance based on the France of Jean Moulin. But when Mnouchkine proposed a vast archaeological journey toward Greek tragedy, which she had not yet taken on as a director, the company accepted. Between early 1990 and May 1992, four premieres took place. First came Euripides's *Iphigenia in Aulis* [*Iphigénie*], quickly followed by *Agamemnon*, the first play in Aeschylus's *Oresteia* trilogy, in November 1990. The Soleil then completed the trilogy with *The Libation Bearers* [*Les Choéphores*] in February 1991 and finally *The Eumenides* [*Les Euménides*] in May 1992. The Euripides play was written long after the *Oresteia*, but in narrative order it comes first, providing background (from events leading up to the Trojan War) for what happens in the *Oresteia*: Euripides tells of Iphigenia being sacrificed, while Aeschylus recounts the return of King Agamemnon and his death, followed by the vengeance of his son Orestes and its consequences.

Iphigenia in Aulis was translated by the specialist in Greek philology Jean Bollack and his wife Mayotte. The first two Aeschylus plays were translated by Mnouchkine, and the last by Cixous. Mnouchkine used a word-by-word translation by Claudine Bensaïd, staying as close as possible to the concrete aspects of Aeschylus's poetry and to its rhythm. She worked in close collaboration with another classicist, Pierre Judet de la Combe, who was happy to engage in the "experience of an unusual, non-academic philological debate with both Ariane Mnouchkine and Hélène Cixous."[8] He proposed oral and written commentary on the translations Mnouchkine produced, and they discussed difficult passages together. Jean Bollack went through the same process with Hélène Cixous for *The Eumenides*. This cooperation was an instance of direct collaboration between a theatre director and scholars without any intermediary work by a dramaturg, and resulted in an exchange that was fruitful for all involved.

No interpretation of the plays was laid down at the beginning of the rehearsal process: the opacity of the text was to be confronted day after day in the work of exploring passions on stage. Mnouchkine told the actors to think of "excavations," "digs," "exhumations." Guy-Claude François and she devised a plan to gut the Cartoucherie and dig four deep pits in the floor of the second hall where statues of Agamemnon's companions, the

The House of Atreus Cycle. The Welcome Area with a vast world map made by Didier Martin and Stéphanie Guennessen, facing the entrance to the theatre. Photo by Michèle Laurent.

The stage for *The House of Atreus Cycle*: an immense, empty, smooth space, bordered by low walls that the actors can climb onto or hide behind. Center stage are two doors for entrances. The intense blue of the back wall evokes the Greek sky. The canopies through which shines the Soleil's famous daylight effect can be seen on the ceiling. Archives Sophie Moscoso.

chorus of the *House of Atreus*, would stand in rows. The image was inspired by the 1974 discovery of the Terracotta Army, the 8,000 spectacular statues surrounding the tomb of Emperor Qin Shi Huang in Xi'an, China, dating from 210 BC. The statues created by Erhard Stiefel, with their varied expressions and costumes, were built to resemble figures made of baked earth: they emerged from the ground in orderly lines, sometimes still half-buried in soil. At the end of the excavation field was the raised stage for musicians; at another angle were the dressing rooms located under the tiered seating area, where, behind a thin mesh screen, the actors silently applied their makeup at serried dressing tables. Actors and spectators both had to traverse the excavation field, wandering through the semidarkness to reach the main stage, flooded in sunlight. This short journey materialized as lived experience the idea of traveling back in time toward ancient tragedy, progressively stripping off layers of interpretation imposed by intervening centuries. In this way the Soleil's own quest for the most essential forms of theatre, from Shakespeare to the Greeks by way of Asian stagecraft, was also given striking representation. In the history of the Soleil, *The House of Atreus* productions marked the height of temporal distance between the present and the action on stage.

The form imagined by the Soleil was neither a partial reconstruction of ancient theatre practices, of the type produced by the Classical Theatre Group at the Sorbonne, which Mnouchkine had been part of before creating l'ATEP (The Association for Parisian Theatre Students), nor a modernization, as in the work of German director Peter Stein (in his 1980 *Agamemnon*, for example). Instead, the Soleil aimed to renew the experience of their *Shakespeare Cycle*, accompanied by an even more demanding theatrical process. As Mnouchkine put it:

> Theatre is the art of the symptom. Actors are people who can show the symptoms of every sickness of the soul. Their responsibility is to suffer those symptoms bodily, and to play them. The audience will recognize its own passions in the actors' suffering. In order to find the symptoms, actors agree to work with a fever. Tragic characters experience anguish in the depths of their bodies.[9]

The empty stage was bordered on three sides by an enclosure made up of low walls arranged to make the whole stage resemble an arena, with two central doors upstage that opened and closed. The intense blue of a Greek sky lent color to the back of the playing area, and the Soleil's artfully created sunlight poured through the overhead canopies. Under the tiered seats a vomitorium was installed, similar to those in ancient Roman theatres. Actors could enter through this new narrow underground corridor. On stage, theatrical creatures appeared who looked totally unfamiliar, even though their main sources of inspiration were clearly Indian: the Soleil drew on kutiyattam, kathakali, and bharata natyam, but also Central European traditions and Caucasian folklore, elements introduced by Simon Abkarian (who is of Armenian descent). All these influences were also perceptible in the performances' music and dance. The company cast around widely to find the theatrical tools they needed. Rehearsals began with masks which were quickly replaced by faces made up in ways inspired by kathakali, which the actress Catherine Schaub had studied for some time in India: very white skin, swaths of thick black paint beneath the eyes, and heavy eyebrows. High headdresses and thick woolly beards framed and enlarged the faces. The thick layers of makeup nevertheless allowed the actors to show changing expressions. The heavy costumes for the men characters with their broad skirts recalled Edward Gordon Craig's concept of the Über-marionette or super-puppet. The women's costumes were conceived differently: in *Agamemnon*, Clytemnestra wore baggy trousers tucked into boots and a belted white blouse. She was played by a newcomer to the Soleil: Juliana Carneiro da Cunha, a Brazilian dancer who had trained at Mudra (a dance school in Brussels, founded by Maurice Béjart) and had worked with choreographer Maguy Marin's company. Other new actors skilled in dance had joined the company, including Duccio Bellugi-Vannuccini, who had worked with actor and mime artist Marcel Marceau and trained with Pina Bausch before arriving at the Soleil for the Asian epics, and Nirupama Nityanandan: she played Iphigenia as a small, fragile child, dressed in white; and from that play she went on to play Cassandra and Electra.[10]

The cycle's treatment of the choruses, both spoken and danced, was particularly striking. The chorus members (of whom the majority were men) were directed in each play by Catherine Schaub, "coryphaeus of the dance." The choruses took many shapes: a chorus of leaping young girls in light-colored skirts for *Iphigenia in Aulis*, a chorus of old men dressed in red and carrying walking sticks for *Agamemnon*, a chorus all in black and saffron of *Libation Bearers* breathing hate and clamoring for vengeance, a chorus for *The Eumenides* of growling wolf-dog men, directed by three Furies (Catherine Schaub, Nirupama Nityanandan, and Myriam Azencot), who appeared as toothless old women.

By their reactions, the chorus members accentuated the protagonists' emotions. Using choral dance with its spins and stops, the chorus of old men, for example, expressed weakness, age, exhaustion, but also astonishment, suffering, and even renewed energy, depending on whether they were interacting with Agamemnon or Clytemnestra, who danced with

Erhard Stiefel and Ariane Mnouchkine in front of several statues before they are lowered into the pits. Archives Sophie Moscoso.

Agamemnon. The chorus of old men works with Ariane Mnouchkine in the rehearsal room (on a temporary set). Photo by Michèle Laurent.

them. Trembling hands, facial expressivity, slight movement preceded the chanted, rhythmic diction with its special stress laid on consonants, all of this performed frontally by the principals. Liberating individual dance moves became necessary as the only way to express the outpouring of emotions provoked by the cruelty of the stage action.

The most majestic entrances – dancing and plunging chorus members, Agamemnon's high chariot draped in red – took place through the centrally placed doors. Another kind of entrance was realized on the long, sloping, moveable platform that emerged from the vomitorium facing the stage: actors stood on the platform, immovable as statues, only coming to life by placing their feet on the main stage. From out beneath the seats, too, came the bloody bodies of the wax dolls in the image of the dead.

The alliance between related arts: a conversation

The exchange reproduced below focuses on the notions of a "shared work of art" and a "total work of art." These characterize the Soleil's attempts in *The House of Atreus Cycle* to translate Richard Wagner's famous ambition to create a *Gesamtkunstwerk*, inspired in part by his reflection on Greek theatre.[11]

Ariane Mnouchkine: *"The linkage of the stage with other arts is no longer subject to question at the Théâtre du Soleil. Yes, actors are always at the center of theatre work, in any theatre. But without music, without lights, theatre wouldn't be the theatre I love. It quickly became clear with* The House of Atreus *project that such an alliance was necessary. And if* The House of Atreus Cycle *involves particularly interpenetrated forms of music and dance, it's because Aeschylus and Euripides demanded it of us. Until we'd run that gauntlet, they wouldn't abandon the fight. And until our bodies understood that necessity, we simply suffered. For me, true theatre – I mean the place and the works – is made first of all of encounters. I would never have done* The House of Atreus Cycle *if we hadn't had Jean-Jacques Lemêtre with us. Working with someone doesn't mean imposing anything on them: it's a very mysterious exchange, very deep, very anchored in interiority, which is like the circulation of blood; and where the feeling that someone is not "in on it" can be a source of alarming suffering for everyone. Circulation doesn't come easily: there's a lot of sweat, a lot of work. We have needed to cross some rivers, some deserts, and some mountains together."*

CATHERINE SCHAUB: "*The actors are the center, they're the light. But what's so rich about this way of working is that all the arts – all the artists – are together. We know we all bear a part of the responsibility for how things move forward on stage. The goal we're asked to strive for is what determines our performance. And the set will be as it is because this or that movement came up while rehearsing. It's not a pre-established, fixed set that we have to perform in. We all move forward together.*"

A. MNOUCHKINE: "*And the presence of a particular voice calls for the use of a particular instrument. Sometimes Jean-Jacques follows a voice, picks up on a certain tone or key. And who's to say whether a few days earlier he could have already heard that theme in his mind, or whether it really does come to him as we work, or whether he said to himself: 'Hmm, here we're not making progress, I'm going to try something different.' One time an audience member said: 'In this play, music is the second lung.' She'd been speaking earlier about text as the first lung.*"

JEAN-JACQUES LEMÊTRE: "*I think in this case music and set design are both 'fighting together' for theatre. There's no subjection of one expressive activity to another. I have no need to defend my music, since it's very clearly theatre music – that is, it takes the theatre as its starting point, beginning from the body of the actor performing a text. The term 'musical theatre' wouldn't be accurate here, because that would imply that the music sometimes leads, takes over. Writing a score for the Soleil means first finding the articulations and shifts in the text I hear, and then making them correspond to transitions of timbre and theme, and so to changes in instrumentation. The next step is to indicate, in the margins of the text, a codified version of those changes that can be memorized, which will include both melodic and rhythmic notations.*"

BÉATRICE PICON-VALLIN: "*So during the creative process there's no hierarchy among the arts at the Théâtre du Soleil?*"

A. MNOUCHKINE: "*Theatre is what leads. It's a quest. When we're doing well, when something is alive and circulating that's both magnificent and totally humble, theatre happens very naturally; it's artistically natural. There are no assumptions; there are no theories or whims in the music or in the staging. Something is present at each instant that's indispensable, vital. That's what makes us 'primitive.' We're often called primitive.*"

GUY-CLAUDE FRANÇOIS: "*It's important to stress that the Soleil has given itself the means to take theatre as far as it can go: it's the only theatre company that lets itself get everyone together and simply say: 'We're going to do the-atre' – just like that. To take an architectural image that comes more easily to me: if there's a wall in our way, we knock it over. That image is true for every actor in the troupe. I think the Théâtre du Soleil is the place where collective art as an idea goes all the way. The work we do is a ping pong game with 15 players (or more). The idea for the arena, for example, came from an actor who was lurking behind one of the flats in the rehearsal space when Ariane didn't know what to do with the chorus. From that point, his idea bounced outwards and made everything come together. Even the text benefits from this process. People think the text comes first, but in fact it takes shape along with the rest of the process, and it can be reworked in response to what happens on stage. This is perhaps less the case with the Greek tragedies, but it's true of texts by Hélène Cixous, who is present when we put together her plays."*

A. MNOUCHKINE: *"When I read a play, I have lots of 'visions.' But when the first rehearsal day comes, I feel instead a kind of emptiness inside me, as if I were sitting on the roof of the world. I try to see a convex stage curving upwards, that's an expression we used for* The Shakespeare Cycle. *What might appear there? It's more than a vacuum – and in any case it isn't really a vacuum."*

B. PICON-VALLIN: *"Would you say it's a space that invites something to appear?"*

A. MNOUCHKINE: *"Yes, a space for something to come forward, a kind of dawning. One needs exceptionally brave actors to bear that idea. There are people who draw strength from waiting for something to appear. Others just want to say their text and don't have the courage to wait. Our troupe is made up of actors who are more or less trained, who are more or less professional, or who are not trained at all. So their training has to happen during rehearsal time. The possibilities for discovery are different for each person. Some of them have to be taught to open up to what's coming: that's also part of what a 'shared work of art' means. So we have to make sure different levels of skill are in tune with each other, just as different arts must find common ground. Musicians have notes, a precise language, almost a scientific one. An actor doesn't. When I say: 'You say you're crying, but you're not crying,' and the actor answers: 'But I am crying,' I have no scientific proof to show that someone is lying to me and lying to themselves. With Jean-Jacques, with Guy-Claude, there's no need for proof, we don't even have to explain our thinking to each other. We work in total complicity."*

Actors warming up (probably led by Marc Pujo) in the performance space. The actors rolled a bridge out of the gaping mouth of the vomitorium beneath the public's seats so that their companions could reach the stage from their shared dressing rooms. Archives Sophie Moscoso.

The Libation Bearers. Orestes (Simon Abkarian) enters, towering, on the blue sloping bridge. He is about to kill Clytemnestra (Juliana Carneiro da Cunha). Photo by Michèle Laurent.

Iphigenia in Aulis. The chorus of young women enters. When rehearsals began, two of the actors were pregnant, hence the little round-bellied apron on the costumes. Each actor made their own decorations on the aprons and on the headdresses inspired by the Indian art *kutiyattam*. The yellow sheaths that go from foot to knee are inspired by the Japanese martial art kendo – they had already been used in *The Shakespeare Cycle*. In the picture the following actors can be identified: Duccio Bellugi-Vannuccini, Éric Leconte, Brontis Jodorowsky, Silvia Bellei, Maurice Durozier, Serge Poncelet. Photo by Michèle Laurent.

Agamemnon. The chorus of stick-wielding old men enters. In the center is the coryphaeus (here, Simon Abkarian). The others include Brontis Jodorowsky, Nirupama Nityanandan, Serge Poncelet, Catherine Schaub, Jean-Louis Lorente, Asil Rais, and Silvia Bellei. Photo by Michèle Laurent.

The Libation Bearers. Dance – called a "paean" at the Soleil – by the chorus of young women. In the center is coryphaeus Catherine Schaub. Flanking her are Duccio Bellugi-Vannuccini and Brontis Jodorowsky. Maurice Durozier recalls that this dance became, for the chorus members, a kind of murderous trance, as the chorus incited Orestes to kill his mother. Photo by Martine Franck, Magnum Photos.

The Eumenides. The chorus of wolf-dogs seated before the doors. Actors (both men and women) are covered in a "total mask." See also the section on animals in Transverse Perspectives of this study. Photo by Michèle Laurent.

J-J. Lemêtre: "*The Théâtre du Soleil offers us the privilege of being able to start from square one. The music really starts from that place, that is to say from hands, feet, and heart. From feeling what's there on the stage, feeling the actors, the way they move, breathe, speak. Everything starts with drums. Why? Since no parts are distributed to begin with, since everything remains open, and since I have no preconceived ideas of what to do, I start not with a melodic or harmonic theme but with the beat, the pulse, with what is the actor's fundamental vibration. Then comes the 'drone,' which is an extremely simple melody that begins to fit with the pitch of the actor's voice. I'm learning at the same time as everyone else. There's an evolution in the music that initially involves very simple work: creating a rhythm in such a way that the tempo of the actor on stage doesn't become too prosaic or realistic, as it might if it were supported by too slow an accompaniment. A certain speed is necessary for us to begin working and for a scene not to collapse. And bit by bit everything takes shape, the characters awaken, and the music awakens with the characters, because the casting happens progressively. What I like about the work here is there's no need to start off by theorizing. The creation of the score happens as we go along; it comes together 'live.'*"

B. Picon-Vallin: "*When you began working on* The House of Atreus Cycle, *did you really only have this space of open invitation? Anything was possible?*"

A. Mnouchkine: "*Anything, anything. It's hard to believe, but it's true, we could go anywhere. My great problem was, of course, the chorus. The only thing I was sure of was that I didn't want a chorus wearing bed sheets. Starting with the first entrances of the chorus members, even though we knew, since the text said so, they were meant to be homogeneous groups of women or old men, we had, instead, a Japanese princess, an Indian, two Eskimos. The whole world entered the chorus, and nothing worked, of course, but we had to go through that process to understand. I'm convinced that because we had that Japanese princess, that Indian, and those two Eskimos at that moment, we didn't act like clones: we were able to put together a chorus of old men who were all the same, but not identical, all together, but each different. 'Ground zero' is not just a figure of speech for us. We would sometimes even imagine that Aeschylus had just sent us his play to put on, and sometimes during exercises, I would tear out pages of the text and hand out sentences one by one, just to clear away the heap of clichés about Greek theatre that dogged us.*"

SIMON ABKARIAN: "*With great dramatists, and with Aeschylus in particular, one gets the impression that they are themselves surprised by what they write. So we were doubly surprised. And then, when something happens with the music, with the space, with how the actors are directed, there are more surprises, some pleasant, some painful; for example, when we saw the temporary fences arrive... For four or five months, we acted behind little fences five centimeters wide, which weren't very stable. But we managed to sit on them. The day the low walls were built, we were able to dance on them, since we'd already learned to act with the narrow five-centimeter fences.*"

A. MNOUCHKINE: "*Improvisation represents a significant portion of our work. We don't improvise with the text when we're working from play scripts, whether they are by Shakespeare, Aeschylus, or Hélène Cixous. There's too great a difference between our poor language and the strength of theirs. But everything that isn't text is improvised.*"

S. ABKARIAN: "*Beginning with the first 'dawning' that came over me, what I felt was that faced with Aeschylus's text, I had to shrink, to become small again, and then suddenly to grow, to awaken. To emerge from the earth. We'd talked a lot about exhumation, and we'd always struggled behind the fences to prepare our entrances, but that was a poetic journey that lasted ten meters. For the costumes, we each did our own searching: I had to build a costume over a period of a month. I made a headdress that was seventy centimeters tall. And I went on stage with that costume, and my improvisation lasted a total of 30 seconds – so you see what kind of critical work we did. In the end, Achilles just wore a stocking on his head. But it was necessary for me to try all that, and for Ariane to see me trying it.*"

J-J. LEMÊTRE: "*For me, it's really a question of improvisation in the Eastern sense. There's always a point when you have to return to basic techniques because you're lost, and after that you can head off to something much more poetic, more mysterious, more grandiose. There's no transposition necessary: I propose things that are listened to, an answer comes, and then that process is repeated in reverse.*"

A. MNOUCHKINE: "*It seems to me that for the arts to be in communion, or for the artists within each art form to come together, they mustn't seek hegemony or even superiority: the arrogance of arts and artists has to disappear, everyone must give way. In the end, everything, at a certain point, yields to the strange small solitary suffering in the middle of the stage, including fear, because fear too must give way.*

The character never gives way, but the actor must give way to the interests of the ensemble."

B. Picon-Vallin: *"Give way in order to help each other?"*

A. Mnouchkine: *"Yes, to help each other, you must give way, a kind of compromise. If you don't, you never free yourself of power relations."*

On theatre music

J-J. Lemêtre: *"Theatre music is not film music, in that we've banished certain words, words like ambience, illustration, atmosphere."*

B. Picon-Vallin: *"Apart from the presence of instruments within the theatrical space – and I don't know if we can speak of an orchestra in this case, since there are only two musicians – do you think that 'orchestra' might serve as metaphor to describe the relationship between the different arts on stage?"*

A. Mnouchkine: *"The word 'orchestra' isn't quite right. Initially the orchestra, if I remember correctly, is the floor itself, the space where the chorus stands and acts. I think what happens with us is closer to the relationship between musicians and actors in forms such as kathakali or even Noh. In our case, once everything is set up, certain rules come into play; we don't do whatever we feel like, and if the performance were to last four or five minutes longer than usual, I would criticize it. But if the actors take an extra breath, the musicians accompany them, and in the same way, if Jean-Jacques is more brutal on a given day with certain themes, the actors go along with him in turn. This doesn't mean they add something to what he's doing. Against the current meaning of 'accompaniment,' which is often used to mean 'addition' or 'accompanying,' we mean 'going with,' 'being the companion of.' That's why I don't really agree with the image of an orchestra which is first and foremost an ensemble led by a baton, even though we do go through moments of that to find the play. By the time of the performance – if it's a good performance – it's theatre, it's listening that leads us. I think something spiritual connects actors, audience, and music, and that this is linked to the possibility of a moment when people forget themselves and become nothing but listening, when musicians, actors, and audience are pure listeners. This state emerges from total discipline, from absolute rigor, and from magical freedom."*

G-C. François: *"An orchestra is made up of people who practice the same single art, which is very different from what happens in theatre."*

J-J. LEMÊTRE: "Bars and barlines were created in order for orchestral musicians to be able to speak to each other through the conductor. But they introduce a certain rigidity. At the Soleil, since we don't have those barlines, we avoid the notions of symmetrical phrasing, of downbeat, and of repetition. And that allows the actor to be more flexible. The beginning of the theme is the same in each performance, so the actor senses I'm with them, but the end can be different every night; new adaptations occur. Separate and different from the word 'orchestra,' there is also the Greek term 'orchestics,' which has been completely forgotten, and which is appropriate here because it refers to the affinity between acting, dancing, and music. If we take the Greek definition, I think acting speaks to the heart, dance to the body, and music to the soul. And the whole speaks to the entire human."

S. ABKARIAN: "Under his tutelage, Jean-Jacques helped us learn all of this. He didn't want to use the technical language of musicians, so he gave us very simple directions: he was looking for an instinctive, poetic relationship to music. He never said: 'Why don't I add a flat there'; but he did say: 'This instrument is tuned to the voice of such and such, or to your voice.' At the beginning, we didn't know how to listen to the music; we'd even say lines over what Jean-Jacques was doing. Or it happened sometimes that an actor hadn't stopped a movement before he began speaking, and so Jean-Jacques would keep playing, since he was following the actor's body. We had to do all this work until we learned to discipline ourselves and observe pauses, and discover how to move from one pause to the next."

A. MNOUCHKINE: "There is no movement without pause. If you look closely at dancers, they are going from immobility to immobility, even in the air: they stand still in mid-air! Music reveals and denounces the absence of pauses, since if Jean-Jacques is playing to a movement and the actor speaks while still moving, nothing works. I think that's a law that applies to all meaningful gestures and movements. In the theatre, our perception is extremely deep but very narrow. The audience can't see more than one thing at a time, and even if they see ten things in a single second, they see them in succession, one after the other. Music imposes an order on gesture, movement around the stage, and text, and that order is essential. Music prevents the actors from stuttering – with their feet, with their mouths, with their eyes, and most of all with their hearts."

The Libation Bearers. The coryphaeus (Catherine Schaub). Observe the details of her headdress, costume and makeup, with its "tears of blood" that were the last layer to be applied. Photo by Michèle Laurent.

S. ABKARIAN: "*Once you've begun this learning process, you don't quite feel comfortable, but then you begin to understand some things, and another aspect of the music appears to you. Sometimes, when Jean-Jacques 'came in' during rehearsals for* The House of Atreus, *he'd begin playing the theatrical situation, the scene, the characters on stage, and then emotion would come. One day I said to Ariane that if Jean-Jacques played like that in that particular scene, even a stone would start acting at that moment. Except that if the stone can't hear, it can't act. For us, it was a question of learning to listen to the music and also of learning to listen to each other; we're often so preoccupied by what we're about to say that we don't hear our scene partner anymore, or we don't see what's being built.*"

A. MNOUCHKINE: "*We can talk a lot about the relationship between the actors and Jean-Jacques, because it's almost a skin-on-skin relationship; but we don't talk much about the actors' relationship with Guy-Claude, because it's very strange. I think actors don't understand anything about set design. I remember that in the very beginning of our work, when there wasn't yet any idea of a set (not even the fences Simon mentioned earlier for* The House of Atreus Cycle*), we rehearsed in an empty room. Which meant that when the time came to rehearse in the set that was being built, there was always a terrible traumatic moment when the actors realized they were going to be acting in a space that seemed gigantic. Actors (when they are really actors) have a sense for music and costumes, but space is always disturbing to them, even if in the end they become very at home in it. Now, in rehearsal, we make a little simulacrum of the set, as soon as we know what it will look like.*"

G-C. FRANÇOIS: "*The location of the performance, the Cartoucherie, plays a very important role. I feel I'm building something that is more to be used as a tool than to be seen as beautiful. A tool is invented in response to needs; and those needs are dictated by Ariane and the actors. The aesthetic aspect isn't added. A thing that's perfectly functional, that corresponds perfectly to a need – first the needs of a poem, of a text, and then of an actor – that thing becomes beautiful. Anyway, that's how I'd define beauty in theatre.*"

J-J. LEMÊTRE: "*Guy-Claude also works with more constraints than we do. If I make a mistake, I pick up another instrument. Ariane or the actors do something wrong, fine, they stop, and we try something else. But Guy-Claude can't tear down a whole wall and then fix it again in ten minutes.*"

A. MNOUCHKINE: *"That can happen, but it's best if it happens less to him than to us. Guy-Claude arrived at the Cartoucherie at the same time I did; he was technical director of the company, and for a long time he shared our 14 hours of daily work. Later, and even though it was a disappointment to me, it became clear there wasn't enough work for him, with a set to create every year or two, and so, without ever leaving us, he went his own way. But he knows every stratum of the Cartoucherie, from the depths of the plumbing to the tip of the roof. Rather than 'set designer,' I prefer to call him a builder or an architect. When we discuss sets, our first terms are taken from construction. Then comes the language of touch, of color... after that, we look for a type of sensual pleasure."*

G-C. FRANÇOIS: *"But nothing is laid out in advance about the relationships between materials, colors, and sounds."*

A. MNOUCHKINE: *"It comes together as a result of the work we do, of the time we take to do the work! And then also the fact that at a certain point there's someone who can say: 'No, this doesn't really work.' I remember a costume from* The Eumenides *– the costume for the dog chorus – we had a lot of trouble figuring it out. It was a problem of material. That's where the time factor is important. When you think about other ways of working, or the types of obligations that other directors have, it's as if they don't put their money to the right use. They put it into quantity, they do 18 plays instead of doing one. In our situation, we need time, because we have to learn to walk again with every production. I learned so much with* The House of Atreus Cycle, *and also with* The Indiad. *But the fact remains that for the next play, once again, I won't know a thing, and what's more, I don't want to know. Because the day I say to myself 'I know' is the day I'll start repeating myself."*

J-J. LEMÊTRE: *"It's very difficult, incidentally, to take the timbre of one character and use it again for another. The harp, for example: its timbre was so completely assimilated to the Congress Party of* The Indiad *that I found it impossible to reuse it, just as it was impossible for an actor playing a Congress Party member to hear it again in the next play. But I have a lot of choice in terms of instruments. Little by little, in the course of our work, we've eliminated most modern and contemporary Western instruments because of the images they provoke, which are too realistic or cinematic. I wanted to say, too, that sometimes the music acts as a set, though never as a constraining one."*

A. MNOUCHKINE: *"Yes, sometimes Jean-Jacques is the sky, the sea, the clouds... destiny."*

Iphigenia in Aulis. Achilles (Simon Abkarian) hands a knife to Iphigenia (Nirupama Nityanandan). Photo by Michèle Laurent.

The Libation Bearers. Orestes (Simon Abkarian), helped by Pylades (Brontis Jodorowsky), drags Clytemnestra (Juliana Carneiro da Cunha) by force to the vomitorium. Orestes says to Clytemnestra: "You have killed he whom you should not have killed, suffer what you should not have to suffer." (Aeschylus, *Les Choéphores*, trans. Ariane Mnouchkine, notes Jean Bollack, Théâtre du Soleil, 1992.) Photo by Martine Franck, Magnum Photos.

The Libation Bearers. The chorus surrounds the deathbed of Clytemnestra, undressed and bloodied, on the moveable bridge. Erhard Stiefel made a mold of the actor's body and then cast it in wax. He made other corpse-mannequins for Agamemnon and Aegisthus. Photo by Martine Franck, Magnum Photos.

J-J. LEMÊTRE: "*And there are times also when an actor manages to create a set.*"

A. MNOUCHKINE: "*What we call the set is exactly that space in which something can come forward, the space we were talking about earlier: my internal state has to resemble that space, and it's not always easy to maintain. This space of possibilities definitely concerns Guy-Claude. But he works toward a concrete space of possibilities, a hard one (even if it's made of fabric), a 'real' one. But if Guy-Claude makes too much sky, neither Jean-Jacques nor the actor will be able to play the sky, and so the audience will see only a single sky, that is, Guy-Claude's, whereas the apparent absence of sky – or land, or sea, or boat, or onions, or ham hanging from the tavern wall – makes everything possible. What I'm saying here is extremely banal. But the funny thing is that this rule, which is banal and which is true in a theatre without sets or music, remains true when there are sets, music, and dance.*"

G-C. FRANÇOIS: "*It was with the Soleil that I learned what emptiness could mean in architecture, the emptiness that makes it possible to bring out everything that humans – in this case, actors – have to offer on their own.*"

"The actor may well be king..."

A. MNOUCHKINE: "*The other day, I saw the very beautiful Pina Bausch production based on Gluck's* Orphée et Eurydice, *and I asked her: 'Have you done other operas?' She said: 'Yes,* Iphigenie auf Tauris.' *'Would you like to do any others?' And she answered: 'I listen and listen, but I can't find any operas where there's room for me.' Verdi doesn't need anybody but Verdi. You have to get used to the idea of giving in, you must make space. Hélène Cixous says: 'If writing for the theatre doesn't stop before the end, if you don't remember, as you write, that in any case the work will be completed by the text's incarnation on stage, then you will write text in excess, unnecessary text.' The author too must ... be suspended.*"

B. PICON-VALLIN: "*Knowing how to give way to others, not taking up too much space: how do you direct actors according to these principles?*"

A. MNOUCHKINE: "*I think that's the only way you can direct actors. But 'giving way' doesn't mean letting the other party do anything they like.*"

C. SCHAUB: "*Giving up space, letting things come. If we're too far forward, if we want to advance too fast, we tear through the text, that piece of paper, and we collide with*

Jean-Jacques; we crash, we crash into the set. The important thing is to listen. We have to be concave."

A. MNOUCHKINE: *"Which doesn't mean being limp, having no energy. Actors must have as few obstacles in front of them as possible, so as to be as rich, as free as possible, but even actors must give way to theatre, to text, to meaning. They must give in: the actor may well be king, but there will nevertheless be a moment where a poor, little, ordinary, everyday character is more of a king than the actor is."*

B. PICON-VALLIN: *"In* The House of Atreus Cycle, *there's a search for a total vision without monumentality: a cycle of plays – of 'complete works' – and an appeal to all the arts: poetry, music, dance, circus, acting, visual arts, makeup. The orchestra includes dozens of instruments. The casting brings together actors of different nationalities, of contrasting physical appearance (look at the diversity of heights, for example). It also includes animals, the chorus of wolf-dogs in* The Eumenides. *Was this total vision your objective from the start, or did it take shape gradually?"*

A. MNOUCHKINE: *"We weren't looking for total theatre, we were looking for Aeschylus and Euripides. There were barking sounds at the end of each play, but the idea for the chorus of animals didn't appear until we were in rehearsals for* The Eumenides. *For the actors, I never distribute anything in advance. When Juliana arrived, she worked on the part of Clytemnestra, which Simon had initially rehearsed. They are both very tall. Height should have no importance: that's realist data. But it was a welcome gift to have that contrast between the mother Clytemnestra and her child Iphigenia[12]: it worked well for Iphigenia really to be treated like a tiny creature. We only gradually became aware of how painfully difficult it all was; the project went beyond anything we could have imagined. People laughed: 'The Eumenides are un-stageable.' But all the problems people run into stem from not taking the text at its word. Or worse: from not believing the text and from focusing on the complexity of the task at hand, getting stuck staring at a kind of huge barrier of foolishness that has accumulated over the centuries. Everything you'll find in our plays was found in the text at one point or another."*

C. SCHAUB: *"The references in the text are very sensual, not intellectual at all. You find indications like: 'Bile rises near my heart.' It's very physical."*

The Libation Bearers (rehearsal). Ariane Mnouchkine and Simon Abkarian search for the right movement. Photo by Michèle Laurent.

Theatre and images

A. MNOUCHKINE: *"There's a great difference between creating a beautiful image on stage by lighting someone, not necessarily an actor, and creating theatre by finding the right lighting for an actor, or rather a character. Personally, I like to light people, and I like them to be really seen. I can't bear someone I can't see, and I think that an actor who's not lit can't act. If you leave actors in the dark for too long, they can't act, and it's not because of their exacerbated narcissism: they can't act because if they're not seen, they can't see either."*

G-C. FRANÇOIS: *"At l'École des arts décoratifs, where I teach, the scenography students have good visual arts skills, but they have to learn to imagine with and for others (the author, actors, and technicians) so as to avoid creating artistic works that are static and sometimes introverted. Theatre can't be made alone. Each thing in theatre has value only insofar as others interact with it, allowing expression to happen."*

A. MNOUCHKINE: *"To return to the idea of a theatre of images: it's narcissistic; it says: 'Look at me, look at my world.' I want, instead, to know about how you share my world, about how much we live in the same world, and about what I can do in such a world. Plays must stimulate us: theatrical texts should call on people to understand, sometimes to react, to learn, to receive. In* The House of Atreus Cycle, *the chorus enters and speaks to us: 'Try to understand, you are such fools, you don't understand. I, old man, I, serving woman, I am telling you something useful, something you have forgotten, I am telling you what you are, hurry up and understand, because if not, you will wind up killing your mother, your daughter.'"*

B. PICON-VALLIN: *"In terms of collaboration between the different arts, film isn't often featured in the Soleil's productions. Though in* Mephisto, *there were projections."*

G-C. FRANÇOIS: *"We'd thought about using film for the play about the Resistance that was meant to precede* Mephisto, *which we still haven't put on."*

A. MNOUCHKINE: *"I love cinema. One day perhaps, in one of our plays, there will be cinema; a character will go to a cinema or watch a film. But our goal is not to compete with cinema, which is something else entirely. I think no art, in fact, can compete with any other. They can only keep each other company for a while: for example, Charlie Chaplin owes everything to theatre, and at the same time he's the greatest cinema actor the world has ever known. I do theatre; I love theatre. If one day there's a cinema on stage, if one day characters are watching a screen, the screen will only remain on stage if it becomes theatrical, and if the cinema acts like a theatre actor. I'll try it out and after a week, if it's still cinema, we'll say: 'Goodbye, Another time.'"*[13]

"If you don't want to suffer, don't enter here!"

A. Mnouchkine: *"I understand that we're here to discuss our work and the convictions we share. But it's important we don't appear too triumphalist. We're convinced this is the right way to proceed, but we mustn't forget the months and sometimes years of doubt, the days and weeks during which this space of possibilities, this magnificent vacuum, remains a lethal emptiness that puts actors on the brink of a nervous breakdown. At those moments I think I'm wrong: we shouldn't work this way; I'd do better to say to the chorus: 'Line up, all of you, in single file, enter slowly, stop there, say your lines and sit down.' This art, this 'shared work of art,' which is an expression I like, the actors must know that it comes about through spurts of very intense work and renunciations that can be very cruel. There is 'yielding' which is one thing, and 'renouncing' which is much worse. In* The House of Atreus Cycle, *the human cost isn't visible, and that's as it should be: the audience shouldn't know. I find it immodest, indecent to show the audience what the play cost us. However, I don't see how we cannot admit that for a play like this you need real actors, who accept doubt, darkness, black holes, who accept a director who says to them: 'I don't know what a chorus is, I want to know, but I don't know. All I know is what it isn't.' It's important to say this because otherwise people might imagine there's a kind of recipe, without understanding that to have this recipe come out right, we have to burn our arms up to the elbows. Today we're gathered here with two of the actors who were the 'locomotives' of the play, and who therefore suffered, though not so much, because they were creators.*[14] *But there are all those who weren't creators in the same way, and those who weren't creators at all. We should inscribe on every pediment: 'If you don't want to suffer, don't enter here. If you're afraid of pain, don't do theatre.'"*

S. Abkarian: *"To follow up on what Ariane is saying, I talked with one of Pina Bausch's dancers about physical injuries. I'm wary of people who are intact, who are innocent of any pain. Even if you walk away from a battlefield unhurt, you at least have the blood of others on you. If you walk*

The Libation Bearers. Face-to-face confrontation between Clytemnestra (Juliana Carneiro da Cunha) and Orestes (Simon Abkarian). On the floor, the knife. Photo by Michèle Laurent.

Agamemnon. Dance of the chorus of old men, each with what energy he can still muster. Photo by Michèle Laurent.

away unscathed, immaculate, then somewhere along the line there's a commitment problem. This dancer, too, had scrapes and scratches everywhere; they all have small injuries all over. And then, to be sure, we actors like to complain, to talk about the wounds. I'm proud of my war wounds, and heaven knows how much I would've liked to avoid them, even so! But to get to where we need to be, we have to stumble; we have to fall; you can't learn to ride a bike without falling; you can't remain intact."

C. Schaub: *"It's the price to pay, and it's worth it, but you have to know you'll have to pay it. It's not enough to plan to spend three months in India at Kalamandalam, at the center for performing arts in Kerala."*

A. Mnouchkine: *"There's a misunderstanding among actors. Many young actors, even in our company, want to find the recipe, the one that makes everything easy and fast. What Catherine means is that Kalamandalam – and first of all, she spent two years there, not three months – isn't a recipe, but just the beginning of a difficult path: from the moment you decide you want to follow that path, everything becomes very difficult. As soon as you start knowing something, the great danger is the illusion of ease, of facility. Theatre is difficult; and even though it's not the audience's business, they often realize it. They say to us: 'You've done so much work, so much work!' And of course the audience, too, must work in these plays, as in all our plays. Future professionals are very surprised by the intensity of what is asked for in training sessions at the Théâtre du Soleil. But nobody is forcing them to be there. So, total theatre or not, or total theatre and, better, shared creation … People ask me: 'How does Jean-Jacques manage the music?' 'He's there, from the first to the last day of rehearsal.' 'I see… and at what time?' 'At nine a.m., sometimes at two p.m. if there's something else planned for the morning.' And my interlocutor expresses great surprise: he wouldn't be able to do it, he has too much else to do."*

Dances in *The House of Atreus Cycle*

C. Schaub: *"I remember that when in rehearsal the old men in the chorus of* Agamemnon *started dancing, the dances were spontaneous, neither dictated nor premeditated. They emerged out of the music and the text, of course, but they always took place at moments when emotion was at such a peak the chorus couldn't express itself in any way except through the body, through …"*

A. Mnouchkine: *"We called it … little 'therapeutic frictions'…"*

Agamemnon (rehearsal). Working on dance with Catherine Schaub and Juliana Carneiro da Cunha (Clytemnestra). Carneiro da Cunha, who arrived in the middle of rehearsals, must join the chorus's dance at the moment of Agamemnon's return (in the red chariot visible in the background). The choreographic work is collective, with the most advanced helping the rest. Archives Sophie Moscoso.

The Libation Bearers. Orestes (Simon Abkarian) dances his emotions before the corpse-mannequins of his mother Clytemnestra and her lover Aegisthus. Photo by Martine Franck, Magnum Photos.

C. SCHAUB: "... *yes, through those 'therapeutic frictions,' exactly. I think that's a phenomenon that can't happen in ordinary theatre, because there isn't enough space. But during the work on* The House of Atreus Cycle, *there were always violent rushes of momentum we were able to express, and the music, whether it was following us or pushing us, was always there like a magic carpet. It allowed us to develop emotion through our bodies, through sound, in what is perhaps a primitive way. All the dances by the chorus were born in this way.*"

A. MNOUCHKINE: "*Orestes' dance in* The Libation Bearers *is one of the most flamboyant, dazzling, taxing moments, both for the actor and for the audience. But it's a collective moment – which steals no credit from Simon, because it's also a very great actor's moment. It's completely collective because it's a dance that brings everything together: music – very grand music – percussion, very specific lighting, the whole chorus, and Aeschylus too, even if there's no text, because we feel all the weight of the preceding scene. At that moment, you're only watching Simon, and Simon deserves to be the focus of every gaze; but that moment is the meeting point of the three plays that came before that. In* The Libation Bearers, *the scene between Clytemnestra and Orestes, the murder of Clytemnestra, and that dance are, for Aeschylus, the tragic summit of his trilogy. Afterward, he tries to put some salve on the wounds; he writes* The Eumenides. *But I think the dance of Orestes is really a 'shared work of art.' If you don't see that, it's a bit as if you said the person who arrives bearing the torch to Olympia carried it alone. I'm all the more glad to say this because Simon had a role as creator in these productions, a role which went far beyond those he eventually played on stage. If we acknowledge that we're creating a 'shared work of art,' then it must exist at every instant, whether there's a single actor on stage or all of them. In a way, when nobody is left on stage and the lights go down, the stage is still peopled with all the ghosts, all the sweat of the characters, the blood of Iphigenia and of Clytemnestra. For an actor to be total at a given moment, everyone else must give way.*"

S. ABKARIAN: "*You can't speak after having killed someone on stage. Something theatrical must happen, translated by dance, by shouts, by a bloody sword. In terms of props, I can't tell you how many swords we must have made – twisted swords, swords with a blade like a kris ... One day, Ariane said to me: 'We need a sword to tell the story, the most ferocious sword we can find.' And in the end it was the simplest sword possible, without even a guard. For* The

The Eumenides. Two of the three Furies (Catherine Schaub in tennis shoes, and Nirupama Nityanandan). Photo by Michèle Laurent.

The Eumenides. Facing the audience, the Furies (Myriam Azencot, Nirupama Nityanandan, and Catherine Schaub) in traveler-vagabond costumes, with sticks and sacks, and four wolf-dogs from the chorus. The work performed by the actors (mostly men) in this chorus was extremely physical. Photo by Michèle Laurent.

House of Atreus Cycle, *everyone had the same knife, in different sizes, but made of the same metal, for the same blood. Which means we gave ourselves something; we yielded something. I know I had difficulty with the idea of 'yielding.' It's true, because when you get used to wanting to act... Until the day Ariane said to me: 'It's Cassandra's story right now, it's Cassandra we want to watch. Not you!' But it takes time to stop, to 'yield,' so as then to give of yourself, to transmit to others. Sometimes you can't help saying: 'It's mine.' But no, it's hers, it's his, it's ours, it's the audience's. And the dance of Orestes is also Clytemnestra's, the dance of the coryphaeus, of the chorus, it's the dance of Jean-Jacques, it's Ariane's dance too."*

The need for extremes

A. MNOUCHKINE: "*For* The House of Atreus Cycle, *we were dealing more with kathakali forms than with kabuki. But it's common knowledge there are foundational elements that connect kathakali, kabuki, Noh,* topeng, *and Greece. Now that I look at the documents, I realize that, indeed, we found Greece again, but we returned to it intuitively: our documentation, which began in Turkey and progressed through the Caucasus, did not involve the Greeks. I didn't want to consult documents on ancient Greece, because I was afraid of falling into clichés from Greek vases, from togas, from elegantly draped cloth. I continue to believe that in the West there is the dramatist's art, but in the East there is the actor's, which I cannot do without and on which I will continue to draw with no qualms. Recently I saw* La Zone,*[15] a film where you see, at the edges of Paris, dump trucks literally pouring garbage onto rag-and-bone men, with their pitchforks and their cloth caps. It hits them in the face, and then they start picking around in it. There's a little assembly line set up, and the women sort the rags. It's like India. You see the same eyes, the same pauses, something universal that has to do with extremes. Why am I using this example for a play that has nothing to do with India? Because everything that's worse is worse there, and everything that's beautiful is even more beautiful. We need these extremes, extreme imbecility, extreme cruelty, because here at home, for the moment it seems that everything is tepid, blurred. Since I don't have very much time, since I'll only live once, I need the extremes to feed on. In the 'Far East,' [*Extrême Orient *in French, trans.], *it's not the East I'm looking for, it's the Extreme. I sense something absolutely generative in India, something I don't know, but that I recognize, which helps me, which nourishes me. The worst*

The Eumenides. Athena (Juliana Carneiro da Cunha) seated cross-legged on a chariot. The luminous goddess founds the first citizens' tribunal, which here she presides. Photo by Michèle Laurent.

in India helps me recognize the worst here, the beauty of everything there helps me recognize beauty here, because I recognize myths. There's an underground river that connects cultures."

J-J. LEMÊTRE: *"In India, you can find elements of music theory that are exactly the same as in ancient Greek music theory. I use modes that I believe to be Greek, and as I do so, I can't prevent them from also being Indian. I begin with the idea that Greece, at a given moment, must have thought it was the center of the world, and swarmed over the rest. The advantage of Greece is that it had within it East and West, in music in any case. A Brazilian or a Turk will recognize a phrase, and so will a Greek, a Chinese person, a Cambodian. It's remarkable, and there's certainly something universal there."*

"There is no last word"

B. PICON-VALLIN: *"What is the director's role?"*

A. MNOUCHKINE: *"I think I've never been able to give a good explanation, and also, I think her role varies from play to play. Sometimes the director is a guide, sometimes a wall, other times a boxer."*

G-C. FRANÇOIS: *"The director harmonizes all the arts, because there are enormous risks with this kind of confrontation between arts."*

A. MNOUCHKINE: *"Maybe the director's role is to have the strength to insert herself?"*

G-C. FRANÇOIS: *"I've never been able to find a comparison that rings true … For one thing, the director is the only person in the group who doesn't produce anything in the physical sense. And her freedom of discernment is heightened by not having the constraints instrumentalists have (actors using their bodies, set designers with their structures and materials)."*

J-J. LEMÊTRE: *"The director is one of the pillars of the work triangle – apart from the author – whose other pillars are the actors and the music. I say 'music' because in my case, composer, performer, and instrument-maker are one and the same."*

B. PICON-VALLIN: *"Is it the director who has the last word? Does someone have to have the last word?"*

A. MNOUCHKINE: *"When you say 'have the last word,' it sounds as if there's permanent conflict. I think that, in fact, if there has to be a last word, it's too bad. If all is well, there's no need for a last word: there should be clarity so obvious that a last word is no longer necessary. That said, and I emphasize this so as not to be misunderstood by very young companies, sometimes a last word is necessary, and in those cases, it's best that it be uttered by the director. Otherwise there will be immeasurable loss of time, and personal factors will come to the fore. When something is very obviously right, that feeling of obvious rightness is shared, by definition. Sometimes we're very pleased with what we've done, but then the obviousness is no longer there – often as soon as the next day. That's one bad thing that can happen. There's also the case where, faced with difficulties, we discover a solution to which almost everyone agrees, but then I say: 'No.' But it never goes as far as an actual conflict, insofar as everyone is ready, as long as it's possible to do better, to keep on going. The most serious situation would be if I said: 'No, we're not there yet,' and the actors became stubborn and stamped their feet and persisted. I think that would be the end of the Soleil. If I found myself working alongside someone who wasn't determined to go absolutely all the way, I think I'd go make... shoes."*

S. ABKARIAN: *"The director faces a different solitude from the solitude of the set designer or the composer. She has to know how to keep things in reserve for the right moment, when, for example, some actors enact ideas that arrive too early for the others. Ariane has to know how to keep much more inside herself than we do. She has to encompass all 'five arts' (just like 'the five senses'), whereas we encompass only one thing, though I have no wish to depreciate what we do."*

A. MNOUCHKINE: *"Think about the way work was divided during the construction of a cathedral. There was a conceiver, an architect who made the plans, and then there were the people who sculpted this or that ornament or sculpture or gargoyle; and the people who worked on the stained glass. And all those different arts had to be extraordinarily well coordinated for the right stone to arrive at the right moment, for example. What's notable in our work is the mobility of the relationship between whole and detail, all the time. Some are working on details, some are working on the whole, and then suddenly the person working on a detail has to consider the whole, and I end up focusing on a detail. We are constantly moving from close-ups to long shots and back. I sometimes wonder if what we're doing when we're all there working on the preparation of a play might resemble the work of cathedral builders, on a smaller scale, and over eight months rather than 90 years, even though those months seem immense to us."*

Triumphs and miseries

The House of Atreus Cycle was awarded the *Grand prix de la Critique*, a major French theatre prize. The production toured for long periods – in the Netherlands, Germany, England, Austria, Canada, the United States, Sicily, and France. These tours made it possible to reach more than 300,000 audience members, a total which exceeds (by a slight margin), according to the "account books" of the Soleil, the number of audience members for *1789* and *The Shakespeare Cycle*. Nothing was simple. There were disagreements within the troupe about the Gulf War. Rebelling against their "foreman" and resenting their "anonymous work" in the choruses, some members of the troupe left; others left too, for more personal reasons – after a long stay they considered a period unequaled in their lives. An extended workshop during the tours brought together fervent new postulants who would learn[16] by working on the dances of the chorus members, the very dances that had wearied those who had created them. And it may be that, animated by the joy the "novices" felt at being admitted into the heart of their dreams, the choruses of *The House of Atreus Cycle* became even more compelling.

The House of Atreus Cycle. The performance space being set up in a natural outdoor setting in Sicily (Orestiadi da Gibellina). In the center is one of the wheeled entrance chariots, manipulated from within by "drivers." Photo by Stefano Fogato.

Notes

1 Ariane Mnouchkine, in *Au Soleil même la nuit*, a film by Éric Darmon and Catherine Vilpoux, AGAT Films & Cie, La Sept Arte, 1997. In this chapter any unattributed quotations will come from interviews Béatrice Picon-Vallin conducted with members of the Théâtre du Soleil and Ariane Mnouchkine from 2010 to 2014.
2 See also Chapter Three of this study.
3 See *Lettre au public*, October 3, 1988, Archives Théâtre du Soleil.
4 The Soleil put out a leaflet announcing the opening of the play for March 1991 (Archives Théâtre du Soleil). The play was never published in France, but an English version exists, translated by Donald Watson in Eric Prenowitz, ed., *Selected Plays by Hélène Cixous* (London: Routledge, 2004). The play has been put on multiple times outside of France.
5 Troupe meeting, January 16, 1989, from Sophie Moscoso's notebooks, Archives Sophie Moscoso.
6 One of the reference works used for this project was the volume edited by Antoine de Baecque, *L'An I des droits de l'homme* (Paris: Presses du CNRS), 1988.
7 See Pierre Judet de la Combe, "Ariane Mnouchkine and the History of the French *Agamemnon*," in Fiona Macintosh, ed., *Agamemnon in Performance 458 BC to AD 2004* (London: Oxford University Press, 2005), 273–289.
8 Ibid., 274.
9 Ariane Mnouchkine, "Écorchement et catharsis," in Odette Aslan, ed., *Le Corps en jeu* (Paris, CNRS Éditions, 1993), 296.

10 See also Chapter Four of this study.

11 The following pages reproduce excerpts from Béatrice Picon-Vallin, "Une oeuvre d'art commune," March 1993 interview with members of the Théâtre du Soleil, *Théâtre/Public*, no. 124–125 (1995), 74–83. Skipped passages are not indicated.

12 In the Soleil's credits, certain characters' names change from play to play due to different translation decisions. In *Iphigenia in Aulis*, traditionally French spellings were used (Clytemnestre, Iphigénie). For the other plays, the translation used spellings closer to the Greek: Clytemnestra, Cassandra.

13 See Chapter Seven on how cinema is treated in the Soleil's plays from the beginning of the twenty-first century: *The Last Caravanserai* [*Le Dernier Caravansérail*], *Ephemera* [*Les Éphémères*], and *The Survivors of Mad Hope* [*Les Naufragés du Fol Espoir*].

14 Simon Abkarian, who had already played numerous parts in *Sihanouk* and *The Indiad*, possessed "the flower," according to Georges Bigot (an expression meaning that he acted exceptionally well, borrowed from kabuki culture – see Chapter Three). During rehearsals for *The House of Atreus Cycle*, he was able to play all the roles. In performances, he played Agamemnon, Achilles, the Nurse, Orestes, a coryphaeus, and a herald.

15 Documentary by Georges Lacombe from 1928. The film was among those screened at the Vidéothèque de Paris during the preparation of the Soleil's 1994 play *The Perjured City, or the Awakening of the Furies* [*La Ville parjure ou le Réveil des Érinyes*].

16 While the *House of Atreus* plays were touring in Sicily (in the small town of Gibellina), the choreographer Maïtreyi had the aspiring company members work at the Cartoucherie by showing them the danced sequences on videotapes.

Drums on the Dam: In the Form of an Ancient Puppet Play Performed by Actors. Mnouchkine would make a film of this very theatricalized production in which actors became puppets manipulated by their fellow actors. In this picture, perched high up on a metal beam, two *kokens* dressed in black (A. Canto Sabido and J. Poirot) hold the strings of the actor-musicians who skillfully play Korean drums (*salmulnori*). In the middle: Duan (R. Ramos Maza), the daughter of the soothsayer, is the captain of the dam's lookouts who execute the different alarm signals on the drums. Around her: V. Mangado, D. Jambert, F. de Melo e Souza, S. Beheshti, M-A. Cardoso Ferreira, Maïtreyi, E. Doe Bruce, M. Rauchvarger, J. Marvan Enriquez, M. Jacques, J-C. Maricot. Photo by Michèle Laurent.

Chapter 6 The Soleil brings in a camera

"My wealth is the world. I'm neither selfless nor altruistic in wanting the world to be preserved as best as possible."
Ariane Mnouchkine[1]

"What next after The House of Atreus Cycle?*"* Hélène Cixous asks: *"Where are we going? We're on the way – we're starting toward ... What will happen to us?"*[2] Theatre is already happening when the Soleil embarks on the urgent adventure of selecting the next subject.

"From 3500 BCE to 1993": the *Awakening of the Furies*

In 1992, the fall of the Berlin Wall and the Soviet Empire suggested how to answer the question "what next?" – prompting conversations, exchanges of "what if ..." readings, and research. But then a news story suddenly overwhelmed public discourse in France, and definitively scotched the initial project. In October 1992, the trial of Michel Garetta, Director of the National Center of Blood Transfusions, rocked readers and listeners by exposing details of a scandal dating back several years, dubbed the "contaminated blood scandal." Numerous health care, medical, judicial, and political groups were blamed. The victims were primarily hemophiliac children, killed by blood transfusions containing the HIV virus from unregulated (or barely regulated) donor sources. It was a hot topic, with blood carrying immense symbolic weight, the kind of symbolic weight conferred on blood in *The House of Atreus Cycle*. The scandal of mortal contagion was both real and a metaphor for the moral crisis and extreme negligence of France's power structure. That which should have saved lives instead killed children. The politicians wouldn't be tried until 1999, and the media and film industry didn't dare address this unresolved, taboo subject. But the Soleil courageously took it on, asked questions, and made accusations.

"Contemporary characters have not been allowed mythic standing." (Ariane Mnouchkine, rehearsal notes from *The Perjured City or the Awakening of the Furies*, compiled by Charles-Henri Bradier, Théâtre du Soleil Archives.)

Hélène Cixous wrote *The Perjured City, or the Awakening of the Furies* [*La Ville parjure ou le Réveil des Érinyes*] between December 1992 and September 1993, while investigating the French medical community. She was "exploring medicine" as she had explored Asia; but lacking geographical or historical distance, she had to seek a metaphoric support, a way to create distance by giving the story a particular form. Her translation of *The Eumenides* (the third part of Aeschylus's Greek tragedy, *The Oresteia*) would end up providing the solution. As for Mnouchkine, she conjured up the setting: it would be a cemetery, more precisely Cairo's City of the Dead, where those cast out of society live together, surrounded by the deceased. Such a setting allowed the Soleil to delve into a subject that had completely overwhelmed them.

The Eumenides, Part IV of *The House of Atreus Cycle*, staged Athena's creation of the tribunal that judged Orestes and acquitted him, making her the goddess-founder of modern law, voting, citizenship, and justice – all the institutions of democracy. Thus were defeated the three ancient Furies – those forces responsible for avenging familial crimes. Dressed in tatters, in hues of mud and smoke, they accepted their banishment to the underground and thereafter their new name "the gracious ones." But the wolf-dog chorus that accompanied them kept its ferocious masks and growled all the way to the end: democracy was seen to be fragile; the chorus had to stay vigilant.

In *The Perjured City*, the Furies, also vigilant, reappeared, accompanied by guides who were also border crossers. The character Aeschylus (Myriam Azencot) became the magical and essential guardian of the cemetery,[3] connecting generations and groups of characters; the character Night (Shahrokh Meshkin Ghalam) was the allegorical mother of the Furies; and two "ghosts" gave form to the child victims. Cixous borrowed Aeschylus's heightened language and the tenor of the voices of "prehistoric weepers"[4] to move the story of the scandal, an alleged state crime, into theatrical form. She either gave fictional names to the real, although transposed, characters, or simply designated actors in the real-life drama by their roles: King, Queen, lawyers, doctors, medical researchers, and ministers. Wielding a surgeon's knife, she operated on reality, a reality which continued to unfold while she was writing, using as guide Anne-Marie Casteret's exposé, *L'Affaire du sang* [*The Business of Blood*].[5]

The Perjured City presented a tragedy of contemporary times, spun out of the energy of *The House of Atreus Cycle* and staged during six months of rehearsals. A chorus of miserable and dispossessed beggars, cloaked in beige or gray jackets, some wearing expressionist make-up, confronted the perpetrators of the crime. They supported the Mother's (Renata Ramos Maza's) revolt, "a metaphor for all mothers' sorrows." Embraced by the united Furies, the Mother became the center of a great debate about justice and forgiveness.

Mnouchkine wanted to have the chorus dance, perhaps even breakdance – and urban dancers came to demonstrate their technique at the Cartoucherie – but the chorus's slow, simple progression across the stage was what stuck. Enclosed behind the cemetery gates salvaged from a former hospital, the chorus moved between the tombs, located stage left and stage right. The living thus slipped in among the roughcast, jagged stones. Certain scenes, in which the living and the dead conversed in the old cemetery, were reminiscent, if unintentionally, of *A Night in the Old Marketplace* by I. Peretz, a 1925 production of the Moscow State Yiddish Theatre.

The Perjured City was one of the Soleil's least popular shows, and the actors voted to close it. For one thing, it was too long (two parts, each three hours long); in retrospect, Mnouchkine thinks she should have made cuts. For another, the subject matter was challenging and misunderstood. *The Perjured City* was seen as a show about AIDS, while it was really a story about unregulated blood transfusions and their terrible consequences. Two scenes were particularly striking: the end, offering the image of a possible future, when the characters broke through the doors to heaven and the upstage wall lit up like a "celestial plain," as King Sihanouk had described heaven in *Sihanouk*. Hundreds of tiny shimmering lights comforted the audience as they left the theatre, with the Mother's last words in their ears: "Our play is over, but yours has just begun. It is your turn to insist that justice occurs justly."[6] The second memorable scene was the one in which the two dead little boys, dressed in red sweaters, returned to the living: they manipulated marionettes while themselves being piloted by *kokens* (Japanese puppeteers) dressed in black. They walked slowly toward the audience and the Mother to a recorded version of Handel's aria *Rinaldo*, sung by the children's choir of the Viennese Sängerknaben.

This was the first time that children appeared on the Soleil's stage, although they had been coming to the Cartoucherie with their parents and had thus been schooled there since the Soleil's beginning. Ever since *The Clowns*, children had visited in elementary or high school groups, and the Soleil had been making theatre just as much for them as for adults. Soon after *The Perjured City*, children would be on stage very often: their fragile and confident presence having the potential to intensify actors' work and transform the audience members' gaze.

"All great works become more relevant from time to time." (Ariane Mnouchkine, *Figaro Lyon*, July 1995.)

The Perjured City, or the Awakening of the Furies. Stage right: the cemetery with its open tombs, its stairs, and its murals. Archives Guy-Claude François.

The Perjured City. Mise en abyme of the return of the deceased. The two children, D. and B. Ézéchiel (L. Charron and M. Beslon), victims of transfusions of contaminated blood, come back to earth, guiding their marionettes. Behind them, the *kokens* are black shadows who guide them. Photo by Michèle Laurent.

The Perjured City. The Furies (N. Nityanandan, J. Carneiro da Cunha, and V. Grail) address the audience from a wooden footbridge. The chorus stands behind them. Photo by Michèle Laurent.

Tartuffe versus the Fundamentalists

The coffers once again empty, the Soleil rehearsed Molière's *Tartuffe* in the same space, slightly modified, as *The Perjured City*. In a relatively short period of time, the production was ready to go. Bernard Faivre d'Arcier had commissioned it for the Avignon Festival, in repertory with the Cixous play. Opening in June 1995 in Vienna at the Vienna Festival, it was remounted in October, after Avignon, at the Cartoucherie. This *Tartuffe* was truly a question of survival for the Soleil, but the Soleil refused to compromise in any way. While Molière was summoned at just the right moment, the Théâtre du Soleil also affirmed its reputation as a free and courageous company by treating the play as a commentary on the burning question of religious fundamentalism.

The poster for the production was black and white, composed solely of printed text. Although it featured Molière's words: "This is a highly stirring comedy, which has been persecuted for a long time ... ," the effect was that of a contemporary newspaper editorial that had been crumpled and blown about by the wind. The theatre was now at the heart of the modern world, no longer the erupting cosmic volcano represented on the dazzling poster for *The Shakespeare Cycle*. The Soleil interpreted *Tartuffe* by returning to the sense of urgency in which Molière wrote it, even if the Welcome Area immersed the audience in Rameau's festive seventeenth-century music; and a *trompe-l'œil* mural of the mischievous author seemed to watch over the crowd from the scaffolding affixed to the theatre's façade. For Mnouchkine had substituted the threat of Muslim fundamentalism for that of Molière's "cabal of bigots," which she had folded into the concept of Inquisition. And indeed there had to be a police presence, with security checkpoints and bag searches during the first part of the run, because of the threat of terrorism that followed the wave of Islamist attacks in France in 1995.

The show was transposed and transported to an imaginary South, evoking Algeria or Morocco. This simultaneously provided distance and familiarity. Between the upstage wall of windows filled in with cinderblocks and the tall gates that had bordered the cemetery of *The Perjured City*, the Soleil's designers created a road. This road, running past the gates, helped delimit in *Tartuffe* a vast downstage terrace, the main playing space. It was from the road, outside the gates, that a street vendor (Sergio Canto), in a red Tunisian felt cap, delivered the show's inventive prologue, occurring before Madame Pernelle's entrance. He clicked his castanets and waved his transistor radio, from which the *raï* song *Mani, Mani* emanated, sung by Cheb Hasni, who had been assassinated in Oran, Algeria in September 1994.[7] Pink bougainvillea spilled over the black gates from which white veils also hung: the cicadas' constant hum suggested how hot it was. The sound of the castanets drew out the dwellers of the Orgon household in a swirl of spotless clothing, and the women fondled cloth, magazines, and oranges in the peddler's dilapidated cart in anticipation. The recorded music filled the theatre with exuberant rhythm.

Madame Pernelle (M. Azencot), covered in black and grey from head to toe, had only to burst into this joyous ruckus to stop it short with an enraged whistle. She was accompanied by her usual companion – doubled for the occasion by two chubby gossips, Flippe and Pote,[8] both enveloped in voluminous skirts. These creatures came into being because two actors had had fun rehearsing the role together, and the company decided they should both play the part. The wordless prelude, underscored by the *raï* music,[9] set up the oppressive situation.

Molière's poetry is lyrical when spoken aloud, saturated with its own interior music – which didn't leave much room for the usual musical work of Jean-Jacques Lemêtre.[10] Molière's language, spoken by foreigners (there were a dozen different nationalities on stage), acquired a shimmering beauty thanks to their varied accents, especially after the October remount, when, because of criticism levied at the production in Avignon, a new focus was placed on diction.

Mnouchkine had thought about staging *Tartuffe* twenty years earlier when, she says, she would have treated the play as a critique of Stalinism. In 1995, her thematic interrogation concerned what happens when "an ideology, instead of offering an ideal, becomes an instrument of oppression and serves to monopolize power."[11] Thus coursing through the narration of events that took place in Orgon's (Brontis Jodorowsky's) home, were themes of fundamentalism, religious fanaticism, and the violence suffered by women and families (rape and arranged marriages). These thematic undercurrents called to mind actual acts since 1992 of extreme violence against intellectuals and women, tied to the rise of Islamism in Algeria – as well as gesturing to the case of Taslima Nasreen, put to death in Bangladesh. Mnouchkine wanted to suggest that like Orgon, the West was complicit with those who assumed the right to kill, imprison, and rape in the name of God.[12]

Between 1995 and 1999, l'AIDA's activities also picked back up: the association to protect artists in danger took action on over 100 cases of artists or journalists who had been victims of Islamist fundamentalism.[13] The theatre program for *Tartuffe*, printed in a five-column newspaper format, assembled historically and geographically diverse texts, including the Edict of Nantes, Molière's preface to *Tartuffe*, philosophical texts by Pierre Nicole, Bossuet, Voltaire, Saint Paul, and Boileau, alongside press summaries and articles. All touched on the subjects

Tartuffe. At the beginning of the performance, behind the front gate, the traveling merchant (S. Canto Sabido), with his oranges, his vials, and his music. Photo by Michèle Laurent.

Tartuffe. The joyful white world of this Mediterranean family's women contrasts with the somber world of men. Seated on the ground, Dorine (J. Carneiro da Cunha) and Mariane (R. Ramos Maza). Photo by Martine Franck, Magnum Photos.

Tartuffe. Cléante (D. Bellugi-Vannuccini), Valère (M. Jacques), Flippe and Pote (V. Crouzet and M-P. Ramo Guinard). White shade veils are attached to the house's gates, which are covered in bougainvillea. Photo by Michèle Laurent.

Tartuffe. Tartuffe (S. Meshkim Ghalam) enters, accompanied not only by Laurent, his servant, but by several henchmen who wait at the door. The warm and welcoming atmosphere of the house, where floral carpets have been laid over the white flooring, has quickly changed. Photo by Michèle Laurent.

of tolerance and intolerance and provided information on religious fanatics' threats and crimes, be they Muslim or Catholic, as well as on the baleful consequences for culture and women's rights of such acts.[14]

Through the production of *Tartuffe*, the Soleil proclaimed itself in service to a cause – that of the freedom of thought of artists and women – rather than at the service of a political party. It thereby aligned itself with engagement, not militancy, even if the Soleil sometimes demonstrated alongside activists. In 1972, Georges Bonnaud had already understood this: "Actually, we wanted to bear witness, not to fight, refusing to become the sort of theatre makers caught in an endless cycle of political meetings."[15] The Soleil's work with l'AIDA embodied this attitude. Mnouchkine had long thought that denunciation becomes legitimate and convincing through creative acts: "We will do [our protests] with the tools we have: with theatre, cinema, song, painting, and books."[16]

The fight for justice extends through the Soleil's entire history, including several productions and staged readings of "trials." First, there was *The Nancy Trial* [*Le Procès de Nancy*] with the group for prison reform (GIP), mounted during the run of *1793*, in which Mnouchkine played the role of a lawyer. Other members of the troupe, as well as Gilles Deleuze and Michel Foucault, also participated. Then, there was *The Prague Trial* [*Le Procès de Prague*], staged bi-frontally between facing audiences, in December 1979, using the leaked, secretly recorded audio transcript from the closed hearing in which the Czech dissident Vaclav Havel was condemned to five years in prison.[17] Finally, in 1984, came *The Trial of Wei, Maker of Springtime* [*Procès de Wei, le faiseur de printemps*], in defense of the Chinese dissident Wei Jingsheng. Quickly staged, these intervention-style productions responded to an identifiable crisis with a creative act. The Prague Trial was remounted once in Munich (February 1980), in German by Mnouchkine and Patrice Chéreau (with Simone Signoret and Yves Montand among the cast), and moved directly to television, programmed for Czech citizens. In 1982, a whole night in Avignon was consecrated to Havel during the run of the Soleil's *Richard II*.

The urgency of creative intervention has never meant mediocrity. In 2010, for example, the Théâtre du Soleil participated in Parisian protests for retirement reform: it fashioned a giant puppet, an allegory of Justice, whose head was sculpted from the model in Prud'hon's painting, *Justice and Divine Vengeance Pursuing Crime*. The puppet moved to the sounds of a Soleil orchestra, guiding the crowd of demonstrators and dancing at intervals, while fighting off crow puppets that attacked it from their perch, trying to make it bow down. (During the May 1, 2002 massive protest against the far-right National Front,

The Trial of the Nancy Mutineers. Filmed as an action by GIP (for prison reform) and presented several times in June 1972, following performances of *1793*. The trial of six mutineers from the Charles III prison ended in a severe sentence. The show used the crux of the arguments at their trial to stage "justice." On the left: J-C. Penchenat, A. Mnouchkine as the lawyer. At the table, G. Bonnaud. (The text is published in the review *Esprit*, October 1972.) See also the picture of the great puppet of Justice in Transverse Perspectives of this study. Photo by Martine Franck, Magnum Photos.

Malian families are welcomed at the Cartoucherie (1996) after having been evicted from the Saint Bernard Church. This experience would plant the seed for the following show: *And Suddenly, Sleepless Nights*. Photo by Stefano Fogato.

the crows had made their first appearance – attacking the French flag.) Magnificent banners, fabricated by Soleil actors, surrounded the Justice puppet in 2010. Rather than displaying political slogans, the banners quoted from great authors (Shakespeare, Hugo, Rousseau, and others). The Justice puppet made five theatrical appearances that autumn. In May 1973, the Soleil had already marched under a Marat quote; and in 1980, actors demonstrated for the liberation of pianist Alba Gonzalez Souza, imprisoned in Colombia, beneath the words of Seneca: "As long as we are among humans, let us be humane."

To define the Soleil's engagement, one must evacuate ideology from the word "political," and leave only its Greek sense, that of citizen theatre. As such, the Soleil reflects on its role in the city and then incarnates it – as lookout, awakener, questioner, resistance fighter, and facilitator of both individual and group transformation. Profoundly convinced of the accuracy of the National Resistance Council's (CNR) ideals, Mnouchkine thinks it necessary to know how to differentiate between Good and Evil.[18] Some accuse her of being a goody-goody and of Manichaeism for this simplification, but she could undoubtedly rebut those who proffer their ideological arguments under a veil of complicated theory. The Soleil's engagement indicates another way of thinking about politics, just as its productions show another way of making theatre: a complete commitment, simple, but not simplistic, where morals, ethics, and beauty anchor and infuse engagement.

To return to *Tartuffe*, Evil was certainly there, and possibly even the Devil, all living in the bearded man with red ears and eyes lined in black. This scary Tartuffe entered the stage after intermission, at the beginning of the third act, introduced by the relentless din of streets echoing Islamist slogans. He crossed the threshold of Orgon's home in terrifying silence, surrounded by a gang of six mute henchmen who looked just like him.

Situating Orgon's terrace on top of the City of the Dead's cemetery from *The Perjured City* left its symbolic mark. While the reasoning behind this was primarily economic, it was also the Soleil's art at play. The theatrical past and History are never completely erased from the company's work or their acting, but instead occupy the background and nourish the work. The present can't exist without the past's conscious and subconscious dimensions: the layering of the stages in *Tartuffe*'s case metaphorized this relationship.

The playing space of *Tartuffe* was therefore somewhat odd, yet it communicated its own truth. The openings of certain tombs were closed by doors or blinds, while the frescoes and sculptures from *The Perjured City* still decorated the rough-cast walls. The lateral stages formed mini-terraces that served as spaces for acting, or for storage of objects that represented daily life: piles of sheets to fold and place in baskets, piles of rugs to spread out on the beige flooring, chandeliers, cooking utensils, and low beds. The set was a luminous white; Oriental carpets were often covered by white sheets. Everyone sat on the ground, until Tartuffe suddenly entered (S. Moshkin Ghalam, an actor and dancer originally from Iran). Ever more nervous at Tartuffe's appearance, the characters then installed themselves on two benches of roughcast stone, placed center-stage, or on the elevated parts of the stage's periphery.

Entrances were made through the upstage gate or from downstage stairs, with actors emerging from the depths of the theatre, that is, from beneath the tiered seating. As in *The House of Atreus Cycle*, the actors gradually took over the entirety of the playing space. The house of Orgon became, then, the house of the Soleil, and in the end, the "police" threatened the audience just as much as they did the characters when "police officers" blocked the exits.

The costumes, invented by the actors, were not "of a period, but of a world," some inspired by a photo album from an Iranian family, others with more contemporary touches. Traditions blended together: Dorine (J. Carneiro da Cunha) wore a turban and pants, as did Elmire (N. Nityanandan), who completed the look with a fitted belt. White clothing united the group of women and Damis (H. Cinque), while black clothing united the men.

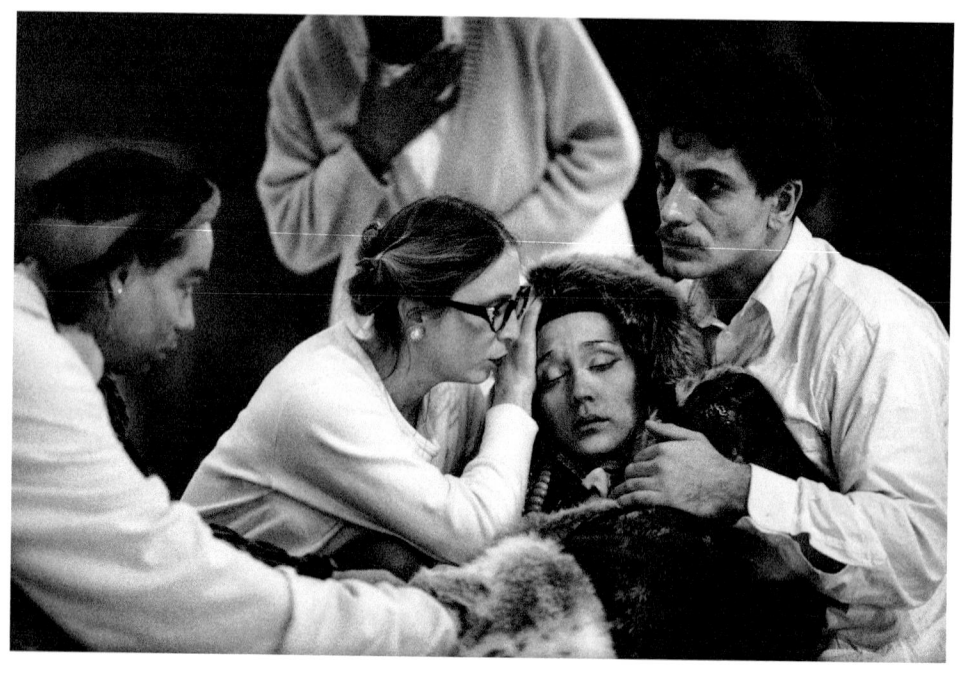

And Suddenly, Sleepless Nights. A Tibetan (R. Ramos Maza) from the visiting theatre troupe is sick. The theatre director (M. Jacques) and Clarissa from International Medical Solidarity (C. Pecheny) gather around her. Photo by Martine Franck, Magnum Photos.

Finally the camera …

The actors' performance was mobile and dynamic, first developed, as always, through working with *commedia dell'arte* and Indonesian *topeng* masks that would not, however, appear in the production. To reinvigorate the actors and encourage them to feel Molière's presence, Mnouchkine would sometimes throw them pages she pretended Molière had faxed. And the effect on performance of the black and white costumes? The style of performance that emerged in this *Tartuffe* resembled that of classic silent film. It was visible in the actors' expressions, the physical staging, the finely powdered white faces, and the faces exaggerated by black make-up. Flippe's and Pote's gags evoked Chaplin, a major reference for the Théâtre du Soleil. One could already see this tendency in *Mephisto* and *The Perjured City*, but the cinematic research appeared more noticeable in *Tartuffe* – in the theatrical composition of a cinematic style that referenced distant or extreme long shots, close-ups, tracking shots, and cutaways.

Because of a timely meeting with Éric Darmon, a filmmaker trained as an ethnologist, who had filmed several minutes of *The Perjured City* for the television channel TV5, Mnouchkine was prompted to bring a camera into the theatre during rehearsals. Appreciating his discrete, non-obtrusive efficiency, she decided Darmon should film the process of creating *Tartuffe*, since he knew how to make himself invisible. This effectively created a two-pronged entry for film at the Soleil: Mnouchkine would study the rushes in the evening during the rehearsal process before the actors saw them; and the completed and edited film of rehearsals would become a way to transmit an aspect of the Soleil's theatrical work to the public.

Tartuffe introduced a new way of working to the Soleil: allowing theatre in process to develop through the camera's eye. The film of rehearsals, *At the Soleil, Even at Night, Birthing Scenes* [*Au Soleil même la nuit, scènes d'accouchement*], would be followed by three films of full productions, *Drums on the Dam* [*Tambours sur la digue*], *The Last Caravanserai* [*Le Dernier Caravansérail*], and *The Survivors of Mad Hope* [*Les Naufragés du fol espoir*]. In the meantime, other filmmakers filmed some of the Soleil's other shows.[19] Mnouchkine's opinion on the role of cinema or video in relation to live performance had started to change. Of viewing the few filmed minutes (from around 1926) of Gogol's *The Government Inspector*, directed by Meyerhold, Mnouchkine said:

> It really touched me. Because it was proof that the show existed. I didn't dwell on the beauty of the staging, but the moment when the actor takes his partner's pinkie finger

in a teaspoon in order to woo her ... I understood that, maybe, all the same, for high-schoolers, college students, young actors, you need to leave a trace.

The process was evolving, and it had become less challenging to secure money to finance more substantial cinematic projects. For Mnouchkine, it wasn't a question of making an exact recording of her productions. Her deep ties to cinema inspired other goals.

With the experience gained during the *Tartuffe* rehearsals, filmed by Darmon's "sponge-like" camera, and with the troupe's agreement, cinema became part of the Soleil's process. Filming, editing, and the completed film work itself[20] marked the beginning of a new chapter, and the troupe took on new cinematic partners. *At the Soleil, Even at Night* not only depicted the preparation of a show but also was Mnouchkine's unwritten theatre manual (she appeared in the credits as "in harmony" with É. Darmon and C. Vilpoux) on the joys and pains, duties and risks, finances and day-to-day tasks of a life consecrated to theatre and to the unsettling and uncertain investigation of its laws. Two brief inter-titles in the *Tartuffe* film added suspense to the narrative drive, composed of sudden developments and surprises, everything geared toward opening night, at which point, of course, the film stopped. On screen, life and art mixed together without romanticism; the film moved from stage to office, kitchen to workshop, from arguments to marvels. After a 20-year period, she who said she was not a writer had in fact written her second training film on the role of theatre, troupe life, and the actor's performance, both based on "Molière material."

If the Soleil's shows had been in dialogue with one another since *1789*, through the cycles they formed and their various engagements with fiction and reality, accepting the traces that film provided served to intensify this dialogue. The company's post-*Tartuffe* works, rendered permanent through digital or film media, would now coexist with the older productions to form a kind of repertory.[21]

Displaced people: the news invades the theatre

The Soleil's political commitments during 1995 – taking a position against fundamentalism, the Avignon Declaration, and a hunger strike for the defense of Bosnia – were reinforced in 1996, when the theatre welcomed into its midst undocumented African families evicted from the Saint-Ambroise Church in Paris's 12th arrondissement. For two weeks, and then again at the end of July after another very violent eviction from the Saint-Bernard Church, where they had been camping since the

And Suddenly, Sleepless Nights. The stag dance, a feat of balance, performed by D. Bellugi-Vannuccini. Upstage, on either side of the door, two musicians blow into the long Tibetan trumpets that accompany the dance, with drumming by J-J. Lemêtre. A strange and magical moment. Photo by Michèle Laurent.

And Suddenly, Sleepless Nights. The *tashi shölpa* dance. On an empty stage, smooth and white, the Tibetan troupe shows its art to the French troupe. In the middle, Madame Tsültim (R. Ramos Maza) introduces six dancers, their faces covered by flat masks (S. Canto Sabido, D. Bellugi-Vannuccini, C. Pecheny, N. Sotnikoff, S. Nicolaï, and S. Lolov). They sing in Tibetan while dancing, accompanied by drums and bells. Photo by Martine Franck, Magnum Photos.

And Suddenly, Sleepless Nights. The Soleil's creativity in summoning the animal kingdom knows no bounds. H. Cinque, a child (A. Caoudal), and S. Canto Sabido sit on a horse caparisoned in gold. In the background, the Wandering Beggar (J. Carneiro da Cunha). Photo by Michèle Laurent.

end of June, 300 people, most of them from Mali, lived at the Soleil, sleeping in the Welcome Area or in tents, as well as in other theatres at the Cartoucherie. They were accompanied by representatives from a variety of aid organizations, such as Doctors Without Borders and the group, GISTI,[22] with whom the Soleil formed solid ties.

Mnouchkine drew together a mediators' association, composed of 26 people – former resistance fighters like Stéphane Hessel, anti-nuclear activist Admiral Sanguinetti, historians, legal experts, lawyers, magistrates, and philosophers – tasked with negotiating between the French state and immigrant families. Their meetings took place on stage, on the set of *Tartuffe*. The Soleil became temporary shelter as well as headquarters for the undocumented immigrants' fight, lodging adults and children who took care of themselves in a kind of joyful disorder, while also organizing protest actions. Fanta Koïta, a Malian-French woman and an aid to the undocumented, has stayed on at the Soleil as a living reminder of this period, selling ginger and hibiscus juice at every show from behind her cart in the Welcome Area. *And Suddenly, Sleepless Nights* [*Et soudain des nuits d'éveil*] was born out of this intense experience, the poster for this show reusing the newspaper dispatch-style already seen in the *Tartuffe* poster. But this time, the newspaper was on fire.

Writing "in harmony with ... "

The desire to speak about the theatre of Tibet, a kingdom brutally crushed by China, had inhabited Mnouchkine since her first trip to Nepal, even before the founding of the Théâtre du Soleil. It showed up in unpredictable fashion as she started contemplating how to defend undocumented immigrants in France. Hélène Cixous had already interviewed Father Henri Coindé, vicar of the Saint-Bernard Church, and dozens of Africans, in preparation for their new production. But Tibet slipped into the heart of the debates between the author and the director. Mnouchkine's interior world was Asian, and the "author function" had become less urgent: rather, a devised approach with actors' improvisations would anchor the new work.

The central theme would be hospitality, the gesture of welcoming strangers into the halls of a theatre that could only be the Soleil's. This was Mnouchkine's old dream for her theatre-house. But the strangers in the story would be Tibetans, and what's more, members of a theatre troupe. Thus, she molded together the story of engaged theatre artists (an engagement which every member of the troupe hadn't yet experienced because there were, as always, newcomers to the company), and the story of a martyred country. The Soleil amassed an abundance of information about Tibet in the theatre program and in the Welcome Area. The resulting production demonstrated how invasive an entire population's pain can be; how difficult, perturbing, and problematic engagement is; and how engagement itself raises doubts, hesitations, fears, and suffering, even when the victims are as discrete as Tibetans.

The preparation for *And Suddenly, Sleepless Nights* – created out of collective improvisations guided by Lemêtre's music, improvisations initiated by "concoctions" (agreements between the actors about where to start each improvisation) – involved meetings with Tibetan refugees, many of whom were living in France.[23] The actors also attended festivals at the Vincennes Pagoda, featuring dances, music, and songs; read Palden Gyatso's book[24] and even met this extraordinary Buddhist monk who had spent 33 years in Chinese prisons and had lived in exile in Dharamshala since 1992. For three months, they attended lectures; and every day they were taught songs and dances by Dolma Choeden, a teacher from Dharamshala's Tibetan Institute of Performing Arts. They became familiar with the Tibetan language and with Buddhism. They "Tibetified" themselves, H. Cixous explained, whose role in the production primarily concerned rewriting certain lines and proposing complementary scenes (notably the prologue and epilogue). Some scenes, like "The Delegation" ["La délégation"], were almost documentary, drawn from the troupe's meeting with Palden Gyatso, who came to speak about the torture he experienced in prison. Erhard Stiefel copied authentic Tibetan masks to use on stage; shoes required for spectacular masked dances were flown in.

The story, developed through improvisations, was as follows: rejected by the French government, a Tibetan delegation occupies a theatre, with the support of French actors, to protest against France's sale of military planes to China. Some characters stake their lives on winning recognition for Tibet's claims. Others, after the exaltation of the first moments, return to their daily occupations. *And Suddenly, Sleepless Nights* ends somewhat tragically: we hear the thrumming of French airplanes taking off for China. This provided, in fact, an ironic counterpoint to the fight of the real undocumented Malian immigrants, which ended for many of them on a positive note (immigration papers and a change in status).

For some French critics, the absence of a sustained dramatic text made the production boring, a judgment far from the audience's passionately moving experience, to which many letters received by the Soleil testify. Mnouchkine has responded by commenting that the text of a great work "can [indeed] nourish the actor's body, [but for *Sleepless Nights*] the process is the inverse: it's the actor's body that produces a more modest text. The poetry is elsewhere." And if the text was "haphazard,

accompanied by Tibetan blessings of good luck (*tashi delek*) –
light, happy, economical, urgent, and allusive,"[25] it was never
gratuitous. It was informed by the stage work that preceded, followed, and accompanied it; it vibrated with the music, colors,
and dances of the production. The language of *And Suddenly,
Sleepless Nights* shouldn't be perceived independent of these
factors, no more than the texts of the Soleil's great collective
creations of the 1970s. However, a significant difference from
those early works was visible in the construction of scenes that
didn't deal with Tibet, but rather with the actors confronted by
Tibet. The presence of "actor-characters," the input of Tibetans
whose traditions and language were welcomed and studied by
the Soleil's performers, and the children who played a role in
the fable all contributed to the story's several layers, constantly
turning it into meta-theatre.

As the "performers from the host-theatre" didn't only play
their own roles, but also that of "the others," it was easy for
the audience to misunderstand who the Tibetan characters
were. The Soleil's Duccio Bellugi-Vannuccini performed the
very old and difficult stag dance (*shawa chakar*), pushing his
and his lama-character's body to the limit: his performance was
deemed to be more authentic than when the dance was performed by real Tibetan monks later on.[26] This shared human
experience gave the audience the opportunity to traverse a full
range of emotions and, at the same time, experience a variable
rapport with the story being told – from illusion to distance,
from a feeling of strangeness to marveling, from laughter to
tears. During the Moscow tour, the audience was even offered
beignets or baguettes to share in the morning after their "sleepless night." The space between fiction and the realities of Tibet
and the Soleil, meant to have been transposed, appeared to be
very thin. The "absence of literature," as Mnouchkine called it,
decreased that distance even more, since the dialogue was taken
from everyday life.

In fact, the distance the show continually played with should
be understood more as "disruption,"[27] that is, evidence of how
an important event's repercussions transform daily life and
cause perspectives to shift. Disruption also allowed the Soleil
to introduce theatrical wonders, for example, Tibetan dances
(*tashi shölpa*); and moments of dissonance, such as the apparition in the "Yak Hunt" scene of the masked characters, the
Dames Pantalon (H. Cinque and M-P. Ramo Guinard). The
yak itself took the form of a total body mask created by E.
Stiefel, as did the Wandering Beggar (J. Carneiro da Cunha),
a marginalized figure – border-crosser, poet, and woman of
the people. In this production, the coexistence of Tibetan and
commedia dell'arte masks served to spark a conversation about
theatre. The occurrence of two fictional troupes face-to-face

gave shape to the eternal question of the Théâtre du Soleil: how can Western theatre welcome Eastern theatre and be nourished by it? This was accompanied by another question: how do you avoid becoming too realistic when approaching the real so closely? The responses, sometimes tinged with humor and self-parody, were staged beneath the enormous eyes of Buddha, painted on the bleached upstage wall of the playing space.

Stylized without being caricatured, the characters often had the panache of characters from classic silent films. The actors created them at the intersection of sculpture, which carved them into space, and music. J-J. Lemêtre and his orchestra of 15 Tibetan instruments, as well as 30 other invented ones – not to mention others which came from 30 different countries, including a piano, since the action concerned Europeans – breathed rhythmic life into all the characters. The resulting work has been described as a "symphony of approaches."[28] "One doesn't walk on a theatre stage, one advances," said the character, the Intern (Delphine Cottu). And, indeed, each actor's individual pilgrimage across the sparkling white stage converged to form the troupe's common advance, in which several new actors appeared – part of an anxious progression of more than 30 years across a continent called Theatre. The actors confessed to the terror that took hold on the first days of rehearsals in front of the void, where they had to find themselves: a sacred terror, without which it would have been impossible to start the ritualistic journey that precedes the creation of every show.[29]

Voice of Duccio Bellugi-Vannuccini

> "It was a magnificent experience, among the most beautiful roles I've ever had the chance to play. Touring in Moscow, it was so moving to meet a small group of Tibetan refugees. For them, the show was an illumination and they, in turn, enlightened us in the restaurant where they brought us to eat Tibetan food. Those are the kinds of nights when you say to yourself: this is what theatre is for."

While Thinking about Lanterns

The breadth of the Soleil's research can be better understood in comparing *And Suddenly, Sleepless Nights* with *Drums on the Dam: In the Form of an Ancient Puppet Play Performed by Actors* [*Tambours sur la digue, sous forme de pièce ancienne pour marionnettes jouée par des acteurs*]; the two played in repertory in 1999.[30] After getting extremely close to lived experience, the company took a tremendous step back from it. For the production that closed out the century, the Soleil returned to the epic form of *The Shakespeare* and *House of Atreus Cycles*.

Drums on the Dam. The stage is surrounded by a strip of white pebbles, like a Noh stage. Its central part is submersible. The river is present: there is real water, that of the final flood in which the little puppets resembling the characters will float, but there is also water represented by the waving of vast swaths of silk. Two footbridges upstage allow for back entrances and exits. The music is located stage right. The footlights are rectangular lanterns. On the back wall, diversely painted silk backdrops change the color of the sky and the countryside. There are 17 different silk drops, painted by Y. de Maisonneuve and D. Martin. Archives Guy-Claude François.

Drums on the Dam. The actor-puppets and their *kokens.* The Chancellor (D. Bellugi-Vannuccini) is assassinated by Lord Hun (S. Lolov). Manipulators: V. Mangado, S. Decourchelle, M. Jacques. One of the *koken* pulls a red string from the Chancellor's clothing to symbolize flowing blood. Photo by Martine Franck, Magnum Photos.

"I believe the theatre should be political and historical and sacred and contemporary and mythological. It is only the proportions which change from production to production." (Ariane Mnouchkine, press conference in Moscow, *Nezavissimaja Gazeta*, February 24, 1998.)

It invented its own bunraku, based on traditional Japanese form. What's more, it rediscovered in this imaginary form a type of kabuki rarely staged, in which the kabuki actors who so admired the great bunraku puppets would sometimes act as though they were puppets, right in the middle of their show.

As we have observed, the composition of the group had changed. Sophie Moscoso, Mnouchkine's assistant, left the Soleil.[31] The person who replaced her, Charles-Henri Bradier, was a student, as she had been when she first arrived, but his journey resembled a rite of passage. First enthralled by *The House of Atreus Cycle*, which he had seen several times, Bradier became involved with the movement surrounding the *Avignon Declaration* in July 1995. That fall, he oversaw the Declaration office and also helped at the bar in the Welcome Area and with administrative work, sharing the load. He returned to the Soleil for the adventure with the undocumented immigrants, and again in 1997, for the Epopea movement ("utopian" meetings of the cultural world, outside of corporate and geographical boundaries). He then produced the troupe of actor Christophe Rauck, who had recently left the company, at the Soleil. He also organized a huge training course, at the conclusion of which new actors joined the troupe – several of whom are still present today. Mnouchkine asked him to transcribe *And Suddenly, Sleepless Nights*' improvisational texts from cassette recordings, which were then transmitted by email to Cixous for editing.

Voice of Charles-Henri Bradier

"One day, in the kitchen, Ariane, reflecting on her next project, told me she would like to go to India, and asked me to accompany her on this preparatory journey. I was extremely surprised! I think that demonstrates one of her best qualities, trusting her youngest collaborators very quickly and very easily. She proposed I be like Siddhartha and partake of an initiatory trip to the country of theatre – so I went along in the company of one of theatre's greatest servants! The gift of a lifetime. We first went to Sri Lanka, where Ariane had discovered an unsophisticated, very ancient form of traditional dance, then to Kerala, to the origins of theatre, to rediscover what had survived and what had been left behind in the shadows."[32]

Drums on the Dam. The masks of a girl (J. Marvan Enriquez) and of the mother of the puppet master (E. Doe Bruce). Photo by Michèle Laurent.

Upon returning to France, Bradier officially became the new assistant. With him, computers and video cameras arrived at the Soleil as tools of creation.

In Cixous's archives, preparatory notes for the next work, dating from August 1998, indicate two possible directions: showing a world in peril, and being part of the world of theatre. The ritual "debates" between the director and the author are preserved in the exchange of notes from this period. In one of them, Mnouchkine intones: "The whole world is a *Cherry Orchard*, the earth is a *Cherry Orchard*, the planet is a *Cherry Orchard*." Later on, she imagines a certain M. Six-Hou, an old Chinese poet, who would narrate the opening of a puppet theatre, a theatre of resistance.[33] In a more developed, sophisticated musing on the same topic, Six-Hou would become M. Hsi-Xou, and Mnouchkine would suggest to Cixous (as recounted in a published essay):

> How about you write a play, an ancient play, which would have been written by the poet Hsi-Xou, which would sometimes be enacted by puppets, sometimes by actors, who would sometimes be women playing all the roles, sometimes men, depending on which kingdom the show was presented in, under which laws, and which prohibitions? [And Cixous adds:] This is what the director said to the author one day. And so the author started to write the play which would have been written by her ancient predecessor and master, the poet Hsi-Xhou.[34]

Cixous accordingly drafted a first version, entitled *While Thinking about Lanterns* [*En contemplant les lanternes*], in which a young (perhaps Noh) actor, the inheritor of his line, has to choose between armed resistance, vital for the future of his country, and his fidelity to his ancestral art, which also has to be protected. With this story in mind, all the actors went on a trip to Asia, financed by the Soleil. "We had never done it before," says Mnouchkine, "because we didn't have the means, even if certain actors had already been to India when we were working on *The Indiad*."[35] The trip provided an education for the renewed troupe – both collective and uniquely personal for each member.

Voice of Charles-Henri Bradier

> "*Before starting rehearsals, which she had wanted to base on the disciplined connection between body, music, and performance practiced by traditional Asian theatres, Ariane asked the actors, as she herself had done in 1964, to 'lose themselves' in Asia, in this 'continent of theatre.' We had*

Drums on the Dam. A fitting of a flexible mask, created by each actor and by M-A. Cardoso Ferreira. Making and fitting masks was part of the research process. On the table, the heads of little puppets, doubles of the characters, which S. Nicolaï would finish constructing. (See also Transverse Perspectives of this study.) Photo by Martine Franck, Magnum Photos.

provided them with leads, itineraries, and contacts in the countries we suggested they survey, because we believed these aesthetic terrains were particularly 'rich' in potential discoveries, countries such as India, Japan, Taiwan, China, Korea, and Bali, as well as Cambodia, Vietnam, and Indonesia. Ariane traveled as well. It was the beginning of email, and the troupe would sometimes connect and meet up here or there for particular events, those discovered by a few actors and immediately shared with the others. Our special relationships with Taiwan (Wu Hsing Kuo and the Contemporary Legend Theatre) and Korea (Kim Duk Soo and the traditional orchestral ensemble SamulNori Hanullim) date from that period."[36]

The Soleil's *Cherry Orchard*

The creation of the definitive version of *Drums on the Dam* took over nine months; it was "stitched together" in a back-and-forth between writing and acting that had no equivalent in any known writing for the stage. The central story addressed the very recent news from China of the catastrophic Yellow River floods and the destruction of the largest dam in the world, the Three Gorges. But it was placed in a far-off past. From the first week of rehearsals, it became obvious, although mostly unforeseen, that the actors should enact puppets. These puppets, who also had handlers, were developed at first as string marionettes, using filmed improvisations as aids. A *samulnoria* (Korean drums) teacher, Han Jae Sok, sent by master drummer Kim Duk Soo, whom they had met in their preliminary travels, came to teach his art to the actors, who became virtuosos. They produced a spectacular drum performance for a key episode of the show. The troupe also re-watched Kenji Mizoguchi's[37] and Akira Kurosawa's entire cinematic output. It was not until right at the very end of rehearsals that they discovered the need for a different kind of puppet. This also necessitated the presence of the puppeteers or *koken*[38] found in bunraku, dressed and veiled in black. The cast, then, had to be doubled.

The Soleil dug deep into Asian legends and sophisticated theatrical techniques, perusing the ancient history of China whose floods and natural disasters would be used for this ecological fable without referencing any precise historical characters. It adapted bunraku and Japanese Noh as its form. But the issues raised were contemporary, tied to corruption, urbanization, poorly regulated deforestation, dams constructed like the defective walls of modern buildings, political decision-making and the fratricidal wars it produces, as terrible as any natural disasters – internal floods against which there are no dams.

The company traveled a great distance to address subjects that touch us very closely.

Radical and splendid, the production appeared to emerge from the dawn of time: it explored the heart of theatre, seeking its "essential oil."[39] The text seemed to be polished by Noh's greats, whose works, translated into English, Hélène Cixous had plunged into in Chicago while teaching there, during the troupe's pilgrimage to Asia. The text was given a particular rhythm and simplified for the strange voices which slowly spoke it, emerging from actors playing the roles of huge puppets manipulated by their fellow actors transformed into *koken*. An unprecedented genre was born from the ancient traditions, in which the puppet found its voice.[40] To arrive at this result, 27 versions of the script were drawn up, maybe more – written, unwritten, and rewritten with the help of computer, fax, and video – tested on stage, with multiple experiments in diction (haiku, gibberish, lyric song), and according to the constraints mercilessly required by puppet form.

Mnouchkine's art sought a peaceful and at the same time troubling shape, as though a suspended performance of life, death, and History, following the path of the great thinkers/theatre makers Edward Gordon Craig (with his reflection on the puppet as the ancestor of the actor[41]) and Vsevolod Meyerhold (with his affirmation that he who masters the "art of directing the puppet theatre actor [knows] the secrets of theatrical marvels which we as theatre people unfortunately don't know"[42]). The Soleil created superb and terrifying "über-marionettes," as Craig would have said. Multiple forms of distancing made them mysterious, simultaneously separating and drawing together the characters, puppets, actors, and puppet handlers – the latter of whom were also like on-stage representatives of the director and musician.

Was it the actress or her handlers (J. Carneiro da Cunha; Jean-Charles Maricot, Sergio Canto Sabido, and Alexandre Roccoli) who made the squat and silky silhouette of old Lord Khang quaver?[43] Was it the handlers who activated the puppets' rippling clothes, or was it Lemêtre's orchestral music – music in which the bunraku shamisen coexisted with the oboe – or was it the powerful bellows suggesting a rising storm? The *koken*'s gaze, beneath their black veil, was riveted to their puppets, following the movements of the live actors who often led them. But it was they who supported the actor-puppets for entrances and exits, when the "puppets" progressively lost the acting energy that had animated them, becoming once again inert material, pure objects. *Koken* also guided the puppets when they needed to overcome an obstacle or navigate a complex route through the set; they lifted them in fabulous classical dance moves when puppets triumphed, commanded, or agonized and died, leaking a thin red thread from their wounded sides. The *koken* also supported some of the actor-puppet's weight to help achieve the gliding step of Noh, while the music almost visibly raised the actors' feet, or shook a carpet of air behind them. "The director must clean the ice in front of the actors, so they can skate freely on it," Mnouchkine says.[44] An actress in roller-skates (Dominique Jambert) traversed the stage, twirling, during *And Suddenly, Sleepless Nights*. In *Drums on the Dam*, the actors metaphorically skated, escaping their weight and flying, inhabiting the form of the puppet they'd invented.

A young "rebel girl" found aesthetic sanctuary in a colorful but worn doll with delicate white porcelain hands, which looked as though they had been broken and repaired (Duan, the daughter of the soothsayer: R. Ramos Maza and her manipulators: S. Canto Sabido and V. Mangado). Artistically stiff, fine and immobile, all the puppet hands were overwhelming in their delicate inertia. Most often, it was the *koken* who carried the props (fans, umbrellas, swords, lanterns), and who manipulated them. The incessant movement came from the rest of the puppet's body, from its articulated zones – swinging, swaying, staggering from left to right, always seeking equilibrium, which was constantly lost and then found again.

Everything was precise, drawn as though an etching. The *koken* sometimes faded away beneath their black uniforms; other times, they suddenly appeared from afar, flattened by the colorful backdrop, and seemed to be nothing but the shadows of the huge puppets, which suddenly became completely autonomous. The action took place between the sky and a river. The elements were represented by silk backdrops: 17 vertical wall coverings with subtle color gradients, regularly leafed through, painted with clouds or the countryside. "The colors of the sky change so quickly," says Duan, and two cloths are spread out to make waves, blue water which would soon be reddened with the fighters' blood.

The light, always so sunny at the Cartoucherie, was dimmed: the production was installed in the Welcome Area and thus the "sky" was less able to be lit than what might have been accomplished in the third nave of the Cartoucherie, with its glass roof and fluorescent lights. In addition, the *koken*'s black uniforms darkened the color palette. In this creation, for which the troupe had risked a great deal and conquered its fears and frequent despondency, the mood was somber. At the end of the performance, a flood submerged everything; water invaded the stage and carried away the puppet master's puppets. Up to his neck in water and watched over by his *koken*, the puppet master saved, one by one, the dolls representing all the puppet-characters in the show – his dear artists –and placed them side-by-side on the edge of the flooded stage, facing the audience. At that point, the

Drums on the Dam. The lantern seller (R. Ramos Maza; manipulators: S. Canto Sabido and V. Mangado) and the Chancellor (D. Bellugi-Vannuccini; manipulators: V. Mangado, S. Decourchelle). Photo by Martine Franck, Magnum Photos.

Drums on the Dam. Lord Hun (S. Lolov; manipulator: M. Jacques) and the Chief Intendant (M. Azencot; manipulator: S. Canto Sabido). The delicate hands of the actor-puppets hold the fans. Photo by Martine Franck, Magnum Photos.

Drums on the Dam. Duan (R. Ramos Maza) and Wang Po (S. Lolov) have a "flying kiss." The characters, executed by the actor-puppets and their *koken*, are in a double lift, requiring tremendous physical effort. In the film of the production, the "flying kiss" would be transformed, after a long exploration, into an "underwater kiss" (under waving red silks). Photo by Michèle Laurent.

Drums on the Dam. Opposite: Madame Li, noodle seller (J. Carneiro da Cunha; manipulators: S. Canto Sabido and J-C. Maricot) and above: her servant Kisa (S. Raynal), who juggles Chinese plates. Photo by Martine Franck, Magnum Photos.

audience might have also remembered the innumerable rows of dolls that stared at them from the top of the walls of the set in *Sihanouk*. They might have thought of the theatrical figurines made of soft bread from Vilno, the Jewish ghetto, during the Nazi reign of terror, signs of art that Mnouchkine often evoked. Resistance through art alone? Or was the Soleil speaking of the immortality of the art of theatre, beginning with puppets?

What was brought to incandescence were the greatly disturbing, grotesque dialectics of the living and the motionless, of the animate and the inanimate, at the very heart of actors' work. The public was seized both ethically and aesthetically, their emotions intensified by recognizing the sum of the actors' efforts, actors' daily and individual research prior to the communal work of theatrical creation, the latter completely dependent on the former. The work of art happens, as Craig tells us, by animating precious material.

The emotion produced by *Drums on the Dam* bordered on the sacred. "The face of the puppet is motionless. Yet innumerable expressions of our passions flicker across this mirror, this motionless face. The space is all the larger for it," writes Hélène Cixous.[45] Tears fell on the young woman's face who sat next to me in the audience one night. In response to my questioning, she murmured: "The eyes, it's the eyes," because the hands were not the only parts of the body to have conquered immobility. The faces of the actors were covered with flexible masks, which they had sewn by hand with gauze and nylon, stuffed with wool, and painted or decorated. This deformed them, gave them another shape, and made the actors unrecognizable. In *Drums on the Dam*, where it was less a matter of constraint than conquest, the sunken eyes seemed to be made of wood or stone. "It's the ecstasy that overcomes the face that makes us understand the immensity of the gods," Cixous continues. A meta-puppet body in ecstasy, which Craig defined as an actor with more fire and less ego; those brilliant and steady puppet gazes, which were actually the living actors' eyes, offered the representation of a transcendent dimension. It's the transcendence of art, the art of theatre, which carries with it, conjures up, and communicates the energy necessary to confront obscurity. This gives wings to audience members, those same wings that Mnouchkine, by making them walk the puppets' path, bestowed upon her actors.

With this frequently performed and grandly toured production, it seemed the Soleil had finished with the Asian forms that had nourished it. Nevertheless, these forms continue to dwell in the foundation of the company's work, even if they are no longer directly summoned. And this farewell, far from being an ending, was a source of inspiration. During *Drums on the Dam*'s 2001 Tokyo tour, bunraku masters thanked the Soleil for bringing their lost treasure back to them, for offering leads on how to keep developing their tradition. Reinvented freely but respectfully by others, a tradition can come back to life; this is one of the welcome results of intercultural exchange. And if Mnouchkine noticed the disappearance of certain traditions in her 1998 trip to India, she could also delight in knowing that after *Drums on the Dam* passed through Tokyo, the kabuki theatre Shinbashi Embuyo produced *The Temple of the Golden Pavilion*. There, for a long time, the celebrated *onnogata* Bando Tamasaburo V, who played the princess Yuki, would perform as a bunraku puppet manipulated by a *koken* – a kabuki *koken*, the same as at the Soleil – amidst a snowfall of pink petals falling from a cherry tree.

Notes

1 Ariane Mnouchkine, in *Le Monde*, February 26, 1990. In this chapter, unattributed quotes by Soleil members and by Ariane Mnouchkine come from one of the several interviews Béatrice Picon-Vallin conducted with them and recorded from 2010 to 2014.
2 Hélène Cixous, in the preface of the republished Hélènc Cixous, *La Ville parjure ou le Réveil des Érinyes* (Paris: Théâtre du Soleil/Éditions Théâtrales, 2010), 9.
3 Guard and guardian characters are recurrent in the Soleil's work. See *And Suddenly, Sleepless Nights*, 1997, or the Atfaab's *Nightwatch*, 2013. The Théâtre du Soleil's guard, Hector Ortiz, was listed in the credits as "Director of Shadows." Today his replacement, Azizullah Hamrah, responds to the title "Nightwatch."
4 Hélène Cixous, *La Ville parjure ou le Réveil des Érinyes*, 15.
5 Anne-Marie Casteret, *l'Affaire du sang* (Paris: La Découverte, 1992).
6 Hélène Cixous, *La Ville parjure ou le Réveil des Érinyes*, 202.
7 It was most likely local Islamist groups who carried out this killing.
8 These two characters will continue to appear in the Soleil's work, notably during a training course in 2009.
9 *Raï* is a popular form of Algerian music.
10 For *Tartuffe*, there was a recorded soundtrack.
11 Ariane Mnouchkine, "Mettre en scène," *Le Monde*, Avignon special edition, July 1995.
12 See *Le Monde*, July 6, 1995.
13 See also Chapter Seven of this study.
14 This criticism also includes the "white supremacist Christian order" in the United States. Persian and Indian poems praising tolerance and castigating ethical defeat were also included in the program.
15 Georges Bonnaud, in "Chronique de l'illusion efficace (1968–1980)," *Le Théâtre d'intervention depuis 1968*, vol. 1 (Paris: l'Âge d'homme, 1983), 38.
16 Ariane Mnouchkine, in *AIDA, Argentine, une culture interdite* (Paris: Maspero, 1981).
17 See Ariane Mnouchkine and Patrice Chéreau, "La liberté est une peau de chagrin," *Le Monde*, December 21, 1979. See also Sarah Guthu, www.jsis.washington.edu.

18 See Béatrice Hamidi-Kim, *Les Cités du théâtre politique en France depuis 1989* (Paris: l'Entretemps, 2013).

19 Bernard Sobel (whom A. Mnouchkine had liked for his televised adaption of *Lulu*) filmed *Mephisto* (1980) and *The Indiad* (1987).

20 For the *Tartuffe/rehearsals* film, there were 524 hours of rushes in beta-numeric video; edited by Catherine Vilpoux, who became a faithful and essential film partner to Ariane Mnouchkine as director.

21 The experience of filming *Tartuffe* would have an immediate impact: *The Perjured City*, which was playing at the same time as *Tartuffe*, would be rapidly filmed, thanks to the appearance of an additional camera for one day. But these are two very different types of films.

22 The GISTI is an information and aid group for immigrants.

23 Cixous and Mnouchkine met Jetsun Pema, the sister of the Dalai Lama, and Matthieu Ricard at Dharamshala. Mnouchkine, Sophie Moscoso, Charles-Henri Bradier, and actors also went to the Alexandra David-Néel Foundation in Digne, France.

24 Palden Gyatso, with Tsering Shakya, *Le Feu sous la neige* (Paris: Actes Sud, 1997).

25 Hélène Cixous, in "Un moment de conversion," *Et Soudain des nuits d'éveil* [*And Suddenly, Sleepless Nights*] theatre program.

26 In 2001, the Soleil welcomed monks from Shechen, a monastery in Nepal where Matthieu Ricard had taken up residence and revived the spectacular practice of sacred dances. Their dance performances were accompanied by a two-week long conference on "Must we really dance with China?" reuniting the best international specialists on the relationship between China and Tibet, as well as the Chinese dissidents Harry Wu and Wei Jingsheng, whose trials l'AIDA had denounced at the time.

27 Ariane Mnouchkine, "Plus on avance, plus on doute," *Journal du théâtre*, February 9, 1998, 4.

28 Ariane Mnouchkine, in an oral interview with R. Kretchetova, Moscow, June 13, 1998.

29 Soleil actors, during an audience talkback at the Red Army Theatre, Moscow, June 11, 1998.

30 *And Suddenly, Sleepless Nights* played from December 1997 to May 1998. The show was reprised in 1999 in repertory with *Drums on the Dam*, created in September that same year.

31 Having left after *The Perjured City*, Sophie Moscoso returned to the Soleil while the undocumented immigrants were there and oversaw the relationship with the mediators' association. One could thus say that she was Mnouchkine's assistant for a period of 28 years (but not during *Molière* or *Tartuffe*).

32 Charles-Henri Bradier, in an interview on January 14, 2012 with authors Roberta Gandolfi and Silvia Bottiroli, published in Italian, in Gandolfi and Bottiroli, *Un teatro attraversato dal mondo: Il Théâtre du Soleil oggi* (Pisa: Titivillus, 2012).

33 See Hélène Cixous Archives, *Tambours sur la digue* [*Drums on the Dam*] Dossier, Bibliothèque Nationale de France.

34 Hélène Cixous, "L'auteur soufflé," www.theatre-du-soleil.fr.

35 Ariane Mnouchkine, interview with Béatrice Picon-Vallin, www.theatre-du-soleil.fr.

36 Some made the choice (R. Ramos Maza and N. Sotnikoff) to stay in one village to study Hebei's Chinese opera with Mrs. Pei Yanling.

37 During her first trip to Asia, Ariane Mnouchkine had interviewed Mizoguchi's collaborators; she published upon her return "Six

entretiens autour de Mizoguchi" in *Les Cahiers du cinéma*, no. 158 (1964), 5.

38 The term used by the Soleil is also used here somewhat improperly because *koken* are the stagehands in kabuki. But their function is also to help the actors in their performance, and they are also often dressed in black.

39 See Edward Gordon Craig, "L'Acteur et la surmarionnette," in *De l'art du théâtre* (Paris: Circé, 1999), 79–106.

40 The puppets spoke, rather than having a singer-narrator as in bunraku.

41 See A. Héliot, "La quête spirituelle d'Ariane Mnouchkine," *Le Figaro*, August 27, 1999.

42 Vsevolod Meyerhold, "Dédicace à S. Obraztsov," in *Écrits sur le théâtre*, vol. IV (Paris: l'Âge d'Homme, 1992), 279.

43 See Hélène Cixous, in the theatre program notes of *Tambours sur la digue* [*Drums on the Dam*].

44 Ariane Mnouchkine, in R. Doljanskij, "Ariane Mnouchkine, je dois nettoyer la glace," *Kommersant*, February 20, 1998.

45 Hélène Cixous, in the theatre program notes of *Tambours sur la digue*.

The Last Caravanserai (Odysseys): Origins and Destinies, Narrative Thread 8, "En route to Australia." Enveloped by the immense silks set into motion by their comrades, the Soleil actors (D. Bellugi-Vannuccini, M. Durozier, S. Nicolaï, D. Jambert, V. Mangado, S. Brottet-Michel) perform the dangerous and often tragic crossings (here of the Indian Ocean) undertaken by migrants on makeshift boats. Photo by Michèle Laurent.

Chapter 7   Ten years of collective creation: between cinema-theatre, documentary theatre, and the lyrical epic

"It was a first draft. We had named it, for that matter, The Golden Age: First Draft. *I consider it today the first draft of other plays, like* The Last Caravanserai *or* Ephemera.*"*

Ariane Mnouchkine[1]

"One makes the choice to share, to remain a collective."

Ariane Mnouchkine[2]

The first decade of the twenty-first century – marked by September 11, 2001, which occurred during the Japanese tour of *Drums on the Dam,* marked as well by the troupe's discovery of the Sangatte refugee and migrant camp[3] and the Australian refugee internment camps[4] – landed Ariane Mnouchkine and the Soleil in an increasingly brutal present. Of course, ever since *Sihanouk,* the major political themes of the end of the twentieth and the beginning of the twenty-first centuries – the massacres, fratricidal wars, and exoduses – had figured in the Soleil's work; and the question of loss, disappearance, separation, and in particular, the exile of "migratory humans" had tormented Mnouchkine. Having first appeared as a potential danger for Orgon's family in *Tartuffe,* exile would inspire the three collective creations that followed (2002 to 2010). This inspiration worked on different levels—on a more sociological level (the contemporary flux of migrants in *Le Dernier Caravansérail* [*The Last Caravanserai*], 2003), a more intimate one (the tearing apart of families in *Les Éphémères* [*Ephemera*], 2006), and a more historical one (the great expeditions of the new "conquistadors" at the beginning of the twentieth century to the "promised land" of Patagonia in *Les Naufragés du Fol Espoir: Aurores* [*The Survivors of Mad Hope: Dawn*], 2010). Exile also influenced the work that Mnouchkine undertook with Hélène Cinque and the Aftaab Theatre of Kabul,[5] whose *Nightwatch* [*La Ronde de Nuit*] was rehearsed and performed at the Cartoucherie.

The political and social engagement of the Soleil, through its plays, its public stances, and the support it had given to different

"Asia – I'm still there through the stories we stage; I can also lose track of it – but the treasure is in me now and I can never really lose it." (Ariane Mnouchkine, interview with H. Cixous and B. Picon-Vallin, 2004, www .theatre-du-soleil.fr.)

"I think that with *Ephemera* we prove in a way that theatre doesn't need to fear cinema. This play carries the mark of cinematic writing, but without a screen or special techniques, other than theatricality." (Ariane Mnouchkine, from notes taken by C-H. Bradier during the filming of *Ephemera*, April 2005.)

causes, completes the image of a theatre continually touched by the bumps and jolts of a world in motion. During this first decade of the twentieth century, the activity of l'AIDA[6] was more and more closely linked to the troupe's artistic work. The Soleil lent its support to Chilean artists, to the imprisoned heroes of the Prague Spring, to Argentine artists, and to Algerian artists and journalists; in 1997, when Christophe Floderer took up the reins of the association's activities, he negotiated numerous cases for asylum seekers, while also establishing mechanisms to organize tours of the Soleil's plays. In 2003, after *The Last Caravanserai*, Elaine Méric took on the leadership of supporting certain refugees whom the Soleil had met at Sangatte, helping other refugees "escape" Australian camps, guaranteeing the regular entry into French territory of Aftaab Theatre company members, and responding to immigration problems encountered by the non-European actors of the troupe.

The attention afforded these crises by Mnouchkine, a conscience-driven traveler, and undoubtedly, the memory of her father's exile from Leningrad in 1923 – an autobiographical detail that she rarely addressed in her work before *Ephemera* – has profoundly influenced this recent decade of the Soleil's work. A haunting vision, transmitted to the young Mnouchkine by her aunt Galina, inflected her approach: the image of Asian soldiers, frozen to death, filing by on their wagons and pulled ever onward by trotting horses. Alexandre Mnouchkine had witnessed this from the window of a train, stopped by the White Army as it crisscrossed Siberia on its errant journey. The vision inscribed itself in Mnouchkine's father and "then, forever, in her."[7]

Ariane Mnouchkine's cinema-theatre

We recognize the new face of the twenty-first-century Théâtre du Soleil by the "films of theatre" produced at the Cartoucherie, each of which influenced the play that would follow. However, it's important to note that the films are not the plays; they are cinematographic recreations of theatrical works, for which Mnouchkine sought effective methods of rendering the plays acceptable on screen. For *Drums on the Dam*, for example, she accentuated the highly theatrical aspect of the play while filming it, thus re-injecting theatre into film through purely cinematographic means. It is difficult, here, to account for the considerable work of transposition these "films of theatre"[8] necessitated.

The artistic and technical experiments of the filmmaking – writing the script, organizing the filming, framing the shots, adapting the scenery, and completing the montage and post-production work – were in part shared by the troupe, which

The Survivors of Mad Hope (filming). *Mise en abyme* of the play: the Cartoucherie is transformed into a film studio; the tiered seating has disappeared; the stage is enlarged; new sets are created. The troupe performs for today's camera the 1914 filming, as well as characters actively engaged in technical work. In the center: Jean Salvatore (S. Nicolaï) and Alice (G. Kraghede-Bellugi). On the left: A. Mnouchkine and J-P. Meurisse, the cameraman. Photo by Michèle Laurent.

The actors, in costume, review the day's shots with Mnouchkine. From left to right: M. Larrañaga y Ausin, D. Jambert, J. Carneiro da Cunha, A. Mnouchkine, C-H. Bradier. Back row: J. Jancsó, A. Simma, S. Nicolaï, A. Milléquant, J-S. Merle, P. Giusti, O. Corsini, V. Mangado, M. Bauduin, S. Bonneau, P. Poignand, M. Durozier, E. Doe Bruce, A. Sarybekian. Photo by Michèle Laurent.

The Last Caravanserai (filming). Mnouchkine views on her computer the rough cut she has created with the actors. Around her, from right to left: P. Guarise, D. Santonja-Ruiz, S. Masson, J. Marvan Enriquez, J. James. Back row: E. Dorand, V. Mangado. Photo by Michèle Laurent.

The Survivors of Mad Hope (Dawn). Jean Salvatore (S. Nicolaï) revives Anna, the freezing schoolteacher (D. Jambert), by rubbing her body with snow. On the left, the camera and the film crew in charge of special effects. From left to right: A. Sarybekian, M. Durozier, S. Jailloux, J. Carneiro da Cunha, A. Borsari, A. Milléquant, P. Giusti, F. Voruz. Photo by Michèle Laurent.

performed in front of the camera, and then gathered around the test screens to review and comment on the shots before retaking them. In this, another facet of the practice of collective creation, the actors worked side by side with film professionals close to the troupe. This process contaminated the theatrical work, which itself had been nourished since the first days of the Soleil by the great masterpieces of cinematic history, as if each play were conceived of and nurtured in a carefully chosen program of cinematic influences. With its films of theatre, the Soleil breathed new life into its approach to theatrical interpretation and collective creation, especially as the new digital tools generated and continue to generate new methods of searching for what "works" theatrically.

Cinema itself finally found its legitimate place on stage in the eyes of Mnouchkine through small onstage screens (showing excerpts of *The Kid* in *The Last Caravanserai*, of *King Kong* and *Stagecoach* in *Ephemera*),[9] or more directly through onstage representations of filmmaking: for example, the central narrative of *Mad Hope* portrays the shooting of a silent film, the action of which is simultaneously acted and projected live. Indeed, there has been a constant exchange between the disciplines of film and theatre, in the same space, within the same company – the computer safeguarding the memory and the animated traces of the filmed investigatory improvisations and experimentations. The Soleil's films of theatre nourished the collective creations *The Last Caravanserai*, *Ephemera*, and *Mad Hope*. For instance, subtitling, the simplest of cinematic techniques, was employed during international tours and in different versions of the *Drums on the Dam* DVD; it undoubtedly inspired the subtitling (actually supertitling) in the play-version of *The Last Caravanserai*. Furthermore, the increasingly cosmopolitan composition of the troupe, the characters created and languages used – each of the actors having a go at speaking the language of the other – also made supertitling an obvious solution to comprehension issues. Likewise, the voice-overs of *The Last Caravanserai* and *Mad Hope* grew out of the voice of the narrator-director in the *Drums on the Dam* film, while also sharing a genealogy with the tradition of the *benshi*, the commentator in early Japanese cinema, whose function is still performed in Tokyo today.

The origins of the rolling platforms that populate the scenes of these three plays can be attributed to several sources: the camera dolly that was mounted on a rolling platform to film *Drums on the Dam*, but also the actors' trestle tables in *Captain Fracasse* and *Molière*, the trucks on which migrants begin their journeys, and the Greek *ekkyklema*.[10] The superposition of sources highlights the organic validity of the Soleil's scenic solution to framing: the rolling platforms suffused the history

The Survivors of Mad Hope (rehearsal). Yuras, the young Alacalufe (Seear Kohi), loyal companion of Kaw-Djer/Jean Salvatore of Hapsburg-Tuscany (Serge Nicolaï), Jules Verne's hero, leaps in the snow during a storm. A *koken* – dressed in white in order to be "invisible" among E. Stiefel's blocks of ice and the white blankets that represent the snowy ground – manipulates Yuras's clothing by the threads attached to it. The *koken*, thus, adds the force of the wind to the snow and the cold. This is a condensed example of the Soleil's collective athleticism in which the energy of some must adjust to the gestural efficiency of others. Photo by Michèle Laurent.

of theatre with that of the troupe, with cinematographic techniques, with objects of modernity, and with vehicles giving shape to *diegesis*. As for the rolling platforms in *Mad Hope*, they occupy a logical place in the context of a play about filmmaking, a play that is truly "cinema-theatre."

As the twentieth century came to a close, early forms of Western cinema, in particular silent film, took the place of, or rather overlaid, Asian forms in the Soleil's work. After having seen kabuki on tour in Leningrad in 1928, Einstein himself analyzed the relationship between this ancient art and cinema. The film stage that "takes over" the theatre stage in the Soleil's later productions was itself born of the "Asias" that have influenced the company.

In *Mad Hope*,[11] the popular forms of theatre, reminiscent of fairground comedy with tumblers, brawls, and pies in the face, that had earlier been reintroduced on the Soleil's stage, were reflected in the highly physical work of the silent film body. The culture of silent film was, furthermore, able to re-enchant the art of theatre by staging its collective craft, as viewed by a theatre troupe. Independent and archaic, silent film, as seen by the Soleil, was thus not only capable of multiplying the physical expressivity characteristic of popular forms of theatre, but it also linked to the political, social, and scientific utopias at the beginning of the twentieth century.

And Suddenly, Sleepless Nights and *Drums on the Dam* inaugurated a return to collective creation through the improvisations of the actors-authors, while at the same time pointing to the possible transformation of collective methods through the addition of computer and video technology. These tools made collective writing both easier and more complicated. All these transformations of theatrical creation, which led to new filmic records of the plays and to the use of video as a rehearsal notebook, have influenced the work of more than one theatre company; but rare are those who, like the Soleil, developed these into a method over the course of a decade. Moreover, this method has been organically tied to the working procedures the Soleil had established from the start: a "house of theatre," capable of becoming a "house for the world," as well as a "house of film."

A new laboratory for collective writing: organization

A larger team had surrounded the director by 2002. Besides Charles-Henri Bradier, there was someone, dubbed "the visual memory,"[12] who was specifically in charge of filming rehearsals. As director's assistant, Bradier would progressively be relieved of his initial tasks of transcribing improvisations and of subtitling the touring productions and the plays, including for francophone audiences (when languages other than French were used). He was charged, however, with the substantial task of keeping a logbook of what was said and what was done at the Soleil – photographing and organizing the materials that had been amassed (writings, photos, and films). He collected the documentation and acted as the constant interlocutor of the actors when Mnouchkine was already at work on future projects and not available for their questions.

Voice of Charles-Henri Bradier

"[For Drums on the Dam], *Ariane very quickly asked me to make the rehearsal notes accessible, so that she could reread them at her leisure and so that each one of us could benefit from them. Each evening, I took up my transcription from the day to add to it and highlight whatever had been particularly important. The following day, it was available in binders that also contained corresponding photos. It was a concrete logbook, intended to be immediately useful to the actors. I indicated in the log if we had been working with the text or in an improvisation. I noted precisely which actors were playing which characters, and above all, I scrupulously recorded Ariane's notes to the actors. Each week, I wrote a summary, a recapitulation of the 'strong moments' of the work. Every day, I had to transfer the rehearsal images onto VHS so that the shots could be reviewed with the actors. The improvisations or the work on the scenes were grouped; then after several months, regrouped – a real work of montage: through this work, we arrived at a series of improvisations that showed the origin and the continual development of a character or a situation, or that revealed the first chronological sequences of scenes.*

For The Last Caravanserai, *with our tools further developed, we organized the images from the improvisations directly on the editing software, Final Cut. We could then choose more precisely from within filmed moments, assemble bona fide short montages, and afterwards burn them much faster onto DVDs. This also confirmed that our working method corresponded well to dramaturgical attempts at constructing plays: this narrative and poetic montage, entirely virtual, even a little dangerous, of the improvisations allowed us to glimpse at the not yet finished play, and see what it could become.*

For Ephemera, my note-taking work became even more active, and pursued an aim that could, in a less obvious way, be understood as dramaturgical. I habitually organized my notes according to the narrative threads introduced by the actors' propositions, as well as by the worlds amassed on stage. Part of my work, alongside the person who was in charge of the video, was to draw up a list of improvisations, then to select them according to Ariane's indications, to name them, and finally, to organize them so that they could easily be found for subsequent viewing. When we realized that a particular improvisation was not developed enough, or on the other hand, that its material was divided into two propositions, too independent of one another, I would match each proposition with similar improvisational threads.

For The Last Caravanserai, there were stories to follow, even if they were by nature incomplete, fragments of life, stages of ongoing voyages, stopping places or routes. Behind this impression of a profusion of stories, there was still a solid structure; we couldn't mix in just anything, there were paths to follow, including the progression of history. For Ephemera, the material was more diffuse, stemming from the unconscious and uncategorizable. We quickly realized that in order to ensure that the work maintained its explosive quality, its relative emotional brutality, we shouldn't set up any links between improvisations or weave any relational backdrop."[13]

The videos produced thus provided the complete scenic text of an improvisation, "the written score" as Mnouchkine puts it,[14] "tangible evidence" which was missing from the collective creations of the 1970s. As she insists, an improvisation *can* be reworked, but the right improvisation must also be well-filmed in order to be reworked. The organization of filmed improvisations allowed for sorting, tracking, and thus, easy viewing – collective viewing on the big screen in which the actor's eye was trained to become like a director's. From *Ephemera* on, when the actor's eye had sufficiently developed, this process of collective and directed viewing also became a productive practice of personal critique.

The Last Caravanserai. Image of collective work. Photo by Charles-Henri Bradier.

Ephemera. In the second nave, preparation of the rolling platforms (D. Cottu, D. Belluggi-Vannuccini, and F. Ressort). The rectangular door platform was used for the episodes "The Nasty Business" and "Forgiveness." The round platform on the right is a doctor's office, used for the episodes "The Sonogram" and "Mesopotamia." Photo by Michèle Laurent.

the music proposed. As he has said, when the actors are "in the music," they are prevented from playing "psychologically."

Mnouchkine and Lemêtre have spoken to one another through headsets since *Ephemera*, when the musician's position high on a balcony necessitated it; and these secret exchanges have now perhaps become necessary for the collective creation in which they are engaged. Equally secret are the "concoctions" of the actors with the musician, palavers that precede each improvisation – when the actors inform Lemêtre of some elements of what they intend to improvise. He grasps the rest on the fly and accompanies the actors as they invent.

Finally, the space for collective creation, "dreamed up" by Mnouchkine, had, until his death in 2014, always been rapidly established through the complicity she enjoyed with G-C. François. The longtime set designer had only to hand over to the actors the task of populating the proposed space. During the creative process in the 2000s, the actors became decorator-constructors and a large part of the work they did to prepare for improvisations consisted in inventing their space, a space that became the frame, in the cinematographic sense of the term, for their appearance on stage. Moreover, these frames were often composed of rolling platforms of different sizes and shapes[16] – a device discovered during the first improvisations for *The Last Caravanserai*. In this kind of work, actor Serge Nicolaï called himself an actor armed with a hammer and drill. Acting on these rolling platforms also presented the opportunity for a new kind of training.

> "The theatre can say everything, do everything. I've never felt this as much as during the creation of *The Last Caravanserai*."
> (Ariane Mnouchkine, interview with B. Picon-Vallin, Cartoucherie, September 18, 2004.)

Working together on living documents: *The Last Caravanserai (Odysseys)*

The genesis of *The Last Caravanserai* started while *Drums on the Dam* was on tour, at the moment when Jean-Pierre Alaux, from the GISTI,[17] took Mnouchkine to Sangatte, close to Calais. In the immense abandoned Eurostar construction hanger, she discovered a world different from that presented by the media: Red Cross team members and their generosity; families, and people hailing from Iran, Iraq, and Afghanistan; travelers without luggage, without documents, fleeing a war-torn country; a government that hunted them; a dictator; the Taliban – which flouted women's rights and forbade universal education – and misery. These were refugees filled with their world and its stories: a contemporary caravanserai, buzzing with richly human odysseys no matter how poor the voyager.

At the last performance of *Drums on the Dam* in Sydney, a sentence, projected on the precious silk backdrop: "Free the refugees," rang out in the Antipodes like the announcement of the next play. Also in Australia, Mnouchkine spent the sun-blistered

The Last Caravanserai: Origins and Destinies, Narrative Thread 330, "Return to Jalalabad." Zpojmai (A. Grant) and Kazhal (V. Le Coënt), two Afghan women in niqab, gliding on a small platform, return to see the ruins of their house, itself situated on a larger platform. Photo by Martine Franck, Magnum Photos.

The Last Caravanserai: Origins and Destinies, Narrative Thread 337, "Alice in Wonderland." In Georgia, Svetlana (D. Cottu), standing on her black dirt-covered platform, speaks to Abaï Kalgan (S. Lolov), the Ossestian shepherd, who rides his donkey. The donkey has its own platform. Crouching on the larger platform is Assia, Svetlana's daughter (M. Larrañaga y Ausin). The "pushers" (from left to right): E. Doe Bruce, S. Brottet-Michel, O. Corsini, V. Bianchini, D. Santonja-Ruiz, É. Gruat. Photo by Martine Franck, Magnum Photos.

afternoons of January, accompanied by Shaghayegh Beheshti, an actress who speaks Farsi, in Villawood, a detention camp in a Sydney suburb. There, hundreds of refugees were shoved together, waiting on the miracle that would be their regularization in Australia, the "promised land" they'd finally reached. However, more often than not, what actually transpired was either their forced return to the war or misery they'd risked their lives to escape from, or deportation to countries they'd already crossed – like nearby Indonesia, and its islands of Lombok or Bali, where Mnouchkine would also travel and meet other refugees facing desperate fates.

It is in Asia that Mnouchkine collected the first round of interviews, centered around a question she posed to those who had left everything: what story should be passed down to your children? The transmission of these lives, fragile shells on the roads and seas of the world, would also be the focus of her next production. Once back in France, Mnouchkine and the troupe hosted another large acting workshop, which allowed them to meet new actors and to increase the cultural diversity of the troupe. Mnouchkine continued to go regularly to Sangatte, always with Shaghayegh Beheshti, and also with Sarkaw Gorany, a Soleil actor and Kurdish refugee, who would guide her through the labyrinthine camp where he, himself, had lived. He would later perform in the play. Certain other actors, who during the *Drums on the Dam* tour had seen Groupov's *Rwanda 94* about the Rwandan genocide, also went to the camp and committed themselves to the plight of the refugees.

The documentation that would support the troupe's improvisational work was essentially made up of the accounts of men and women met in the camps, to whom the project aimed to give both a public and a personal voice. In the final stage of creation of *The Golden Age*, the improvisations had been tested, guided, and corrected by an audience implicated in the events represented. In *The Last Caravanserai*, this encounter was accomplished at the beginning of the work. Political engagement and artistic practice mixed so thoroughly as to become barely distinguishable – for example the case of Jean-Charles Maricot. While performing in *The Last Caravanserai* the role of "Parviz," a refugee from Sangatte who lost his leg jumping onto the Eurostar, Maricot also took care of the amputee, until the real Parviz received his papers. Scenes like the videoconference questioning of the Iraqi refugee, Al Bassiri, by the tribunal of Melbourne, were entirely true to life.

The "living documents" thus assembled over a long period of time were of three types: interviews recorded by the director, encounters of the actors with refugees, and the actors' personal experiences in the different parts of the world from which they hailed (for example, Iran, Bulgaria, and Russia).

Mnouchkine would not give the recordings to the actors right away, and Shaghayegh Beheshti was tasked with saying nothing. But, according to C-H. Bradier, knowledge about various camp detainees seemed to seep out of her. When Mnouchkine finally gave the actors the recordings, it was clear to everyone that these voices had to be heard. The recordings nourished a second stage of the production's creation and provided the play's structure.

The immense saga, coproduced by Ruhrtriennale[18] with the support of the Belgian opera director Gérard Mortier, lasted six hours in its full version (with necessary intermissions so that spectators could take a breather and eat). The full production played on weekends. The play was composed of two parts: "The Cruel River" ["Le Fleuve cruel"] (created in April 2003) and "Origins and Destinies" ["Origines et destins"] (created in November 2003). Each part was subdivided into chapters or sequences in which the same characters reappeared; most of the 37 actors, not including the children, played several roles.

The burning question was what form to invent so that the document didn't lose its impact and so that this work of documentary theatre would also be a work of art. The Soleil's solutions were very different from those proposed by Peter Sellars, who, on the same subject, the same year, presented *The Children of Herakles* by framing the representation with debates and films in order to open up Euripides's play to current events. At the back of the empty stage – refinished with a layer of smooth cement, the mass of which was colored by gradations of black and grey – a grey silk backdrop (a survivor from *Drums on the Dam*) was hung. This silk would be raised and lowered at the end of each sequence for entrances and exits of the actors, which could also be accomplished via the two ramps that ran laterally alongside the stage. Downstage, there was a long rectangular pit. On the empty stage, both somber and luminous, everything was dedicated to movement: the play spoke only of wanderings, travels, and lost roots. The actors performed on rolling carts, put into motion or stopped by "pushers" who witnessed the scenes and represented the spectators, forming a silent but expressive chorus. Each location had its own rolling platform that entered, laden with its decor and characters. Other characters could enter the scene positioned on smaller rolling platforms. The actors were, thus, elevated above the surface of the stage, constantly moved and put off balance.

One of the recurring episodes was the attempt to cross the border, represented by the large platform positioned on the edge of the pit. On the side of the platform was a chain-link fence that the smugglers snipped to allow the refugees to slip between the cracks and jump into the void below – representing at once the risk of the voyage, the hiding place searched by police, and the train for England that the refugees had to grab hold of as it slowed down entering the Chunnel. Other rolling platforms evoked, among other places, a French port, a road in the Caucasus mountains, a beach, an Afghan and Chechen house, a secret workshop, the Charles de Gaulle airport tarmac, an Australian tribunal, a British cliff. Some of the platforms carried a container for contraband, or they featured a donkey, a motorcycle, a lamppost, or simply trees indicating different seasons. The partitions or walls erected on many of these theatrical "caravans" were equipped with openings (windows, doors, etc.) that framed the actors' faces as if in "close up." The reference to cinema – silent, fictive, documentary[19] – was constantly present: it was felt in the acting, in which speech was rare; just as in the treatment of space, segmented and mobile; in the movement of the rolling platforms; and also in the diversity of the frames and shots proposed; in the non-linear narrative; and in the multitude of languages used – all tools the theatre further "polished with all its poetic power."[20]

The spatial configuration, ready to receive dozens of stories of departures and painful separations, was combined with a visual and musical framework that belonged just as much to the dramaturgy as to the scenography. The text in *The Last Caravanserai* was of two sorts: recorded accounts and, also, the dramatic lines of the characters – played by actors of many nationalities, speaking 22 languages (Farsi, Russian, Bulgarian, English, Ukrainian, German, Turkish, Arabic, Dari, Chechen, and more). The refugee accounts, spoken in their original languages, were very moving, thanks to the particular timbre of the voices, the beauty of the sounds, and the profound emotions inhabiting them. They were translated into French in a beautiful script that was projected onto the silk cyclorama; the text ran across the silk as the refugee voices sounded. The translations of the actors' lines for the performed scenes, when not in French, were projected on any part of the set where they could be legible. The result was a powerful association between the oral and the written.

At the Soleil, the music is always the sonorous "carpet" on which the actors perform. Here, it also served as stage directions – evoking the place and the moment or identifying a political event. The music built a layered sound space that completed the text in essential ways and deepened the narration. Lemêtre's grandiose musical souk, with live musical instruments, electronic machines, and samplers, was distanced a bit from the audience by a large scrim.

Each of the two parts of *The Last Caravanserai* started by representing exiles' tribulations in violent waters – specifically, a river and the sea. During these sequences, platforms rolled and tilted underneath meters of silk fabric, furiously shaken by

The Last Caravanserai: The Cruel River, Narrative Thread 136, "An Afghan love." On their rolling terrace, the lovers, Fawad (S. Brottet-Michel) and Azadeh (S. Beheshti), converse with the bird of happiness. The young woman will later be hanged by the Taliban. Photo by Michèle Laurent.

The Last Caravanserai: The Cruel River, Narrative Thread 122, "The Great Raid on the Refugees." Eurotunnel security agents (F. Ressort and V. Mangado) mistreat Clavdia (E. Loukiantchikova-Sel), who wants to jump onto the Eurostar. The "pushers" (S. Masson and D. Santonja-Ruiz). Photo by Michèle Laurent.

The Cruel River, Narrative Thread 332, "The Last Protest." In Tehran, in their living room (on a rolling platform), the father Mirza Zamani (M. Durozier) and his children Eskandar (J-C. Maricot) and Parastou (S. Beheshti). Their dialogue is in Farsi; the translation is projected on the façade. Photo by Michèle Laurent.

Origins and Destinies, Narrative Thread 331, "Wedding Present." Milenka, the young Serbian bride (here V. Bianchini), is stretched out, dead, on her platform. Around her, Liszitsa, a Serbian thug (S. Brottet-Michel), and on the motorcycle, Vuk (S. Nicolaï), a Serbian pimp. The "pusher" of the rolling platform (J. Marvan Enriquez). Photo by Michèle Laurent.

the actors. This theatrical form created a hymn to the words of the refugees. To open each part, Mnouchkine's voice, first live and then recorded, announced in a letter addressed to one of her principal interlocutors during the interviews that the promised play was finally finished. Her words were translated orally, and simultaneously, into Farsi, by Shaghayegh Beheshti, while the text in French appeared as a projection across the grey silk cyclorama. Mnouchkine's letter also asked for news.

"Dear Nadereh," these words still resound in my ears, addressed not only to the play's audience, but also to the refugee, Nadereh – Nadereh, located again by the company during its Melbourne tour. Just as they located and celebrated during a performance in Lyon, Captain Rinnan, commander of the cargo ship Tampa, who had, against orders, rescued shipwrecked children off the Australian coast. The form of this play was, in its genesis as in its performance, a hymn to fraternity, materialized during the bows when, after so many scenes of violence and hate, the 37 Soleil actors, men on one side and women on the other, ran center stage and threw themselves into one another's arms.

Voice of Ariane Mnouchkine

(First farewell to *The Last Caravanserai* in a letter to the troupe, July 29, 2006, during a break from *Ephemera* rehearsals, while the troupe was on tour with *The Last Caravanserai* in Greece.)

"My very dear friends,

The dog days of summer have just ended. Finally, we can breathe. It was almost frightful. A sort of stubborn cataclysm crouched over the city, assailing it from the sky, giant feet weighing on its chest, determined to asphyxiate it. Finally, a divine order came to make the monster rise. He withdrew with regret. He will be back.

The Cartoucherie is cool, astonishingly cool. The Welcome Area is wide open. To the left, through the plastic curtain, the workshop's light sparkles, to the right the deep dark of the performance hall. And the white dust that covers everything, as if in mist. The Chaos necessary for all beginnings, for every sunrise. Yes, you, in Greece, you are living the harmony of a sunset. In its near perfection, and probably also in its melancholy. And me, I'm in the disorder of birth. In its cacophony. And in its anguish. I wish The Last Caravanserai the most glorious sunset that a constellation like ours can dream of. I believe, without boastfulness, that this play did some good. And if it did, it is also because we have done our work well. We have been silent, we have listened, we have believed, we have received, and almost every evening, down to the last evening, we have meticulously pursued excellence. And then above all, almost every day, we have remained united and, almost every day, we have loved one another.

I embrace you more firmly than you could truly stand,

Ariane."

Another epic play: *Ephemera*

Ephemera surprised its audiences and seemed to go against the tide of the Soleil's habitual forms. For that matter, the familiar space of the Cartoucherie was no longer recognizable: the third hall had been totally restructured in a bifrontal configuration in which the spectators, themselves staged, faced each other for the duration of the six-and-a-half-hour play. Seated in tiered seats, the audience members' torsos and faces were "framed" by lines of little festive and watchful lights that ran along the border of each row. The play was a montage of slices of life, sketched from the everyday. In the play, the actors did dishes, cooked, ate; the air smelled like bleach or grilled rosemary; a doctor did a sonogram; a man made fresh-squeezed orange juice for his mother; characters dressed children and celebrated birthdays; a little girl learned to ride a bike; a mother did herself up for her daughter's wedding; a man abused his wife; and the death of loved ones prowled ceaselessly. The spectacle ventured into new territory – that of the intimate, the familial, and the everyday. The famous distance present in the Soleil's work seemed to be totally reduced to zero: Mnouchkine's focus was once again adjusted, this time to approach the individual or, rather, the "we" by way of the "I." *Ephemera* was clearly in dialogue with *The Last Caravanserai,* developing themes present at the heart of the great epic – precious, simple moments of a past life from which exile had forever separated the protagonists – intimacy piercing through the epic's shape, thanks to the stories of those bearing witness to multiple forms of exile. The observed was no longer first and foremost the foreigner/the other, belying one of the Soleil's central maxims: "The more one places one's imaginary at a distance, the better one is able to speak about oneself."[21]

In *Ephemera*, the focus was, then, on one country, France, and on four generations of French people – the same generations that coexist today in the company. Instead of the epic thrust of survival that drove *The Last Caravanserai*, it was a certain era (from 1940 to today) that animated *Ephemera*. The experience accumulated by the actors and transmitted within the troupe proved crucial; it allowed the company to forge

Ephemera, Volume 2, Episode 15, "In the Archives." Recalling Ariane Mnouchkine's Breton village, Stang Bihan, during the war, the little girl (R. Jodorowsky) reads while lying on an old mattress. *Ephemera*'s attic of intimate memories, a kind of personal archive, will be paralleled in the archive of *Mad Hope*, the place where the traces of collective adventure are found. Photo by Michèle Laurent.

Ephemera, Volume 1, Episode 1, "A Marvelous Garden." A small platform, with a garden gate and a sign, is pushed forward into the playing space. The young woman (D. Cottu), who has just lost her mother, climbs onto the platform. Her posture renders the pain of separation communicable, as does the gaze of the "pusher" (É. Gruat). Photo by Michèle Laurent.

ahead, rich with an aesthetic of precision and a strong sense of scenic design, both gleaned from Asian traditions.[22] Ultimately, the minimal distance between the theatre and its subject matter was inflected by the mode of creation and by a specific scenic configuration, one that avoided all timorous withdrawal into oneself. Naturalism and voyeurism were avoided, and a layered gaze constructed: the spectators mutually examined one another, all while watching the actors, who were, themselves, watched by the attentive "pushers" of the rolling platforms.

"An intimate story told by thirty voices"[23]

The challenge this time lay in how to write a theatrical narrative inspired by childhood memories of company members, at once very personal and mutually recognizable. The actors performed both under the watchful eye of Mnouchkine and in comity with her: she gave of herself in the process just as much as did her actors. The director went all the way back in her family history to her grandparents' experience during the Occupation, sharing a delicate and fragile personal history. In this process, collective creation took place without a safety net; each person was exposed to the maximum. They allowed their unconscious to speak. They worked – and here the word "rehearsal" is no longer appropriate – but, rather, they shared with one another and then improvised, throwing themselves into the stories of others. The work was about secrets, trial and error, experimentation without a text, without a linear or guiding narrative, with no material but oneself, and sometimes, photo albums. Over the course of the complex creative process, the Soleil appealed to literature (Anton Chekhov, Edmond Jabès, Pablo Neruda, Marcel Proust, Raymond Carver ...), history (Marc Bloch, Simone Weil, Primo Levi, Hanna Krall ...), encounters (with Caroline Piketty,[24] who would inspire the character of the archivist in the play), and documentary or auteur films (Bergman, Kurosawa,[25] Rossellini, Scola, Wells, Sirk, *Night and Fog* by Resnais, *The Murder of a Hatmaker* by C. Bernstein, etc.) to guide their work.

The "vision" requested of the actors was 1) that human beings discover they are mortal and 2) that separation is unavoidable. Silent for a long time, the improvisations were carried out to music by Lemêtre, who had composed a notebook of musical compositions – also visions, all in minor tones on themes chosen with Mnouchkine from which he pulled according to the indications given to him by the improvising actors. Mnouchkine requested transparency, restraint, simplicity, knowing how to peel away one's layers, as well as operating with a scalpel, receiving others' visions, looking for the concrete, and being meticulous.

Ephemera, Volume 1, Episode 9, "The Long-awaited Letter (The People's Paradise)." A moment of intimacy between the couple Roxana (J. Carneiro da Cunha) and Manolo (M. Durozier). Photo by Michèle Laurent.

Ephemera, Volume 2, Episode 29, "A Marvelous Place." A German soldier interrupts a family gathered together in their Breton home to watch a John Ford film. The screen is on another platform. From left to right: M. Durozier, V. Colemyn, J. Carneiro da Cunha, A. Simma, E. Loukiantchikova-Sel, R. Jodorowsky. The "pushers" (É. Gruat and M. Larrañaga y Ausin). In *Ephemera*, there are moments that theatricalize the Resistance. Photo by Michèle Laurent.

Ephemera, Volume 2, Episode 23, "Candied Apples." Exhausted, the parents have brought their children (R. de Miranda and Ruben Delgado) home from the fair. It's as if they are being gently rocked by the "pushers" (D. Belluggi-Vannuccini and S. Mahmoud-Vintam). From behind, D. Jambert, V. Mangado, V. Colemyn, and the children. Photo by Michèle Laurent.

Ephemera, Volume 2, Episode 25, "Forgiveness." Odette Rivière (C. Grandville) prevents her sister Fanny (M. Larrañaga y Ausin) from opening the door to their neighbors, Tatiana and Alexei Menuhin, the victims of a Nazi raid. Above the playing space, the musician J-J. Lemêtre. Photo by Michèle Laurent.

Ephemera, Volume 1, Episode 11, "The Darling Son." A bourgeois living room on a rectangular platform. On the telephone, the daughter of the family (D. Cottu) learns of her brother's fatal accident. The family had been waiting on him for lunch. The "pusher" (M-L. Crawley), attentive and full of empathy, pushes the platform with care. Photo by Michèle Laurent.

Ephemera, Volume 1, Episode 14, "My Mother's Room (Christmas)." The departure of Kate, the British mother (A. Grant), upsets her daughter Liliane (D. Cottu), who is held back by her father (M. Durozier). This photograph was taken during a rehearsal: in the tiered seating of the bifrontal space we can see the serious faces of A. Mnouchkine and C-H. Bradier. Photo by Michèle Laurent.

This play was also composed of objects, a flood of objects – furniture, knick-knacks, lamps, telephones, toys, dishes – collected on sidewalks, bought at Emmaüs,[26] found in one or the other's attic and lent for use in the play. The objects told the story of the characters. Chosen and arranged with the care of a set dresser (Mnouchkine uses this word, pulled from film vocabulary) by the actors whose work also consisted, as in *The Last Caravanserai*, of creating the scenic frames for their improvisations themselves, the objects became actors and partners. They spoke, and their language was vociferous. Used, dirty, out of fashion, cobbled together, reemerging from the past – from the places where they had been stored away – the objects brought with them the innumerable lives, anonymous or identified, of which they were the witnesses.

Intimate stories, collective improvisations, music, objects, videos – these were the instruments in this laboratory of scenic writing. Of nearly 400 scenes, roughly 50 were kept. These would become the chapters of the two "Volumes" that made up the play, as the theatre program indicated. Concentrating on the essence of several intimate stories, the two parts of the play told the story of "a group, a class, a country."[27] Yet the parts also contributed to "weaving a web – French, European, and ultimately, global."[28] One of Mnouchkine's heuristic principles: "Search for the particular to find the universal," was in play.

One can imagine the sadness of those whose improvisations were not retained for the final version of the play. Mnouchkine had already thought for a moment that it would be possible to add a third part to *The Last Caravanserai*, but – just as her plan to perform sequences in different orders on different nights for *Caravanserai* – adding more scenes to *Ephemera* never came to be.

A configuration of vision and recall, between cinema and novel

Ephemera was conceived during *The Last Caravanserai* tour and the epic's subsequent filming and editing.[29] The bifrontal, tiered seats overlooked an elongated space that Mnouchkine called in turn an "autopsy table, arena, magnifying glass, and the Piazza Navona." On either end of the long, playing space, two elevated stages – the musician's and an "attic" where authentic archive boxes were piled up – faced one another. Underneath these, the playing space opened up – designated as a passage, a corridor of time through which the rolling platforms glided. It very quickly became clear that a new shaped rolling platform, this time circular, would be necessary. Spheres of intimate worlds, these platforms advanced loaded with characters, furniture, and objects. Carpeted and wired with electricity, they entered and traversed the length of the corridor, its floor a variegated grey; the round platforms revolved constantly in a strange yet ordered ballet, offering the totality of their volume to the audience's view. The "pushers" – feline, attentive, delicate, and anxiously watching – controlled the speed and rhythm of the movements, unveiling the actions of the characters embodied by their colleagues. Like *koken*, they made possible the performance of the actors, pushing them into the playing space. And the action *rolled* in very long sequence shots, improbable in cinema because they allowed the spectators to view, in one glance, the interior of each furnished room, unencumbered by walls, as well as the backside of the decor.

Without ever losing sight of the other spectators – who made up the background and, thereby, prevented any total identification with the characters or action – audience members witnessed the performance of human passions in their multiple stopping places. This theatre of images, in constant movement, with little dialogue, was a theatre of memory – musical, gestural, a sort of live, athletic cinema. Repeated close ups of characters (actors and objects) were shown in detail by the rounds made by the scenic configuration; long shots were accomplished when the platforms disappeared under the curtains, whose grey folds swelled at each end of the performance corridor as in Noh theatre. Each object, pulled from everyday life, elicited the astonished recognition of the spectators, who talked to each other, stammered, cried, laughed (the actors heard them and were not bothered by these reactions). The slow, repetitive, turning motion and the acting out of the character's flashbacks on the rolling platforms also provoked sudden recollections, inviting spectators to take the time to remember their own formative experiences. And the stories that they followed from one entrance to another – rendered fictive through the sculpting and curating work of collective creation – did their retrospective magic. Frequent pauses in the action, during which the empty space was filled only by sound, reinforced for the audience the impulse to work on oneself.

The theatre can do anything, can dare anything: here it found the means of lingering over the relationship between an old woman – dirty, crazy, and sick – and her doctor (Perle and Nelly, respectively performed by S. Beheshti and J. Carneiro da Cunha). It can show a fatal traffic accident, the indignation of a court bailiff at the situation of an overly indebted couple. It can discover, ingeniously in this case, how to stage children, those fragile and strong little people who are everywhere in the play – our past and our future.

"An entire day, it's still too short!" wrote a spectator in one of the numerous letters that audience members regularly address to the Soleil. Indeed, one would have happily and

"The combination of the formalism of the rolling platforms with the absolute authenticity of each object, of each bottle, is remarkable. The way in which, starting from a small empty platform, the play develops grandiose images when six platforms or more turn together; and then, the play shrinks back into this little 'ovum' – it's truly remarkable. It's really a novel: we might evoke Thomas Mann, Marcel Proust, Joyce ...." (Lev Dodine, in "Un regard d'ailleurs sur *Les Éphémères*," interview with B. Picon-Vallin, *ThéâtreS*, no. 26, 2007.)

"[It's] a theatre of compassion in the true sense of the word." (Lev Dodine, in "Un regard d'ailleurs sur *Les Éphémères*," 2007.)

The Survivors of Mad Hope (Dawn). Film poster recreated as a fresco by M. Lefebvre and E. Gülgonen on the walls of the Welcome Area. Other silent film posters were created as well. Photo by Frédéric Mastellari, Archives Théâtre du Soleil.

The Survivors of Mad Hope. A "film kiss." Everyone, astonished and joyous, witnesses the kissing scene between Mademoiselle Marguerite (O. Corsini) and Shubert (S. Brottet-Michel). From left to right: J-S. Merle, F. Voruz, V. Mangado, E. Doe Bruce, V. Panikkaveettil, A. Milléquant, M. Durozier, A. Simma, D. Belluggi-Vannuccini, S. Nicolaï, and J. Carneiro da Cunha. Photo by Michèle Laurent.

lucidly stayed on the banks of this time-river to roll out with the actors our own platforms: childhood bedrooms, those of our parents, mothers always present, those of our children and grandchildren. *Ephemera* was a ritual of collective evocation: the intimate weaving together of everyone's vulnerable present. The great Russian director Lev Dodine described this play as "revolutionary." Here, the Soleil experimented with a new form of urgent engagement: re-centering its focus on ordinary persons, the grains of sand that globalization has exiled far from themselves. It tries to understand them and to understand itself, without the cloak of egotistical narcissism, without vast problems or ideologies. Where do we come from; who are we? In a period of rapid change, the quest for the essential thread that links human beings to the world is resolutely necessary and political. And this would be the objective of *The Survivors of Mad Hope*. While preparing this next play, Mnouchkine said in 2009:

> I think the most political play we can currently do is a play that gives some enthusiasm, lightness, and hope to human beings. Today, there is nothing else to say; and yes, it's a work of the collective body. [We are making a work] on the strength of joy, of laughter, of humanity [...] for those who want to live together and who still believe – who believe in socialism and in the future.[30]

The Survivors of Mad Hope (Dawn): a large-scale play

The history of the relationship between the Soleil and the cinema was intensified in this production, which testified to the friendly confrontation of the two art forms. The play recounted the saga of a filmmaking crew who, during the oppressive months leading up to 1914 and World War I, filmed the political utopia recounted in a posthumous novel by Jules Verne (*Magellania* [*En Magellanie*]). After having addressed familial memory, with a local and personal preciseness that allowed them to grasp the universal, the Soleil refocused on the beginning of the twentieth century and threw itself into a different kind of archive – the archives of Western civilization – to speak of a group united by its faith in the dawning century, in the progress that it promised, in socialist ideals, and in a new popular art form, the cinema.

Mnouchkine had first thought to return to Shakespeare with *Othello*, but that turned out to be the wrong direction. The support she gave to presidential candidate Ségolène Royal and the questions the politician posed about the functioning of democracy probably helped inspire her new choice. Her chance

"You have to let yourself be engulfed in the music in order to respond to it. I look at the text, and I see these horrible old words; it's as if we were plunging them in a regenerative liquid. It's the beating heart of the music and your beating hearts that must accomplish this; and at the same time, all this must beat together rhythmically." (Ariane Mnouchkine, rehearsal notes for *The Survivors of Mad Hope*, compiled by C-H. Bradier.)

encounter with Verne's *Magellania* did the rest. A story as a point of departure: the troupe once again needed its author, who had remained present during all these years, ready to intervene on one matter or another when asked. Cixous thus began writing "magellanesque stories," and then a group of "scriptwriters" among the most seasoned actors got together to imagine the possibilities for transposing Verne's utopian story of a voyage to Patagonia to the stage; they introduced into the narrative visionaries, artists, and finally a filmmaker. Documentation was collected on the beginning of the twentieth century and its utopias. The actors watched a number of silent films.[31] The work on stage began with very long improvisations that led to a many-layered and complex dramaturgical structure.

J-J. Lemêtre doubled his role as musical director, a role without which nothing that had happened on the Soleil's stage since the Shakespeares would have come into being: he became the fictional character Camille, the pianist and sound engineer. The act of filming and the projection of the film of the voyage were brought together by what we might call a fantastic theatrical narrative, a story subtly layered, comprising four interconnected levels. The first was that of the Mad Hope dance hall, whose owner, Félix Courage (E. Doe Bruce), a lover and unwitting patron of the seventh art, symbolizing faith in the future, opened his attic to a filmmaker at odds with the major production company Pathé. Jean LaPalette (M. Durozier), and his film crew: his sister Gabrielle (J. Carneiro da Cunha) and his childhood friend Tommaso (D. Bellugi-Vannuccini); and the employees of the Mad Hope itself, taken on as actors, would make the film. The second level was that of the fictional ship, which in the heat of creation took on the name of the hospitable cabaret, the Mad Hope. The Mad Hope ship carried emigrants from all walks of life to South America where it shipwrecked. The third level was the embedded story of Jean Salvatore (S. Nicolaï), who crossed paths with the survivors of the shipwreck on one of the frozen islands of Magellania where they washed up. In the fourth layer – the history of colonialism and the First World War – Queen Victoria (A. Grant) and Darwin (D. Bellugi-Vannuccini) were introduced, Jean Jaurès was assassinated, and mobilization for the war obliged the artists to rush the end of their film and process the remaining sequences. We might also speak of another layer – that of the Soleil troupe itself, giving life to a film crew (after shooting two films as a company), and humorously staging its own creative methods in a meta-discourse that culminated in a splendid stage metaphor on the role of art – through the final image of the "lighthouse, a beacon in the tempest."

During the scenes in which they performed film actors, the Soleil's actors borrowed the style of the greats of silent film. As

The Survivors of Mad Hope. In Félix Courage's attic, the actors prepare for a shoot. Stage left, under the orange lamp, Camille sits at his piano. The snow-making basket has been loaded. Photo by Martine Franck, Magnum Photos.

The Survivors of Mad Hope. The screen for the text to be projected has been installed. The painted flats are being placed. The snowy surface, the white blankets, are being adjusted. Stage right, the filmmakers' table. In a white work coat, Gabrielle will turn the crank handle of the camera. Photo by Martine Franck, Magnum Photos.

The Survivors of Mad Hope. A barrier and the panels representing the boat cabins are being installed. Pieces of sea ice are being brought in. The space, with all its hoists, evokes the image of a large ship. Photo by Martine Franck, Magnum Photos.

The Survivors of Mad Hope. Finally, the emigrants, shipwrecked on the Island of Hoste, remake the world to their ideal. In white against a black background – in reference to the text panels of silent film – their inaudible words appear little by little. Photo by Michèle Laurent.

they pantomimed speech, their words about the political and social utopias of the beginning of the twentieth century were projected on elements of the set or on panels held in place by a system of guides and pulleys suspended above the immense stage. In the "dance of silent film" that the play set into motion – with its chorus of 35 actors, each of whom created characters and none of whom were simply extras, where the "employees of the dance hall" also functioned as stagehands and film crew – the incredible happened. The Soleil was able to re-infuse words with meaning, the height of paradox in a play about silent film. The projection of the lines (pantomimed by the actors) during the shooting of the film, a magical subterfuge, gave life back to words trampled by the sordid history of the twentieth century: words that had made the actors of *1793* thrill in 1970, words that in 1996 were projected on the façade of the theatre during the Soleil's activism for undocumented immigrants. "Liberty, equality, fraternity, humanity, socialism," words which might have seemed ridiculous given the sociopolitical context of the twentieth century, had made spectators jubilant. Mnouchkine reported this happily during rehearsals. These words would once again become credible and meaningful, once projected on the stage of a theatre that, in 2010, played fraternally with the birth of cinema.

The acting combined different source material: Félix Courage performed as a Harlequin; Tommaso danced his role with infinite grace. With the crank-handled camera being false, *Mad Hope* referred back to the treasures of burlesque jokes. Actors played the love scenes like those that had first made cinema successful. When the stage was empty, the voice over or *benshi* recounted the goings-on of the film crew or announced the historical events that punctuated the action.

The play was immensely successful: film professionals hurried to the Cartoucherie, eager to see early cinema as recreated by a theatre company enamored of the infancy of the seventh art. They were able to witness all of the rudimentary special effects of an art that had invented itself as it developed: the paper snowstorms, snowdrifts created with white blankets; the rescue of convicts drowning in the bottom of the ship's hold; the darting fish; the graceful rhea; a "real" shipwreck in a basin of water; and a special effect worthy of the spectacular Châtelet Theatre of years past – the bow of an enormous ship splitting the stage. The success was so total that one of Mnouchkine's best-known critics, the theatre director Patrice Chéreau, finally won over, admitted in a letter that it was she who had been right. And his emotion made him wonder: "Should he, himself, give up doing theatre?"[32]

With this project, a loop seemed to have been closed: Ariane Mnouchkine totally fulfilled her personal utopia, her dream of

The boat taking the emigrants away is named for the dance hall where Jean LaPalette's (M. Durozier's) team films. A canvas prow, a sail, and painted panels of a cloudy sky suffice to indicate the departure of the boat on film. Jean gives directions to his amateur actors. From left to right: J. Jancsó, M. Bauduin, D. Jambert, A-A. Dosse, V. Mangado, S. Jailloux, P. Giusti, A. Grant, A. Sarybekian, P. Poignand, O. Corsini, S. Bonneau, A. Milléquant, J-S. Merle, A. Simma, D. Belluggi-Vannuccini, S. Nicolaï. Photo by Martine Franck, Magnum Photos.

The Survivors of Mad Hope. The special effects for the shipwreck. In a rectangular basin full of water, stirred up by wooden spoons, the magnificent and fragile miniature boat is filmed during lightning and thunder. Everyone is passionately focused on their respective tasks (projector, fan, water bucket to throw waves …) From left to right: P. Poignand, O. Corsini. A. Simma, E. Doe Bruce, S. Jailloux, M. Bauduin, D. Belluggi-Vannuccini, J. Carneiro da Cunha, M. Durozier, S. Nicolaï, A. Milléquant, J. Jancsó, D. Jambert, V. Mangado, A-A. Dosse, F. Voruz, A. Grant. Photo by Martine Franck, Magnum Photos.

joining together a theatre and a cinema troupe, years after the difference between the two had led her to opt for the theatre. She equated Felix's attic and the Soleil's dimly lit stage in the opening scene of *Mad Hope* to an archival reserve and, thus, made the theatre a space for the memory of cinema (and of theatre). She could, for example, finally show in all its plenitude the extent of the work she had demanded of her actors for *The Last Caravanserai*. The "operas" or moments of choral work used to prepare the stage and serve as transition from one story to another now made up, thanks to the principle of filming, the center of *Mad Hope*, instead of only its interludes. Thus the utopias devalued by the tragic history of the twentieth century were paradoxically fulfilled on the Soleil's stage: the "actors" played by actors and the "characters" played by "actors" worked side by side, practically without leaving the stage, to make the play work. The shooting of the film, the service at the cabaret, the "actors," the "cameramen," the "special effects artists," the "technicians," the "stuntwomen," the "extras," all equally important, presented the impressive image of a realizable and free collective. As a counterpoint to the war that broke out during the play, the stage showed a utopia, dreamed and achieved though the collective engagement of the artists, who – even though life as a troupe is not easy and provokes crises just as in ordinary life – know what it means to believe in discipline, agreement on shared objectives, attention to others, knowledge, and expertise.

In this production, as in *The Last Caravanserai*, the theatre was at work to serve the world through the extreme attention and care the actors gave to one another, a spirit carried collectively beyond them by compassion and hospitality or fervor for and faith in the art they communicated. The lyricism of these epics transported the spectators beyond their everyday, opening them up to encounters with others. This phenomenon of empathy, the capacity to see from another's point of view while remaining oneself,[33] allowed the audience, just like the actors, to form an "us," to reach a universal plane, while remaining individuals. After a performance of *Mad Hope*, my neighbors for the evening, seated on the white benches of the Soleil, murmured: "Thank you," while applauding. This moving appreciation, which allows us to understand something of the particular atmosphere of the Soleil, could be an appropriate closing for this chapter.

Nonetheless, after a long tour and the filming of *Mad Hope*, "Shakespeare insisted," confesses Mnouchkine, and a lengthy rehearsal period was again launched in order to tackle in 2014 *Macbeth*. Cixous also wrote a companion play centered on this evil character – a criminal politician, power hungry and, as in Shakespeare, ready to do anything to satiate his passion, even upend the natural order. While the companion piece would have used the same scenic configuration as recent plays – a black stage, its empty space delineated by grey silks with the Cartoucherie halls draped in red, Cixous' play was never staged. The new "cycle" limited itself to Shakespeare.

The Soleil thus came back to one of its greatest inspirations, dedicating the entire decor of the Welcome Area to him. This decoration was at once a celebration of the Elizabethan genius, an inscription of the Soleil in the history of productions of his plays (painted reproductions of cinema and theatre posters of Shakespearian productions covered the walls), and an image of the world as it could be in the beauty of its infinite diversity. But audience expectations were not met. This *Macbeth* had nothing in common with *The Survivors of Mad Hope* or *The Shakespeare Cycle* of the 1980s. As with *1793* and *Ephemera*, the audience was at first surprised; and it took two weeks during which the actors and spectators "rehearsed together" before the play found its wings (which happens when the stage is totally supported by the public's attention). The new translation by Mnouchkine was precise, rhythmic, and immediately intelligible to today's audiences. The energy for life that had inhabited the demi-god characters of the Soleil's *Richard II* or *Henry IV* disappeared. Macbeth (S. Nicolaï) was a sick man; and the Soleil used the elements of its scenic vocabulary to unveil the symptoms of his destructive leprosy.

The Buddhas on the walls of the second nave were covered over with red fabric, the whole space was rendered in blood-red. The multiple scene changes required by the writing were choreographed for a tribe of stagehands, who worked closely with *koken*, dressed all in black. At times, the latter carried out the changes. In both cases, the rapid precision of the set changes gave the play the rhythm of a thriller. The scenic configuration reemployed for entrances and exits the vomitorium of *The House of Atreus Cycle*. Groups of characters – leaping and running to percussive music, somewhat like in *The Shakespeare Cycle* – flew from under the bleachers onto the stage via a sloping footbridge. Circular platforms, borrowed from *Ephemera*, turned a ballet of banquet tables into witchcraft during the famed Banquo ghost scene (*Macbeth:* Act 3, Scene 4). The witches, sharing a lineage with the Furies, danced to the praise music from *The House of Atreus Cycle*, composed by Lemêtre to unite the four Greek plays. As for the closing music, which pealed out from the musician's stage—itself gently lit by the brilliance of many small lights outlining the shapes of instruments—it was the Gandhi theme from *The Indiad*.

The constant presence of Lemêtre was more discrete than usual – the habitual musical work with the actors hadn't taken place, and the music became more cinematographic.

Macbeth (rehearsal). At the Soleil, Shakespeare's three witches have become a wild, dancing chorus. They open the performance with a frantic ritual on the red hemp heath, to the sound of J-J. Lemêtre's percussions, which call the audience to their seats. Photo by Anne Lacombe.

Macbeth (rehearsal). The ghost of Banquo appears to Macbeth (S. Nicolaï) from a trap-door shrouded in smoke. Behind him are four round chariots (rolling platforms) from *Ephemera*, with the banquet guests seated on them in transparent chairs. Photo by Lucile Cocito.

The *koken* or the servants of the stage (S. Beheshti and J. Jancsó, M. Chaufour and A. Milléquant), in contemporary clothes, trace with red rose petals the path that leads to the crime. This image contains the memory of the *hanamachi*, the kabuki footbridge dubbed the "path of flowers" that has so inspired the Soleil. Photo by Michèle Laurent.

He nonetheless found powerful harmonies to score central moments, like Fauré's *Requiem* for the scene when Birnam Wood comes to Dunsinane, or the montage he developed of cosmic sounds recorded by NASA to orchestrate the harrowing sonic world of this particular *Macbeth*. In this production, the tragedy became that of an ordinary man, devoured by ambition and media attention, harassed by microphones and dazzling flashes – the tragedy of a character from a television series, devoid of grandeur but perpetrator of an evil larger than himself. The costumes mixed periods and countries. And for the monstrous (but banal today) character's final crushing moment Mnouchkine created images that evoked the French Resistance. She shifted the final verses of Shakespeare's play to end the Soleil's production on the moor of red hemp that covered the dimly lit stage. (Here we heard echoes of her long ago *Midsummer Night's Dream* with its floor of goatskins.) Her rearrangement offered a generous invitation to take action together, each of us in our own way and to our own ability. Could *Macbeth* have had any other ending at the Soleil? Faced with evil in action ("Things bad begun make strong themselves by ill," *Macbeth*: Act 3, Scene 2), our choice is to join the resistance. "*Macbeth* [is] a tragedy of power," wrote C-H. Bradier in a letter to the actors. And he continued, echoing Hélène Cixous: "And [where are] the people in this story?" He answered: "Well, you have summoned them. Watching you, I see we become more and more that very collective."[34]

Notes

1 Ariane Mnouchkine, in Jean Chollet, *Construire pour le temps d'un regard: Guy-Claude François scénographe* (Paris: Fage éditions, 2009), 79.

In this chapter, any unattributed quotes by Soleil members and Ariane Mnouchkine come from research in the Soleil Archives or from one of the several interviews Béatrice Picon-Vallin conducted with them and recorded from 2010 to 2014.

2 Ariane Mnouchkine, interview at the Foundation Pierre-Bergé, April 20, 2012.

3 Sangatte, a refugee and migrant camp near Calais, France, was set up by the Red Cross at the request of the French government in 1999. Its aim was to house the growing number of migrants who were sleeping in the streets of Calais and the surrounding towns while they waited to attempt the crossing into England via the Channel Tunnel or ferries. The camp, initially set up to house 600 refugees, was soon overpopulated. By 2002, it housed 2,000 people living in wretched conditions. Racial tensions, violence, and police harassment and repression plagued the camp. It was eventually shut down in 2002 by French president Nicolas Sarkozy. More recently (2002–2014), Calais has been the site of the "Jungle," or makeshift migrant and refugee camps, which have been met with force and repeatedly razed to the ground by French authorities.

4 The system of Australian Immigrant Detention Centers (IDCs), or internment camps, according to their detractors, located throughout the country, are designed to detain, in addition to those who have breached the conditions of their visas, refugees claiming asylum who have arrived "irregularly" by sea. Mnouchkine did a series of interviews at the center in Villawood that would inform the creation of *The Last Caravanserai.*

5 This theatre company, a sister company to the Soleil, was founded with the help of Mnouchkine and the troupe during a workshop they held in Kabul in 2005. The Aftaab Theatre of Kabul shares a name as well as kinship with the Soleil, "aftaab" being the Dari translation of "soleil," or sun.

6 Founded in 1979 by Ariane Mnouchkine and Claude Lelouche, the Association Internationale de Défense des Artistes victimes de la répression dans le monde [International Association for the Defense of Artists Victims of Repression] works to bring about the release of politically imprisoned artists.

7 Ariane Mnouchkine, in Fabienne Pascaud, *L'art du présent: Entretiens avec Ariane Mnouchkine* (Paris: Plon, 2005), 44–45.

8 See concerning the relationship between theatre and cinema at the Soleil the long study that Béatrice Picon-Vallin has dedicated to the subject: "Parler du monde, parler au monde. *Le Dernier Caravansérail* et le 'ciné-théâtre' d'Ariane Mnouchkine," in *De la scène à l'écran, Théâtre aujourd'hui*, no. 11 (Paris: CNDP, 2007), 746–775.

9 These films are by Charlie Chaplin (1921), Merlan C. Cooper and Ernest B. Schoedsack (1933), and John Ford (1939).

10 The *ekkyklema*, a wheeled platform that was rolled through the skênê of ancient Greek theatres, was a technology used to unveil interior scenes to the audience.

11 The subtitle of the play (*Dawn* [*Aurores*]) evokes Murnau's film *The Dawn* (1927). The subtitle was excluded from the film title.

12 The following have performed the role of "visual memory": Judith Marvan Enriquez (for *Drums on the Dam*), Marie Heuzé (for *The Last Caravanserai*, in which J. Marvan performed), and once again J. Marvan Enriquez (for *Ephemera*), and Lucile Cocito (for *The Survivors of Mad Hope*).

13 Charles-Henri Bradier, in Roberta Gandolfi and Silvia Bottiroli, *Un teatro attraversato dal mondo: Il Théâtre du Soleil oggi* (Pisa: Titivillus, 2012).

14 Ariane Mnouchkine, in Béatrice Picon-Vallin, "Écrire au présent: un récit intime à trente voix," *Alternatives théâtrales*, no. 93, 2007, 56–62.

15 Ariane Mnouchkine, interview with Béatrice Picon-Vallin at the Cartoucherie, June 5, 2010.

16 See for more details on the actors' work, Béatrice Picon-Vallin, *Ariane Mnouchkine* (Paris: Actes Sud-Papiers, 2009).

17 Groupe d'information et de soutien des immigrés [Information and Immigrant Aid Group] is a French non-profit organization supporting human rights. Founded in 1972 through an association of social workers, lawyers, and activists who were in regular contact with foreign populations in France, its aims are to protect the rights of immigrants and to advocate for free movement across borders.

18 Ruhrtriennale is an annual music and arts festival in the Ruhr region of Germany.

19 The actors viewed, in particular, the documentary film *Clandestins, Le Voyage infernal* by Jean-Paul Mudry, Télévision Suisse nomade, 2001, and consulted albums of photographic documents.

20 Ariane Mnouchkine, rehearsal notes on process from *The Last Caravanserai*, November 2004, dossier of the film production, complied by Charles-Henri Bradier, Théâtre du Soleil Archives.

21 Maurice Durozier, interview with B. Picon-Vallin, Paris, March 23, 2007.

22 For example, the *Ephemera* actors had taken a *Salpuri* purification dance workshop at ARTA (Association for Research on the Traditions of the Actor [Association de la recherche des traditions de l'acteur]), located at the Cartoucherie, with the Korean dancer Kim Ri-Hae.

23 Ariane Mnouchkine, in Béatrice Picon-Vallin, "Écrire au présent: un récit intime à trente voix," *Alternatives théâtrales*, 59.

24 Caroline Piketty's book, *Je cherche les traces de ma mère* (Paris: Autrement, 2006), was an important source.

25 One of the first titles of the play was *To Live* [*Vivre*] in homage to Kurosawa's 1952 film.

26 The equivalent of the American Goodwill, Emmaüs is a charity organization that aims to support the impoverished and the homeless. As part of its operations, Emmaüs accepts donations and sells goods at low cost.

27 Ariane Mnouchkine, working notes from rehearsals of *Ephemera*, collected by C-H. Bradier, April 18, 2006, in theatre program.

28 Ibid., April 24, 2006. The non-referenced citations are also excerpted from this same theatre program.

29 See Béatrice Picon-Vallin, "Parler du monde, parler au monde, *Le Dernier Caravansérail* et le ciné-théâtre d'Ariane Mnouchkine," *De la scène à l'écran: Théâtre aujourd'hui*.

30 Ariane Mnouchkine, from rehearsal notes for *The Survivors of Mad Hope*, compiled by C-H. Bradier, August 25, 2009, Théâtre du Soleil Archives.

31 These films included *The Wind* by V. Sjöstrom; *Way Down East* by D.W. Griffith; and *Sunrise*, *The Last Laugh*, and *Taboo* by F.W. Murnau. Certain Sundays there were film projections at the Soleil.

32 Ariane Mnouchkine, in "Changement de décor," radio program dedicated to Patrice Chéreau, France-Culture, October 13, 2013.

33 See Alain Berthoz and Gérard Jorland, eds., *l'Empathie* (Paris: Odile Jacob, 2004).

34 Bradier is referencing H. Cixous's musings about the production, from her e-mail on June 21, 2014.

The Survivors of Mad Hope. A small hot air balloon, with an effigy of the character Jean Salvatore in it, welcomes the audience at the entrance to the cabaret The Mad Hope; also the entrance to the Théâtre du Soleil. (The balloon was created by Elena Antsiferova.) Photo by Michèle Laurent.

Transverse perspectives: six thematic illustrations

Several themes and essential motifs have been present at the Soleil from the beginning; they have nourished its work and its aesthetic. The discovery of a drawing by Roberto Moscoso for *1789*, with a giant marionette and a bird at the end of a perch, immediately evoked for me the figures of Justice and the crows that the Soleil paraded through the streets of Paris as part of a 2010 demonstration against retirement reform. And then there are all those white birds, manipulated on stage, that appear from play to play …. The drawing of a rolling platform, cheerful and colorful, from the hand of the same Moscoso for *Captain Fracasse* led me to consider the long lineage of platforms used by the Soleil, including the chariots of *The House of Atreus Cycle*. And since *Fracasse*, the troupe has performed in front of stunningly painted backdrops, developing from *The Shakespeare Cycle* to *The Survivors of Mad Hope* into fluttering silks, furious or delicate, precious material bought in Asia and handled artfully.

The following selection of images on several choice themes – marionettes, animals, rolling platforms, backdrops and silks, children, and bows – will give the reader some points of entry into the world of the Soleil. Ariane Mnouchkine affirms: "Among the great teachers of actors, there are marionettes." Marionettes have been so present and so powerful that they've even transformed the actors into their image. Mnouchkine has constantly asked her actors to preserve a piece of their childhoods. And the Soleil children have shared the lives of their actor-parents, who first created the plays for them, and later would have them as acting partners. And even if there were not any children on stage during *The Survivors of Mad Hope*, Mnouchkine summoned them for the shooting of the film. Are they not also the future, those for whom the troupe strives? Finally, the experience of the bows as expressions of sharing and brotherhood has always been an integral part of all the Soleil's productions.

THE MARIONETTES

A research sketch by R. Moscoso, *1789*. Archives Roberto Moscoso.

The bird-puppeteer in waves of blue silk (V. Mangado), *The Last Caravanserai*. Photo by Michèle Laurent.

The marionette of Justice carried by four of the Soleil members and attacked by one of the crows, Paris, 2010. Photo by Béatrice Picon-Vallin.

The ghost-children from *The Perjured City* and their puppeteers. Photo by Michèle Laurent.

The actor-marionettes from *Drums on the Dam* and their puppeteers/manipulators. Photo by Michèle Laurent.

A rehearsal for *1789*. Photo by Martine Franck, Magnum Photos.

The large marionette of the Queen, *1789*. Archives Sophie Moscoso.

Madame Cléopâtre's baby-clowns, *The Clowns*. Photo by Claude Bricage.

The little marionettes from *1789*. Photo by Gérard Taubman.

The minuscule marionettes, effigies of the characters, from *Drums on the Dam*. Archives Théâtre du Soleil.

The dummies, effigies of the actors, *The Miraculous Night*. Photo by Marie-Hélène Bouvet.

THE ANIMALS

The rhea from *The Survivors of Mad Hope.* Photo by Michèle Laurent.

A horse from *And Suddenly, Sleepless Nights.* Photo by Michèle Laurent.

The fish from *The Spirit of Mount Tan Vien* (a Vietnamese story performed for children by the Soleil actors, 1973). Archives Georges Bonnaud.

The Georgian donkey from *The Last Caravanserai*. Photo by Michèle Laurent.

The wolf-dogs of the chorus from *The Eumenides, House of Atreus Cycle*. Photo by Martine Franck, Magnum Photos.

The horses from *Macbeth*. Photo by Michèle Laurent.

Moona Baloo the Female Bear from *The Indiad or India of their Dreams*. Photo by Michèle Laurent.

The yak from *And Suddenly, Sleepless Nights*. Photo by Michèle Laurent.

THE ROLLING PLATFORMS

A research sketch by Roberto Moscoso for *Captain Fracasse*. Archives of Sophie Moscoso.

Rolling platforms in *Molière*. Photos by Michèle Laurent.

Rolling platforms in *Molière*. Photos by Michèle Laurent.

The entrance of two rolling platforms in *The Last Caravanserai* (the trees, outfitted with wheels, could also travel), rehearsal photo. Photo by Michèle Laurent.

The scene "A Marvelous Garden" in *Ephemera*. Photo by Michèle Laurent.

The actors' rolling platform/stage from *Molière*. Photo by Michèle Laurent.

A rectangular rolling platform from *Ephemera* and its "pushers." Photo by Michèle Laurent.

A rolling crate for Madame Gabrielle who films the film within the theatre piece, *The Survivors of Mad Hope*. Photo by Michèle Laurent.

THE BACKDROPS AND SILKS

The Last Caravanserai: panels of painted silk for the sky and for the river water. Photo by Michèle Laurent.

The drying of the silks to be dyed and painted (Y. de Maisonneuve and D. Martin) for *Drums on the Dam* in the Buddha hall. Archives Ysabel de Maisonneuve.

The installation of panels painted for the film set in the play *The Survivors of Mad Hope*. Photo by Michèle Laurent.

One of the painted backdrops for *1789*. Photo by Lesly Hamilton.

The Spirit of Mount Van Tien (in a tent). Archives Georges Bonnaud.

One of the silks from *Henry IV*. Photo by Michèle Laurent.

A sketch on cardstock by G-C. François for *Twelfth Night*. Archives Guy-Claude François.

Two of the 17 painted silks for *Drums on the Dam*. Photo by Michèle Laurent.

Two of the 17 painted silks for *Drums on the Dam*. Photo by Michèle Laurent.

The Survivors of Mad Hope. Photo by Michèle Laurent.

The silks in movement, *Macbeth*. Photo by Michèle Laurent.

THE CHILDREN

1789: behind the big table, the caravan-day-care that would become their school. Archives of Georges Bonnaud.

A break for a pie-in-the-face during the shooting of *Mad Hope*. Photo by Michèle Laurent.

The filming of *Molière*. Photo by Michèle Laurent.

On tour in Saint Étienne in the tiered seating of *Ephemera*: Mnouchkine addresses the actors, the adults above and the children below. Photo by Bettina Brinkmann.

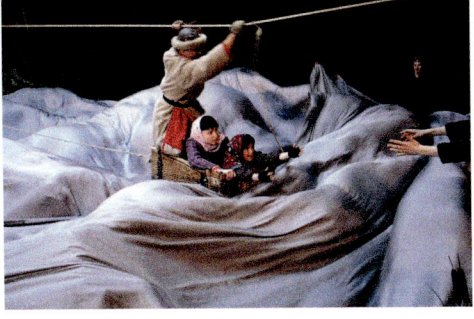

In front of the enormous ship, wrecked among icebergs (filming of *Mad Hope)*. Photo by Michèle Laurent.

The children in the small basket that crosses the raging river: *The Last Caravanserai*. Photo by Michèle Laurent.

The Survivors of Mad Hope/film: Gabrielle, the adult, meets Gabrielle, the child. Photo by Michèle Laurent.

Mnouchkine speaks to the child playing Parastou during the filming of *The Last Caravanserai (Odysseys)*. Photo by Michèle Laurent.

Ephemera: Volume 1, Episode 5, "Pasta shells." Photo by Bettina Brinkmann.

Ephemera: a moment of preparation is necessary, the actors' tête-à-tête with their child partners. Photo by Bettina Brinkmann.

Macbeth: Banquo and his son. Photo by Michèle Laurent.

THE BOWS

A Midsummer Night's Dream. Archives Sophie Moscoso.

Mephisto. Archives Théâtre du Soleil.

Richard II. Archives Monique and Daniel Cordin.

Twelfth Night: the actors' bows in Berlin. Photo by Liliana Andreone.

Twelfth Night: bows with bharata natyam steps in Munich in 1983. Archives Sophie Moscoso.

The Terrible but Unfinished Story of Norodom Sihanouk: the actors, the audience, and the marionettes (the Khmer people). Photo by Liliana Andreone.

The Eumenides: bows with the technical team. Archives Sophie Moscoso.

The Last Caravanserai (Odysseys): the actors come down into the auditorium and are on the same level as the spectators. Photo by Michèle Laurent.

The Survivors of Mad Hope (Dawn): the final show (306th) in Taiwan, bows with the whole troupe. Photo by Liliana Andreone.

Tartuffe: bows in the style of a family photo. Photo by Liliana Andreone.

Ephemera: bows, with the children, to both sides of the tiered seating. Photo by Bettina Brinkmann.

The Survivors of Mad Hope: Dawn. The filming of Marguerite's false flight. Notice the astonishing back and forth between theatre, craftsmanship, special effects, and film images. Photo by Charles-Henri Bradier.

First Epilogue (2014): the galaxy of the Soleil

"The theatre's influence is boundless. Every evening, in a house of some 600 people, you never know where the fires will be lit."

Ariane Mnouchkine[1]

I've reached the end of this book, and like Jean La Palette and his production team for the film *Mad Hope*, who decided on the eve of World War I to film without breaks, I, too, feel authorized to take this story to the end without summing up. The Soleil is a path, and any summary should heed the words of Spanish poet Antonio Machado: "Traveler, there is no path, the path comes in the walking."[2] Yet, there is more to say about the Soleil's fellow travelers: its public, the companies it invites and encourages, and those who stand by its side.

The public: weaving connections

No theatre company functions without thinking about its public; but the place of the public is special to the Soleil, for it owes its very existence, at least in part, to its audience. Let's not forget that it was the tremendous enthusiasm of the spectators who kept flocking to the Cartoucherie that kept the young company alive in the early 1970s when, after its colossal success in Milan with *1789 or The Revolution Must Only Stop at the Perfection of Happiness*, no other theatre in France would produce them. The devotion has been reciprocal; and it dates to a period even earlier that *1789*. Gérard Hardy talks about how, during the run of *The Kitchen* in 1967, he spent hours speaking with the people whom Sonia Debeauvais[3] had sent him to:

> I ended up really knowing all those folks whose names I'd gathered, because I spent all my time working on it. What was really interesting was going to see the people in charge of the cultural committees in the factories, or the heads of associations, to speak to them about what it meant to be an artist, about what we did and how we did it, to have a

"Often, during our ritual daily meetings with the actors, before we begin, we remind ourselves that there might be among the audience people who have never been to the theatre before. And for others, this might be the last performance they'll ever see." (Ariane Mnouchkine, in Fabienne Pascaud, *L'Art du présent*, 2005, 125.)

The Office at the Théâtre du Soleil, 1987. Pictured are Liliana Andreone and Eve Doe Bruce, who would become an actor. Photo by Stefano Fogato.

real relationship with them. Then, they'd go off and speak to their members about us.[4]

The Soleil's files of addresses and connections, growing little by little, exploded when *1789* came back to Paris. The public relations system that Hardy and Odile Cointepas had put in place was eventually handed over to Liliana Andreone, who joined the company in 1976 for the film *Molière*. First, she worked in the costume shop, then, after *Mephisto*, on running the housekeeping – which led to the "Office," while Hardy went back to acting.

Voice of Liliana Andreone

"*Gérard had assembled a huge file, what we called the 'round' file.[5] He's the one who taught me the job. So our contact file is entirely made up of people who asked to be part of it. Gérard would say: 'Never just take the names off the checks; it will have the opposite effect of what you want. If people really want to be on your contact lists, when they receive the letter you send – because they have asked to have it sent to them – they'll open it! When you steal an address, it just feels like one more advertisement, and they'll put it in the garbage.' For* Mad Hope, *reservations were so overwhelming that we were worried about how to keep things feeling human. We asked for help from people around us because there weren't enough of us working the telephones. Gérard came back to the Soleil and worked for free; and it was a marvelous moment for everybody to watch what he did … . He transmitted to all the younger people how to speak to the public.*"

This patient, personalized, but non-intrusive relationship with the public, this friendly and open way of listening (a relationship that has never functioned by subscriptions), has resulted in a large, computerized database of "Individuals," "Groups," and "Internationals." It is constantly evolving. Sylvie Papandréou, who joined the Soleil in 1997 and is the second in command of the Office, acknowledges with Andreade that today the number of "Individuals" surpasses the number of "Groups."[6] This certainly reflects the state of the society we live in.

Voice of Sylvie Papandréou

> *"There are definitely fewer cultural committees from factories and fewer local associations in our 'Group' files these days. Now we have 'groups of friends' and networks who always plan to come together. We spend a lot of time on the phone with them … . But this kind of trial and error organization is magical. It's only at the Soleil that ticketing works like this. After having worked more than 20 years in this kind of position in the theatre, I've learned that everything is possible at the Soleil. And there are no people more important than any others."*[7]

The Office, which is responsible for welcoming the public and filling a house of 555 seats,[8] is thus supple and flexible – finding solutions when a spectator has a problem, re-ticketing an entire evening when Mnouchkine delays the opening, never cashing a check before the date of the performance – always later, and always keeping a few seats free, the number depending on the evening. School trips for students are more than welcome; as children are, we know, tomorrow's public. But the Soleil never fills the house with them: students never make up more than a fifth of the evening's audience. For *The Last Caravanserai* (2003), the Soleil did organize, exceptionally, a series of school matinees, bringing in more than 1,500 students from Paris, its suburbs, and from the provinces.

Almost from the start, the company communicated directly and intimately with its audience members through a "Letter to the public" – addressing how the company was doing, what its projects were, and where it was in terms of its forthcoming production. This missive, which expresses the Soleil's sense of responsibility toward the public monies that help keep the company afloat, also bears witness to its affection for all those faithful and future spectators, destined to receive the coming production. For their part, the spectators write to the Soleil to describe how they felt about the show they saw, thank them, or let them know how they plan to come to the next production. For example, some long-time adherents of the Soleil initiated a trip from Château-Renault to attend in 2010 *The*

Survivors of Mad Hope: they rented the buses themselves and brought some 500 theatre "guests" from the Loire Valley along with them.

A Letter from Château-Renault

> "*On Saturday, March 13, just ten days away, you'll have 320 of our high school students with you, in your theatre, to attend a performance. There'll also be my colleagues: teachers and proctors, the school counselor, the super Yvette, and Rabiaa who works in the kitchen, the principal as well. Some of the parents wanted to come too and they wanted to come with their friends, and their friends brought in their friends. Some of them were in high school with me 25 years ago when we all went to the Théâtre du Soleil. We were just 13 years old then. So we'll be 420 people, and we'll come in eight buses.*"[9]

This kind of affectionate exchange helps build a network with the public, as does the Soleil's Internet site, conceptualized to be attentive to users' needs. There is a "Palaver Tree" under which the public can post its comments and thoughts; an information column on the Soleil's activities: "Our News;" as well

Gérard Hardy and Ariane Mnouchkine speaking to children at a school in Avignon, during the run of *The Clowns* at the Avignon Theatre Festival, July 1969. Archives Jean-Claude Penchenat.

as a column on what else is happening at the Cartoucherie: "In Our Hangars." There is a space for commentary on the more serious social and political questions: "Sentinels and Warning Bells"; and a promotional summary of upcoming productions and activities of theatre friends – companies both nearby and far away, called "Active Propaganda" – a term borrowed from Jacques Copeau. And there are articles, interviews, and all kinds of information on past productions and the Soleil's history, initially uploaded for the three years during which the Théâtre du Soleil was one of the subject areas for the French high-school leaving exam (*le baccalauréat*).

"I'd say that the public makes theatre with us."[10]

The simple and direct relationship established by the Office is further enhanced from the moment one enters the theatre, where each spectator is welcomed as though a guest and not a customer. Speaking of *1789*, Jacques Delcuvellerie puts it this way: "Before the opening scene, we [found] ourselves in a very different role from that of ordinary spectator: we [were] there to support an effort, a new project; we [were] included in a world of solidarity and not just consumerism."[11] That type of relationship continues to this day, while finding different forms of expression; for example, the help given by spectators to the Afghan theatre company, Théâtre Atfaab, or the contributions donated to top up the budget for the film of *Mad Hope*. For *Mad Hope*, as had happened for *The Shakespeare Cycle* (1990), spectators had to go to the Cartoucherie and line up in order to purchase their seats, as the telephone system had broken down. (The Soleil didn't take reservations through the Internet in 2010). The Office team, the actors, and Mnouchkine herself reciprocate these forms of solidarity by being present in the Welcome Area during intermission, where the public can either purchase an inexpensive meal or get a drink of water from one of the many carafes at their disposal, and also by being there at the end of the production to interact and converse with spectators.

In 1993, Ariane Mnouchkine said:

> The public is king. When it enters, it will decide if it was right to pay to come here. The public should be able to say: "You fed me; you gave me strength; you are allowing me to go back to the city a little better, a little more aware, a little more sure, a little more generous, a little stronger." It's the public's reaction that counts, the way they come to tell us what they've experienced. They give us back our strength. They nourish us in all the ways it's possible to nourish, and first of all materially. The fact that people take the bus, the subway, spend 135 francs (now 30 euros), come to us instead of sitting in front of their television … By their witnessing, their

recognition, they justify what we do; they elect us again. And by that I mean they agree that we can represent them.[12]

The crowd of people gathering in the Welcome Area every night, excited to be at the Soleil, still moves and delights Mnouchkine. A kind of fourth creator, the Soleil's audience is particularly reactive to what happens on stage – wonderment, tears, fainting during *The Shakespeare Cycle* and *Ephemera* (2008), nostalgic whispers about the children's toys piled on the circular glides of the latter, humming softly, then more loudly the melody of the "Internationale" when the ship Mad Hope arrives at port during *The Survivors of Mad Hope*. Here is how the actor Catherine Schaub describes the public's emotional rollercoaster during the touring of *The House of Atreus* in Bradford, England (1993): "It was so hot that all the spectators had fans; we had a human ocean of fans in front of us; and it was extraordinary to see the effects of this in the production's moments of greatest tension or relaxation: it was like waves coming in, and it always seemed orchestrated."[13]

Individual reactions become collective, especially for the bows – where face to face with the many actors and the technical and Office crews who join them toward the end of the run, all of them hand in hand after the deployment of their art – the public, like a mirror of the artists, also forms a collective. Spectators become a group united by often prolonged clapping, not to say ovations. After the performance, many audience members need to speak, searching for the right words to express what they've experienced both intimately and through sharing. Their world has grown bigger through these giant and stimulating productions. The public's emotions are felt corporeally; and spectators always recognize the enormity of what has been accomplished so generously and without pretense.[14]

At the Cartoucherie in the Vincennes woods, just as during touring, everything contributes to creating this kind of exchange, which is the definition of what their theatre is – where all senses are appealed to, and not just the intellect. Mnouchkine explains:

> I remember evenings in Bali in a village. The children would come to watch a bit of the show being performed, then go buy a packet of fried shrimp, or fall asleep in their mothers' laps. [It's like] the two approaches that have always tempted us: completely captivating the spectators or allowing them to feel free. They have to breathe; they shouldn't feel oppressed or constrained. But at the same time we want them to be so involved in the show that they don't move or speak. To arrive at that kind of balance, we need a certain kind of space, a certain kind of music, a particular rhythm. It's really all deeply organic. A matter of uniting mind and

body. In the theatre, if the body isn't comfortable, the mind can't function as it should. But if you only speak to the mind, then the body feels nothing; there's no emotion.[15]

People's theatre in action

Voice of Ariane Mnouchkine

"The public's response to our work felt like a kind of benediction. I don't think we were saying, when we started out, that we were certainly going to have an audience. In truth, we didn't really know what that meant when we got launched. What the public's love could mean... What that would elicit from me in terms of gratefulness, love, responsibility, feelings of danger and guilt. Always being afraid that the public would be disappointed, sad. Every time I talk about it, I think about something that happened when I was a kid. I must have been about 12 years old. We were living in the sixteenth arrondissement, on the rue Lalo, next to the Porte Maillot, which was still a kind of vacant lot. Circuses used to set up there. One day we went to the circus with our housekeeper. It was springtime; we were in a line to buy tickets to the Pinder Circus. Three or four places in front of us an old lady got to the ticket booth and whispered something. She turned around and left the line, saying: 'So that's how it goes, at my age not having enough money to buy a ticket to the circus. Just think about it!' – and then she went on her way. It stayed with me like a shaming. Why didn't I dare pay her ticket or ask our housekeeper: 'Can't we pay for her?' I didn't dare. I think that woman lives in my relationship to our audiences. When you get right down to it, I've been trying for forty years to compensate for that child's shame of not daring. Not daring to speak to her: I was afraid the housekeeper would say 'no.' I didn't dare either take on what might have been the woman's dignified refusal. I remember the light at the end of that afternoon, toward eight o'clock at night, those long shadows. That old lady for whom the little bourgeois girl didn't dare buy a ticket ... I didn't do it and it became a kind of crime. When older women come to speak to me after a performance, I often think of that old lady."[16]

The people's theatre practiced by the Théâtre du Soleil isn't undergirded by a particular ideology, but by maintaining affectionate connections with a very diverse and numerous public. These days, Mnouchkine likes to use director Antoine Vitez's phrase "an elite theatre for everybody." That means theatre that everybody can afford, but also that anyone can grasp intellectually, but realized at the highest level of art. A theatre at

Setting up the stage for *Ephemera* in the Park Avenue Armory in New York, at the invitation of Lincoln Center, 2009. The red and white striped cloth that surrounds the set reminds us of the material that surrounds the sets of Japanese Noh theatre, when it is performed outdoors. It was after this production that the Armory, which belongs to the U.S. Army, became a major arts venue. Photo by Stéphanie Berger.

In Bochum, Germany, at the Jahrhunderthalle Ruhrtriennale, in June 2004. A meeting of the company before a performance of *The Last Caravanserai*. Photo by Étienne Lemasson.

once simple – that is the simplicity acquired after many years of experience – and intelligent, where everyone, regardless of their age or their origins, finds something personally meaningful. It's theatre work that brings together different generations – at least four today – different nationalities, and different social classes – especially among its high-school public and all those within the realm of National Education to whom the Soleil is directly connected. Indeed, ever since *The Kitchen*, specialized journals not given to speaking about theatre review the work of The Soleil. Transgenerational, transsocial, international – these are the characteristics that describe, without theorization or dogmatism, the Théâtre du Soleil's notion of popular, that is, people's theatre.

Mnouchkine likes to say: "In a theatre company, one is responsible for souls."[17] The members of the company who have worked in public relations, while also moving between stage work and administration, embody that attitude. For its part, the Soleil's public takes on responsibility for the Soleil: it's often word of mouth that, from the very beginning, circulates information about productions, as well as conveying enthusiasm and the emotional tenor of a performance. What really characterizes the state of the Soleil's spectators – and Mnouchkine says this as well – is active hope, rather than passive waiting.

The planets circulating around The Soleil

There's an entire planetary system around the Théâtre du Soleil, comprised of many people coming from different horizons in France as well as abroad. The circles of friends and acolytes are added depending on themes and concerns expressed in each show. There are ancient and traditional theatre companies as well as interns and young troupes whom Mnouchkine mentors. All of them encounter each other, sooner or later, on the bleachers – where one always makes room for other spectators – or during the Soleil's long weekend workshops.

Might it be possible that the Théâtre du Soleil provides, as one of the Afghan characters in the Théâtre Atfaab's *Nightwatch* [*La Ronde de nuit*] proposes, "a shelter for the world's archives?" These archives are both material and immaterial. The former are composed of all the costumes, innumerable musical instruments, and masks that Ariane Mnouchkine presents to her interns as the theatre's treasures. The latter are the men and women who have entered and crossed through the theatre's hangars: to perform or to teach, to watch or to work on sets and paint frescoes, to cook, to solve problems, to invent projects – knowledge, savoir faire, and wisdom being transmitted thanks to the space's fluidity.

Nightwatch. A production by the traveling Afghan Theatre Aftaab, created at the Soleil, in French and in Dari, in 2013. An illegal Afghan immigrant becomes the night watchman at a theatre located in a woods, a dream space where during a long winter's night a multitude of characters parade. The screen, which permits the character Nader to speak to his family, serves as frame. Photo by Michèle Laurent.

The history of popular theatre in France is linked, in part, to the Soleil and its "home school." First of all, there is the Théâtre du Campagnol, directed by Jean-Claude Penchenat, who created the Campagnol's first production at the Cartoucherie in 1971. In 1997, Christophe Rauck, who had joined the company during the run of *The House of Atreus* (1990), founded his own company, Terrain Vague. It was welcomed for six weeks at the Soleil for a production of Brecht's *The Caucasian Chalk Circle*, before he took the show to Berlin to perform at the Berliner Ensemble. When he was artistic director of the Théâtre Gérard Philipe of Saint-Denis, Rauck engaged many actors who had been part of the Théâtre du Soleil (Philippe Hottier, Juliette Plumecoq-Mech, Virginie Colemyn, Myriam Azencot). Jean Bellorini, who became the director of the Saint-Denis theatre after Rauck, had had his work produced at the Théâtre du Soleil as well, indeed produced from the time he graduated from the Claude-Mathieu Theatre School. His company, Air de Lune, first performed *The Seagull* at the Soleil in 2003, then in 2010 *Tempest in a Skull* [*Tempête sous un crane*], an adaptation of Hugo's *Les Misérables*.

The actor Simon Abkarian – who also has a career in film – writes, performs, and directs shows with his company TERA, founded in 1998. These are directly connected to his experience as an actor with the Soleil – for example, his *Penelope, Oh Penelope* [*Pénélope, ô Pénélope*] in which former Soleil actors Georges Bigot, John Arnold, and Catherine Schaub performed.

He also performed a solo show influenced by his work at the Soleil, *Menelaus's Rembetiko Rhapsody* [*Ménélas rébétiko rapsodie*][18] in which he danced and dialogued with on-stage musicians. Actor Georges Bigot transmits what he learned at the Soleil both at Au Petit Théâtre du Pain, located in the Basque country, and at The Actor's Gang, located in Los Angeles. His remounting, with Delphine Cottu, of the Soleil's *The Tragedy of King Sihanouk* (2013) in the khmer language in Cambodia speaks to how long the reach of the Théâtre du Soleil has been, but also of the depth of its impact. The actor Hélène Cinque, with her company l'Instant d'une Résonance, presented at the Soleil *Love's Labour's Lost* and *Cymbeline*, projects that had been abandoned by the Soleil during their work on *The Shakespeare Cycle*. And, in 2012–2013, the young street performers Les Lorialets (now called Baraque Liberté) performed under the linden trees at the Soleil *Our Commune: A Little Known History Recounted on a Wagon* [*Notre commune – Histoire méconnue racontée sur un char*]. The Soleil subsequently asked them, after its own run of *The Last Caravanserai*, to perform at Paris's Museum of Immigration some of the interviews it had carried out with refugees.

Andrés Pérez Araya, who passed away in 2002, came to the Soleil as an intern in 1983 for *The Shakespeare Cycle*, in which he performed the role of a black guard; he stayed on as a company member to perform in the Asian epics (Zhou Enlai and Khieu Samphan in *Sihanouk*, and Gandhi in *The Indiad*). He returned to his home in Chile and founded the company Gran Circo Teatro, which was both extremely innovative and highly indebted to his work at the Soleil. As a well-known director in Latin America, he always said about his time with the Soleil troupe: "For a theatre person coming from a developing country, it was a place where you could learn many useful things."[19] The Soleil was pleased to honor the man and his work while touring in Chile in 2012. And this is just the beginning of the genealogy we could establish for the Théâtre du Soleil.[20]

As time has gone on, the Soleil's responsibility to transmit its methods and philosophy has loomed larger and larger. It has thus offered free workshops at the Cartoucherie. More than 1,500 young people applied, for example, to the 2009 iteration, for which the actor Philippe Caubère returned to teach. Four-hundred-fifty people participated in the workshop, which lasted eight days.[21] The methods of the Soleil are also taught elsewhere – since 1984 in workshops given by Soleil actors while touring internationally (Georges Bigot and Maurice Durozier in Los Angeles and in Brazil), and by former actors with the Soleil, still close to the company, who offer workshops at various festivals or in theatres or universities that privilege artistic exchange.

A workshop in Afghanistan in 2005. Afghan actors perform for Ariane Mnouchkine in *commedia dell-arte* masks or in Balinese masks that the Théâtre du Soleil brought with them for the workshop. Photo by Everest Canto de Montserrat.

The Soleil's musical director Jean-Jacques Lemêtre also teaches workshops in many parts of the world.

One workshop stands out among the many: in 2005 Mnouchkine and 40 company members went to Afghanistan to teach, despite the very obvious dangers involved in working in Kabul. This was the origin of the Afghan company, the Théâtre Atfaab, "atfaab" meaning "sun" in the Dari language. The Soleil has god-mothered this company, which already has a striking history. After its first productions, *Romeo and Juliette* in Kabul, *Tartuffe* in Paris (based on Mnouckine's staging), it produced in 2006 *On That Day* [*Ce jour-là*], based on the kind of improvisations that gave shape to *The Last Caravanserai*. In *Nightwatch*, an Afghan inflected *commedia dell'arte* piece staged by Hélène Cinque, the Afghan actors invented the text in order to perform their own exile, as if in the Cartoucherie, with one of their actors performing the role of guardian of the theatre. This piece was both a meta-theatrical exploration of theatrical transmission and an echo of the questions raised in *And Suddenly, Sleepless Nights*.

Voice of Maurice Durozier

"In Kabul, we were faced with events that went way beyond what we were equipped to handle. We were participating in the renaissance of a society that had been destroyed by war. The work allowed us to give to certain people a reason to live. That's what art can do in this world. They saw what a troupe was: men and women working together. It was

possible to live like that. And when we started to rehearse
Ephemera, *they were present. We had been able to have*
them come. When we talked about our first idea for the
project – a comet that meant the end of the world – their
eyes grew big. I can still see them: they murmured: 'Yes, the
end of the world.'"[22]

In 2003, the Soleil launched the Festival Premiers pas, also
known as a festival for "the children of theatre troupes;" and
Mnouchkine tapped Alexandre Zloto, the head of the young
company, TAF Théâtre, for the artistic directorship. The festival harkened back to what Jacques Copeau had imagined
in his *Solicitations [Appels]*: it held events in tents or in the
Cartoucherie's hangars, depending on what was free at the
time. The festival was meant to bring in groups who believed in
the importance of theatre companies, and whose members were
committed to each other for the long term, as well as committed
to finding a new rapport with their publics.

Founded in 1989, again through Mnouchkine's initiative,
l'ARTA (or the Association for Research in Acting Traditions),
was created to organize workshops helmed by masters of various theatre arts. ARTA was initially led by Lucia Bensasson,
who acted with the Soleil from *1789* until *The Shakespeare
Cycle*, and by Claire Duhamel – the latter having been both
an actor and administrator of the Renaud-Barrault Company,
who, after being named Cultural Attaché to Santiago, Chile,
during the dictatorship, worked to bring artists in danger to
France. Duhamel was eventually replaced by Jean-François
Dusigne, who had performed in the Soleil's Asian epics – and
who is now, also, a theatre professor at the University of Paris.
ARTA has invited scores of Asian, Russian, and British professionals to teach in its building; and often members of the Soleil
participate in these workshops.

The Soleil's hospitality extends to invitations to theatre
companies from far away, especially those whose traditions
have inspired the work of the company. It works with Milena
Salvini's Mandapa Center, the Maison des Cultures du Monde,
and ARTA to bring in from India, for instance, kathakali
and *kutiyatam* troupes (the Sopanam and Kalamandalam
Schools). It has brought in great dancers, such as the *odissi*
dancer Kelucharan Mohapatra, the *kuchipudi* dancer Shantala
Shivalingappa, the Ceylanese dancers Khema de Costa and
Upekha da Silva. From Japan, the Soleil has invited *kyogen*
families (the Nomura Family and the Shigeyama Family) and
kabuki families (Fujima Kanjuro); and from Cambodia, the
royal troupe of *Sbek Thom* (shadow theatre with leather puppets). There has been the *wayang kulit* or shadow theatre of
Java from Indonesia, and from Bali the *Calon Arang*; from

Korea, Kim Ri-Hae has come to demonstrate the *Salpuri* dance and Kim Duk-Soo has come with an ensemble of traditional percussionists (SamulNori Hanullim). The Tipa, or dancing monks from Tibet, have come in from the Monastery of Shechen; and Gyuto monks have also taught. Wu Hsing-Kuo, an actor trained in Chinese Opera, arrived from Taiwan to teach a master class, and worked on excerpts from *King Lear*: the experience helped him return to Taiwan to rebuild his own troubled company, Contemporary Legend Theatre. The Soleil also welcomed a company (Siah Bazi) performing *siah bazi*, a popular comic form from Iran, tightly controlled by the Islamic Republic and now almost nonexistent, as well as the great Iranian singer Shahram Mazeri and the Israeli jazzman Giora Feidman. In 1993, the Soleil produced an Indian show, based on an idea of Mnouchkine's with Rajeev Sethi: *India, from Father to Son, from Mother to Daughter* [*L'Inde de père en fils, de mère en fille*]. A popular theatre form, this piece featured storytellers, musicians, dancers, acrobats, and magicians – all in the spirit of keeping transmission alive. And there has been so much more …

The Soleil opened its theatre to "twin company," Eugenio Barba's Odin Theatre of Denmark in 2000 for *Mythos* and *Ode to progress*; in 2005 for *Salt* and *Andersen's Dream* – whose set greatly inspired the scenography for *Ephemera*. And in 2012, the Odin came with *Chronicle of Life*. It offered its stage to the Russian director Anatoli Vassiliev for his *Dom Juan*, and all of its hangars for entire nights of Indian music (northern ragas in 2000, Carnatic chanting from the south of India in 2010). The Quebecois artist Pol Pelletier came in with her solo show, *Joy* [*Joie*] in 1994; the Radeau company with *Cantatas* [*Les Cantates*] in 2001; Patrice Chéreau for a reading of *The Legend of the Great Inquisitor* [*La Légende du Grand Inquisiteur*] in 2008. The company sponsors myriad encounters and colloquia on contemporary issues, on the question of how best to train artists, on the history of theatre, as well as opening its doors for various festivities. The list is long: enumerating everything would get boring; and because there is not enough room, this accounting is ultimately incomplete.[23] The examples above are simply meant to give an idea of the many exchanges the Soleil has encouraged and of the networks of friendship and intercultural knowledge it has fostered.

> "I don't have the feeling of having lost. I'd say, rather, that we haven't won yet." (Ariane Mnouchkine, in *Le Monde*, February 26, 1998.)

Another way

"Another way" might have been a good title for the Soleil's production *The Survivors of Mad Hope*. It is certainly a good title for my closing thoughts. For we must ask, what's the secret behind the longevity of the Théâtre du Soleil, which has established itself outside of all known theatrical institutions and structures? Is it the periodic, necessary, but never premeditated renewal of the company – brought about by departures – that has guaranteed its youthfulness, a kind of meshing of utopian dreams of the 1960s with the ideals of renewable energy? Is it the basic stability provided by a commitment to public service, combined with personal engagement with the ethics of a collective project? Is it Mnouchkine's lucid optimism? Her unflagging energy, her rare and determined personality in which "the artist and the teacher, the inventor of beauty and the educator never cease to coexist and dialogue?"[24] Could it be the quality of the group's work, the quality indeed of the majority of the members of the Soleil? The egalitarian organization of intensive research? The success abroad as well as in France? The desire to always go farther? No doubt it is all of this, but above all, trust in theatre as a contemporary art form and as a possible model for a society still in the making – and the actors' trust in the company leader, even when she herself doubts. And, also, the fact that if the troupe has lasted, it's because "there was always someone to breathe on the coals."[25] Fire was also engraved on the logo of the Taganka theatre in Moscow, and the brazier provided a good image for their collective creation, but internal quarreling caused by the political context in Russia got the better of them; and the fire went out. This has never been the case at the Soleil, and Mnouchkine has never left her company, despite the fact that she had wanted to make a "real" film at the close of *The Last Caravanserai*. She has, instead, made her films in the theatre.

There have been periods in which some have been wary of the Soleil: it has been critiqued for not being dialectical enough. But a total work should be judged by the rhythm of its realizations; and what might have seemed weaker should be understood by what followed – a first iteration that grew into something more powerful. Bernard Faivre d'Arcier says that Ariane Mnouchkine should be thought of as a "national living treasure," the title given to the greatest masters of art in Asia. Devoted to her commitment to theatre, Mnouchkine intervenes in the social fabric of the country: the Soleil is a theatre of resistance. For *Macbeth*, while people were being laid off everywhere, Mnouchkine had 42 actors on stage from 24 different countries; and the entire company boasts 80 people, 100 when extra help comes on-board.

Twenty-eight productions and seven films, and a public exhorting: "Continue!" "Don't stop!" The hangar where the Soleil has installed itself, buildings that everyone finds beautiful, is a space that is neither public nor private, but common – connected to the world by a whole arts network, by adventures and friendships, a utopian space which, according to Mnouchkine, is "the possible not yet realized." In fact, it's

Ariane Mnouchkine at the Cartoucherie in 2014. Photo by Michèle Laurent.

a festive spatiotemporal universe. And it is political because it is festive. Going to the Soleil is itself a celebration, for some even a wonderland; and the troupe knows how to organize a good party outside of the performances themselves – in order to regenerate energies and celebrate what should be celebrated. Their way, this other way, is still long, but the Soleil has many exceptional companions. For, as Simon Abkarian says:

> You never really leave the Théâtre du Soleil. There's always something that remains through the sieve of time: a per-petual questioning, a love of actors, a love of the public, rigor, respect, delicacy, a quest for a never-obtained but always sought for perfection. This theatre makes us mutu-ally human.[26]

Ariane Mnouchkine writes to the students at ENSATT (The National School of Theatre Arts)[27]

"*You're lucky.*

You're lucky to have gone to school – to high school, perhaps to university, without restrictions, without quotas.

You're lucky, yes, because elsewhere in the world this couldn't happen – that on this Monday, September 30, 2013, young men and women, even if just like you, could not come together in a theatre school.

Without having to hide, without fearing for your lives, without risking being burned alive, you're lucky to commence today your studies at this prestigious theatre school where you will be taught to mime, to perform, to incarnate acts driven by unfathomable emotions – or pure, obscene, sublime, diabolical, atrocious ones. Human, that is.

And if you're not here to perform those feelings, because this isn't the theatre path you've chosen – those of you here to become theatre technicians – don't think you're off the hook. The bridges from which the others will jump, the balconies off of which they'll hang, the storms that will shipwreck them, the shore, the urban jungle, the king's cell, the orchard, the sound of an axe cutting it down, the thunder of anguish and remorse, the sun downs and sun rises, dusk – all of that is you. You will embroider the pillow that smothers. The handkerchief as well. You will sew the lethal tunic. You will make the blood flow. The suns, the obscure lights, the aphrodisiac moons – you're the ones who will hang them.

So all you 'virile' ones, you future technical directors, those of you who don't 'have to do it,' don't show off. For you'll be on the battlefield. You'll fight. You'll tremble and you'll choke as well. In any case, that's what I hope for you.

But, my God, why am I saying all this. It's almost aggressive.

I'm saying it because I'm afraid. I'm afraid for you. I'm always afraid that someone will keep you from imagining, from dreaming, from flying. I'm afraid of cynics, of vulgar people, of those destroyed types with their 'I know everything' allure. I'm afraid that some man, some woman, maybe someone among you, yes, especially someone among you, will disenchant you. A noisy lug with their stash of beer, a screamer with their plastic bags. Nasty comments between two cigarettes. And it's over. The moon is down. It, too, made of plastic.

But what am I trying to say to them? … Talk about a welcome speech! Be nice! They're young. Encourage them!

But that's what I'm doing. I am encouraging them, in my own way, by telling them what I'm worried about and by pointing out the enemies.

The School's Director now reading this letter chose me – me – to be your "godmother." Your teachers agreed and that's not nothing. It's an honor, but it's more than that: it's a responsibility. Enormous. I can't proffer a phony greeting that doesn't represent what I believe, that doesn't name the tools you must absolutely have and share in order to be launched into the epic story that starts this very day. And that started for me 55 years ago.

I believe in imagination, in freedom, but also in being on time. I believe in the inventiveness of language, but also in being polite – the least one can be in the ritualization of daily life.

I believe in the generosity of performance and action, but even more I believe in the generosity of listening.

Above all else, I believe in friendship that will be your secret medicine, your magic potion.

I believe that your school must not divide you into actors, on the one hand, and technicians, on the other, but, rather, simply make you into men and women of the theatre. A boom, a projector, a hammer, a drill, an emotion, good diction, a cautious silence, a melody, a verse, a well-placed ladder – those belong to everyone. You need each other desperately. If you don't want to share your knowledge and your practice, you will be less good, less happy, less proud. I'm telling you that. I'm sure of it.

I believe that your school should not be preparing you for the Market, but for the immense worksite of a better world, which, thanks to your art, you now begin to work on.

I believe that all the bureaucracies of France, Navarre, and Europe must stop associating the help they're proposing to young people with the cages in which you would be forced to enter – if you think 'realistically.' Your school must not teach you to succumb to resignation.

You must not enter any preordained box, any cage; your only limits are those imposed by your heart and your conscience: respect for others, Justice, solidarity, and human tenderness.

I hold you close,

Ariane"

Notes

1 Ariane Mnouchkine, *Le Nouvel Observateur*, September 15, 1999.
2 Antonio Machado, "Caminante no hay camino," *Proverbios y cantares, XXIX* (1909–1937).
3 See Chapter One of this study.
4 Gérard Hardy, Interview with M. Faye, Master's thesis, Paris III-Sorbonne Nouvelle, April 26, 2011.
5 This file has the same round form as that of Sonia Debeauvais's audience file. We might think of this roundness as the image of the audience surrounding the Théâtre du Soleil.
6 Naruna de Andrade was also a long-time member of the Office team before she returned home to Brazil.

7 Sylvie Papandréou, in an interview with Béatrice Picon-Vallin at the Cartoucherie, June 2010.

8 When the vomitorium entrances from under the bleachers are used, there are only 500 seats available.

9 From the Archives of the Théâtre du Soleil at the Cartoucherie.

10 Ariane Mnouchkine, in an interview with Béatrice Picon-Vallin at the Cartoucherie, June 2010.

11 Jacques Delcuvellerie, in "Sur la limite, vers la fin/Groupov," *Alternatives théâtrales*, 2012, 379.

12 Ariane Mnouchkine, in "Une oeuvre d'art commune," *Théâtre/Public*, no. 124–125 (1995).

13 Ibid.

14 See Béatrice Picon-Vallin, "Les longs cheminements de la troupe du Soleil," *Théâtre/Public*, no. 152 (2000).

15 Ariane Mnouchkine, in an interview with Guy-Claude François and Béatrice Picon-Vallin, www.theatre-du-soleil.fr.

16 Ariane Mnouchkine, in an interview with Béatrice Picon-Vallin at the Cartoucherie, June 2010.

17 Liliana Andreone and Sylvie Papandréou use similar terms when they talk about their work in the Office.

18 These two plays have been published by Actes Sud-Papier in 2009 and 2012, respectively.

19 Andrés Pérez Araya, in "En plein Soleil," *Fruits*, no. 2–3, June 1984, 29.

20 In Rio de Janeiro, Brazil, the Amok Theatre has organized its space in a way that resembles the Soleil's.

21 See the film by Catherine Vilpoux, *Ariane Mnouchkine: l'Aventure du Soleil*, ACAT films and Co./ARTE France (2009).

22 Maurice Durozier, in an interview with Béatrice Picon-Vallin in Paris, March 23, 2007.

23 We can add to this list the welcome given to other former and current members of the Soleil who have produced their plays at the Soleil: Georges Bigot and his Compagnie de l'Étoile Peinte with *The Dispute* [*La Dispute*, 1997] and with Au Petit Théâtre du Pain, *Embedded*, 2006; Catherine Schaub with *Gilgamesh, an Archeological Dig* [*Gilgamesh, chantiers de fouille*, 2006] – mounted with young Syrian actors who had asked the Soleil to do a workshop for them; Maurice Durozier with *Kalo* in 1993 and *An Actor's Word* [*Parole d'acteur*] in 2013; Myriam Azencot with Compagnie/Chachjaroni performing *Family Stories* [*Histoires de famille*, 2006]; Paul Golub with Cyrille Bosc and Clémentine Yelnik and the Théâtre du Volcan Bleu performing *Hamlet on the Road* [*Hamlet sur la route*] in 2000; Valérie Grail with *1962* in 2001 and *The Luck of My Life* [*La Chance de ma vie*] in 2007; Guy Freixe and the Théâtre du Frêne with *Dancing at Lughnasa* in 2004.

24 Claude Roy, "Ariane Soleil," *Double Page, Le Théâtre du Soleil: Shakespeare*, no. 21 (1982).

25 Ariane Mnouchkine, in F. Darge, "Retour sur cinquante ans de création," *Le Monde*, April 23, 2014.

26 Simon Abkarian, in "Changement de décor," radio program, France Culture, March 30, 2014.

27 Ariane Mnouchkine accepted the position of "godmother" for the class entering in 2013 l'École nationale supérieure des arts et techniques du théâtre, also known as the "Rue Blanche School," a national arts school. She welcomed them with this letter. The class will carry her name.

Second Epilogue (2019): returning to Asian sources, expanding, and transmitting

Voice of Ariane Mnouchkine

> *"Theatre belongs to the world. When theatre doesn't cut itself off from the world, when it accepts the simple fact that it's part of the world, it has the power to make the world better. Theatre, like art in general, is one of those places that can really improve our world, like an orange grove. It's a small light. Every night, a few people exit the theatre a little stronger, with their eyes a little more open."[1]*

No, you never leave the Théâtre du Soleil. And I return again to the company to write this last chapter for the English-language edition of my study. Nearly five years have gone by since its publication in French; and during this time, instead of stopping, the Théâtre du Soleil has pursued an ever wider and longer path. The world's political situation has grown more worrisome: with an increase in wars, terrorism, Islamic fundamentalism, the rise of populisms all over the globe, and the immigration/migration crisis – foreseen remarkably by the Soleil in its 2003 production. The Soleil's adventures, however, have put its "explorers" in dialogue with even more cultures. The company didn't create, as planned, a piece on the Karachi Affair, which would have treated one of the most serious financial and political scandals of the last several decades.[2] The subject was no doubt too limited and couldn't begin to grasp the abyss that seemed to open up in France in 2015 with the bloody attack by Islamic fundamentalists on the satirical newspaper *Charlie-Hebdo*. Thus, two-and-a-half years of questioning, of traveling, and of unending research would separate the creation of *Macbeth* from *A Room in India* [*Une Chambre en Inde*], which premiered on November 5, 2016.

Traveling as part of the creative process

Voice of Ariane Mnouchkine

> *"First of all, there's the traveling. So I'll speak about our last voyage, not just mine but a voyage of the entire company,*

our voyage to India. All the Théâtre du Soleil: [...] techni-
cians, the Office staff, everybody – at my request, maybe I
should say my insistence, and not without some astonish-
ment – everybody went to India."[3]

On November 14, 2014, at a company meeting during one of
the performances of *Macbeth* – a show that closed on March
1, 2015 – Ariane Mnouchkine spoke to the members of the
Soleil about a supposed article on George Orwell, titled: "An
Unknown Episode in the Life of Orwell." Orwell is an author
Mnouchkine had always and often read, someone she calls her
"guard rail," someone who had, she believes, "the courage to be
skeptical of destructive progress."[4] This document, mysteriously
found in the archives of Oxford's Bodleian Library, explained
how Orwell, during his time as colonial officer in Burma (now
Myanmar) in 1922–1927, had encountered a "miniscule but celebrated tribe from the Rakhine mountains," known by nomads
as "the enlightened people" or "the questers of light."

As the story goes, sparked by the account of a Burmese pris-
oner, Orwell planned and executed an exploratory trip to try to
locate this tribe in order to understand the experience of human
beings who were ready to question themselves continuously to
achieve what they believed to be a "noble happiness," common
to all and based on sharing. The company members accepted
this story as authentic,[5] but, in fact, someone had dreamed
it up. For Mnouchkine, it was a reflection of her own quest-
ing and a metaphor more generally for the visionary work of
Orwell, himself. Invented or not, the "article" made the actors
dream as well, opening wide the doors of their imaginations.

While looking for a new starting place for the next production,
Mnouchkine set off on the "Orwell path." She left to explore
Burma during the months of March and April 2015. And she
was disconcerted by how much the country had changed since
she'd first been there, "progress" having violently dug a chasm
between rich and poor, the always poor become even more so –
while also being distanced from their traditions and customs.
She continued on her way, stopping at police stations in hopes
of finding a trace of His Majesty's officer and his voyage to find
the "enlightened people." And then she left for nearby India,
meeting up with Hélène Cixous in May 2015 and discovering with her in the state of Tamil Nadu, near Pondicherry, the
terukkuttu art form, a Tamil performance tradition, the oldest living theatre in the world. It's a theatre emanating from
castes on the lower end of the caste spectrum, a kind of popular cousin to kathakali; and it energizes its surroundings with
bright colors, songs, music, and dancing. During ritual periods,
terukkuttu players perform episodes from the great Indian epics
the *Mahabharata* or the *Ramayana* outdoors and all night long.
For Ariane Mnouchkine, *terukkuttu* was a salutary shock.

The Shock: a representation of *terukkuttu* in the village of Mosavadi, Tamil Nadu, May 2015. Photo by Ariane Mnouchkine.

The trail had become "hotter": if the tribe she'd been looking for was undiscoverable in Burma, lost in some fuzzy memories of Orwell, who had, all the same, nourished her first vision, it could, nevertheless, be found in the *terukkuttu* company she'd just encountered. Pushed to the outskirts of towns, guardian of ancestral knowledge, a concentrated site of resistant theatricality, *terukkuttu* was also funny, even insolent, thanks to the presence of a buffoon, or *katyakkattan*, a delegate of the public itself with whom he was in constant dialogue. Mnouchkine instinctively knew that somehow this theatre had to be present in the Soleil's next production – and, indeed, in *A Room in India*, *terukkuttu* became the object of an artistic quest – a theme that would become clear over time.

On her return from India, Mnouchkine urgently organized at the Cartoucherie a research laboratory on *terukkuttu*, a form no one knew. The actors examined photos and watched videos; they developed their first short improvisations, completely understanding "the ridiculousness of their ignorance but also the beauty of their curiosity and confidence."[6] To her delight, Mnouchkine also discovered in the costume shop, carefully preserved, a *terukkuttu* costume she had bought 20 years earlier to help out an Indian performer who was short of money.[7] Later, she would learn that this costume had belonged to Kalaimamani Purisai Kannappa Sambandan Thambiran, the master teacher of the small theatre that had caught her heart, and of which we will speak more later.

In Pondicherry, in addition to the shock of discovering *terukkuttu*, or rather rediscovering it – because she had, in fact, seen some performances a long time before,[8] she had the task of leading a session of the Soleil's "Nomadic School." This would be the fourth stage of a long, ongoing workshop for actors from all corners of the world, a more formal version of what the Soleil was in the habit of organ-

The first *terukkuttu* workshop at the Cartoucherie after the Soleil returned from India, May 28, 2015. In the Welcome Area, where we see traces of the production of *Macbeth*, the actors improvise with what is available to them. Photo by Charles-Henri Bradier.

izing before every new theatrical cycle or project.[9] Sometimes these workshops were held while on tour, or by special request, as for the Kabul workshop in 2005. In 2015, the Soleil had begun thinking about multiplying the number of workshops, offering regularly educational sessions, rather than master classes – anywhere in the world where there was a demand or a need for them. Mnouchkine and some ten members of the company wanted to share their collective practices, the moments when all queried what theatre was, a kind of *testing of their working methods through transmitting them*: looking at vision, choral work, masks, improvisation, music and performance, and collective creation. The first Nomadic School took place in July 2015 in Santiago, Chile, where the Soleil had already been invited by the Santiago a Mil Festival Foundation in 2012 to perform *The Survivors of Mad Hope*. Three-hundred-fifty students showed up from many parts of Latin America (Brazil, Argentina, Bolivia, Columbia), not only Chile, and partici-pated for an entire month, working in three languages (French, Spanish, and English). The second iteration of the Nomadic School was held on Faro Island in Sweden, followed by a ses-sion in Oxford, before the one in Pondicherry.[10]

The Nomadic School in India, slowly assembled with the aid of the Alliance Française in Pondicherry, with the French Institute of India, the French Embassy, and friends from the French community who offered to lodge the actors, was planned for December. Twelve members of the company would participate. After this, the rest of the troupe would join them to begin working on the next show. But on November 13, 2015, a terrorist attack at the Bataclan Club and surrounding neighborhoods killed over 130 people in Paris. Mnouchkine hesitated, paralyzed, traumatized: should she stay in Paris rather than go to India, stay to work on the horror just experienced? That seemed to be the most pressing need. Was there any other possible reaction? But no doubt she also remembered her own flight to Nepal in 1963, during her first trip to India, an escape from the cruelty and religious conflict taking over Calcutta.

So she said nothing of her concerns and decided to stick to the project. Wouldn't it be better to take some distance, to get away from Paris in order to understand what had happened and act on it? The Nomadic School of India did, then, take place in Pondicherry at the Indianostrum Theatre, founded by Koumarane Valavane, a former Soleil actor. One-hundred students participated.

And when it was over, the rest of the troupe travelled to Pondicherry. They started their work on their new show there: but without a story, without a clear subject, and with no particular vision (Mnouchkine was at a loss). There was only doubt, which slowly imposed itself as one of the leitmotifs of the play to come – doubt that would have to be embodied. And, then, there were four more catalyzers: *terukkuttu*, "the tribe of light," as Mnouchkine explained to her actors on January 11, 2016;[11] the European chaos seen from the vantage point of the local chaos; India itself as a foreign but also generative source, regenerating theatre by its long practice of the art; and the brotherhood of actors, reinforced by their distance from France and the anxiety provoked by recent events. In India, during this difficult passage through a creative void, their rehearsals, also taking place at the Indianostrum, focused on observing life all around them, and on the body. Mnouchkine had foreseen this: the new production would be very physical. Each morning, master teacher Sambandan and his nephew, the dancer and actor Palani Murugan, taught the Soleil actors how in *terukkuttu* to use their eyes, their arms, their feet, what the rhythm of the dances required. In the afternoon, actors worked on improvisations in French, modeling them on *terukkuttu*, but not finding anything that really stuck.

In the course of the work in India (from January 4 to January 26) and upon their return to the Cartoucherie on February 15, their improvisations were continually fed by "the sounds of India," this "continent that never sleeps."[12] They finally decided that they would, after all, speak about everything they'd worked on in India, that they wanted to make their audiences laugh, and that they would create a comedy. Already on January 25, Mnouchkine had advised: "Let the comedy come; it's a noble genre, especially at times like this. [...] The most courageous and beautiful thing would be to make the public laugh at its fears."[13] She later said of this show: "the actors were heroic,"[14] as it was truly difficult to believe in comedy, even if she herself felt on some level how necessary it was, given the trauma everyone was going through.[15] Faithful to its genesis, the fiction would take place in India. But it would not be a play about India.

Voice of Hélène Cixous

> "We were like refugees from History. Around our room, the Times had turned wild. We were asking ourselves, what was happening to us, we people so different, yet united by the same concerns; we were wondering how to name That Thing, that chaos. The air was boiling. [...] We felt like the whole world was imploding in order to parade in our room. The world's peoples were calling out. It was truly overwhelming. They were crying: Help! Or: Never again! And in how many languages? All of them! We were looking for a way to answer them, We, members of the Troupe."[16]

Such was the atmosphere for their collective creation. The company would answer, speak to all the world's upsets: terrorism; ISIS; the radicalization of adolescents;[17] refugees; brainwashing; how women are treated in the world, but especially in India and in Muslim countries;[18] schooling; ecological disaster – and Syria, Iraq, France itself. And, perhaps above all else, of the challenges posed by such disorder to the theatre and through the theatre to art. That would be the cement that would hold together this montage of a thousand faces, itself supported by a scenic strategy of dream sequencing. This was what Mnouchkine saw in introducing the dream:

> The more true it is, the more it will appear as a dream ... with some exceptions. Because, in fact, a dream is always a profound truth communicated with incredible freedom; and it's the freedom that's unbelievable, not the feelings, not the passion. Everything feels free but with the freedom of illogic ... That's what a dream is.[19]

"What purpose do we serve when the devils are at the door?" A Room in India

Voice of Ariane Mnouchkine

> "You have to know how to be happy, if that's at all possible! The world doesn't give a damn about our complaints and disillusionment. Nostalgia serves no purpose, but only makes us weak. We wanted to triumph over our anguish through laughter!"[20]

A Room in India. The Welcome Area is decorated by brightly colored frescoes and paintings representing characters from Hindu mythology. At the back, there is a forest, and on the side walls, texts in Hindi and in French. Photo by Michèle Laurent.

"One day you'll produce my plays," Anton Chekhov says to the "Assistant" lost in the worries and uncertainties of collective creation. He queries in Russian: "Why look so far when there are so many beautiful plays, like mine?" And he adds, ironically: "You want to speak about the status of women? Why not do my *Three Sisters* ...." He insists: "it's a comedy," and then compares different stagings by Stanislavski, Nemirovitch-Dantchenko, Peter Stein – all of them too sad, too dark. But Giorgio Strehler's – oh yes! And the "Assistant" remembers dreamily his *Cherry Orchard* and calms down.

The above was one of the many scenes, a particularly moving one, of *A Room in India* that examines the ups and downs of the Soleil under the leadership of Ariane Mnouchkine – but transposed to the stage as Cornélia (an echo of Cordelia), the third daughter of King Lear. And Lear is present as well, but his first name is Constantin; and Constantin Lear is Japanese.[21] Lear is the fictional head of a fictional company and he has gone mad because of the world's craziness and the terrorist attacks on Paris in 2015. Once in India, he deserts everyone, handing off to Cornélia, his assistant, the direction of the actors and of their audacious project to stage a production inspired by the *Mahabharata*, that great Indian epic.

As we can see, *A Room in India* talks a lot about theatre. This particular collective creation is without a doubt one of Mnouchkine's most personal, and the scene described above, with Doctor Chekhov (Arman Saribekyan) dressed in black and white, his shirt and vest immaculate, with a pince-nez and doctor's bag – preceded in the room by "three sisters" in white blouses and long black skirts – is one of the most intimate. For with it, Mnouchkine admits how much she loves Chekhov, even though she has never staged him. But on the huge stage of *A Room in India*, Chekhov makes an appearance, as does Shakespeare a few scenes earlier – Shakespeare, the master whom she *had* staged several times in her career with great success.

Called "visitations" in the program notes to the show, numerous characters also appear, as do visions and fantasies, dreams and nightmares. These apparitions seem at first to be Cornélia's, whom we see stretched out or curled up in a great white bed, covered by a sheet – a bed that fills the left side of the stage. There, she sleeps or wakes up, and moves nervously about, always in her nightgown, in wonderment or in terror. We never really know if she's dreaming or if she's working with her actors, watching and commenting their improvisations.

The challenge of this show was to account for the state of the world, its tragedies, confusion, and uncertainty, but in a form both comic and poetic. The Soleil did so by asking unanswerable questions. The production required more than nine months of work in collective imagination.

Another question quickly emerged: what would be the best space for this show-in-the-making? It quickly became clear that the idea of a room and of India should be merged: the room would allow an exploration of intimacy – and even bodily intimacy: the upstage toilet permitting the public to witness the intestinal upset caused by various characters' anxiety and stress. "India," as the stage of History, would illumine the work of theatre itself: for India presents the immensity of a churning world and provides the necessary distance to look at the present metaphorically – which has always been one of Mnouchkine's formal concerns. This choice also reflected the fact that the kinds of Islamist conflicts roiling Europe and the Middle East were being replicated in India in another way: radicalized Hindu nationalists, supporting the BJP Party, daily refuse women their rights and violate their Muslim compatriots. *A Room in India* would, then, show several forms of radicalized, fundamentalist thought, avoiding simplistic categories for good and evil.

So there would be a double fictional space, but one single scenic stage, inspired by the guesthouse in Pondicherry where some of the troupe had been housed. This space was vast and luminous, with eight different openings: doors, and windows

A Room in India. Luminous and open, the stage has some ten entrances and exits. Rather than being a protected space, we are in a space of waiting – fragile, and easy to invade. The emptiness of stage center allows for dance numbers. Stage left is for musicians, where doors also open to other parts of the guesthouse. From stage right, guarded by the statue of a small Asian horse, come the sounds of the city and the tumult of the crowds, as well as "visitations" of such characters as Krishna and Shakespeare. Photo by Étienne Lemasson.

A Room in India. "The Death of Karna," a scene which, with "Goodbye to Ponnourovi," would be part of the later show, *Our Little Mahabharata*. We see part of the *terukkuttu* musical ensemble (here Quentin Lashermes and Shafiq Kohi) setting up behind Karna. A phone call from Paris will interrupt this scene; Karna (Sébastien Brottet-Michel) will come back, but no one, except the sleeping Cornélia, will be on stage. Karna, annoyed, wakes her up by sounding his ankle bracelets, and the whole *terukkuttu* company rushes on stage to finish the scene. Photo by Michèle Laurent.

shaded by Persian blinds, through which the city – with its noises, commotion, and crowds – as well as the world of imagination, entered the room. There were few furnishings: a bed, a white armchair, a refrigerator, fans, two worktables, and moveable trunks. Upstage, housing the bathroom and thus recalling Mikhail Bakhtin's theory of the grotesque, was a small arched structure made of beige cloth, resembling the stage of *terukkuttu* performances. It became also, at different moments in the show, the space of poetic vision. There was also a series of steps downstage, leading from the room and open to the audience. This made it possible to multiply unexpected entrances, rapid exits, and the vast circulation of visions haunting the characters (the fictional theatre troupe and their Indian hosts) and the actors of the Soleil, themselves – visions presented as improvisations one after the other to the "Assistant" and from which the show, itself, was built. Thus we see that *A Room in India* was *a play about a play in construction*, a kind of endless *mise en abyme*, an auto-fiction reminiscent of *And Suddenly, Sleepless Nights*, but much more complex.

And an epic wind blew through the room, a furious world of news. We heard many languages and many different accents: French, English, Russian, Arabic, Japanese, Hungarian, Tamil, even German ... We might be hearing the mother tongue of a Soleil actor or we might be hearing a language they had learned for the show. On-stage projections translated directly the actors' lines (on a wall, on a stage element – a rickshaw, for example) and, also, on a screen high up toward the middle of the bleachers where the audience sat. Polyglotism, a multiplicity of languages, had become (and remains) the natural language of the Théâtre du Soleil; and the super-titling was very unobtrusive, as if floating.

During four hours, we saw the workings of a theatre world: this room in an immense India was the way of achieving "the great by the small," that old Brechtian adage which had long been one of the principles of the Soleil. Languages cohabited; and all the realms of the living appeared: humans, gods (Krishna), animals – without mentioning the vegetal world of the bougainvillea, tumbling down around the windows and doors. Two curious monkeys leapt into the room; they complemented Gandhi's appearance, crossing the stage while one of his speeches was voiced from the wings. A small white cow stuck its lovely and sacred muzzle out of the upstage opening. The scenic space was transformed with each entrance and exit, not so much because stage elements were moved around, but because of the windows that opened, the lighting that changed, the music and sounds that Jean-Jacques Lemêtre and Thérèse Spirli performed live, and because of the layered visions that interlocked and then uncoupled in this loosely structured plot.

The underbelly of the stage played a part as well: a trap opening allowed one of the "actors" (Martial Jacques) to slip inside to explore the polluted water table, and another one (Duccio Bellugi-Vannuccini) to travel away and thus send a video, projected on stage, of "Syrian actors" in Aleppo performing *Richard III* in a dust-filled tunnel – a bombed, shaken, and war-torn shelter. These were fantastic "documentary" images in black and white of how art is, indeed, resistance.

Wide and oriented frontally, convincing in its simplicity, fluid and dreamily changing, the scenic space of *A Room in India* shared some similarities with the desire for immediate impact of Robert Lepage's project *Playing Cards: Spades* (2012). But the Soleil's production didn't overcharge itself with the kind of hyper-technological, ingenious and complex, mobile and transformable circular box used by Lepage. Technology was, of course, present: laptop computer, fax machine, smartphone, Skype, video camera were employed to transport the action from one continent to another, from Saudi Arabia to Iceland, from Pondicherry to Paris. The Internet allowed the audience to hear in Arabic, translated onto one of the white walls, the dangerous rants of an Islamist website. It was, however, an old model hard-resin telephone and its strident ring that brought the dreamers back down to earth, interrupting a number of scenes by a call from "Astrid" in Paris, the fictional company's administrator, wanting to know how the show was progressing under the sponsorship of the Alliance Française.

Among the numerous themes running through the show, the concern about disappearing cultures, and particularly theatre, came back again and again. Cornélia says: "I'm afraid for theatre. Will it still exist in 20 years?" She asks directly the endless question of what theatre's purpose is: "If all the theatres in the world were demolished, who would miss them?" And throughout the work, the optimistic and feisty answer was that theatre must live – just as *terukkuttu* lived in the production, proving its vitality through noisy eruptions, contaminating characters and actors who became, as soon as they appeared, both public and chorus.

The *terukkuttu* master Sambandan, from the village of Purisai, a tiny speck on the map of the Indian sub-continent, spent several months at the Cartoucherie working with the Soleil actors on their form, while the actor Nirupama Nityanandan, born in Madras, acted as interpreter. This was an exemplary act of cultural and artistic transmission – the Soleil actors themselves hailing from many different nations. The actors became so proficient they couldn't be distinguished from the Tamil performers in the production: they spoke, sang, danced, and played traditional percussion, as well as cymbals, oboe, and harmonium. The chief difference was the Soleil women who also performed *terukkuttu* on stage, which is not permitted in India. "For actors to accept that kind of very difficult training, there has to be a great master. And Sambandan," said Mnouchkine, "is a very great one."

The rigorous daily training, which focused on language as well as gestures and singing, gave the actors a common and solid vocal and corporeal basis for their improvisations. *Terukkuttu*'s highly colored, strange, but also conventional and lyrical, grandiose and comic theatricality helped give shape to the production, while at the same time tying *A Room in India* to the long history of a particular kind of world theatre, evoked, also, by gestures to Shakespeare, to Noh, to Chekhov – and by allusions to Lear, Molière, Stanislavski, Artaud, Peter Stein, and others. This was a new way of welcoming and transferring esthetically Asian forms on the Soleil's stage, a stage that had already seen so many other manifestations of Asian aesthetics. There was, nevertheless, a striking similarity between the actors' working methods for *A Room in India* and the way they learned to play traditional Korean percussions for *Drums on the Dam*.

Working with Sambandan, Mnouchkine had selected two specific stories from the rich repertory of *terukkuttu* to insert into the flow of dreams and visions. These two echoed the play's concern with the difficult and subservient situation of women in parts of today's India, and the violence inflicted upon them. Thus the Soleil performed, "The Rape of Draupadi" (Judit Jancsó), in which the wife of the Pandava clan is dragged by her hair in front of her five husbands by Dushasana (D. Bellugi-Vannuccini or Omid Rawendah), then undressed on the orders of Duryodhana (Sébastien Brottet-Michel or Seear Kohi), but finally saved by the god Krishna, who made it impossible to carry out the act by turning her gold-ornamented red sari into an infinite stream of cloth. The other story staged the farewell scene between Karna (Sébastien Brottet-Michel) and his wife Ponnourouvi (Shaghayegh Beheshti) before battle, in which her lamentations and self-pummeling achingly translated what it would mean to be a widow, alone on earth, abandoned, with no possible future: "In this earthly world, why was I born a woman?"

A Room in India, uncompromising and courageous, played to sold-out houses from the beginning. Mnouchkine held out against the worries that the play was too long, believing the *longueurs* indispensable. The public agreed.[22] The production captured today's anguish, asking questions everyone is still asking about the galloping regression in human community and corresponding increase in violence and hate – all represented through the turbulence of the show's construction. It communicated a reinvigorating energy, emanating from the presence

A Room in India. "The Death of Karna," the last moment in which Ponnourouvi (Shaghayegh Beheshti) dances and sings her anguish at being left alone and abandoned by Karna, who has gone off to fight Arjuna. Seated cross-legged on various trunks, the musicians accompany her: Aziz Hamrah on harmonium; Andrea Marchant on the tamil oboe; Ya-hui Liang on percussions; Marie-Jasmine Cocito, vocals; Thérèse Spirli, choral director, on cymbals; Palani Murugan, Sayed Ahmad Hashimi, and Omid Rawendah also on vocals. Photo by Michèle Laurent.

A Room in India. Each time the *terukkuttu* scenes interrupt the action, all of the actors, costumed for their last scene, appear and sit or stand on each side of the stage. Enhancing the chorus, making it a kind of world choir, they sing with the *terukkuttu* musicians who sit on trunks. Here we see (higher up): Nirupama Nityanandan, Seear Kohi, Farid Gul Ahmad, Hélène Cinque, Maurice Durozier, Duccio Bellugi-Vannuccini, (lower): Alice Millequant, Wazhma Total Khil, V. Baskaran, Dominique Jambert, Man-Waï Fok, Vijayan Panikkaveettil, Agustin Letelier. Photo by Anne Lacombe.

of 35 actors who constituted not just one theatre company, but three: the Théâtre du Soleil; the auto-fictional troupe; and the *terukkuttu* company. And we might add a fourth: the filmed "Syrian company" performing Shakespeare under bombardment – inspired, in fact, from the peril faced by the real Afghan company, the Théâtre Aftaab.

We should also speak of the unexpected energy exploding from the satirical sketches that ridiculed incompetent terrorists and brainwashed Islamists. Laughter became a theatrical arm for burying fear, maintaining hope, installing a temporary reprieve to the awfulness, or just staying alive with dignity. Mnouchkine would say later: "Did we have the right to laugh at such serious things? Censorship is insidious; it slips into everything, especially your own fear. But we decided together that even if we were afraid, we had to forge ahead."[23] Even the controls established to check bags in public places were theatricalized. The Soleil built a small pagoda in front of the entrance to the theatre, an entrance glittering with a hundred fairy lights; and there, costumed actors from the Soleil searched people's bags with the necessary tools. (Elsewhere, as in all Parisian theatres and as required by Vigipirate, the national protection code against terrorism, other precautions had been taken to make sure actors and audiences were safe.)

In their search into comic forms, it was logical that Charlie Chaplin take his place among the ancestors haunting the Soleil's grand theatrical fresco. He had always been one of Mnouchkine's most important inspirations. In this production, Chaplin was omnipresent in the final scene. "Charlot" (D. Bellugi-Vannuccini) appeared as yet another avatar – here a fragile and hesitating imam, dressed in black, head wrapped. He stepped onto a small stage and spoke into a microphone the lines that end the celebrated 1940 Chaplin film, *The Great Dictator*. The English text had been recorded by the actor, imitating Chaplin's rhythm, and super-titled on stage; but the actor's slight accent could still be heard in the recording:

> We want to live by each other's happiness, not by each other's misery. We don't want to hate and despise one another. In this world there is room for everybody and the good earth is rich and can provide for everybody. The way of life can be free and beautiful. But we have lost the way.

Chaplin's pressing appeal to responsible action and democratic union, offered almost in its entirety, was interrupted by two armed terrorists who shot the speaker at close range. The furious "Assistant" rushed in: "It can't end like this!" A moment of suspense: would this be a comedy or a tragedy? We were looking at three temporal modes brought together:

A Room in India. A satirical scene: "ISISwood" "[Daeshwood]." Shooting a propaganda film in the desert. Photo by Michèle Laurent.

A Room in India. Another satirical scene: "Two Worlds." Four Saudis, members of the Advisory Committee for Human Rights of the Kingdom of Saudi Arabia, are asking in English by Skype for advice from people working at Iceland's Ministry of Communication – Iceland being the country ranked number one for equality between men and women. The Saudis hope to advance up the rankings, finding themselves currently at the bottom of the scale. Pictured: Samir Abdul Jabbar Saed, Duccio Bellugi-Vannuccini, Arman Saribekyan, Martial Jacques, and on the screen Dominique Jambert. Photo by Michèle Laurent.

the Chaplin film, the show being performed, and the fictional rehearsal in which the "actors" had been proposing their visions. What would wrap this up? The "Assistant" tenderly whispered to the actor collapsed in front of her Mnouchkine's key phrase – Mnouchkine the director of the auto-fiction rehearsing with her actors – "Let's do it again." Magic words: the assassinated Charlot got up, stumbling a bit, picked up his lines, but fell down again after one more round of shooting, kalashnikovs sounding. However, he arose for a third time. And, in a choral circular movement, the gloriously colored and multi-national crowd of 35 actors, who had just performed more than 100 characters and told 1001 stories, gathered around him. The theatre of the world came to life one last time in a flash of solidarity, as short as it was stunning. It was an image of our awkward humanity, wanting to understand, to find answers, to believe against all odds in a possible future of united action.

A Room in India. The Imam/Charlot (Duccio Bellugi-Vannuccini), called "The Revenant" in the theatre program, has been shot. He's lost his headdress. Here he returns to his little stage and, fragile, speaks his lines again, while being watched by the director Cornélia (Hélène Cinque), seated on the bed. Two "theatre troupes" are present (French and *terukkuttu*). Pictured from left to right: Azizullah Hamrah, Seear Kohi, Shafiq Kohi, Sayed Ahmad Hasimi, Agustin Letelier, Farid Gul Ahmad, Seietsu Onochi (Lear), Omid Rawendah, Shaghayegh Beheshti (Ponnourouvi). Photo by Michèle Laurent.

Kanata: First Episode (The Controversy), a show by Robert Lepage with the Théâtre du Soleil

Voice of Robert Lepage

"Theatre gives permission to perform the other. To allow you to tell the other's story. There was something that really touched me in the Rocky Mountains: the [First Nations people] offered us a dance workshop. You should have seen the reaction of the Afghan actors: their mother country came back to them in full force. It's not just characters and situations, but also the earth, the land itself, that allows us to recognize ourselves in the other's situation."[24]

Voice of Duccio Bellugi-Vannuccini

"What I thought was interesting in the creation of Kanata *is that while Ariane works first on the acting, on its rightness, the truth of the characters, and then develops the dramaturgy, Robert begins by constructing the dramaturgy and then develops the characters."*[25]

In 2014, Ariane Mnouchkine asked the Canadian director Robert Lepage if he would like to mount a production with the actors of the Soleil. This would be a major event in the Soleil's history, the first time the actors would work with an invited director, someone from the outside.[26] Both artists had followed closely and admired each other's work for a long time.[27] Mnouchkine had particularly appreciated *The Seven Streams of the River Ota*. Their working methods were different, but both were committed to telling great epic stories. Mnouchkine certainly recognized Lepage's mastery in the use of new technologies. She didn't feel the same need, but realized: "It's in the same vein, the same theatrical family. He opened doors for me."[28]

The actors were as enthusiastic as Lepage about collaborating, and so the work began. A first, very short workshop took place at the end of *Macbeth* in March 2015, followed by a September 2015 workshop. The working sessions from then on would be more or less long, with great stretches of time in between, structured according to Lepage's approach. The title of the new production was quickly found: *Kanata*, an old, sixteenth-century Laurentian name for Canada – this was fitting as Lepage wanted to work with the multi-national troupe of the Soleil on the history of his country, starting with the original genocide of First Nations peoples. In August 2016, he invited the actors to Quebec, to his theatrical home, Ex Machina. This was the first step in an exploratory voyage through Canada, focusing especially on the Western provinces, notably around

Banff in Alberta, where Soleil actors would meet artists, activists in the cause of First Nations peoples, inhabitants, and also some of the important indigenous Chiefs. They would also travel to Vancouver to see the tough neighborhoods of downtown Eastside. *Kanata*, however, was not meant to be documentary theatre, although one of the actors (Martial Jacques) would play a documentary filmmaker – which added a meta-theatrical layer to the production.

The strong fictional narrative, full of surprising twists, but based on documentary research, was partially created before the Canadian travels; it was enriched through improvisations, themselves rewritten by the dramaturg working with Lepage. The similarity and difference between Lepage's approach and that of the Soleil were quite apparent: both are interested in auto-fiction, but Lepage's work with the actors was more directive, particularly since he was working for the first time with some 33 actors and had never handled more than nine people on stage prior to this production.

Kanata was meant to be an enormous three-part fresco that spanned three historical periods. The Soleil's costume workshop had thus worked ceaselessly to produce costumes for the several hundred characters who emerged during rehearsals. However, in July 2018, after three years of work, a violent polemic about the piece erupted in Montreal, on the heels of another controversy around the production *SLAV*.[29] Lepage and Mnouchkine (who had just returned from Japan) tried to calm things down by holding open meetings and by dialoguing. Lepage was accused of cultural appropriation – which might seem ironic, given that he had chosen to work with the Soleil, itself a multicultural company that has for years been telling the world's stories, and whose actors sometimes found their own stories, or the stories of their cultures, taken over and performed by someone else, someone from an entirely different background. Moreover, the Soleil had already addressed in *The Survivors of Mad Hope* the terrible history of Patagonian native peoples (the Alakalufs, a group that has completely disappeared) through the story of Yuras, Anju, and their mother – the latter killed by a bounty hunter paid according to how many ears he could collect.

Without being able to see the finished product, a collective of indigenous artists – supported, sometimes despite what they would have wanted, by violent accusations over a social media campaign gone viral – contested the production's legitimacy. The feeling was that Indigenous People had to be the ones to perform Indigenous People. Several co-producers became anxious and withdrew their financial support. Ex Machina, Lepage's company, gave up. But a combination of the Festival d'Automne in Paris, which had already programmed and helped finance the show, and Mnouchkine's own tenacity kept *Kanata* alive. Lepage went to Paris in November, as had been scheduled, to direct the last rehearsals before the opening.

Kanata, whose title had been modified to *Kanata: First Episode (The Controversy)* [*Kanata – Épisode I – La Contraverse*], opened on December 15, 2018. The violence of the attacks against the work and the shortage of time made it impossible to maintain the production's epic scope. Only the last part was kept, with a few framing scenes from the first two parts inserted at the beginning. The auto-fictional aspect of the work, however, was developed. The polemic that had so impacted the work's creation was examined within the play itself: we thus see the threat of a world where everyone retreats "into a circle where no one can leave and where no one has the right to enter. To each their own cell. Well, me," says the character Miranda (Dominique Jambert), a young French painter discovering Vancouver, "I don't want anything to do with that kind of jail."

Condensed from what had been a long process, the show focused on the contemporary period, and, especially, on the treatment of indigenous women: scenes of mothers whose children had been snatched from their arms by priests; Tania (Frédérique Voruz), an indigenous girl from a complicated family who runs away and ends up in the streets with a drug problem – and is eventually murdered by a serial killer (Maurice Durozier, playing the role of an actual and infamous pig farmer, Robert Pickton, now in prison for multiple murders in Vancouver). In its shortened form, one might think of *Kanata: First Episode (The Controversy)* as a response to the new movement to "decolonize the arts,"[30] which would, it seems, forbid white artists from speaking the words of First Nations peoples. This is, in fact, the opposite of what the troupe had heard from Ceejay, Shining Eagle Woman, of the Beaver clan of the Carrier Nation. Meeting the actors during their travels in Canada, she told them: "I've come so that you will hear my voice. I'm a survivor." And she added, speaking to actors overwhelmed by her story: "Carry my voice for me, to all the nations from which you come from, so the world learns how important we women are."[31] Here, we might recall the voices heard in *The Last Caravanserai*, the witnessing of Iranian and Afghan refugees who had also asked the Soleil to bring their stories to as many people as possible.

Kanata places on stage to be heard and learned about the situation of Canada's First Nations (and we know there are many tribes and traditions within); it alerts spectators to the devastating history that is theirs and that many people do not know. To provide documentation about what was shown on stage, the Soleil's bookstore displayed and sold studies and collections of articles about Canada's indigenous peoples. But the production

Kanata: Episode I (The Controversy). In rehearsal: a medicalized injection room in Vancouver, where Tania (Frédérique Voruz) goes for the first time. A staff member (Eve Doe Bruce) helps her. Upstage, we can catch a glance behind the translucent windows of the downtown Eastside neighborhood. Photo by Michèle Laurent.

Kanata: Episode I (The Controversy). In rehearsal: the scenic space is "planted" with cylindrical trunks which, when moved elsewhere on their rolling platforms, establish very distinct spaces. They can frame, create a much bigger space, or focus the action – which gives a cinematic rhythm to the show, accented by musical transitions. Here, we see one of the final scenes, where in his canoe the indigenous documentary filmmaker (Martial Jacques) protects the young painter arrived from France (Dominique Jambert) during her first drug trip. Archives Théâtre du Soleil.

also moved its audience by staging intensely emotional scenes, such as the tragic moment when the character Louise, performed by the Asian actress Nirupama Nityanandan (filmed live off-stage and projected on screen to the public) recounts life in residential schools, where First Nations children were forcibly sent, once abducted from their families, and browbeaten into assimilation. Her words were taken directly from an interview[32] with a First Nations person from the Tl'azt'en Nation, in North Prince George, British Columbia. While the Soleil actor spoke in English with the accent and rhythmic characteristics of the interviewee, another actor (Camille Grandville), playing an interpreter speaking into a microphone, repeated the words in French on stage. This simple and dignified witnessing was without sentimentality, occupying the entirety of the immense stage by the quality of the image and the sound.[33]

Mnouchkine was and has remained lucid about her position concerning the staging of *Kanata*, a controversy that has also found echoes in France:

> Cultures belong to no one. No border should limit them, because, in fact, they have no known geographical limits and certainly no temporal limits. Cultures are not isolated; they fertilize each other and have done so since the beginning of time. No more than any farmer can stop the wind from sending to their field the healthy or sick seeds from their neighbor's sowing, no people, not even the most insular one, can claim their culture as definitively pure. The histories of hordes, clans, tribes, of ethnic or other groups, of peoples, even nations can't be patented, as certain people would like to believe, because they all belong to the great story of humanity. It's that great story that's the artists' territory. Cultures, all cultures, are our source, and, in a certain way, they're all sacred. We must drink from them carefully, with respect and gratitude, but we can't accept that someone forbids us to approach them, because that would exile us to the desert. It would be an intellectual regression – an artistic, political, and terrifying step backwards. *Theatre has doors and windows. It tells of the whole world.*[34]

Kanata is also that rare phenomenon in which the aesthetic universes of two artists, according to a code of intimate hospitality, weave together, adapting to each other. Thus the number of languages spoken on stage was increased: Chinese found a place. And accents were kept and foregrounded – by sequences in which an indigenous language (Mohawk, in this case) was translated through a dictaphone; or American English was acquired by working with a coach. And we saw at work the rolling platforms seen elsewhere in Mnouchkine's work (here, tree trunks pushed on stage). And we saw also the remarkable transitions between scenes in which all of the actors participated – transforming, as if in a ballet, the stage. Lepage accelerated these moments, using a system of atmospheric images (landscapes, interiors, rain, sunset, storms, farms, airport), projected on the back wall, that instantaneously modified the space, without, however, depriving the audience of the pleasure of watching the actors work. His minimal and poetic use of technology in no way contradicted the Soleil's aesthetic. And, at the end, when all those characters who had disappeared returned to the stage, we experienced a flashback to the starry heavens that in 1994 concluded the Soleil's *The Perjured City*.

Invitations and escapades before the next production

Voice of the Soleil

> "*While our show* A Room in India *is getting ready to take off for New York where we'll perform from December 5 to 20, 2017, before we reprise the play at the Cartoucherie (next February 23), our theatre will once again become the home and the stage for young or less young companies come by to share with us their work. All this coming year, and as always when we are able when the company is traveling outside its own naves, we'll welcome no less than 12 new artistic adventures.*"[35]

At the same time that the Soleil expands its galaxy by organizing Nomadic Schools in Europe, Latin America, or India, it continues to nurture a program of invitations to the Cartoucherie. In April 2015, there was a great kathakali evening by the Kalamandalam, produced with the Mandapa Center; in June, there was Chinese opera: *A Chaste Woman* and *The Great Melancholia*, with the remarkable actor Zeng Jingping of the Liyuan Theatre.[36] From October to December, there was *Nightwatch* (created in 2013) by the Théâtre Aftaab, and *Bouk de là* by the Baraque Liberté Company, as well as the Samul Nori Company of Kim Duk Soo, with is shamanistic rituals and Korean percussions.

In 2016, the Odin Theatre returned with *In the Skeleton of the Whale* and *Great Cities under the Moon*. Another great evening, this time of *kutiyattam*, took place just before the opening of *A Room in India*: it provided a kind of consecration. In 2017, Koumarane Valavane's Indianostrum Theatre, which had hosted a Nomadic School, brought three shows to the Cartoucherie: *Karuppu*, *Kunti Karna*, and *Land of Ashes*, accompanied by Jean-Jacques Lemêtre's music. A mix of traditional forms, such as *kalaripayatt*, an ancient Indian martial art, and dance theatre, the Indianostrum courageously addressed, and continues to address, themes pertinent to contemporary issues in Indian society. In July 2018, the Kodo Next Generation Company from Sado Island, came to perform Japanese *taïko* percussions, in conversation with Japanese modernity. They caused a sensation.[37] We can add to this long list the names of Bernard Bloch, Bernard Sobel, Chantal Morel, the Atélier Hors Champs, the Studio Théâtre with its *Cherry Orchard*, Yann Reuzeau, the Majaz Théâtre, and so many others, including Li-Yu You, who performed on the Chinese sitar.[38]

In 2018, after a performance of the Odin Theatre's *Tree*, the Soleil welcomed some of its former actors to its main theatre space. Simon Abkarian came with his two-part piece: *Above the shadows: The Last Day of Fasting* [*Au-delà des ténèbres: le Dernier jour du jeûne*] and *The Storks' Flight* [*L'Envol des cigognes*], two "neighborhood tragi-comedies."[39] It was easy to recognize in these Middle Eastern family stories – trapped in patriarchy and the torment of a country at war – an authentic disciple of the Théâtre du Soleil. The force of the women's voices, the punch of the laughter, and Abkarian's poetic choices clearly indicated, as he says himself: "A promise kept." He, indeed, opened the 2019 season with his staging of a rewritten *Electra* [*l'Electre des bas-fonds*]. Catherine Schaub-Abkarian also performed twice in the Soleil's rehearsal space, with two other kathakali performers, *The Foot's Song* [*Le Chant du pied*, 2018 and 2019], a poetic initiation to kathakali practice. These three performers constitute the chorus for Abkarian's *Electra of the Lower Depths*. Other actors, for example Serge Nicolaï and Olivia Orsini, demonstrated what they'd learned at the Soleil by adopting the use of the Japanese stage servant, or *koken*, when they performed at the Théâtre Montfort in 2018 *A Bergman Affair*.

Voice of the Public

> "*And while you're not in rehearsal or not performing at your place – at our place, the Cartoucherie – what are the technicians and actors doing? Where are the people we want to see, as soon as possible, in your naves?*"[40]

In 2018–2019, while at the same time working at the Soleil, some of the actors launched other projects, creating breakout troupes, performing in Italy (Duccio Bellugi-Vannuccini), in Brazil (Sébastien Brottet-Michel), in Taipei and Macao (Shaghayegh Beheshti), or in Armenia and Kosovo (Arman Saribekyan). Or they made films, based on some of the Soleil's work (Dominique Jambert and Vincent Mangado in Brittany;

Duccio Bellugi-Vannuccini and Martial Jacques in India). Some made albums (Maurice Durozier in Brazil). The Théâtre Aftaab was eventually absorbed into the Théâtre du Soleil, but some of its members returned to Kabul to make a film (*Kabullywood* with Louis Meunier).[41]

In June 2019, some of these break-out projects were presented to the public at the Soleil, for instance, an adaptation of Pablo Neruda's *I Confess that I've lived* [*J'avoue que j'ai vécu*], by the Train de Nuit Company. The trio of performers evoked musically how much the great poet had inspired the Soleil. Actor-singers close to the Soleil (Virginie Le Coënt, Frédérique Voruz, and Emmanuelle Martin) invited other, similarly inclined artists to a festival called "Nothing But Women."

Perhaps this last event gestured to Mnouchkine's own musical adventure: for in 2019, she presented the first work she'd directed with actors other than the Soleil's. It was a musical adaptation of Quebecois author Michel Tremblay's 1965 work *The Step-Sisters* [*Les Belles Soeurs*], originally written in Joual. The work, *As Comadres*, premiered in Brazil (Curitiba, Rio de Janeiro, and Sao Paulo) in Portuguese – after two years of periodic rehearsals. Mnouchkine had seen the creation in Paris in 2012 (book, decor, and staging by René Richard Cyr and music by Daniel Bélanger), and had proposed the idea to a group of Brazilian actors – some of whom had worked with the Soleil before (Fabianna Melo e Souza, Juliana Carneiro de Cunha). These women had been searching for something to perform with only women; and they very much wanted to be able to create a show, despite the disastrous situation of the arts in Brazil under Jair Bolsonaro.

As Comadres was a new experience for Mnouchkine, as she didn't try to reinvent the staging. Rather, she sought to copy what René Richard Cyr had done, the way that apprentice painters used to learn to paint by copying Great Masters in museums. She had to be both modest and exacting in her work in order to find something powerful that also recognized the double strangeness of the linguistic charge: both Joual and Portuguese. Julia Carrera translated the piece into Portuguese; and then the words had to be fitted to the music. Mnouchkine called herself "the artistic supervisor," and she and the actors watched a video of the show many times in order to study what René Richard Cyr had accomplished. While each phase of the work presented a new challenge (financing, constructing the set, costumes), the actual rehearsals (acting with Mnouchkine; singing with Wladimir Pinheiro) felt utopic. And in Curibita, as well as in Rio, the translation was a hit: the audiences laughed uproariously at each line.

And yet, what a portrait of sadness, pettiness, and tragedy: a play in which women, aged 22–87, gather in a kitchen to help a character named Germaine (now a legend in Quebec) glue her green stamps in the books that would bring her all kinds of goodies. But these women end up showing how bigoted, jealous, and mean they really are, stealing the stamps of a person who has had, they whine, a little more luck than they. And they slip the stamps into their pocket books, a costume prop from the 60s that never leaves their sides.

Structured in long monologues, the play allows each of the women to have her moment to confide and confess. Because Mnouchkine's production was a musical, the monologues were sung, very much in the mode of Brecht; and they were expertly executed, even by those who had never sung before. Mnouchkine increased the cast by five, thereby creating a choral unit who sat stage left, reacting to everything that happened on stage and singing with the other women in the ensembles. There were two actors for each role, and the women alternated roles every night, which created an exceptionally strong ensemble and a joyous collective energy. Certain details evoked the situation in Brazil today, while the songs and the fantastic story line kept the play from falling into realism.

After the second performance in Rio, almost the entire audience stayed for the conversation following the show, despite the anxiety of returning home late at night in such a dangerous city. Person after person spoke, thanking Mnouchkine for offering them the possibility of seeing energizing theatre, especially in light of the situation in Brazil, and for bringing them all together. The multiplicity of languages in Mnouchkine's other productions might be read here in the exacting work of moving Quebecois French into Brazilian Portuguese. And we might see in the hospitality offered in Brazil to a mythical Quebecois work, a continuation of the hospitality experienced in the creation of *A Room in India* – a triumph, also, over difficult material conditions.

Our Little Mahabharata (Fall 2019)

Voice of Kalaimamani Purisai Kannappa Sambandan Thambiran

> *"We even have a troupe in Paris!"*[42]

In November and December 2019, the Soleil troupe gathered for 15 performances of *A Room in India*. It was an exceptional occasion, after tours at the Festival du Printemps des Comédiens in Montpellier, in New York at the Armory, and at the Théâtre Kléber-Méleau in Lausanne, which was meant to be the last performance. But *A Room in India* came back to the Cartoucherie, where the Welcome Area still bears signs of its passage. And it was accompanied, every other night, by *Our Little Mahabharata* [*Notre Petit Mahabharata*], which picked up the work from two evenings in the spring of 2018

(May 12 and 13), when Sambandan's company and the actors of the Soleil had performed together, very experimentally, four episodes of the *Mahabharata*.

Those two evenings and the performances in 2019 constitute a key cultural moment: two cultures meeting for reciprocal enrichment thanks to a form of theatre Mnouchkine calls "immortal and invincible" – the only sure thing in the whole process of creating *A Room in India*. Thanks to the actors' long pedagogical training, the production fully satisfied the master teacher, Sambandan. The actors had worked to perfect their craft and, says Mnouchkine: "We managed to sing and dance with [the *terukkuttu* performers]. We really did well; becoming indistinguishable."[43] The polemic about cultural appropriation would take place a year later, but the Soleil had already experienced an exchange in which two sides had both won and been renewed, each absorbing the identity of the other.

During the first Nomadic School in Pondicherry, Mnouchkine had seen that the hundred students who had come from there, but also from Kerala or from Calcutta,

> had all forgotten their treasure: the sources of Indian theatre. These are all of our sources, and those young people had forgotten them, crushed by the destructive forces of television. But now, things buried in the depth of their unconscious and their pride were coming back, the memory of things they'd seen when they were four or six years old. We were giving them back their tools. We'd come earlier not to steal them, but to borrow them. And now we were bringing them a tool kit they were no longer aware of.[44]

Ariane Mnouchkine speaks of tools, but perhaps we might use the word "soul," or a kind of vital energy that the Soleil was giving back in a cultural transfer that worked in both directions.

The master of *terukkuttu* returned home from his experience with the Soleil full of confidence in his art. The experience had allowed him to introduce women performers into the shows he would do in India and had suggested that he could change the traditional script, as Ariane Mnouchkine had done while working with him on the episodes that were introduced into *A Room in India*. We might remember a similar exchange, when, during a tour in Tokyo in 2001, the quality of the work on bunraku in *Drums on the Dam* had inspired certain Japanese masters to rethink their own work.[45] There is also the example of *Sihanouk*, which presented to the khmer people their own story in such a way that many years later Cambodian actors would use Hélène Cixous's text and Mnouchkine's *mise-en-scène* to reconquer their past and even perform before a French public.[46] This is similar to what happened to Seki Sano, a young director of the theatre company Toranku Gekijô of Tokyo, who went

A Room in India. Behind the *terukkuttu* curtain, Draupadi (Judit Jancsó), while turning, begs Krishna to help her. On the orders of King Duryodhana (Seear Kohi), his brother Dushasana (Duccio Bellugi-Vannuccini) is trying to undress her. But Krishna multiplies the red cloth of her sari, which exhausts Dushasana. His brother encourages him, while the chorus sings the song of Draupadi's sari. Photo by Michèle Laurent.

The Evenings of May 12 and 13, 2018. Kalaimamani Purisai Kannappa Sambandan Thambiran (Drona) and Palani Murugan (Abhimanyu) perform a *terukkuttu* scene (*La Mort d'Abhimanyu*). The Soleil actors and the Purisai school musicians form the orchestra. Photo by Anne Lacombe.

to study the new Russian theatre with the experimental director Meyerhold, and who rediscovered with him the treasures of kabuki that he had once disparaged.[47]

Mnouchkine had long dreamed of directing the *Mahabharata*. She admits that one can't keep on going to India and not dream about it. For his beautiful version in 1985, Peter Brook had borrowed the story and the myths, but not the versification, the music, and the sense of India itself. The initiation and apprenticeship of *terukkuttu* have allowed Mnouchkine to approach the great epic differently. *Our Little Mahabharata*, resulting from an intensive period of work, has been electrified by the exchanges and the back-and-forth between cultures. It is a collective, holding out against the disappearance of forms and cultures, an ode to cultural diversity, a victory against loss and death. At the end of the year 2019, this show became part of the larger repertory of the Théâtre du Soleil, with its four acts: *The Dice Game* [La Partie de dés], performed by Sambandan's Purisai school; *The Rape of Draupadi* [*Le Viol de Draupadi*], performed by the Théâtre du Soleil; *The Death of Abhimanyu, Arjuna's Son* [*La Mort d'Abhimanyu, fils d'Arjuna*], performed by the Sambandam group; and the *Death of Karna: Goodbye to Ponnourouvi* [*La Mort de Karna: Les Adieux à Ponnourouvi*], performed by the Soleil. More than a performance, the combined work is meant

Master Kalaimamani Purisai Kannappa, surrounded by his Indian students, E. Prakash Raj (left) and Palani Murugan (right), takes a bow. Photo by Anne Lacombe.

as a mark of gratitude to Sambandan, and reciprocally, a space for Sambandan to recognize, in turn, "how precious it has been for him to work with Westerners, how much that has given him new strength, and how proud he is of his Indian and French students."[48] Tradition only lives if it transforms; culture only survives through exchange. After profoundly absorbing the essence of so many traditions, after having adapted them to fit the company's own imaginary, or after copying traditions while transforming them on its stages – a crossroads for the world – the Théâtre du Soleil has also been capable of giving back to the source country theatre forms that are true, eternal, *and* transformable.

Voice of Ariane Mnouchkine

"Terukkuttu *is incontestably what reminds us of what art is, of what the light of art means.*"[49]

What is the Théâtre du Soleil preparing for us now – that company, that *school*, that has long prized the equality of men and women in all things? What might the future hold in a trajectory that has brought the company ever closer to the sources of Asian arts? Let's close with a moment of suspense, leaving the last word to Ariane Mnouchkine, the Soleil's instigator and inspired manager: "As always, I have a first scene. Sometimes it flies away; it might also explode in the middle of its flight. But it begins in Japan."[50]

Notes

1 Ariane Mnouchkine, from the theatre program of *Le Dernier Caravansérail* [*The Last Caravanserai*].
2 The Karachi Affair, a major military scandal, concerned kickbacks between lobbyists in France and Pakistan over negotiations to acquire French submarines. The governments of both François Mitterand and Jacques Chirac were involved.
3 Ariane Mnouchkine, from the theatre program of *Une Chambre en Inde* [*A Room in India*], taken from a public conversation between Ariane Mnouchkine and Eugenio Barba at the Théâtre du Soleil, March 8, 2016.
4 Ariane Mnouchkine, in a telephone conversation in Paris with Béatrice Picon-Vallin, February 26, 2019.
5 To reinforce the authenticity of this article, Mnouchkine mentioned that it was found in the journal of a Welsh ethnobotanist by a young researcher in environmentalism. See the program notes for *A Room in India*.
6 Ariane Mnouchkine, in an interview with Béatrice Picon-Vallin at the Cartoucherie, January 12, 2017.
7 Marie-Hélène Bouvet recounts this in an e-mail to Béatrice Picon-Vallin on March 12, 2019.
8 There were *terukkuttu* performances in Paris in 1985 for "The International Year of India" and in 1997 at the Maison des Cultures du Monde, for the first "Festival of the Imaginary."

9 For more information, see https://www.theatre-du-soleil.fr/fr/auto ur/la-transmission/pages/l-ecole-nomade-286. Catherine Vilpoux is also preparing a documentary film on the Nomadic School with Bel Air Classiques.

10 These sessions took place from June 29–July 24, 2015 in Santiago, Chile; from August 10–21, 2015 on Faro Island; from September 14–25, 2015 at Oxford; from December 14–30, 2015 and January 9–26, 2018 in Pondicherry. More sessions have been scheduled for July 2019 (Mayotte) and January 2020 (Pondicherry).

11 Ariane Mnouchkine, in the rehearsal journal cited in the theatre program of *Une Chambre en Inde.*

12 Hélène Cixous, from "Excerpts from Cornélia's journal, May 2016," in the theatre program of *Une Chambre en Inde.*

13 Ariane Mnouchkine, in the rehearsal journal cited in the theatre program of *Une Chambre en Inde.*

14 Ariane Mnouchkine, in a phone conversation with Béatrice Picon-Vallin, February 6, 2019.

15 Other Soleil actors would work independently on a comic approach, as in, for example, the non-Soleil production, Lazare's cabaret, *The Dark River (Sombre rivière),* 2017.

16 Hélène Cixous, from "Excerpts from Cornélia's journal, May 2016," in the theatre program of *Une Chambre en Inde.*

17 In order to better understand how a person could be turned into a terrorist, the Soleil met with specialists who attempt to roll-back the damage done to young people through radicalization.

18 We might remember the many attacks on women in Cologne, Germany, on New Year's Eve, 2016.

19 Ariane Mnouchkine, in the rehearsal notes for May 24 cited in the theatre program of *Une Chambre en Inde.*

20 Ariane Mnouchkine, in an interview with Agnès Santi, in the theatre news magazine *La Terrasse,* August 25, 2016.

21 Constantin is also Stanislavski's first name, and the first name of the character Treplyov in *The Seagull.*

22 Mnouchkine liked to say in the pre-show remarks she would make to the audience that *A Room in India* wasn't even four-hours long, in comparison with some of her other productions.

23 Ariane Mnouchkine, interviewed on the radio program "La Matinale," France Inter, February 21, 2018.

24 Robert Lepage, April 2018, as reported by Mélanie Drouère in the theatre program for *Kanata: Episode I (La Controverse)* [*The Controversy*].

25 Duccio Bellugi-Vannuccini, in an e-mail to Béatrice Picon-Vallin, June 1, 2019.

26 In 1977, two members of the Soleil directed two productions with Soleil actors: Philippe Caubère directed *Dom Juan* and Jean-Claude Penchenat directed *David Copperfield.* In 1998, Irina Brook, not of the Soleil, also directed *All's Well that Ends Well* for the Avignon Festival with the Soleil troupe.

27 See Ariane Mnouchkine's letter to the public, October 22, 2018, https://theatre-du-soleil.fr/fr/notre-theatre/les-spectacles/kanata-ep isode-i-la-controverse-2018–2164.

28 Ariane Mnouchkine, in a phone conversation in Paris with Béatrice Picon-Vallin, February 26, 2019.

29 *SLĀV* was a Lepage production for the International Jazz Festival in Montreal that provoked intense criticism over the issues of cultural appropriation and the non-representation of minority performers. Several performances were cancelled in June 2018.

30 "Décoloniser les arts" is the name of a French association created in 2015 to "fight against discrimination in the arts towards minority and postcolonial populations."

31 See the reporting of this in Hélène Choquette's documentary, *Lepage au Soleil: à l'origine de Kanata*, EMA Films Inc., 2019. See also the site Voix des femmes autochtones: https://femmesautochtones.com. Consulted January 10, 2019.

32 See the testimony of Lucille Mattess, www.lesenfantsdevenus.ca. Consulted January 12, 2019.

33 This sequence can be understood as the crescendo of the theme of violence towards First Nations peoples, seen in the testimony of this First Nations woman, speaking from the screen of a large television placed on a rolling platform and manipulated by pushers.

34 Ariane Mnouchkine, in an interview with Joëlle Gayot, "Ariane Mnouchkine: les cultures ne sont les propriétés de personne," *Télérama*, No. 3584, 2018, 20–21. Our emphasis.

35 Théâtre du Soleil, in its letter to the public, September 16, 2017.

36 The Chinese performances were part of the Festival Standard Idéal organized by Patrick Sommier at the theatre MC93 in Bobigny.

37 "Kodo" means heartbeat. This show was part of the Festival Paris l'Été.

38 See https://www.theatre-du-soleil.fr/fr/demandez-le-programme.

39 This two-part piece won the Prize of the Union of French Critics in June 2019.

40 This reflection was cited by Ariane Mnouchkine in an editorial, May 25, 2019, https://theatre-du-soleil.fr/fr/les-editos/editorial-du-25-mai-2019-34.

41 For more projects, see https://www.theatre-du-soleil.fr/fr/demandez-le-programme.

42 Kalaimamani Purisai Sambandan, cited by his nephew in a video interview, https://www.theatre-du-soleil.fr/fr/notre-theatre/les-spectacles/notre-petit-mahabharata-2018-2146.

43 Ariane Mnouchkine, in a phone call in Paris with Béatrice Picon-Vallin, February 26, 2019.

44 Ariane Mnouchkine, during "Le Prix de l'expérience. Contraintes et dépassements dans le travail de groupe," a public conversation between Ariane Mnouchkine and Eugenio Barba at the Théâtre du Soleil, March 8, 2016. Notes taken by Béatrice Picon-Vallin.

45 See Chapter Six of this study.

46 See Chapter Four of this study and the DVD that will be available from Bel-Air Classiques, July 2019.

47 For more on this story, see Béatrice Picon-Vallin, "Avant-propos," in *Butô(s)*, eds. Odette Aslan and Béatrice Picon-Vallin, Paris: CNRS Editions, 2002, 7–15.

48 Ariane Mnouchkine, in a phone interview on the Eurostar with Béatrice Picon-Vallin, February 16, 2019.

49 Rehearsal Note of January 11, 2016, as cited in the theatre program for *Une Chambre en Inde*.

50 Ariane Mnouchkine, in a telephone call with Béatrice Picon-Vallin, February 26, 2019.

The daily ritual before every performance. Ariane Mnouchkine sounds the three blows that traditionally open a French production. However, rather than signaling the opening of the curtain or the arrival on stage of the actors, the blows are sounded on the wooden doors to the Soleil's hangar. They thus announce the entrance of the spectators. And the show begins: the Welcome Area fills up and comes alive. Photo by Michèle Laurent.

Macbeth (rehearsal). Ariane Mnouchkine shows the rehearsing actors the proposed poster for the performance. Photo by Lucile Cocito.

Appendices: chronology and awards, theatre programs and posters

Timeline: productions and awards

1939: Ariane Mnouchkine is born in Boulogne-sur-Mer.

1958–59: A. Mnouchkine studies in Great Britain.

1958: She attends a Peking Opera performance at the Théâtre des Nations.

1959: Creation of l'ATEP, Association for Parisian Theatre Students.

1961: L'ATEP performs *Genghis Khan* by Henry Bauchau at the Arènes de Lutèce.

1963: A. Mnouchkine's first trip to Asia.

1964 (May 29): The Théâtre du Soleil is founded.

1964–65: The Soleil performs *Les Petits Bourgeois* [*The Philistines*] by Maxim Gorky, adapted by Arthur Adamov, directed by A. Mnouchkine, sets and costumes Roberto Moscoso; performances at the MJC (Maison des jeunes et de la culture) of the Porte de Montreuil and the Théâtre Mouffetard (2,900 spectators).

1965–66: *Le Capitaine Fracasse* [*Captain Fracasse*], based on the novel by Théophile Gautier, adaptation by Philippe Léotard, directed by A. Mnouchkine, sets R. Moscoso, costumes Françoise Tournafond; Théâtre Récamier (4,000 spectators).

1967:
- *La Cuisine* [*The Kitchen*] by Arnold Wesker, adapted by P. Léotard, directed by A. Mnouchkine, sets R. Moscoso; Montmartre circus (63,400 spectators).
- Union of Critics' Grand Prize (France) awarded to *La Cuisine*.
- Brigadier Prize (France) awarded to *La Cuisine*.
- Prize from the Association of Theatregoers (France).

1968:
- *Le Songe d'une nuit d'été* [*A Midsummer Night's Dream*] by William Shakespeare, adapted by P. Léotard, directed by A. Mnouchkine, music Jacques Lasry, sets R. Moscoso, costumes F. Tournafond; Montmartre circus (47,000 spectators).
- *L'Arbre sorcier, Jérôme et la tortue* [*The Magic Tree, Jerome and the Turtle*], directed by Catherine Dasté, music J. Lasry; Montmartre circus, Avignon Festival.

1969–70: *Les Clowns* [*The Clowns*], Théâtre du Soleil collective creation, in collaboration with Théâtre de la Commune d'Aubervilliers, directed by A. Mnouchkine, music Teddy Lasry, sets R. Moscoso, costumes Christiane Candries; Théâtre de la Commune d'Aubervilliers.

Tour: Avignon Festival, Piccolo Teatro (Milan). Reprise, Élysée-Montmartre. (40,000 spectators.)

August 1970: The Soleil moves in to the Cartoucherie de Vincennes.

1970–71: *1789: "La revolution doit s'arrêtter à la perfection du Bonheur,"* Théâtre du Soleil collective creation, directed by A. Mnouchkine, sets R. Moscoso, costumes F. Tournafond; premiere at Piccolo Teatro in Milan, reprise at the Cartoucherie.

Tour (in France and abroad): Villeurbanne, Besançon, Caen, Le Havre, Martinique, Lausanne, Berlin, London, Belgrade. (281,370 spectators).

1972–73: *1793: "La cite révolutionnaire est de ce monde,"* Théâtre du Soleil collective creation, directed by A. Mnouchkine, sets R. Moscoso, costumes F. Tournafond; Cartoucherie. Reprise of *1789* alternating with *1793* at the Cartoucherie. (102,100 spectators.)

1974: *1789*, film of the performance, directed by A. Mnouchkine (DVD released by Bel Air Classiques, 2017).

1975: *L'Âge d'or, première ébauche* [*The Golden Age: First Draft*], Théâtre du Soleil collective creation, directed by A. Mnouchkine, performance space Guy-Claude François, costumes F. Tournafond, masks Erhard Stiefel; Cartoucherie.

Tour: Warsaw, Venice, Louvain-la-Neuve, Milan (136,080 spectators).

1976–77: *Molière ou la vie d'un honnête homme*, film written and directed by A. Mnouchkine with the Théâtre du Soleil. Sets G-C. François, costumes Daniel Ogier, images Bernard Zitzermann, music René Clémencic (DVD released by Bel Air Classiques, 2004).

1977: *Dom Juan* by Molière, directed by Philippe Caubère, sets G-C. François, costumes F. Tournafond. (30,439 spectators.)

1978: Alf Sjörberg Prize awarded to the Théâtre du Soleil by the National Theatre of Stockholm.

1979–80: *Méphisto, le roman d'une carrière* [*Mephisto*], based on the novel by Klaus Mann, adapted and directed by A. Mnouchkine, sets G-C. François, costumes Nani Noël and Daniel Ogier, music Jean-Jacques Lemêtre, masks E. Stiefel; Cartoucherie.

Tour: Avignon Festival, Atelier théâtral de Louvain-la-Neuve, Lyon, Rome, Berlin, Munich, Lons-le-Saunier. Performance filmed for video by Bernard Sobel. (160,000 spectators.)

1981–84: Les *Shakespeare* [*The Shakespeare Cycle*], translated and directed by A. Mnouchkine, sets G-C. François, masks E. Stiefel, costumes Jean-Claude Barriera and Nathalie Thomas, music J-J. Lemêtre. (253,000 spectators.)

1981: *Richard II*; Cartoucherie.

1982:

- Union of Critics' Grand Prize (France) awarded to *Richard II*.
- *La Nuit des rois* [*Twelfth Night*], Avignon Festival. Subsequently, *Twelfth Night* alternated with *Richard II* at the Cartoucherie.
- **1983:** Grand Prize Dominique for Stage Direction (France) awarded to *La Nuit des rois*.

1984: *Henry IV*, 1ère partie [*Henry IV, Part I*]; Cartoucherie. Performed alternating with the two previous plays in the cycle.

Tours 1982–84: Avignon Festival, Munich Festival, Los Angeles Olympic Arts Festival, Berlin (Berliner Festspiele).

1985–86: *L'Histoire terrible mais inachevée de Norodom Sihanouk, roi du Cambodge* [*The Terrible but Unfinished Story of Norodom Sihanouk, King of Cambodia*], by Hélène Cixous, directed by A. Mnouchkine, music J-J. Lemêtre, sets G-C. François, costumes J-C. Barriera and N. Thomas, statues and masks E. Stiefel; Cartoucherie.

1985: Grand Prize for Theatre awarded for 20 years of activity by the Ministry of Culture (France).

Tour 1986: Amsterdam (Holland Festival), Brussels, Madrid, Barcelona. (108,445 spectators.)

1986: *Á la recherche du Soleil*, film réalisé par Werner Schroeter (Ziegler Film, Berlin).

1986: Union of Critics' Prize (France) for best actor awarded to Georges Bigot in the role of Sihanouk.

1987: Europe Prize for theatre (European Union) awarded to Ariane Mnouchkine.

1987–88: *L'Indiade ou l'Inde de leurs rêves* [*The Indiad or India of their Dreams*], by Hélène Cixous, directed by A. Mnouchkine, music J-J. Lemêtre, sets G-C. François, costumes J-C. Barriera and N. Thomas, masks E. Stiefel; Cartoucherie.

1988: Prize for Pleasure in Theatre awarded by Taormina Arte (Italy) to the company for its enduring work.

Tour: Tel Aviv (Jerusalem Festival). Performance filmed for video by Bernard Sobel. (89,000 spectators.)

1989:

- *La Nuit miraculeuse* [*The Miraculous Night*], film directed by A. Mnouchkine, written by A. Mnouchkine and H. Cixous (VHS).
- Arletty Prize (France) awarded to Ariane Mnouchkine for her participation in promoting theatre work.

1990–91: Prize for the Best Theatre Work and Best Company awarded to the Soleil by an international jury of German-language critics.

1990–93: *Les Atrides* [*The House of Atreus Cycle*], directed by A. Mnouchkine, music J-J. Lemêtre, sets G-C. François, sculptures E. Stiefel, costumes N. Thomas and Marie-Hélène Bouvet. (286,700 spectators.)

1990: *Iphigénie* [*Iphigenia in Aulis*] by Euripides, translated by Jean Bollack; Cartoucherie.

1990: *Agamemnon* by Aeschylus, translated by A. Mnouchkine; Cartoucherie.

1991:

- *Les Choéphores* [*The Libation Bearers*] by Aeschylus, translated by A. Mnouchkine; Cartoucherie. Performed alternating with the two previous plays in the cycle.
- Union of Critics' Grand Prize (France) awarded to *Les Atrides*.
- Union of Critics' Prize (France) for the best stage music to Jean-Jacques Lemêtre for *Les Atrides*.

1992: *Les Euménides* [*The Eumenides*] by Aeschylus, translated by H. Cixous; Cartoucherie. Performed alternating with the three previous plays in the cycle.

Tours 1991–93: Amsterdam (Holland Festival), Essen (Theater der Welt), Sicily (Orestiadi di Gibellina), Berlin (Berliner Festspiele), Lyon (Théâtre national populaire), Toulouse (Le Sorano), Montpellier (Le Printemps des comédiens), Bradford (European Art Festival), Montreal (Festival de théâtre des Amériques), New York (BAM), Vienna (Wiener Festwochen).

1992–93: Drama Desk Award and Obie Award (New York) for *Les Atrides*.

1993: *L'Inde de père en fils, de mère en fille* [*India from Father to Son, from Mother to Daughter*], directed by Rajeev Sethi, based on an idea by A. Mnouchkine. (8,414 spectators.)

1994:

- Eschillo d'Oro: awarded by the National Institute of Classical Drama, Syracusa, Italy, for *Les Atrides*.

- *La Ville parjure ou le Réveil des Érinyes* [*The Perjured City, or the Awakening of the Furies*], by H. Cixous, directed by A. Mnouchkine, music J-J. Lemêtre, sets G-C. François, costumes N. Thomas and M-H. Bouvet; Cartoucherie.

Tour: Liège (Théâtre de la Place), Recklinghausen (Ruhr Festspiele), Vienna (Wiener Festwochen), Avignon Festival. (51,200 spectators.)

- Union of Critics' prize (France) for best original French-language play awarded to *La Ville parjure*.

1995–96: *Le Tartuffe* [*Tartuffe*] by Molière, directed by A. Mnouchkine, sets G-C. François, costumes N. Thomas and M-H. Bouvet, music J-J. Lemêtre; premiere in Vienna (Wiener Festwochen).
Tour 1995: Avignon Festival, Saint-Jean-d'Angély, Liège (Théâtre de la Place).
October 1995: Performances at the Cartoucherie.
1996: Medal of Honor Josef Kainz (Vienna) awarded to Ariane Mnouchkine for her staging of *Tartuffe*.
Tour 1996: La Rochelle, Vienne, Copenhagen (Copenhagen 96), Berlin (Berliner Festspiele). (122,000 spectators.)
1996–97: *Au Soleil même la nuit (scènes d'accouchements)* [*At the Soleil even at night (delivery scenes)*], film by Éric Darmon and Catherine Vilpoux in harmony with A. Mnouchkine (DVD released by Bel Air Classiques, 2011).
1997–98: *Et soudain des nuits d'éveil* [*And Suddenly, Sleepless Nights*], Théâtre du Soleil collective creation in harmony with H. Cixous, directed by A. Mnouchkine, sets G-C. François, paintings Danièle Heusslein-Gire, costumes N. Thomas and M-H. Bouvet, music J-J. Lemêtre; Cartoucherie.
Tour June 1998: Moscow (Chekhov Festival). (55,000 spectators.)
1999: *D'après La Ville parjure*, Film based on *La Ville parjure ou le Réveil des Érinyes* by Catherine Vilpoux, images Éric Darmon, music J-J. Lemêtre (Book/DVD released by the Théâtre du Soleil, 2010).
1999–2002: *Tambours sur la digue, sous forme de pièce ancienne pour marionnettes jouée par des acteurs* [*Drums on the Dam, in the Form of an Ancient Puppet Play Performed by Actors*], by H. Cixous, directed by A. Mnouchkine, music J-J. Lemêtre, sets G-C. François, Ysabel de Maisonneuve and Didier Martin, costumes N. Thomas and M-H. Bouvet; Cartoucherie. (150,000 spectators.)
1999: Grand Prize of the City of Paris to the company for their stage work.
2000:

- SACD (Society of Dramatic Authors and Composers) Grand Prize awarded to *Tambours sur la digue*.
- Union of Critics' Grand Prize awarded to *Tambours sur la digue*.
- Molière awards for *Tambours sur la digue*: best creation, best *mise en scène*, best set design (G-C. François).

Tour 2000: Basel (Kaserne Basel), Antwerp (DeSingel).
Tour 2001: Lyon (Célestins-Théâtre de Lyon), Montreal (Festival de théâtre des Amériques), Tokyo (New National Theatre), Seoul (National Theatre of Korea).
Tour 2002: Sydney (Sydney Festival).
2001–02: *Tambours sur la digue*, film by A. Mnouchkine, filmed at the Cartoucherie in 2001 (DVD released by Arte vidéo, 2002).
2003: *Le Dernier Caravansérail (Odyssées)* [*The Last Caravanserai (Odysseys)*], Théâtre du Soleil collective creation, music J-J. Lemêtre, sets

G-C. François, paintings D. Martin, hangings Y. de Maisonneuve, costumes N. Thomas and M-H. Bouvet; Cartoucherie. (185,000 spectators.)

April 2003: *Le Dernier Caravansérail (Odyssées), Le Fleuve cruel* [*The Last Caravanserai (Odysseys), The Cruel River*]; Cartoucherie.

November 2003: *Le Dernier Caravansérail (Odyssées), Origines et destins* [*The Last Caravanserai (Odysseys), Origins and Destinies*]; Cartoucherie.

Tours 2003–05: Rome, Quimper (Théâtre de Cornouaille), Avignon, Bochum (Ruhrtriennale), Lyon (Théâtre des Célestins), Berlin (Arena Theatre), New York (Lincoln Center Festival), Athens, Melbourne.

2005:
- Ariane Mnouchkine receives an honorary doctorate from The University of Rome.
- Ariane Mnouchkine and the Soleil are awarded the Picasso Silver Medal from UNESCO for their contribution to cultural diversity and dialogue.
- Molière awards for *Le Dernier Caravansérail (Odyssées)*: best creation in a public theatre; best company; best set design (Serge Nicolaï, Duccio Bellugi-Vannuccini, G.-C. François); best stage music creation (J-J Lemêtre).

2006:
- *Le Dernier Caravansérail (Odyssées)*, film by A. Mnouchkine, filmed at the Cartoucherie in 2005. (DVD released by Bel Air Classiques – Arte Video, 2006.)
- *Les Éphémères* [*Ephemera*], Théâtre du Soleil collective creation, in two parts (volumes); Cartoucherie.

Tour: Quimper, Athens Festival, Avignon Festival, Buenos Aires Festival, Porto Alegre em Cena Festival, São Paulo, Taipei, Vienna (Wiener Festwochen), Saint-Étienne. (160,000 spectators.)

- *Un Soleil à Kaboul, ou plutôt deux* [*A Soleil in Kabul, or Rather Two*], documentary film directed by D. Bellugi-Vannuccini, Philippe Chevallier and Sergio Canto Sabido. (DVD released by Bel Air Classiques, 2009.)

2007: A. Mnouchkine receives a Golden Lion in Venice for her entire body of work.

2008:
- *Les Éphémères*, filmed in Saint-Étienne by B. Zitzermann. (DVD released by Bel Air Classiques – Arte Vidéo, 2009.)
- Oxford University awards A. Mnouchkine an honorary doctorate.

2009:
- Mnouchkine receives the International Ibsen Award from the Norwegian government for her entire body of work.

Tour (*Les Éphémères*): Lincoln Center Festival in New York.

- *Ariane Mnouchkine. L'Aventure du Théâtre du Soleil* [*Ariane Mnouchkine: The Théâtre du Soleil Adventure*], documentary film by C. Vilpoux. (Arte Vidéo, 2009.)
- *Un cercle de connaisseurs* [*A Circle of Connoisseurs*], documentary film by Jeanne Dosse. (DVD released by Bel Air Classiques, 2009.)
- Obie Award (New York) for *Les Éphémères*.

2010:

- *Les Naufragés du Fol Espoir (Aurores)* [*The Survivors of Mad Hope (Dawn)*], Théâtre du Soleil collective creation half-written by H. Cixous, music J-J. Lemêtre, costumes N. Thomas, M-H. Bouvet and Annie Tran; Cartoucherie.

Tour: Lyon (Théâtre des Célestins), Nantes (Grand T), Athens Festival, São Paulo (SESC Belenzinho), Rio de Janeiro (HSBC Arena), Porto Alegre (Parque Eduardo Gomez), Festival Santiago a Mil, Wiener Festwochen, Edinburgh International Festival, Taipei (National Theatre of Taiwan). (185,000 spectators.)

- Union of Critics' prize (France) for best original French-language play awarded to *Les Naufragés du Fol Espoir (Aurores)*.
- Molière awards for *Les Naufragés du Fol Espoir (Aurores)*: best creation in a public theatre, best costume creation (N. Thomas, M-H. Bouvet, A. Tran).

2011–12: *Les Naufragés du Fol Espoir*, filmed at the Cartoucherie and on tour. (DVD released by Bel Air Classiques, 2013.)
2011: Goethe Medal of Honor awarded to Ariane Mnouchkine from the Goethe Institute in Weimar, Germany.
2012:

- International Stanislavsky Prize (Moscow) awarded to Mnouchkine.
- Critics' Diploma of Honor (Chile) awarded to the Soleil for *Les Naufragés du Fol Espoir (Aurores)*.
- Herald's Angels Prize (Edinburgh) for *Les Naufragés du Fol Espoir (Aurores)*.

2014: *Macbeth*, by Shakespeare, translated and directed by A. Mnouchkine, music J-J. Lemêtre, costumes M-H. Bouvet, N. Thomas, and Annie Tran. Cartoucherie.

- (May 29): Anniversary of the First Fifty Years of the Théâtre du Soleil.

2015:

- Nonino International Prize (Pavia di Udine, Italy) awarded to Ariane Mnouchkine.
- 25th International Hope Prize awarded to the Théâtre du Soleil and Ariane Mnouchkine by the Institute for People's Theatre (Aasen, Denmark).
- Pablo Neruda Medal for Cultural and Artistic Merit (Chile) awarded to Ariane Mnouchkine.
- Ariane Mnouchkine initiates the creation of the Théâtre du Soleil's Nomadic School.
- (June 29–July 24) First iteration of the Nomadic School in Santiago, Chile, invited by the Foundation Teatro A Mil.
- (10–21 August) Second phase of the Nomadic School – on Faro Island in Sweden, invited by Stockholm's Academy of Dramatic Arts and by the Bergman Center, with the support of the Institut Français of Sweden.
- (Sept. 14–25) Third phase of the Nomadic School – in the United Kingdom, invited by Oxford University and Oxford's French House.

- (Dec. 14–30) The Nomadic School goes to Pondicherry, India, welcomed by the Indianostrum Theatre, and sponsored by the Alliance Française, the French Embassy, and the Institut Français of India.

2016: *Une chambre en Inde* [*A Room in India*], Théâtre du Soleil collective creation, directed by A. Mnouchkine, music J-J. Lemêtre, costumes M-H. Bouvet, N. Thomas, and Annie Tran; Cartoucherie.

Tour: New York (Park Avenue Armory), Montpellier (Printemps des comédiens), Lausanne (Théâtre Kléber-Méleau).

2017:
- Beaumarchais Prize (France) to Ariane Mnouchkine for her entire body of work.
- Goethe Prize (Frankfort) to Ariane Mnouchkine for her entire body of work.

2018:
- (January 9–26) The Nomadic School returns to Pondicherry.
- (May 12–13) *Notre petit Mahabharata: Hommage à notre maître et aux origines d' Une chambre en Inde* [*Our Little Mahabharata: A Homage to our Master Teacher and to the Origins of A Room in India*]. Four episodes of the *Mahabharata* performed by the Théâtre du Soleil and the Tamil students of P.K. Sambandan.
- Obie Award/Special Mention (New York) for *Une Chambre en Inde*.
- *Kanata, Épisode 1: La Controverse* [*Kanata, Episode 1: The Controversy*], directed by Robert Lepage, music Ludovic Bonnier, costumes M-H. Bouvet, N. Thomas, and Annie Tran; Cartoucherie.
- Molière awards for *Une Chambre en Inde*: best creation in a public theatre, best *mise en scène*.
- Samuel de Champlain France-Amériques Prize awarded to Ariane Mnouchkine by the France-Canada Institute for her promotion of French culture and her international theatre work, especially in Canada.

2019: *Kanata, Épisode I: La Controverse* [*Kanata, Episode I: The Controversy*] tours in Naples (Napoli Teatro Festival Italia) and Athens (Athens and Epidaurus Festival).

- Ariane Mnouchkine is awarded the Kyoto Prize in the category of Arts and Philosophy by the Inamori Foundation for her lifetime achievement in the arts.
- (June 29–July 20) The Nomadic School goes to Mayotte.
- (November 5) Ariane Mnouchkine receives the National Prize for Secularity from the Committee on Secularity and Republicanism (Paris Hôtel de Ville).

The Soleil programs: casts, credits, and thanks

(Some casts went through multiple changes. The credits reproduced here are primarily from the programs listing the initial cast of each production; cast members of a reprise are indicated with an asterisk [*] when relevant.)

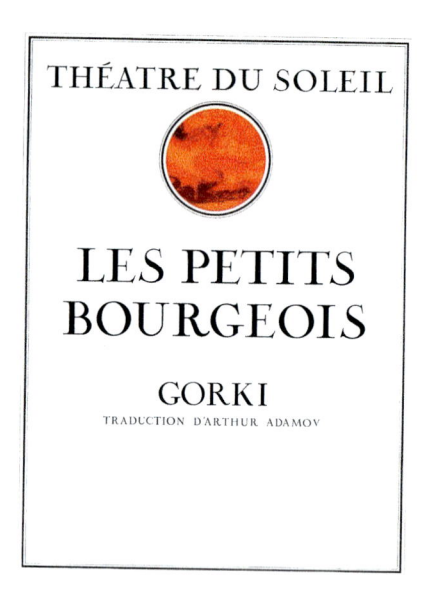

Les Petits Bourgeois [*The Philistines*]

By Maxim Gorky, adapted by Arthur Adamov
Premiere: November 1964, at the MJC (Maison des jeunes et de la culture) of the Porte de Montreuil.

With, by order of appearance:
Tatiana Vassilievna: Sonia Katchadhourian
Polia: Chantal Solca
Piotr Vassilievitch: Jean Sagolce, Jean-Pierre Tailhade*
Vassili Vassilievitch: Pierre Giuliano
Akoulina Ivanovna: Louba Guertchikoff
Stepanida: Cécile Ricard
Pertchikine: Gérard Hardy
Terenti Krisanfovitch Teteriov: Paul Besset
Elena Nicolaievna: Édith Zetlin, Joséphine Derenne*
Nil Vassilievitch: Philippe Léotard, François Joxe*
Maria Nikitchina Tsvetaieva: Cristel Lazarewsky, Anne Demeyer*
Chichkine: Claude Merlin
A peasant woman: Natia Carcelli, Marie Irakane*

Director: Ariane Mnouchkine
Sets and costumes: Roberto Moscoso
Stage manager: Gérard Hardy
Music: Roger Tessier
Pianist: Pierre Audon
Photography: Martine Franck
Poster and program: Catherine Legrand
Administration: Jean-Pierre Tailhade
Treasury: Jean-Claude Penchenat
Publicity: Gérard Hardy
With the collaboration of: Georges Donzenac, Jean-Claude Penchenat, Geneviève Penchenat, Jean-Pierre Tailhade, Françoise Tournafond, Baudoin Bauchau, Liliane Léotard

THEATRE DU SOLEIL

LE CAPITAINE FRACASSE

D'APRES
TH. GAUTIER
ADAPTATION PHILIPPE LEOTARD

Le Capitaine Fracasse [*Captain Fracasse*]

Based on the novel by Théophile Gautier, adapted by Philippe Léotard
Premiere: January 21, 1966, at the Théâtre Récamier.

With, by order of appearance:
Accordionist: Gilles Lecouty
Pierre: Claude Merlin
Baron de Sigognac: Gérard Hardy, François Joxe*
Matamore: Lau Ferreira, Gérard Hardy*
Hérode: Jean Caune, Henry Czarniak*
Léandre: Thomas Leiclier

Scapin: Jean-Pierre Tailhade
Zerbine: Joséphine Derenne
Cowherd: François Joxe, Daniel Bart*
Isabelle: Chantal Solca
Suits of Armor: Max Douchin, Alain Foussat, Yves Beneyton,* Marc Roucout*
Stagehand: François Decaux*
A valet: Alain Foussat, Yves Beneyton*
A caryatid: Pierre Danger, Hans Stark*
Marquis des Bruyères: Michel Barcet
Chiriguiri: Max Douchin, Marcel Robert*
Agostin: Paul Besset, Jean Caune*
Chiquita: Barbara Girard
Scarecrows: Pierre Danger, Alain Foussat, François Joxe, Claude Merlin, Yves Beneyton,* Marc Roucout,* Hans Stark,* Claude Merlin,* Charles Anthony*
A soldier: Max Douchin
Duc de Vallombreuse: Charles Antony
Merindol: Pierre Giuliano
Thieves: Max Douchin, Alain Foussat, Lau Ferreira,* Pierre Giuliano
Gymnastics professor: Max Douchin, Pierre Giuliano*
Barber: Pierre Danger, Pierre Giuliano*
First young woman: Daïna La Varenne
Second young woman: Chantal Baudot*
Procurer: Lau Ferreira, Marc Roucout*
Rakes: Pierre Danger, Lau Ferreira, François Joxe, Claude Merlin, Yves Beneyton,* François Decaux,* Marc Roucout,* Hans Stark*
Innkeeper: Max Douchin, Marcel Robert*
Albert: Thomas Leiclier

Director: Ariane Mnouchkine
Sets and props: Roberto Moscoso
Riser made by: Paul Besset
Props made by: Roberto Moscoso
Costumes: Françoise Tournafond
Costumes made by: Liliane Léotard, Roger Jouan, Louba Guertchikoff, Françoise Tournafond
Makeup: Nicole Félix
Songs: Music, Dominique Brial; Lyrics, Philippe Léotard
Fight manager: Georges Donzenac
Stage manager: Saadi Bahri
Lights: Serge Wolf
Photography: Martine Franck
Poster and program: Catherine Legrand
Administration: Jean-Pierre Tailhade
Treasury: Jean-Claude Penchenat
Publicity: Gérard Hardy
With the collaboration of: Paul Besset, Georges Donzenac, Myrrha Donzenac, Pierre Giuliano, Louba Guertchikoff, Philippe Léotard, Roberto Moscoso, Martine Franck, Françoise Tournafond

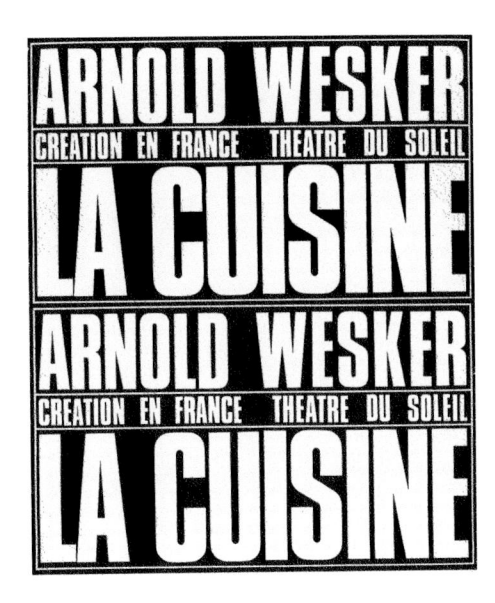

La Cuisine [*The Kitchen*]

By Arnold Wesker, adapted by Philippe Léotard
Premiere: April 5, 1967, at the Cirque de Montmartre.

With, by order of appearance:
Fred, night watchman: Max Douchin, Georges Bonnaud*
Max, butcher: Pierre Forget
Raphaël, kitchen hand: Roger Bardelot, Mario Gonzalès*
Bertha, cold buffet: Maria Iracane, Louba Guertchikoff*
Nadia, waitress: Geneviève Penchenat, Rosine Rochette
Ida, waitress: Françoise Jamet, Daïna La Varenne
Paul, pastry cook: Jean-Claude Penchenat
Raymond, pastry cook: Fabrice Herrero
Liliane, waitress: Daïna La Varenne, Françoise Jamet*
Huguette, waitress: François Fabrice, Élisabeth Hazan, Christine Sandre*
Anne, coffees: Nicole Félix, Lucia Bensasson
Denise, waitress: Mireille Franchino, Liliane Léotard*
Geneviève, waitress: Élisabeth Hazan
Simone, waitress: Anne Demeyer
Youssef, kitchen hand: Omar Hamidechi, Salah Teskouk*
Jackie, waitress: Myrrha Donzenac
Mado, waitress: Josette Boussard, Geneviève Penchenat
Monique, waitress: Joséphine Derenne
Alfredo, roaster: Guy Laroche
Maître d'hôtel: Antoine Delcambre, Georges Lucas*
Philippe, soups, eggs: René Patrignani
Samir, grilled meats: Claude Merlin
Hans, fried foods: Carlos Denis, Jean-Marie Verselle*
Mario, fish: Charles Antoni, Marc Godard*

José, hot vegetables: François Joxe, Jacob Weizbluth*
Peter, fish: Jean-Pierre Tailhade, Philippe Léotard*
Franck, second chef: Gérard Hardy, Roland Amstutz*
Chef: Serge Coursan
Peretti, the boss: Léo Peltier, Roger Weber*
Hobo: Gérald Denizot

Adaptation: Philippe Léotard
Director: Ariane Mnouchkine
Assistant: Nora Kretz
Sets: Roberto Moscoso
Construction: Daniel Pesquet
Outreach: Gérard Hardy, Françoise Fabrice
Photography: Martine Franck
Posters and programs: Catherine Legrand
Stage manager: René François
Administration: Jean-Pierre Tailhade, Jean-Claude Penchenat
Secretariat: Françoise Descotils
Public relations: Gérard Hardy

Le Songe d'une nuit d'été [*A Midsummer Night's Dream*]

By William Shakespeare, adapted by Philippe Léotard
Premiere: February 15, 1968, at the Cirque de Montmartre.

With, by order of appearance:
Musician: Teddy Lasry
Theseus: Paul Besset

Amazon Queen: Joséphine Derenne
Egeus: Jacques Tourane
Hermia: Élisabeth Hazan
Demetrius: Charles Antoni
Lysander: François Joxe
Helena: Rosine Rochette
Amazons: Danielle Chinsky, Michelle Amado, Lucia Bensasson, Dorte Oloe
Theseus's suite: Georges Bonnaud, Philippe Druillet, Marc Godard, Fabrice
     Herrero
Tamias: Jean-Pierre Tailhade
Peter Quince: Claude Merlin
Nick Bottom, the weaver: Philippe Léotard
Francis Flute, the bellows-mender: Jean-Claude Penchenat
Robin Starveling, the tailor: Gérald Denizot
Tom Snout, the tinker: Gérard Hardy
Snug, the joiner: Serge Coursan
Puck: René Patrignani, Jean-Marie Verselle
A Fairy: Jean-Marie Verselle, Georges Bonnaud
Oberon: Germinal Casado, Jean-Frédéric Brossard
Titania: Ursula Kübler
Fairies: Dorte Oloe, Max Douchin, Philippe Druillet, Georges Bonnaud, Marc
     Godard, Fabrice Herrero, Jean-Pierre Tailhade, Jean-Marie Verselle

Adaptation: Philippe Léotard
Director: Ariane Mnouchkine
Technical director: Guy-Claude François
Sets: Roberto Moscoso
Costumes: Françoise Tournafond
Music: Jacques Lasry
Lighting: Roger Leuvron
Makeup: Nicole Félix
Choreographer: Ursula Kübler
Photography: Martine Franck
Poster and program: Annie Briat, Louis Briat
Sets made by: Daniel Pesquet, Roberto Moscoso, François Berthet
Costumes made by: Nicole Bize, Rodolphe Sabourdy
Props made by: Françoise Tournafond, Erhard Stiefel
Music performed by: Yvonne Lasry, Jacques Lasry, Teddy Lasry, Bernard
     Baschet
Stage manager: René François, with the collaboration of Baudoin Bauchau
Sound manager: Anne Demeyer
Administration: Jean-Pierre Tailhade
Central secretariat, treasury: Jean-Claude Penchenat
Responsible for outreach: Gérard Hardy, Myrrha Donzenac
Secretariat: Françoise Descotils

Les Clowns [*The Clowns*]

Premiere: April 25, 1969, at the Théâtre de la Commune d'Aubervilliers.

A play by (pell-mell): Mireille Franchino, Mario Gonzalès, Gérard Hardy, Ariane Mnouchkine, Jean-Claude Penchenat, François Joxe, Jean-Marie Verselle, Rosine Rochette, Anne Demeyer, Georges Bonnaud, Joséphine Derenne, Max Douchin, Teddy Lasry, Claude Merlin, Serge Coursan.
And with the participation of (pell-mell): Josette Boulva, Philippe Léotard, Françoise Jamet, Fabrice Herrero, Lucia Bensasson, Charles Antoni, Liliane Léotard, Gérald Denizot, Ursula Kübler, Jean-Pierre Tailhade.
Madame Patafiole: Anne Demeyer
Monsieur Fiu-Fiu: Jean-Marie Verselle
Monsieur Albert: Max Douchin
Monsieur Pépé la Moquette: Mario Gonzalès
Monsieur Laïobule: Claude Merlin
Monsieur Léopold: Gérard Hardy
Madame Cléopâtre: Joséphine Derenne
Monsieur Appollo: Jean-Claude Penchenat
Mademoiselle Scampouzzi: Ariane Mnouchkine
Monsieur Rigolin: Philippe Léotard

<small>THE MUSICIANS</small>
Head Music-Clown: Teddy Lasry
Piano-Clown: Rosine Rochette
Percussion-Clown: Charles Contri
Tuba-Clown: Michel Derouin
Cymbals-Clown: Jean-François Labouverie
Trombone-Clown: Georges Bonnaud

Technical director: Guy-Claude François
Sets: Roberto Moscoso
Costumes: Christiane Candries
Music: Teddy Lasry
Makeup: Fabrice Herrero
Photography: Martine Franck
Posters and program: Annie Briat, Louis Briat, Catherine Legrand
Props: Roberto Moscoso, Fabrice Herrero
Sets made by: Sébastien Alward, Baudoin Bauchau, Lucia Bensasson, Claude Forget, Guy-Claude François
Costumes made by: Hélène Séris, Christiane Candries, Geneviève Bouchez, Didier Dumas
Costume and prop manager: Liliane Léotard
Administration: Jean-Pierre Tailhade
Central secretariat: Jean-Claude Penchenat
Responsible for outreach: Gérard Hardy
Secretariat: Françoise Descotils.
The Clowns was staged in collaboration with the entire team of the Théâtre de la Commune d'Aubervilliers.

1789, la révolution doit s'arrêter à la perfection du bonheur [*1789, The Revolution Must Only Stop at the Perfection of Happiness*]

Premiere: November 11, 1970, at the invitation of the Piccolo Teatro, Milan; then December 26, 1970, at the Cartoucherie.

A play by (in order of appearance): Jean-Claude Penchenat, Georges Bonnaud, Daïna La Varenne, Rosine Rochette, Roland Amstutz, Françoise Jamet, Gérard Hardy, Marc Godard, Jean-François Labouverie, Serge Coursan, René Patrignani, Mario Gonzalès, Michel Derouin, Geneviève Rey, Luc Bartholomé, Michel Toty, Nicole Félix, Fabrice Herrero, Anne Demeyer, Joséphine Derenne, Louis Samier, Lucia Bensasson, Louba Guertchikoff, Myrrha Donzenac, Philippe Dubois, Gilles Milinaire

Participants in the reprise: Jean-Claude Bourbault, Philippe Caubère, Marie-France Duverger, Philippe Hottier, Maxime Lombard, Clémence Massard, Claude Meunier, Alain Salomon, Franck Poumeyreau

Director: Ariane Mnouchkine
Sets: Roberto Moscoso

Costumes: Françoise Tournafond, Christiane Candries
Musical director: Michel Derouin
Photography: Martine Franck
Poster: Catherine Legrand
Puppets and props: Nicole Princet
Technical director: Guy-Claude François
Sets made by: Baudouin Bauchau, Michel Bricaire, Guy-Claude François, Claude Forget, Louis de Grandmaison, Roberto Moscoso
Costumes made by: Hélène Séris, Michel Dufays, Solange Félix, Odile Cointepas, Christiane Candries, Françoise Tournafond
Props made by: Jean-Claude Barriera, Gilbert Moreaux, Nicole Princet
Record-keeper: Sophie Lemasson
Historical consultant: Élisabeth Brisson
Outreach: Gérard Hardy, Odile Cointepas, Françoise Lemoine

1793, la cité révolutionnaire est de ce monde [*1793, The Revolutionary City is Part of This World*]

Premiere: May 12, 1972, at the Cartoucherie.

Cast:

CITOYENS AND CITOYENNES

Basile Renoir, baker: Gilles Milinaire
Adrien Réveillard, blacksmith: René Patrignani
Germain Fabre, engraver: Georges Bonnaud
Honoré Ferron, clerk: Jean-Claude Penchenat
Agricol Chapette, Marseille *fédéré*: Maxime Lombard
Néné d'Allauch, Marseille *fédéré*: Philippe Caubère
Angèle Lafargue, chambermaid: Geneviève Rey
Henriette Rocancourt, ironer: Nicole Félix
Rose-Marie Quentin, washerwoman: Joséphine Derenne
Louise Cassius de Linval, day laborer: Myrrha Donzenac
Thérèse Barridoux, market worker: Françoise Jamet
Anna Chapuis, embroiderer: Lucia Bensasson
Émilie Retranché, seamstress: Daïna La Varenne
Jeanne Anglivielle, newspaper vendor: Louba Guertchikoff
Léonie Linard, delivery woman: Anne Demeyer
Gabrielle Petit, kitchen maid: Dominique Valentin
Félicien Parent, butcher's boy: Jean-Claude Bourbault
Baptiste Dumont, journalist: Franck Poumeyreau
Charles-Henri Lebreton, mail clerk: Gérard Hardy
Antoine Maréchal, joiner and cabinetmaker: Roland Amstutz
Jean Choux, soldier: Serge Coursan
Joseph Dupril, wine merchant: Philippe Hottier
Simon Catel, musician: Michel Derouin
Participants in the reprise: Marc Godard, Marie Catherine

Director: Ariane Mnouchkine
Sets and lighting: Baudoin Bauchau, Jean-Noël Cordier, Antonio Ferreira, Claude Forget, Guy-Claude François, Louis de Grandmaison, Roberto Moscoso, Alain Salomon
Costumes: Jean-Claude Barriera, Nathalie Ferreira, Chantal Forget, Françoise Tournafond
Musical director: Michel Derouin
Photography: Martine Franck
Poster: Catherine Legrand
Administration: Françoise Descotils, Françoise Lemoine
Outreach: Gérard Hardy, Odile Cointepas, Françoise Lemoine
Record-keeper: Sophie Lemasson
Historical documentation: Jean-François Labouverie
Reception: Betty Coursan, Maurice Coutarel, Christian Dupavillon, Jacques Leroy, Marguerite Vernot

L'Âge d'or, première ébauche [*The Golden Age: First Draft*]

Premiere: March 4, 1975, at the Cartoucherie.

A play by Jean-Claude Barriera, Baudoin Bauchau, Lucia Bensasson, Georges Bonnaud, Jean-Claude Bourbault, Philippe Caubère, Odile Cointepas, Jean-Noël Cordier, Emmanuel de Bary, Anne Demeyer, Joséphine Derenne, Françoise Descotils, Myrrha Donzenac, Nicole Félix, Antonio Ferreira, Nathalie Ferreira, Guy-Claude François, Martine Franck, Mario Gonzalès, Gérard Hardy, Philippe Hottier, Françoise Jamet, Catherine Legrand, Sophie Lemasson, Françoise Lemoine, Maxime Lombard, Clémence Massart, Ariane Mnouchkine, Jean-Claude Penchenat, Alain Salomon, Erhard Stiefel, Jonathan Sutton, Valérie Tisné, Dominique Valentin, Julie Vilmont.

THE ACTORS AND THEIR CHARACTERS

Salouha: Lucia Bensasson
Abdallah: Philippe Caubère
Mimi the sweetheart: Anne Demeyer
Viviane Volpina, M'Boro: Joséphine Derenne
Béatrice: Myrrha Donzenac
Irène: Nicole Félix
Pantalone of Naples, Marcel Pantalon, Ramon Granada, a young man: Mario Gonzalès
La Ficelle, M. Gueulette, a young man: Philippe Hottier

Bernada the old woman: Françoise Jamet
Antoine Raspi, mayor of Naples: Maxime Lombard
Sylvette, lover on the beach: Clémence Massart
The prince of Naples, Olivier, Aimé Lheureux: Jean-Claude Penchenat
M. Dussouille: Alain Salomon
Mahmoud Ali: Nicolas Serreau
Harlequin of Naples, Max, lover on the beach: Jonathan Sutton
Big Lou: Dominique Valentin

Director: Ariane Mnouchkine
Director's assistant: Sophie Lemasson
Stage manager: Emmanuel de Bary
Masks: Erhard Stiefel assisted by Valérie Tisné
Costumes: Françoise Tournafond, Jean-Claude Barriera, Nathalie Ferreira
Creation of the stage space: Guy-Claude François (technical director), Jean-Noël Cordier (lighting designer), Antonio Ferreira (construction), Baudoin Bauchau (stagehand)
Reception: Georges Bonnaud, Françoise Lemoine
Posters: Catherine Legrand
Photography: Martine Franck, Jean-Claude Bourbault
Administration: Françoise Descotils, Jean-Claude Penchenat
Outreach: Gérard Hardy, Odile Cointepas

Méphisto, le roman d'une carrière [*Mephisto*]

Based on the novel by Klaus Mann, adapted by Ariane Mnouchkine
Premiere: May 4, 1979, at the Cartoucherie.

THE CHARACTERS (by order of appearance)
Klaus Mann, then Sébastien Brückner: Christian Colin
Hendrik Höfgen: Gérard Hardy
Carola Martin: Lucia Bensasson
Hans Miklas: Jonathan Sutton
Theresa von Herzfeld: Marie-Françoise Audollent
Otto Ulrich: Jean-Claude Bourbault
Magnus Gottchalk: Yves Gourvil
Madame Efeu: Louba Guertchikoff
Knurr: Roland Amstutz
Juliette: Myrrha Donzenac
Myriam Horowitz: Anne Demeyer
Alex: Norbert Journo
Érika Brückner: Joséphine Derenne
Nicoletta von Niebuhr: Nicole Félix
Théophile Sarder: René Patrignani
Lorenz: Julien Maurel, then Pierre Fatus
Young waiter: John Arnold
Thomas Brückner: Jean Dupond
Émelyne: Odile Cointepas
Ludwig: Claude Forget
Hans Josthinkel: Georges Bonnaud
AT THE CABARET DER STURMVOGEL (THE STORM BIRD)
Master of Ceremonies: Roland Amstutz
General Fonnésique: Jonathan Sutton
Hitler: Christian Colin
AT THE RESTAURANT
Maître d'hôtel: Georges Bonnaud
Officer: Jean Dupond
ORCHESTRA
Musical director: Jean-Jacques Lemêtre
Assisted by: Luciano Moro Marangone
Violin: Roland Amstutz
Guitar: Marie-Françoise Audollent
Percussion: Lucia Bensasson
Trombone: Georges Bonnaud
Cornet, clarinet: Jean-Claude Bourbault
Flute: Odile Cointepas
Piano, harmonica, percussion, glockenspiel: Jean Dupond
Double bass: Yves Gourvil
Piano: Louba Guertchikoff
Percussion: Norbert Journo
Violin, saxophone: Jonathan Sutton
Final song: Martine Rouvières

DIRECTION

Director and adapter (from the French translation of Klaus Mann's novel by Louise Servicen, Éditions Denoël): Ariane Mnouchkine

Sets: Guy-Claude François

Costumes: Nani Noël, Daniel Ogier

Costume management: Liliane Long

Music: Jean-Jacques Lemêtre

Director's assistant: Sophie Moscoso

Masks: Erhard Stiefel

Hair: Bruno

Makeup: Nicole Félix

Documentation: Sophie Moscoso, Lorenz Knauer

Vocal coach: Martine Rouvières

Dance coach: José Vieira

Posters and graphics: Annie Abadie, Catherine Legrand

Photography: Michèle Laurent, Yon Intxaustegi, Martine Franck

Administration: Jean-Pierre Henin

Audience relations: Liliana Andreone, Odie Cointepas, Gérard Hardy

Press relations: Marie-Françoise Audollent

SETS

Technical director: Guy-Claude François

Drawings and color models: Dominique Plait, Dorothée Crosland

Construction in wood: Claude Forget

Construction in metal: Antonio Ferreira

Lighting: Jean-Noël Cordier

Projections: Yon Intxaustegi

Painters: Dorothée Crosland, Christian Delhomme, Thierry François, Fabrice Herrero, Xavier Philippe, Dominique Plait

Sculptors: Christian Delhomme, Raul Gomez, Osvaldo Rodriguez

Light fixtures: Norbert Journo

Builders: Baudoin Bauchau, Frédéric Duperray, Antonio Ferreira, Claude Forget, Patrice Lainé, Justino Lourenco, Élisabeth Sassier, José Vasconcelos

Lighting technicians: Laurence Aucouturier, Jean-Noël Cordier, François Watrin

Interns: John Arnold, Véronique Gargiulo

COSTUMES

Chief costume designers: Marie-Jo Bouton, Victoria Gomes, Brigitte Méllé

Costume details: Joëlle Loucif

Decorators: Nani Noël, Daniel Ogier

Costume designer in charge of cutting: Nathalie Thomas

THE SHAKESPEARE CYCLE
Richard II

By William Shakespeare, translated by Ariane Mnouchkine.
Premiere: December 10, 1981, at the Cartoucherie.

ROYAL FAMILY
King Richard II: Georges Bigot
Queen: Odile Cointepas
Duchess of Gloucester: Lucia Bensasson
John of Gaunt, Duke of Lancaster, uncle to the king: John Arnold
Henry Bolingbroke, son of John of Gaunt: Cyrille Bosc
Duke of York, uncle to the king: Philippe Hottier
Duke of Aumerle, son of the Duke of York: Philippe Blancher
RICHARD'S FRIENDS
Bushy: Julien Maurel
Bagot: Antoine Del Pin
Green: Jean-Baptiste Aubertin
LORDS
Thomas Mowbray, Duke of Norfolk, banished: Maurice Durozier
Lord Fitzwater, marshal: Marc Dumétier
Earl of Northumberland: Maurice Durozier
Henry "Hotspur" Percy, Northumberland's son: Jean-Pierre Marry
Lord Ross: Philippe Carbonneaux
Lord Willoughby: Guy Freixe
Sir Stephen Scroop, dying warrior: Maurice Durozier
Abbot of Westminster: Pierre Fatus
Sir Pierce Exton, assassin: John Arnold
OTHER CHARACTERS
Welsh captain: Marc Dumétier
Gardener: Philippe Hottier
Gardener's apprentice: John Arnold

Richard's fools: Pierre Fatus, Julien Maurel
Queen's lady: Hélène Cinque
Groom: Hélène Cinque
Servants of the stage work: Jean-Baptiste Aubertin, Philippe Carbonneaux, Hélène Cinque, Antoine Del Pin, Pierre Fatus, Véronique Gargiulo, Fabien Gargiulo, Julien Maurel

Translator and director: Ariane Mnouchkine
Assistant: Sophie Moscoso
Sets: Guy-Claude François
Masks: Erhard Stiefel
Costumes: Jean-Claude Barriera and Nathalie Thomas, with Leyla Ates, Victoria Gomes, Geneviève Humbert, Fanny Mandonnet, Michèle Van Ruymbeke, Philippe Carbonneaux, Élisabeth Chailloux, Louba Guertchikoff
Music: Jean-Jacques Lemêtre, with Claude Ninat
Lighting: Jean-Noël Cordier, with Laurence Aucouturier, François Watrin, John Arnold, Myriam Azencot, Maurice Durozier, Guy Freixe, Véronique Gargiulo, Clémentine Yelnik
Masonry: Antonio Ferreira, with Victor Costa, José Vasconcelos, Jean-Baptiste Aubertin, Baudouin Bauchau, Philippe Blancher, Cyrille Bosc, Hélène Cinque, Antoine Del Pin, Anne Demeyer, Marc Dumétier, Pierre Fatus, Fabien Gargiulo, Véronique Gargiulo, Philippe Hottier, Louise Mailliard
Carpentry: Claude Forget, with Georges Bigot, Cyrille Bosc, Hélène Cinque, Anne Demeyer, Véronique Gargiulo, Fabien Gargiulo, Louise Mailliard, Jean-Pierre Marry
Metal construction: Antonio Ferreira and José Vasconcelos, with John Arnold, Philippe Blancher, Hélène Cinque, Pierre Fatus, Fabien Gargiulo, Véronique Gargiulo, Louise Mailliard, Julien Maurel
Machines: Claude Forget, François Watrin
Hangings/Backdrops: Mehmet Ates, with Leyla Ates, Marie-Françoise Audollent, Odile Cointepas, Louise Mailliard
Paintings, patinas and gildings: Gérard Hardy
Props: Georges Bigot, Philippe Blancher, Maurice Durozier, Antonio Ferreira, Claude Forget, Philippe Hottier, José Vasconcelos
Physical training: Philippe Hottier
Vocal coach: Martine Rouvières
Poster and graphics: Annie Abadie
Photography: Martine Franck, Michèle Laurent, Lesly Hamilton
Administration: Jean-Pierre Henin
Housekeeping: Maria Albaiceta
Cooking: Lucia Bensasson and Joséphine Derenne, with Maria Albaiceta
Audience relations: Liliana Andreone, Myriam Azencot
Press relations: Marie-Françoise Audollent, with Véronique Coquet

La Nuit des rois [*Twelfth Night*]

By William Shakespeare, translated by Ariane Mnouchkine
Premiere: July 10, 1982, at the Avignon Festival; then alternating with *Richard II* at the Cartoucherie.

By order of appearance:
Duke Orsino: Georges Bigot
Curio: Hélène Cinque
Valentine: Julien Maurel
Viola: Joséphine Derenne
Captain: Maurice Durozier
Sir Toby Belch: Philippe Hottier

Maria: Hélène Cinque
Sir Andrew Aguecheek: Clémentine Yelnik
Olivia: Odile Cointepas
Feste, the fool: Julien Maurel
Malvolio: John Arnold
Sebastian: Jean-Pierre Marry
Antonio: Maurice Durozier
Fabian: Georges Bigot
First officer: Cyrille Bosc
Second officer: Philippe Blancher
Priest: Cyrille Bosc
Servants of the stage work: Laurence Aucouturier, Cyrille Bosc, Philippe Carbonneaux, Marc Dumétier, Guy Freixe, Véronique Gargiulo

Translator and director: Ariane Mnouchkine
Assistant: Sophie Moscoso
Sets: Guy-Claude François
Costumes: Jean-Claude Barriera and Nathalie Thomas, with Geneviève Humbert, Marie-Hélène Bouvet, Anne Demeyer
Music: Jean-Jacques Lemêtre, with Claude Ninat
Choreographer: Maïtreyi
Lighting: Jean-Noël Cordier, with Laurence Aucouturier, François Watrin
Construction and props: Antonio Ferreira, Claude Forget, Erhard Stiefel, and José Vasconcelos, with Victor Costa, Jean-Baptiste Aubertin, Baudouin Bachau, Philippe Blancher, Cyrille Bosc, Antoine Del Pin, Marc Dumétier, Pierre Fatus, Fabien Gargiulo
Machines: Claude Forget, François Watrin
Hangings/Backdrops: Gérard Hardy, with Mehmet Ates, Philippe Carbonneaux, Véronique Gargiulo, Rui Frati, Guy Freixe
Physical preparation: Maïtreyi
Hair: Madeleine Cofano for Bruno
Photography: Martine Franck, Michèle Laurent
Poster and graphics: Annie Abadie
Administration: Jean-Pierre Henin
Housekeeping: Maria Albaiceta, Rui Frati
Audience relations: Liliana Andreone
Press relations: Odile Cointepas

Henry IV: I [Henry IV: Part I]

By William Shakespeare, translated by Ariane Mnouchkine
Premiere: January 18, 1984, at the Cartoucherie. Performed alternating with *Richard II* and *La Nuit des rois* [*Twelfth Night*].
THE ROYAL FAMILY

King Henry the Fourth: John Arnold
Henry, Prince of Wales, son of the king: Georges Bigot
John of Lancaster, son of the king: Hélène Cinque
THE KING'S FAITHFUL
Earl of Westmoreland: Guy Freixe
Sir Walter Blunt: Philippe Blancher
PRINCE HENRY'S FRIENDS
Sir John Falstaff: Philippe Hottier
Poins: John Arnold
Bardolph: Fabien Gargiulo
Peto: Hélène Cinque

Hostess: Odile Cointepas
THE KING'S ENEMIES
Thomas Percy, Earl of Worcester: Guy Freixe
Henry Percy, Earl of Northumberland: Maurice Durozier
Henry Percy, known as "Hotspur," Northumberland's son: Julien Maurel
Lady Percy, wife of Hotspur: Odile Cointepas
Earl of Douglas: Maurice Durozier
Sir Richard Vernon: Serge Poncelet
OTHER CHARACTERS
Sheriff: Marc Dumétier
First Traveler: Maurice Durozier
Second Traveler: Serge Poncelet
BLACK GUARDS
Cyrille Bosc, Marc Dumétier, Jean-François Dusigne, Fabien Gargiulo, Robert
  Gourp, Jean-Pierre Marry, Andrés Perez, Éric Rey

Translator and director: Ariane Mnouchkine
Assistant: Sophie Moscoso
Sets: Guy-Claude François
Paintings, patinas and gildings: Philippe Carbonneaux, Geneviève Humbert,
  Véronique Gargiulo, Pascale Boutroux
Music: Jean-Jacques Lemêtre
Musicians: Jean-Jacques Lemêtre, Luciano Moro Marangone
Instrument-makers: Claude Ninat, Caroline Lee
Music servant: Véronique Gargiulo
Costumes: Jean-Claude Barriera, Nathalie Thomas, Marie-Hélène Bouvet,
  Thérèse Angebault, Francine Gaspar, Victoria Gomez, Nacira Ouchene
Masks and props: Erhard Stiefel
Lighting: Jean-Noël Cordier, with Laurence Aucouturier, Carlos Obregon
Carpentry and props: Claude Forget, with Thierry Meunier
Masonry and painting: Victor Costa, Joaquim Baptista, Antonio Ferreria, José
  Vasconcelos
Diction coach: François Joxe
Record-keeper: Myriam Azencot
Photography: Martine Franck, Michèle Laurent
Poster and graphics: Annie Abadie
Administration: Jean-Pierre Henin
Audience relations: Liliana Andreone, with Clémentine Yelnik
Housekeeping: Maria Albaiceta
Press relations: Odile Cointepas, with Liliana Andreone
Ticket sales: Louba Guertchikoff, with Pedro Guimaraes
Ticket-taking and maintenance: Baudouin Bauchau

L'Histoire terrible mais inachevée de Norodom Sihanouk, roi du Cambodge
[*The Terrible but Unfinished Story of Norodom Sihanouk, King of Cambodia*]

By Hélène Cixous
Premiere: September 11, 1985, at the Cartoucherie.
(The characters marked with an asterisk appear only in the second era of the
   play.)

CAMBODIA
THE ROYAL PALACE
Norodom Sihanouk, first King, then Prince of Cambodia: Georges Bigot
Norodom Suramarit, deceased King, Sihanouk's father: Guy Freixe
Queen Kossomak, Sihanouk's mother: Odile Cointepas
The Princess, Sihanouk's wife: Hélène Cinque
Madame Mom Savay, ex-first royal dancer: Claire Rigollier
THE KING'S FAITHFUL AND FRIENDS
Lord Penn Nouth, minister and counselor: Maurice Durozier
Captain Ong Meang, aide-de-camp to the Prince: Simon Abkarian
Chea San, Cambodian ambassador to Moscow: Zinedine Soualem
THE KING'S ENEMIES
Prince Sisowath Sirik Matak, cousin of the king: Bernard Martin
General Lon Nol: Guy Freixe
Cambodian ambassador to Paris: Andrés Pérez
THE ROYAL HOUSEHOLD
Dith Boun Suo, servant to the king: Gérard Hardy
Dith Sophon, servant to Queen Kossomak: Zinedine Soualem
Rama Mok, musician: Jean-Jacques Lemêtre

Little musician: Hélène Cinque

Servants: Simon Abkarian, Baya Belal, Mario Chiapuzzo, Christian Dupont, Pedro Guimaraes, Jean-Pierre Marry, Éric Rey

PHNOM PENH

Madame Khieu Samnol, vegetable merchant, mother of Khieu Samphan: Myriam Azencot

Madame Lamné, Vietnamese fish merchant: Clémentine Yelnik

Yukanthor, their adopted son*: Fabien Gargiulo

LON NOL'S HOUSEHOLD

Captain Sim Narang, aide-de-camp: Éric Rey

Captain In Sophat: Mario Chiapuzzo

Soldiers: Jean-François Dusigne, Pedro Guimaraes, Éric Rey

REPUBLIC OF LON NOL

Um Savuth's envoy*: Andrés Pérez

Cheng Heng, president of the National Assembly*: Christian Dupont

Long Boret, prime minister*: Serge Poncelet

Saukham Khoy, president of the Republic*: Jean-Pierre Marry

KHMER ROUGE

Saloth Sâr: Serge Poncelet

Khieu Samphan: Andrés Pérez

Hou Youn: Jean-François Dusigne

Ieng Sary*: Éric Rey

Ieng Thirith, wife of Ieng Sary*: Claire Rigollier

OTHER CHARACTERS

Peasants: Simon Abkarian, Zinedine Soualem

Japan's ambassador to Cambodia: Jean-François Dusigne

Chinese merchant*: Zinedine Soualem

The Kamaphibal, Khmer Rouge cadre*: Bernard Martin

Chorn Hay, Khmer Rouge cadre*: Pedro Guimaraes

THE UNITED STATES OF AMERICA

Henry Kissinger: Serge Poncelet

Melvin Laird, Secretary of Defense: Jean-François Dusigne

General Abrams, Commander in chief of the American Forces in South Vietnam: Simon Abkarian

Robert McClintock, U.S. ambassador to Cambodia: Fabien Gargiulo

General Taber: Marc Dumétier

Hawkins, CIA agent: Mario Chiapuzzo

John Gunther Dean, U.S. ambassador to Cambodia*: Simon Abkarian

Keeley, Dean's secretary*: Marc Dumétier

Pete McCloskey, Republican senator*: Mario Chiapuzzo

US. Envoy to Peking*: Pedro Guimaraes

Secretary to the envoy*: Gérard Hardy

THE U.S.S.R.

Alexis Kosygin, Prime Minister: Simon Abkarian

Interpreter: Éric Rey

CHINA

Zhou Enlai, Prime Minister: Andrés Pérez

Cambodian ambassador to Peking: Fabien Gargiulo

Étienne Manac'h, French ambassador to Peking: Bernard Martin

VIETNAM

Pham Van Dong, Prime Minister of the Republic of North Vietnam*: Serge Poncelet

General Giap, Minister of Defense and Commander in chief of the North Vietnamese Army*: Christian Dupont

General Van Tien Dung, his assistant*: Jean-François Dusigne

Director: Ariane Mnouchkine

Assistant: Sophie Moscoso

Music: Jean-Jacques Lemêtre
Musicians: Jean-Jacques Lemêtre, Pierre Launay
Sets: Guy-Claude François
Costumes: Jean-Claude Barriera and Nathalie Thomas, with Marie-Hélène Bouvet
Masks: Erhard Stiefel
Lighting: Jean-Noël Cordier, with Laurence Aucouturier, Carlos Obregon
Wood: Claude Forget, with Robert Catenacci, Thierry Meunier
Stone, plaster and cement: Victor Costa, with Joaquim Pedrosa, Fernando dos Anjos
Brick: Yannick Girard and Pierre Sauton, with Manuel Cunha, Eugênio Sampaio, Peter Upor
Metal: José Vasconcelos and Caroline Lee, with Benoît Barthélémy
Painting: Mario Chiapuzzo, Véronique Gargiulo, Gérard Hardy, Clémentine Yelnik
Statuettes: Erhard Stiefel, with Beate Blasius, Ly Nissay, Véronique Gargiulo, Baya Belal, Sylviane Veniat
Props: Caroline Lee, Claude Forget, and Erhard Stiefel, with Liliana Andreone
Instrument-makers: Caroline Lee, Jean-Jacques Lemêtre, and Claude Forget, with Pierre Launay
With, for all the work accomplished, the unqualified but indispensable help of: Simon Abkarian, Myriam Azencot, Georges Bigot, Mario Chiapuzzo, Hélène Cinque, Odile Cointepas, Marc Dumétier, Christian Dupont, Maurice Durozier, Jean-François Dusigne, Guy Freixe, Fabien Gargiulo, Pedro Guimaraes, Gérard Hardy, Jean-Pierre Marry, Bernard Martin, Andrés Pérez, Serge Poncelet, Éric Rey, Claire Rigollier, Zinedine Soualem, Clémentine Yelnik
Stage manager: Christian Dupont
Administration: Jean-Pierre Hénin
Audience relations: Liliana Andreone, with Naruna de Andrade, Clémentine Yelnik
Housekeeping: Maria Albaiceta, with Selahattin Öter
Press relations: Odile Cointepas, with Liliana Andreone
Ticket-taking and maintenance: Baudoin Bauchau
Watchman: Hector Ortiz
Poster: Roberto Moscoso
Program: Anne Delbende
Photography: Martine Franck, Michèle Laurent
Some musical instruments were built by Marcel Ladurelle and Robert Hébrard, instrument-makers, and the percuphone was built by Patrice Moullet. The hair styles were by Michel Provini (Claude Maxime). The chairs and tables were built by Gilles Bigot, master carpenter and cabinetmaker.
Over the course of the performances, some characters were also incarnated by the following actors:
The Princess: Sophie Piollet
Madame Mom Svay: Baya Belal
Dith Boun Suo: Mauricio Celedon
Servants: Pedro Celedon, Paul Golub, Jean-Louis Lorente, Bernard Poysat, Catherine Schaub
Captain Sim Narang: Paul Golub
Lon Nol's servant: Ly Nissay
Ieng Sary: Antonio Diaz-Florian
Ieng Thirith: Baya Belal
Saukham Khoy: Mauricio Celedon
General Taber: Mario Chiapuzzo
Secretary to the U.S. envoy to Peking: Jean-Louis Lorente
Interpreter: Pedro Guimaraes

L'Indiade ou l'Inde de leurs rêves [*The Indiad or India of their Dreams*]

By Hélène Cixous
Premiere: September 30, 1987, at the Cartoucherie.

With, by order of appearance:
CONGRESS PARTY AND COMPANIONS
Pandit Jawaharlal Nehru: Georges Bigot
Maulana Abul Kalam Azad: Maurice Durozier
Sarojini Naïdu: Myriam Azencot
Sardar Vallabhbhaï Patel: Serge Poncelet
Mahatma Ghandi: Andrés Pérez Araya
Abdul Ghaffar Khan, known as Badshah Khan: Simon Abkarian
Ghani Khan, his son: Fabien Gargiulo
Hermann Kallenbach: Bernard Martin
Kastourbaï Gandhi, Gandhi's wife: Clémentine Yelnik
Aruna Asaf Ali: Sophie Piollet
Sushila Nayar: Silvia Bellei
Manu, Gandhi's little niece: Catherine Schaub
THE MUSLIM LEAGUE AND COMPANIONS
Mohamed Ali Jinnah: Jean-François Dusigne
Liaquat Ali Khan: Paul Golub
Sir Mohamed A. Iqbal: Asil Rais
Fatima Jinnah, Jinnah's sister: Catherine Schaub
Dina Jinnah, Jinnah's daughter: Nirupama Nityanandan
A messager: Asil Rais
THE PROVINCES
A. K. Fazlul Huq, chief Muslim minister of the provincial government of Bengal, Unionist Party: Maurice Durozier

Sir Sikander Hayat Khan, chief Muslim minister of the provincial government of Punjab, Unionist party: Simon Abkarian

Tara Singh, Sikh minister of the provincial government of Punjab: Mario Chiapuzzo

A Congress Party minister of the provincial government of Bihar: Simon Abkarian

Another Congress Party minister of the provincial government of Bihar: Zinedine Soualem

ENGLAND

Marquess of Linlithgow, viceroy of India from 1936 to 1943: Mario Chiapuzzo

Sir Archibald Wavell, viceroy of India from 1943 to March 1947: Christian Dupont

Lord Mountbatten, Earl of Burma, last viceroy of India, from March to August 1947: Asil Rais

Lord Mountbatten's aide-de-camp: Mahmoud Shahali

ROADS AND STREETS

Haridasi, solitary wandering Bengali woman: Baya Belal

THE NORTHWEST FRONTIER

Goulam, a Pathan: Zinedine Soualem

Tughlak, a Pathan: Jean-Louis Lorente

Masud Khan, Pathan schoolteacher: Mahmoud Saïd

NEW DELHI

Ganga Singh, Sikh driver: Fabien Gargiulo

Inder, rickshaw-wallah, an untouchable: Mauricio Celedon

Lala, Bengali rickshaw-wallah: Éric Leconte

Ahmad, rickshaw-wallah: Pascal Durozier

Rahman, his older brother, rickshaw-wallah: Mahmoud Saïd

Ima, their mother: Nirupama Nityanandan

Guardian of the Sufi saint's tomb: Zinedine Soualem

PUNJAB

Rajkumar, peasant from Sialkot: Jean-François Dusigne

Sikh solider from Simla: Asil Rais

Siddiqui, peasant from Sialkot: Mahmoud Saïd

SIND

Bahadur, bear tamer: Mahmoud Shahali

Moona Baloo, his bear: Catherine Schaub, with Jean-Louis Lorente

BENGAL

Hathihaï Sen, from Noakhali district: Simon Abkarian

Rajiv Sen, his brother: Bernard Martin

BIHAR

Man who sings song from a score (*partition*): Bernard Martin

BOMBAY

Darshan Lal, Mohamed Ali Jannah's Hindu servant: Asil Rais

TAMIL NADU

Hindu soldier from Simla: Bernard Martin

SERVANTS, PORTERS, OFFICERS, SOLDIERS

Sylvia Bellei, Duccio Bellugi-Vannuccini, Beate Blasius, Mauricio Celedon, Pedro Celedon, Mario Chiapuzzo, Christian Dupont, Pascal Durozier, Fabien Gargiulo, Paul Golub, Pedro Guimaraes, Éric Leconte, Jean-Lois Lorente, Ly Nissay, Bernard Martin, Nirupama Nityanandan, Sophie Piollet, Asil Rais, Mahmoud Saïd, Mahmoud Shahali, Catherine Schaub, Zinedine Soualem, Clémentine Yelnik

Director: Ariane Mnouchkine
Assistant: Sophie Moscoso
Sets: Guy-Claude François
Costumes: Jean-Claude Barriera, with Nathalie Thomas, Marie-Hélène Bouvet, Nadia Soualem
Musicians: Jean-Jacques Lemêtre, with Corinne Hache, Pierre Rigopoulos
Mask: Erhard Stiefel
Lights: Jean-Noël Cordier with Laurence Aucouturier, Carlos Obregon
Wood: Claude Forget, with Thierry Meunier, Jean-Louis Lacarra
Stone, plaster, cement, brick, marble: Victor Costa, with Joaquim Pinto Serra, José Vasconcelos, Eugênio Sampaio, Ricardo Vasconcelos, Fernando dos Anjos, José Pais, Patrice Andreopa
Metal: José Vasconcelos, with Antonio Ferreira
Instrument-makers: Jean-Jacques Lemêtre, with Corinne Hache, Daniel Lefebvre, Claude Forget, Selahattin Öter
Bharata natyam coach: Maïtreyi
Phonetics and linguistics coach: Françoise Berge
Physical preparation: Marc Pujo
Stage manager: Christian Dupont
With, for this endeavor, the unqualified but indispensable help of: Simon Abkarian, Myriam Azencot, Baya Belal, Silvia Bellei, Duccio Bellugi-Vannuccini, Georges Bigot, Beate Blasius, Mauricio Celedon, Pedro Celedon, Mario Chiapuzzo, Christian Dupont, Maurice Durozier, Pascal Durozier, Jean-François Dusigne, Fabien Gargiulo, Paul Golub, Pedro Guimaraes, Eric Leconte, Jean-Louis Lorente, Ly Nissay, Maïtreyi, Bernard Martin, Nirupama Nityanandan, Andrés Pérez, Sophie Piollet, Serge Poncelet, Asil Rais, Mahmoud Saïd, Mahmoud Shahali, Catherine Schaub, Zinedine Soualem, Clémentine Yelnik.
Administration: Jean-Pierre Henin
Audience relations: Liliana Andreone, Naruna de Andrade
Audience patronage: Claire Duhamel
Press relations: Sarah Cornell
Poster, program, photography: Martine Franck, Michèle Laurent
Housekeeping: Maria Albaiceta and Selahattin Öter, with Kim San
Ticket-taking and maintenance: Baudouin Bauchau
Watchman: Hector Ortiz
Some musical instruments were built by Marcel Ladurelle and Jacques Venant, instrument-makers, and Didier Hache, carpenter. The Viceroy's seat was built by Gilles Bigot, master carpenter and cabinetmaker. The map in the Reception area was made by the Atelier Passe-Muraille.

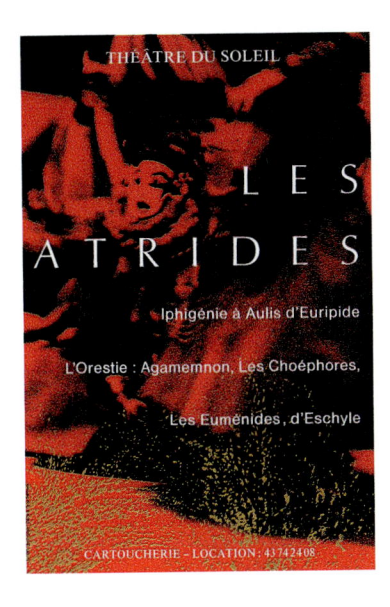

CYCLE DES ATRIDES [THE HOUSE OF ATREUS CYCLE]
Iphigénie [*Iphigenia in Aulis*]

By Euripides, translated by Jean Bollack and Mayotte Bollack
Music by Jean-Jacques Lemêtre
Premiere: November 16, 1990, at the Cartoucherie.

CHORUS
Coryphaeus: Catherine Schaub
Chorus members: Silvia Bellei, Duccio Bellugi-Vannuccini, Georges Bigot, Christian Dupont, Maurice Durozier, Pascal Durozier, Brontis Jodorowsky, Éric Leconte, Jean-Louis Lorente, Serge Poncelet, Asil Rais, Zinedine Soualem
PROTAGONISTS (by order of appearance):
Agamemnon: Simon Abkarian
Old man: Jean-Louis Lorente
Menelaus: Asil Raïs
Messenger: Georges Bigot
Clytemnestra: Juliana Carneiro da Cunha
Iphigenia: Nirupama Nityanandan
Achilles: Simon Abkarian
Director: Ariane Mnouchkine
Assistant: Sophie Moscoso
Sets: Guy-Claude François, with sculptures by Erhard Stiefel
Costumes: Nathalie Thomas, Marie-Hélène Bouvet, Marie-Paule Gaboriau
Musicians: Jean-Jacques Lemêtre, with Sergio Perera
Makeup design: Catherine Schaub
Prop and set design: Simon Abkarian, with Catherine Schaub
Dances led by: Catherine Schaub, Simon Abkarian, Nirupama Nityanandan, supervised by Nadejda Loujine
Lights: Laurence Aucouturier, Carlos Obregon, Marc Semirchal, and Rodrigo Bachler-Klein, with Franck Millara

Set construction:

Masonry (stone, plaster, cement, brick): Victor Costa and Joaquim Pinto Serra, with Pedro Pinto Serra

Carpentry (woodwork, support structures, cabinetmaking): Thierry Meunier, with Jean-Pierre Marry, Aldo Vivoda

Metal: Marc Semirchal and Manuel Pereira da Silva, with Jean-Baptiste Bernatene, Antonio Ferreira, Choukri Gabteni

Paintings: Atelier Passe-Muraille, Karine Lemonnier, Xavier Philippe, Sylvie Espinasse, and Marie Desforge, with Pedro Guimaraes, Nissay Ly

Instrument-making: Jean-Jacques Lemêtre, Sergio Perera

Stage manager: Christian Dupont

Housekeeping: Maria Albaiceta and Selahattin Öter, with Kim San

Ticket-taking and maintenance: Baudouin Bauchau

Director of darkness: Hector Ortiz

Administration: Nathalie Pousset, with Pierre Salesne

Audience relations: Liliana Andreone, Antoine Del Pin, Naruna de Andrade

Ticket sales: Pedro Guimares

Press relations: Sarah Cornell

Physical preparation and care: Marc Pujo

Poster and program: Tatoo

Photography: Martine Franck, Michèle Laurent

Interns: Madeleine Blackwell (Australia), Imor Herman-Andersson (Sweden), Mohammad Hirzalla (Israel), Kyeng-Mee Jung (Korea)

Soundtrack: François Leymarie, from Studio Sinuances.

Agamemnon

By Aeschylus, translated by Ariane Mnouchkine
Music by Jean-Jacques Lemêtre
Premiere: November 24, 1990, at the Cartoucherie.

CHORUS

Coryphaeuses: Simon Abkarian, Nirupama Nityanandan, Georges Bigot

Coryphaeus of the dance: Catherine Schaub

Chorus members: Silvia Bellei, Duccio Bellugi-Vannuccini, Christian Dupont, Maurice Durozier, Pascal Durozier, Brontis Jodorowsky, Éric Leconte, Jean-Louis Lorente, Serge Poncelet, Asil Rais, Mahmoud Saïd, Zinedine Soualem

PROTAGONISTS (by order of appearance):

Watchman: Georges Bigot

Clytemnestra: Juliana Carneiro da Cunha

Emissary: Simon Abkarian

Agamemnon: Simon Abkarian

Cassandra: Nirupama Nityanandan

Aegisthus: Georges Bigot

Director: Ariane Mnouchkine

Assistant: Sophie Moscoso

Sets: Guy-Claude François, with sculptures by Erhard Stiefel

Music: Jean-Jacques Lemêtre

Costumes: Nathalie Thomas, Marie-Hélène Bouvet, Marie-Paule Gaboriau

Musicians: Jean-Jacques Lemêtre, with Sergio Perera

Philologists: Jean Bollack, Pierre Judet de La Combe

Makeup design: Catherine Schaub

Prop and costume design: Simon Abkarian, Catherine Schaub

Dances led by: Catherine Schaub, Simon Abkarian, Nirupama Nityanandan, supervised by Nadejda Loujine

Rehearsal leader: Myriam Azencot

Lights: Laurence Aucouturier, Carlos Obregon, Marc Semirchal, and Rodrigo Bachler-Klein, with Franck Millara

Set construction:

Masonry (stone, plaster, cement, brick): Victor Costa and Joaquim Pinto Serra, with Pedro Pinto Serra, Choukri Gabteni

Carpentry (woodwork, support structures, cabinetmaking): Thierry Meunier, with Jean-Pierre Marry, Aldo Vivoda

Metal: Marc Semirchal and Manuel Pereira da Silva, with Jean-Baptiste Bernatene, Antonio Ferreira

Paintings and patinas: Atelier Passe-Muraille: Karine Lemonnier, Xavier Philippe, Sylvie Espinasse, and Marie Desforge, with Pedro Guimaraes, Ly Nissay

Instrument-making: Jean-Jacques Lemêtre and Sergio Perera, with Caroline Lee, Marcel Ladurelle

Stage manager: Christian Dupont

Stage servants: Viviana Alberti, Odile Delonca, Choukri Gabteni, Ly Nissay

Music servant: Laurence Ossart

Sound management: Rodrigo Bachler-Klein

Costume workshop: Nathalie Thomas, Marie-Hélène Bouvet, and Marie-Paule Gaboriau, with Pascale Guene, Laurence Benoît, Charlotte Guicherd, Annie Tran, Stéphanie Triaud, Ysabel de Maisonneuve

Sculpture workshop: Erhard Stiefel, assisted by Dominique Contesso, with Érika Cixous, Claire Coutelle, Odile Delonca, Claudia Jenatsch, Nathanaëlle Lobjoy, Veronika Medici, Dominique Viars

Housekeeping: Maria Albaiceta and Selahattin Öter, with Kim San

Ticket-taking and maintenance: Baudouin Bauchau

Director of darkness: Hector Ortiz

Administration: Nathalie Pousset, with Pierre Salesne

Audience relations: Liliana Andreone, Antoine Del Pin, Naruna de Andrade

Ticket sales: Pedro Guimaraes, Eve Doe Bruce

Press relations: Sarah Cornell

Physical preparation and care: Marc Pujo, with Nicolas Bounine

Poster and program: Tatoo

Photography: Martine Franck, Michèle Laurent

Interns: Madeleine Blackwell (Australia), Imor Herman-Andersson (Sweden), Mohammad Hirzalla (Israel), Kyen-Mee Jung (Korea).

Soundtrack: François Leymarie, from Studio Sinuances:

Bass guitar: François Leymarie

Violin: Marie-Françoise Viaud

Viola: Marie-Emmanuelle Hérouard

Double bass: Gilles Since

Flutes: Marjolaine Ott

Tabla: Ravy Magnifique

Clarinet, Eastern stringed instruments, percussion, invented musical instruments: Jean-Jacques Lemêtre

Daf, dohol, darabouka (drums): Edmond Zartarian

The map in the Welcome Area was made by Didier Martin and Stéphanie Guennessen.

The Théâtre du Soleil particularly wishes to thank its friend Claudine Bensaïd for her generous help: she took on that most austere of tasks, the word for word transliteration of the Greek texts.

Les Choéphores [*The Libation Bearers*]

By Aeschylus, translated by Ariane Mnouchkine
Music by Jean-Jacques Lemêtre
Premiere: February 23, 1991, at the Cartoucherie.

CHORUS

Coryphaeus: Catherine Schaub
Chorus members: Duccio Bellugi-Vannuccini, Georges Bigot, Christian Dupont, Maurice Durozier, Pascal Durozier, Brontis Jodorowsky, Éric Leconte, Jean-Louis Lorente, Serge Poncelet, Asil Rais, Zinedine Soualem
Orestes: Simon Abkarian
Pylades: Brontis Jodorowsky
Electra: Nirupama Nityanandan
Servant: Pascal Durozier
Clytemnestra: Juliana Carneiro da Cunha
Nurse: Simon Abkarian
Aegisthus: Georges Bigot

Director: Ariane Mnouchkine
Assistant: Sophie Moscoso
Sets: Guy-Claude François, with sculptures by Erhard Stiefel
Costumes: Nathalie Thomas, with Marie-Hélène Bouvet, Marie-Paule Gaboriau
Musicians: Jean-Jacques Lemêtre, with Maria Serrao
Philologists: Jean Bollack, Pierre Judet de La Combe
Makeup design: Catherine Schaub
Prop and costume design: Simon Abkarian, Catherine Schaub
Dances led by: Catherine Schaub, Simon Abkarian, Nirupama Nityanandan
Rehearsal leader: Myriam Azencot
Lights: Jean-Michel Bauer, with Thierry Tournon, Carlos Obregon, Franck Millara
Set construction:
Masonry (stone, plaster, cement, brick): Victor Costa and Joaquim Pinto Serra, with Pedro Pinto Serra, Choukri Gabteni
Carpentry (woodwork, support structures, cabinetmaking): Thierry Meunier, with Jean-Pierre Marry, Aldo Vivoda
Metal: Marc Semirchal and Manuel Pereira da Silva, with Antonio Ferreira
Paintings and patinas: Atelier Passe-Muraille: Karine Lemonnier, Xavier Philippe, Sylvie Espinasse, and Marie Desforge, with Pedro Guimaraes, Ly Nissay
Instrument-making: Jean-Jacques Lemêtre, with Caroline Lee, Marcel Ladurelle
Stage managers: Christian Dupont, with Ly Nissay, Jean-Pierre Marry, Pedro Pinto Serra, Odile Delonca, Choukri Gabteni
Sound manager: Rodrigo Bachler-Klein
Costume workshop: Nathalie Thomas, Marie-Hélène Bouvet, and Marie-Paule Gaboriau, with Muriel Galinie, Isabel Le Guellec, Ta Muy Phong, Annie Tran
Sculpture workshop: Erhard Stiefel, assisted by Dominique Contesso, with Érika Cixous, Claire Coutelle, Odile Delonca, Claudia Jenatsch, Nathanaëlle Lobjoy, Veronika Medici, Dominique Viars

Administration: Nathalie Pousset, with Pierre Salesne
Audience relations: Liliana Andreone, Antoine Del Pin, Naruna Andrade, Pedro Guimaraes
Computer relations: Naruna Andrade, with Marcia Fiani
Press relations: Sarah Cornell
Ticket sales: Eve Doe Bruce, Marie-Christine Bento
Physical preparation and care: Marc Pujo
Poster and program: Tatoo
Photography: Martine Franck, Michèle Laurent
Housekeeping: Maria Albaiceta and Selahattin Öter, with Kim San
Ticket-taking and maintenance: Baudouin Bauchau
Director of darkness: Hector Ortiz
Soundtrack: François Leymarie, from Studio Sinuances:
Violin: Marie-Françoise Viaud
Viola: Marie-Emmanuelle Hérouard
Flutes: Marjolaine Ott, Jacques Riou
Clarinet, Eastern stringed instruments, percussion, invented musical instruments: Jean-Jacques Lemêtre
Bass guitar: François Leymarie

Les Euménides [*The Eumenides*]

By Aeschylus, translated by Hélène Cixous
Music by Jean-Jacques Lemêtre
Premiere: May 26, 1992, at the Cartoucherie.

PROTAGONISTS (by order of appearance):
Prophetess: Nirupama Nityanandan
Apollo: Shahrokh Meshkin Ghalam
Orestes: Simon Abkarian
Clytemnestra's Ghost: Juliana Carneiro da Cunha
Furies: Catherine Schaub, Nirupama Nityanandan, Myriam Azencot
Athena: Juliana Carneiro da Cunha
Chorus members: Duccio Bellugi-Vannuccini, Brontis Jodorowsky, Myriam Boullay, Stéphane Brodt, Sergio Canto, Laurent Clauwaert, Daniel Domingo, Martial Jacques, Jocelyn Lagarrigue, Jean-Pierre Marry, Christophe Rauck, Nicolas Sotnikoff
Black guards: Stéphane Brodt, Nadja Djerrah, Eve Doe Bruce, Evelyne Fagnen, Isabelle Gazonnois, Valérie Grail, Martial Jacques, Brontis Jodorowsky, Samantha McDonald, Nicolas Sotnikoff

Director: Ariane Mnouchkine
Assistant: Sophie Moscoso
Sets: Guy-Claude François, with sculptures and masks by Erhard Stiefel
Costumes: Nathalie Thomas, with Marie-Hélène Bouvet
Lights: Jean-Michel Bauer
Musicians: Jean-Jacques Lemêtre, with Marc Barnaud and Isabelle Gazonnois
Philologists: Jean Bollack, Pierre Judet de La Combe
Makeup design: Catherine Schaub
Prop and costume design: Simon Abkarian, Catherine Schaub
Dances led by: Catherine Schaub, Simon Abkarian, Nirupama Nityanandan
Rehearsal leader: Myriam Azencot
Set construction:
Masonry (stone, plaster, cement, brick): Victor Costa and Joaquim Pinto Serra, with Joaquim Baptista, Pedro Pinto Serra
Carpentry (woodwork, support structures, cabinetmaking): Thierry Meunier, with Jean-Pierre Marry, Aldo Vivoda
Metal: Manuel Pereira da Silva, with Antonio Ferreira

Paintings and patinas: Atelier Passe-Muraille: Sylvie Espinasse, Marie Desforge

Stage managers: Ly Nissay, with Odile Delonca, Eve Doe Bruce, Jean-Pierre Marry, Pedro Pinto Serra

Lighting team: Carlos Obregon, with Cécile Allegoedt

Sound manager: Rodrigo Bachler-Klein

Sculpture workshop: Erhard Stiefel, assisted by Dominique Contesso, with Érika Cixous, Claire Coutelle, Odile Delonca, Claudia Jenatsch, Nathanaëlle Lobjoy, Veronika Medici, Dominique Viars

Costume workshop: Nathalie Thomas, Marie-Hélène Bouvet, Annie Tran, and Marie-Paule Gaboriau, with Muriel Galinie, Isabelle Le Guellec, Ta Muy Phong

Administration: Nathalie Pousset, with Pierre Salesne

Audience relations: Liliana Andreone, Antoine Del Pin, Naruna de Andrade

Computer relations: Naruna de Andrade, Marcia Fiani

Press relations: Sarah Cornell

Physical preparation and care: Marc Pujo

Poster and program: Tatoo

Photography: Martine Franck, Michèle Laurent

Ticket sales: Pedro Guimaraes

Housekeeping: Maria Albaiceta and Selahattin Öter, with Jean-Cyrille Merle Remond, Kim San

Ticket-taking and maintenance: Baudouin Bauchau

Director of darkness: Hector Ortiz

Soundtrack: François Leymarie, from Studio Sinuances:

Violin: Marie-Françoise Viaud

Viola: Marie-Emmanuelle Hérouard

Double bass: Gilles Since

Accordion: François Castellio

Flutes: Marjolaine Ott, Jacques Riou

Tabla: Ravy Magnifique

Clarinet, Eastern stringed instruments, percussion, invented musical instruments: Jean-Jacques Lemêtre

Daf, dohol, darabouka (drums): Edmond Zartarian

The map in the Welcome Area was made by Didier Martin and Stéphanie Guennessen.

The Théâtre du Soleil particularly wishes to thank its friend Claudine Bensaïd for her generous help: she took on that most austere of tasks, the word for word transliteration of the Greek texts.

L'Inde de père en fils, de mère en fille [India from Father to Son, from Mother to Daughter]

Directed by Rajeev Sethi, based on an idea by Ariane Mnouchkine
The Théâtre du Soleil welcomes its masters and their students.

PANDWANI
Bhillaï (Madhya Pradesh)
Storyteller: Teejan Baï (tanpura)
Musicians: Brish Lal (tabla), Tulsi Ram (harmonium), Bishram Singh (sursringar)
Student: Rambha Baï Manjheera
MANGANIAR MUSICIANS AND SINGERS
Jaisalmer (Thar Desert, Rajasthan)
SINGERS
Barkat Khan (sinset)
Chanan Khan (kamaicha, been)
MUSICIANS
Feroz Khan (dholak), Ghazi Khan (khartal)
Pempa Khan (been)
STUDENTS
Manjoor
Talab Khan
MASLETS
Andhra Pradesh
Magician: Chand Baba
Student: Sayed Babu
NATS
Maharashtra
Acrobat: Heera Baï
Students: Bharti, Netal Singh
KATHAK DANCERS

Jaipur (Rajasthan)
Master: Girdhari Lal (harmonium, tabla)
Students: Kamal Kant, Kaushal Kant, Keshav Kant
GOTIPUA DANCERS
Raghurajpur (Orissa)
Master: Guru Shri Maguni Das (pakhavaj)
Students: Panchanand Bhuina, Prabhakar Mudali, Siddeshwar Mudali
BAULS
Bengal
Masters: Nirmala Goswani (ektara), Shri Haripada Goswami
Disciples: Lakhan Das Baul (khamak, ananda lahari), Paban Das Baul (dubki, dotara), Phoolmala Das Baul (ektara, karatalas), Subal Das Baul (ektara, duggi)
Sets: Guy-Claude François
Stone, plaster, cement, and brick: Antonio Ferreira, Joaquim Pedrosa, Pedro Pinto Serra, Manuel Pereira da Silva, Antonio Bonifácio
Wood: Thierry Meunier, Ly Nissay, Jorge Luis Lobos Medel
Painting and patinas: Sylvie Espinasse, Jean-François Espinasse, Didier Pons
Lights: Jean-Michel Bauer, Cécile Allegoedt, Rodrigo Bachler-Klein, Jean-Noël Cordier, Carlos Obregon
Decorations: Erhard Stiefel
Cooking and hospitality: Maria Albaiceta, Christine Hours, Jean-Cyrille Merle-Remond, Pharin Ly, Annie Tran, Estrela Gaspar, Liliana Andreone, Juliana Carneiro da Cunha, Nadja Djerrah, Maurice Durozier, Évelyne Fagnen, Isabelle Gazonnois, Danièle Heusslein-Gire, Ysabel de Maisonneuve, Ariane Mnouchkine, Sophie Moscoso, Nathalie Pousset
Director of darkness: Hector Ortiz
Program: Tatoo, with Anne Laville
Interpreters: Bhagwati Prasad Hatwal, Mimlu Sen, Rahul Vohra
Translations: France Bhattacharya, Lokenath Bhattacharya, Rahul Vohra

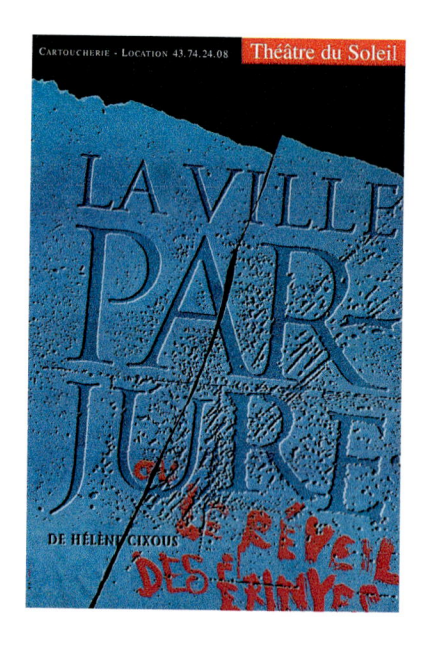

La Ville parjure ou le Réveil des Érinyes [*The Perjured City, or the Awakening of the Furies*]

By Hélène Cixous
Music by Jean-Jacques Lemêtre
Premiere: May 18, 1994, at the Cartoucherie.

CHORUS
First Coryphaeus, Immonde: Juliana Carneiro da Cunha ("With two caskets at her side...")
Second Coryphaeus, Lagadoue: Laurent Clauwaert ("We are all equal before death...")
CHORUS MEMBERS
Éliminé: Sergio Canto ("Were my voice not worn so thin..."), Brontis Jodorowsky ("It's because we are too bright, too lively...")
Abelle: Samantha McDonald ("That's what worries me..."), Valérie Crouzet ("Specialists, they exist!")
Thessalonique: Nicole Chandi Ansari ("Europe's conscience was badly wounded ..."), Évelyne Fagnen ("And since then it is totally deceased ..."), Esther André Konstantellos ("And never, for fifty hears, have you heard the tiny trumpet of conscience ..."), Carolina Pecheny ("That one, if he were to say: Yes, I have sinned..."), Christophe Rauck ("Let's have the lawyer, the proofs and witnesses, if you care about them so much more than about truth ..."), Rainer Sievert ("Thus to a threat so vague, so vast, so absolute ..."), Marc Barnaud, Duccio Bellugi-Vannuccini, Alexandre Ferran, Isabelle Gazonnois, Martial Jacques, Eva Perez, Marie Paule Ramo, Nicolas Sotnikoff, Maria Volodina
PROTAGONISTS (by order of appearance)
Mother (alternating): Renata Ramos Maza or Nirupama Nityanandan
Aeschylus: Myriam Azencot
Maître Brackmann: Jocelyn Lagarrigue
Maître Marguerre: Duccio Bellugi-Vannuccini
Night: Shahrokh Meshkin Ghalam
Furies (alternating): Nirupama Nityanandan or Renata Ramos Maza, with Juliana Carneiro da Cunha, Valérie Grail
X1: Brontis Jodorowsky
X2: Nicolas Sotnikoff or Rainer Sievert
King: Shahrokh Meshkin Ghalam
Queen (alternating): Juliana Carneiro da Cunha or Renata Ramos Maza or Nirupama Nityanandan
Officer of the Court: Laurent Clauwaert
Minister: Christophe Rauck
Systems Maintenance: Sylvain Jailloux
Forzza: Nicolas Sotnikoff or Brontis Jodorowsky
Monsieur Capitaine: Duccio Bellugi-Vannuccini
Professor Cornu-Maxime: Brontis Jodorowsky
Professor Anselme: Jocelyn Lagarrigue
Doctor Berthier: Valérie Grail
Doctor Jumeau: Nicolas Sotnikoff
Professor Lion (alternating): Nirupama Nityanandan or Juliana Carneiro da Cunha or Renata Ramos Maza
Doctor Brulard: Sylvain Jailloux
Daniel and Benjamin Ézéchiel, the children (alternating): Melchior Belson, David Brami, Michaël Couve de Murville, Léo Charron, Thésée Festinger, Ludovic Joyet, Valentin Mazzoran, Alexandre de Meireles, Luciano de

Moliner, Romain Morice, Benjamin Pages, Abenamar Sanchez, Johnny Tran, Charles Vitez **and later** Zacharie Abraham, Niloufar Amir Ebrahimi
Their guardian angels: Juliette Plumecocq Mech, Martial Jacques, Sylvain Jailloux
Kabuki doubles: Juliette Plumecocq Mech

Director: Ariane Mnouchkine
Assistant: Sophie Moscoso
Sets: Guy-Claude François
Assistant to Set Design: Sylvie Espinasse
Costumes: Nathalie Thomas, with Annie Tran, Marie-Hélène Bouvet, Christelle Muller
Musicians: Jean-Jacques Lemêtre, with Morgane
Lights: Jean-Michel Bauer, with Cécile Allegoedt, Rodrigo Bachler-Klein, Carlos Obregon, Jacques Poirot, François Ravinet
Marionette construction: Erhard Stiefel
Marionette instruction: Francis Jolit
Chief makeup counselor: Tamani Berkani
Ambassadress unto the children: Myriam Boullay
Stone, plaster, cement, concrete: Joaquim Pedrosa Baptista, with Mohamed Charkaoui, Michel Dumur, Célestin Granomord, Nascimento Mendes, Joaquim Pereira Gonçalves
Wood: Thierry Meunier, with Jean-Pierre Marry, Ly Nissay, Blasco Ruiz
Metal: Antonio Ferreira, with Alain Brunswick
Paintings and patinas: Sylvie Espinasse, with François Bancilhon, Victor Bonnabel, Pedro Guimaraes, Danièle Heusslein-Gire, Nicole Veilhan
Instrument-making: Caroline Lee
Stage managers: Juliette Plumecocq Mech, Jean Pierre Marry, Thierry Meunier, Ly Nissay
Sound manager: Rodrigo Bachler-Klein
Intern: Ismael da Fonseca
Administration: Nathalie Pousset, Pierre Salesne
Audience relations: Liliane Andreone, with Emmanuelle Henry, Naruna Andrade
Press relations: Mara Negron
Ticket sales: Pedro Guimaraes, with Anna Paula Petitdemange, Jean-Christophe Cardineau
Physical preparation and care: Marc Pujo
Phonetics and diction coach: Françoise Berge
Housekeeping: Maria Albaiceta, with Jean-Cyrille Merle, Remond Estrella, Gaspar Domingues, Zahra Amir Ebrahimi, Catherine Lefebvre
Ticket-taking and maintenance: Baudouin Bauchau
Director of darkness: Hector Ortiz
Photography: Martine Franck, Michèle Laurent
Poster and program: François Richez
We thank Anne-Marie Casteret for her book *L'Affaire du sang* [*The Business of Blood*], which was extremely helpful to us.

Le Tartuffe [*Tartuffe*]

By Molière
Premiere: June 10, 1995, in Vienna (Austria – Wiener Festwochen).

With, by order of appearance:
Merchant: Sergio Canto
Dorine: Juliana Carneiro da Cunha
Elmire: Nirupama Nityanandan
Mariane: Renata Ramos Maza
Valère: Martial Jacques
Flippe: Valérie Crouzet
Pote: Marie-Paule Ramo Guinard
Damis: Hélène Cinque
Cléante: Duccio Bellugi-Vannuccini
Madame Pernelle: Myriam Azencot
Orgon: Brontis Jodorowsky
Tartuffe: Shahrokh Meshkin Ghalam
Laurent: Jocelyn Lagarrigue
Loyal: Laurent Clauwaert
Royal Officer: Nicolas Sotnikoff
The Fundamentalist Gang, the Soldiers: Jamalh Aberkane, Haim Adri, Sergio
    Canto, Sylvain Jailloux, Jocelyn Lagarrigue, Nicolas Sotnikoff
Song: Cheb Hasni

Director: Ariane Mnouchkine
Sets: Guy-Claude François
Costumes: Nathalie Thomas, Marie-Hélène Bouvet, Annie Tran
Lights: Jean-Michel Bauer, Cécile Allegoedt, Carlos Obregon, Jacques Poirot

Soundtrack: Jean-Jacques Lemêtre and François Leymarie, with Yann Lemêtre
Sound manager: Rodrigo Bachler-Klein
Wood: Thierry Meunier, Michel Tardif, Manuel Begbeder, Daniel Lefebvre, Ly Nissay
Metal: Antonio Ferreira, Alain Brunswick, Joaquim Pedrosa Baptista
Paintings and patinas: Danièle Heusslein-Gire and Sylvie Espinasse, with Hadewy Freeve, Pedro Pinheiro Guimaraes
Director's assistant: Judith Marvan Enriquez
Stage managers: Myriam Boullay, Marie-Paule Ramo, Ly Nissay
Administration: Nathalie Pousset, Pierre Salesne
Audience relations: Liliana Andreone, Eve Doe Bruce, Kristos Konstantellos
Press relations: Mara Negron
Ticket sales: Maria Adroher Baus, Pedro Pinheiro Guimaraes, Christian Dumais-Lvowsky
Phonetics and diction coach: Françoise Berge
Housekeeping: Christine Hours, with Hélène Tersac
Ticket-taking and maintenance: Baudoin Bauchau
Director of darkness: Hector Ortiz
Photography: Martine Franck, Michèle Laurent
Posters and program: Louis Briat
Welcome Area fresco design: Dorothée Crosland
Welcome Area fresco construction: Didier Martin, Anne Deschaintres, Charlotte Camus, Joseph Crosland

---

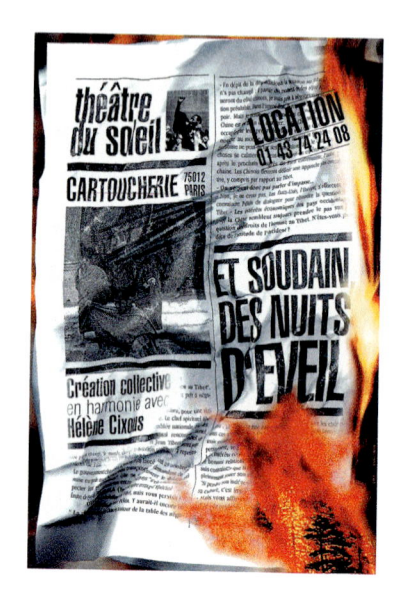

Et soudain des nuits d'éveil [*And Suddenly, Sleepless Nights*]

Collective creation in harmony with Hélène Cixous
Music by Jean-Jacques Lemêtre
Premiere: December 26, 1997, at the Cartoucherie.

With, by order of appearance:

Jacques, director of the theatre: Martial Jacques

Madame Tsültim, dancing master; Yeshe, delegate; Dolkar, singer and dancer:
Renata Ramos Maza

Tashi, singer and dancer: Duccio Bellugi-Vannuccini

Sonam, director of the troupe: Sergio Canto

Koubilaï, singer and dancer; Young man, second provocateur: Nicolas Sotnikoff

Madame Rolanda Pantalon; Marie-Ange, International Solidary Medecine:
Hélène Cinque

Madame Florinda Pantalon; Éléonore, intern; Camille, the Seventh Collective:
Marie-Paule Ramo

Marie-Christine, administrator; Charlotte, intern: Delphine Cottu

Madame Gabrielle, caretaker; Pupul, electrician: Myriam Azencot

Père Gilles, a spectator: Pascal Guarise

Loubna Soltani, a spectator: Shaghayegh Beheshti

Schoolteacher, spectator in solidarity; monk, children's nanny: Serge Nicolaï

Antoine, the chief helper: Laurent Clauwaert

Suzanne Tellmann, geographer: Myriam Boullay

Paloma, actress; Tara, delegate; Dona Ana Amélia, Paloma's aunt; homeless
man: Juliana Carneiro da Cunha

Félicité, seamstress; Germaine, Seventh Collective: Eve Doe Bruce

Zézé, cook: Fabianna de Mello e Souza

Olivia, responsible for community outreach: Maïtreyi

Manuel, disciple: Matthieu Rauchvarger

Monk, secretary; Jean-Baptiste, sick doctor: Guillaume Briat

Urania Kukulis, Tibetologist: Esther André-Konstantellos

Claude Delyon, Belgian spectator; a spectator, nuisance: Jean-Charles Maricot

François, electrician; Georgy, Charlotte's father; young man, first provocateur:
Sava Lolov

Olivier, actor: Vincent Mangado

Mathilde, actress; Marguerite, Charlotte's mother: Dominique Jambert

Clarissa, International Solidarity Medecine: Carolina Pecheny

Dancers of Tashi Shölpa: Duccio Bellugi-Vannuccini, Sergio Canto, Sava Lolov,
Serge Nicolaï, Carolina Pecheny, Nicolas Sotnikoff

Yak: Duccio Bellugi-Vannuccini, Serge Nicolaï

Children: Zacharie Abraham Caillart, Jamel Ben Slimane, Aurélien Caoudal,
Alexandre de Meireles, Marvin Gofin, Bonheur Ly, Pissei Ly, Sam
Sarabandi, Pouya Mohtasham Ansary

Director: Ariane Mnouchkine

Sets: Guy-Claude François

Paintings and patinas: Danièle Heusslein-Gire, with Didier Martin, Kristos
Konstantellos, Pedro Guimaraes, Yael Haber, Maria-Adelia Cardoso
Ferreira, Jean-Charles Sankara

Masks: Erhard Stiefel, with Ana Hopfer

Costumes: Marie-Hélène Bouvet, Nathalie Thomas, Annie Tran, and Ysabel de
Maisonneuve, with Elisabeth Jacques

Musicians: Jean-Jacques Lemêtre, with Catherine Brisset

Lights: Cécile Allegoedt, Carlos Obregon, Jacques Poirot

Stone, plaster, cement, metal, and wood: Antonio Ferreira and Thierry Meunier,
with Alain Brunswick, Amos Nguimbous, Ricardo Garcia Mateos

Director's assistants: Sophie Moscoso, Judith Marvan Enriquez, Charles-Henri
Bradier

Dancing master: Dolma Choden

Dance rehearsal leader: Maïtreyi

Tibetan teacher: Nicolas Silhé

Welcome Area fresco: Didier Martin, with Gaëlle Bernard, Joseph Crosland

Instrument-building: Caroline Lee

Administration: Pierre Salesne
Audience relations: Liliana Andreone, Naruna de Andrade, Sylvie Papandréou
Computer machine tamer: Étienne Lemasson
Kitchenmasters: Christian Dupont, Ly That-Vou, Josephina Rodriguez, and Ly Nissay, with Karim Gougam
Ticket sales: Maria Adroher Baus, Clara Bauer
Director of darkness: Hector Ortiz
Poster and program: Louis Briat
Program design: Sophie Moscoso
Photography: Martine Franck, Michèle Laurent
Soundtrack: François Leymarie, Yann Lemêtre
Ticket-taking and maintenance: Baudoin Bauchau

We would particularly like to thank the Sans Papiers de Saint Bernard (undocumented immigrants of Saint Bernard Church), for the inspiration that their fight has brought us and continues to bring us.

We thank the TIPA (Tibetan Institute of Performing Arts) for having had faith in us, having transmitted so much knowledge, and having delgated Madame Dolma Choden to us, with all her art and sweet patience.

We warmly thank SARTHI, which, from New Delhi, allowed us access to multiple treasures; and Mireille Helffer, Jean-Paul Ribes, Jean Lassale, Marc Riboud, as well as Françoise Rousseau-Benedetti and Lorenzo Benedetti, whose affection and immense generosity have accompanied us and supported us for so many years with complete discretion.

Tambours sur la digue, sous forme de pièce ancienne pour marionnettes jouée par des acteurs [*Drums on the Dam, in the Form of an Ancient Puppet Play Performed by Actors*]

By Hélène Cixous
Music by Jean-Jacques Lemêtre
Directed by Ariane Mnouchkine
Premiere: September 11, 1999, at the Cartoucherie.
This play is dedicated to Jacques Lecoq and Paul Puaux.

CHARACTERS by order of appearance:
Duan, the soothsayer's daughter: Renata Ramos Maza
Her handlers: Sergio Canto Sabido, Vincent Mangado
Soothsayer: Nicolas Sotnikoff
His handlers: Jean-Charles Maricot, Matthieu Rauchvarger
Lord Khang: Juliana Carneiro da Cunha
His handlers: Jean-Charles Maricot, Sergio Canto Sabido, Alexandre Roccoli
Chancellor: Duccio Bellugi-Vannuccini
His handlers: Vincent Mangado, Stéphane Decourchelle
Hun, Lord Khang's nephew: Sava Lolov
His handlers: Stéphane Decourchelle, Martial Jacques
Chief Intendant: Myriam Azencot
His handlers: Sergio Canto Sabido, Stéphane Decourchelle
Architect (in succession): Martial Jacques, Sava Lolov
His handlers: Alexandre Roccoli, Serge Nicolaï, Sergio Canto Sabido
Tshumi, minor court painter: Serge Nicolaï
His handlers: Maïtreyi, Jean-Charles Maricot
Chancellor's standard-bearer: Pascal Guarise
His handlers: Eve Doe Bruce, Maïtreyi, Sergio Canto Sabido
Palace servants: Delphine Cottu, Eve Doe Bruce, Judith Marvan Enriquez, Maïtreyi, Shaghayegh Beheshti
Their handlers: Sergio Canto Sabido, Shaghayegh Beheshti, Matthieu Rauchvarger, Maïtreyi, Eve Doe Bruce, Christophe Noël, Alexandre Roccoli, David Santonja
He Tao, Lord Hun's lieutenant: Nicolas Sotnikoff
His handlers: Matthieu Rauchvarger, Vincent Mangado, Stéphane Decourchelle
Wang Po, Chancellor's secretary: Sava Lolov
His handlers: Martial Jacques, Alexandre Roccoli
Madame Li, noodle merchant: Juliana Carneiro da Cunha
Her handlers: Sergio Canto Sabido, Jean-Charles Maricot
Kina, her servant: Sandrine Raynal
Her handlers: Matthieu Rauchvarger, Judith Marvan Enriquez, Christophe Noël
Monk: Myriam Azencot
His handlers: Stéphane Decourchelle, Sergio Canto Sabido, Alexandre Roccoli
First fisherman: Duccio Bellugi-Vannuccini
His handlers: Vincent Mangado, Sergio Canto Sabido
Second fisherman: Delphine Cottu
His handler: Christophe Noël
Third fisherman: Jean-Charles Maricot
His handler: Matthieu Rauchvarger
Handler of the tiny fisherman: Pascal Guarise
The River: Nicolas Sotnikoff
Its handler: Martial Jacques

Drums: Delphine Cottu, Dominique Jambert, Eve Doe Bruce, Fabianna de Mello e Souza, Jean-Charles Maricot, Judith Marvan Enriquez, Maïtreyi, Maria Adelia, Martial Jacques, Matthieu Rauchvarger, Sergio Canto Sabido, Shaghayegh Beheshti, Vincent Mangado

Their string handlers: Jacques Poirot, Frédéric Potron

Palanquin bearers: Nicolas Sotnikoff, Serge Nicolaï, Sergio Canto Sabido

Their handlers: Matthieu Rauchvarger, Alexandre Roccoli, Sandrine Raynal, Christophe Noël

O'mi, lantern merchant: Renata Ramos-Maza

Her handler: Stéphane Decourchelle

Her apprentice: Nicolas Sotnikoff

His handler: Jean-Charles Maricot

Liou Po, messenger of the breach: Duccio Bellugi-Vannuccini

His handlers: Sergio Canto Sabido, Vincent Mangado

Architect's wife: Renata Ramos-Maza

Her handler: Vincent Mangado

Chief Intendant's henchmen: Matthieu Rauchvarger, Nicolas Sotnikoff

Their handlers: Serge Nicolaï, Alexandre Roccoli

Servants of Lord Hun: Fabianna de Mello e Souza, Shaghayegh Beheshti

Their handlers: Christophe Noël, David Santonja

First guard: Nicolas Sotnikoff

His handler: Jean-Charles Maricot

Second guard: Vincent Mangado

His handler: Matthieu Rauchvarger

Child, brother of Wang Po: Sandrine Raynal

His handler: Christophe Noël

Wang Po's old father: Duccio Bellugi-Vannuccini

His handler: Stéphane Decourchelle

Baï Ju, marionettist: Sergio Canto Sabido

His handlers: Stéphane Decourchelle, Vincent Mangado

His wife: Maria Adelia

Her handler: Christophe Noël

His daughter: Judith Marvan Enriquez

Her handler: Matthieu Rauchvarger

His mother: Eve Doe Bruce

Her handler: Jean-Charles Maricot

Director: Ariane Mnouchkine

Sets: Guy-Claude François

Silks: Ysabel de Maisonneuve, Didier Martin

Costumes: Marie-Hélène Bouvet, Nathalie Thomas, Ysabel de Maisonneuve, and Annie Tran, with Élisabeth Jacques

Masks: the actors, with Maria Adelia

Musicians: Jean-Jacques Lemêtre, with Carlos Bernardo Carvalho, Dominique Jambert

Apprentice: Hsieh I-Jing

Drum master: Han Jae Sok

Lights: Cécile Allegoedt, Carlos Obregon, Jacques Poirot

Assistant to the director: Charles-Henri Bradier

Quartermaster: Martial Jacques

Chief movement consultant: Duccio Bellugi-Vannuccini

Constructors: Antonio Ferreira, Alain Brunswick

Metal: Maël Lefrançois, with Nicolas Dallongeville

Plaster, cement: Amos Nguimbous

Wood: Frédéric Potron, with Amos Nguimbous

Apprentice for all materials: Sébastien Marinetti

Paintings and patinas: Matthieu Lemarié, Pedro Guimaraes

Puppet construction: Serge Nicolaï, Fabianna de Mello e Souza, Shaghayegh Beheshti

Props: Erhard Stiefel, Christian Dupont, Pascal Guarise, Serge Nicolaï, Sergio Canto Sabido, Stéphane Decourchelle, Vincent Mangado

Visual memory: Judith Marvan Enriquez, Josephina Rodriguez, Myriam Boullay

Chief dispenser of care: Marc Pujo

Chief counselor on construction: Erhard Stiefel

Administration: Pierre Salesne

Audience relations: Liliana Andreone, Naruna Andrade, Sylvie Papandréou

Apprentices: Anne Cheneau, Marine Bisaro

Computer machine tamer: Étienne Lemasson

Delegate for humanitarian action: Christophe Floderer

Kitchenmasters: Ly That-Vou, with Ly Nissay, So Sekion, Christian Dupont

Ticket sales: Maria Adroher Baus, Pedro Guimaraes

Poster and program: Louis Briat

Photography: Martine Franck, Michèle Laurent

Phonetics and diction: Françoise Berge

Website captain: Gérard Bagot

Director of darkness: Hector Ortiz

Ticket-taking and maintenance: Baudouin Bauchau

Visiting apprentices having come from afar: Catherine Daele, Anna Hoeg, Lin Tsu-Cheng, Liu Mei-Yin

In remembrance and in celebration of having thanks to give, for we have travelled much, and thus we were much helped:

In Korea, it was Mr. Cheo Junho who opened all the first doors for us, and many other paths as well. It was thanks to him that we met Mr. Khang who allowed us to meet Mr. Kim Duk Soo, musician and artistic director of Samulnori Hanullim, who sent to us he who was to become our drum master, Jae Sok Han. Mrs. Lee Byung Boc was more than a guide to us: she became, as well, our friend and a kind of Muse. Isako Matsumoto, thanks be given to the gods, was a sweet and understanding lantern lighting our way across mysterious Japan. Mrs. Chiu, director of the Centre culturel et d'information de Taipei [Taipei Information and Cultural Center] in Paris, launched our discovery of the extraordinary artistic vitality and inexhaustible hospitality of her country, under the guidance of Mrs. Tai-Fan Pan. Over there, Professor Mingder Chung and his assistant Shu Lin, as well as Shin-Ni, known as Elisa, accompanied us through marvels and typhoons without ever abandoning us, and without ever tiring of our unfathomable ignorances and our insatiable appetite for knowledge. In Vietnam, we wish to thank Marcia Fiani, our great and faithful friend, who took us in and cared for us. Here at home, we would like to express our gratitude to all those we will call "The Light Brigade" and who came through as reinforcements at the crucial moment: Tristan Abgrall, Elisabeth Cerqueira, Solene Delarne, Isabelle Deffin, Anna Gallotti, Laetittia Guichard, Mickaël Gunther, Anna Kamychnikova, Andrea Kelley, Franck Kubacki, Emma Scaife, Laure Seguela, Eun-Ju Song, Vania Vaneau, Claire Lise Vendé, Lorena Zilleruelo, and he who, like Ulysses, had a wonderful journey among us, Gregory Popov. And of course, as always, Françoise Rousseau-Benedetti and Lorenzo Benedetti whose affection and immense generosity have accompanied us and supported us for so many years with complete discretion.

Le Dernier Caravansérail (Odyssées) [*The Last Caravanserai (Odysseys)*]

Premiere of THE CRUEL RIVER: April 2, 2003 at the Cartoucherie.
Premiere of ORIGINS AND DESTINIES: November 22, 2003, at the Cartoucherie.

Odysseys told, heard, listened to, improvised and staged by: Shaghayegh
    Beheshti, Duccio Bellugi-Vannuccini, Virginie Bianchini, Charles-Henri
    Bradier, Sébastien Brottet-Michel, Juliana Carneiro da Cunha, Hélène
    Cixous, Virginie Colemyn, Olivia Corsini, Delphine Cottu, Eve Doe Bruce,
    Maurice Durozier, Sarkaw Gorany, Astrid Grant, Émilie Gruat, Pascal
    Guarise, Jeremy James, Marjolaine Larranaga y Ausin, Jean-Jacques
    Lemêtre, Sava Lolov, Elena Loukiantchikova-Sel, Vincent Mangado, Jean-
    Charles Maricot, Judith Marvan Enriquez, Stéphanie Masson, Fabiana
    Mello e Souza, Ariane Mnouchkine, Serge Nicolaï, Seietsu Onochi,
    Mathieu Rauchvarger, Francis Ressort, Edson Rodrigues, David Santonja-
    Ruiz, Andreas Simma, Nicolas Sotnikoff, Koumarane Valavane

Proposition: Ariane Mnouchkine
Music: Jean-Jacques Lemêtre
Space: Guy-Claude François
Sets: Serge Nicolaï, Duccio Bellugi-Vannuccini
Large paintings for stage and Welcome Area: Didier Martin, with Mathieu
    Lemarié
Large hangings/backdrops: Ysabel de Maisonneuve
Lights: Cécile Allegoedt and Carlos Obregon, with Simon André, Cédric Baudic
Sound: Patricia Cano and I-Jing Hsieh, with Philippe Engel, Yann Lemêtre,
    François Leymarie
Costumes: Marie-Hélène Bouvet, Nathalie Thomas, and Annie Tran, with
    Élisabeth Jacques
Director's assistant: Charles-Henri Bradier

Builders: Antonio Ferreira, with Adolfo Canto Sabido, Karim Gougam, Everest Canto de Montserrat, Roméo Canto Sabido

Metal: Alain Brunswick, with Nicolas Dalongeville

Chief nose consultant: Erhard Stiefel

Wood: Éric Den Hartog, with Matthew Pomerantz

Trees: Francis Ressort, David Santonja, Emmanuel Dorand

Chief makeup counselor: Tamani Berkani

Administrative affairs: Pierre Salesne

Public affairs: Liliana Andreone, Naruna de Andrade, and Sylvie Papandréou, with Myriam Azencot

Apprentice: Christel Laurent

Computer, graphic, technical and floral affairs: Étienne Lemasson

Humanitarian affairs and tours in France and abroad: Elaine Méric

Ticket sales affairs: Maria Adroher Baus and Pedro Guimaraes, with Nirupama Nityanandan, Jessica Rossel

Kitchenmasters: Ly That-Vou, Ly Nissay, Azizullah Hamrah, Gholam Rezah Hosseini

Chief dispenser of care: Marc Pujo

Translation of narratives: Shaghayegh Beheshti

Children: Françoise Berge

Program: Catherine Schaub, Thomas Félix-François

Posters: Thomas Félix-François, with photos by Charles-Henri Bradier

Photography: Michèle Laurent, Martine Franck

Website: Gérard Bagot

Interns and apprentices: Emmanuel Dorand, Alexandre Michel, Pauline Poignand, Xian Rong Chen, Virginie Le Coënt, Marie Heuzé, and Jennifer Sabbah, with Jeanne Dosse, Matthieu Dosse

Little girls: Alba Gaïa Kraghede-Bellugi, Galatea Kraghede-Bellugi, Sarah Gougam, Leah Agranat, Anahid Ruivo, Axelle Zavalichine, Juliette Hutebergue, Suzanne Wachnick

General stage manager: Fabianna de Mello e Souza

Director of darkness: Hector Ortiz

Ticket-taking and maintenance: Baudoin Bauchau

Les Éphémères [*Ephemera*]

Premiere: December 27, 2006, at the Cartoucherie.

Episodes dreamed, invoked, evoked, improvised and staged by:
Shaghayegh Beheshti, Duccio Bellugi-Vannuccini, Charles-Henri Bradier, Sébastien Brottet-Michel, Juliana Carneiro da Cunha, Hélène Cinque, Virginie Colemyn, Olivia Corsini, Delphine Cottu, Marie-Louise Crawley, Eve Doe Bruce, Emmanuel Dorand, Servane Ducorps*, Maurice Durozier, Camille Grandville*, Astrid Grant, Émilie Gruat, Dominique Jambert, Jeremy James, Marjolaine Larranaga y Ausin, Virginie Le Coënt, Jean-Jacques Lemêtre, Elena Loukiantchikova-Sel, Vincent Mangado, Alexandre Michel, Alice Milléquant*, Ariane Mnouchkine, Serge Nicolaï, Seietsu Onochi, Pauline Poignand, Matthieu Rauchvarger, Francis Ressort, Andreas Simma.
And the children: Alba Gaïa Kraghede-Bellugi, Galatea Kraghede-Bellugi, Paco Falgas, Iñaki Falgas, Emmie Poinsot, Emma Zinszner, Balthazar Perraud, Rebecca Jodorowsky, Alice Le Coënt-Salvetti, Ruben Delgado, Raquele de Miranda, Nathan Agranat, Amalia Guis*, Ivan Guis*, Nina Gregorio*, Lucien Jaburek*, Orane Mounier*, Simon Rousteau*, Louise Guy*, Saranya Siegel-Berger*, Alice Eynaud*, Milan Galland*, Jeanne Duquesne*
(Those marked with an asterisk* joined the performance for the reprise in 2008 or for the tour.)

Proposition: Ariane Mnouchkine
Music: Jean-Jacques Lemêtre
Director's assistant: Charles-Henri Bradier
Space passionately desired by Ariane Mnouchkine
Ardently brought into being by Everest Canto de Montserrat
Feverishly painted by Elena Antsiferova
Small worlds obsessively assembled by the actors, under the attentive eye of: Serge Nicolaï, Duccio Bellugi-Vannuccini, Sébastien Brottet-Michel, Jeremy James, Olivia Corsini, Francis Ressort, Eve Doe Bruce, and Seietsu Onochi, with Astrid Grant
Lights: Cécile Allegoedt, Cédric Baudic, Nil Tondeur, Régis Richard, Elsa Revol*
Sound: Yann Lemêtre, Judith Marvan Enriquez, Virginie Le Coënt, Anthony Desvergnes
All other paintings: Marion Lefebvre, Erol Gülgonen, Laure Gilquin, Clarence Boulay, Anna Deschamps
Builders:
Wood: Jean-Louis Guérard, David Buizard, Tanguy Trotel, Jean-Marie Baudinière
Metal: Nicolas Dallongeville, Kaveh Kishipour, Bertrand Mathevet, Alain Brunswick, Julie Kayser, Vincent Bernard
All materials: Adolfo Canto Sabido, Jérôme Sauvion, Samuel Capdeville
Costumes, hangings, and tapestries of all kinds: Nathalie Thomas, Marie-Hélène Bouvet, Annie Tran, Chloé Bucas, Cécile Gacon, Karin Faltlhauser, Élisabeth Leclerc, Laure Rewega, Mhorgane Ribière, Anaïs Tondeur, Pauline Mazeaud
Chief organizer of chariots (rolling platforms): Sébastien Brottet-Michel
Stage managers: Hélène Cinque, Pauline Poignand, Emmanuel Dorand
Hair and wigs: Jean-Sébastien Merle-Barreau
Kitchenmasters: Pedro Pinheiros Guimaraes, Maral Abkarian, Karim Gougam, Mohamed Hemmatjou
Barmasters: Paula Giusti, David Buizard, Lucile Cocito
Major technical and computer affairs: Étienne Lemasson
The paintings in the hall of a thousand Buddhas were created in 1997 for the premiere of *And Suddenly, Sleepless Nights* by Danièle Heusslein-Gire and our team. The guardrails in the Welcome Area were conceived by Juliette Liberman, and constructed by Juliette Liberman, Elsa Laborde, and Hakim Belmatoug.
Public affairs: Liliana Andreone, Sylvie Papandréou, Naruna de Andrade
Administrative affairs: Judit Jancsò, Pierre Salesne
Humanitarian affairs and tours in France and abroad: Elaine Méric
Ticket sales affairs: Maria Adroher Baus, Luciana Velocci Silva, Gaëlle Méric, Boutros El Amari, Dan Kostenbaum
Chief pedagogues: Françoise Berge, Frédérique Falgas
Chief dispenser of care: Marc Pujo
Trainer: Frédéric Roualen
Photography: Martine Franck, Michèle Laurent
Website: Gérard Bagot
Memories, images: Judith Marvan Enriquez, Lucile Cocito, Jeanne Dosse, Marie Heuzé
Transcriptions: Celia Daniellou, Nirupama Nityanandan, Patricia Cano
Archives: Claire Ruffin, Julie Sadeg
Program: Catherine Schaub-Abkarian, Thomas Félix-François, with photos by Pedro Guimaraes
Posters: Thomas Félix-François, with photos by Charles-Henri Bradier
Interns and apprentices: Alice Milléquant, Thérèse Spirli, and Jenny Vernier, with Ainur Camber-Rougé
Ticket-taking and maintenance: Baudoin Bauchau, Fanta Koïta
Night watch: Mohamed Nabbat

Les Naufragés du Fol Espoir (Aurores) [*The Survivors of Mad Hope (Dawn)*]

Théâtre du Soleil collective creation, half-written by Hélène Cixous
Proposition by Ariane Mnouchkine
Freely inspired by a mysterious posthumous novel by Jules Verne
Premiere: February 3, 2010, at the Cartoucherie.

With:
Misses
Eve Doe Bruce who incarnates **Monsieur Félix Courage,** boss of the cabaret
    The Mad Hope.
Juliana Carneiro da Cunha who incarnates **Madame Gabrielle,** sister of Jean
    LaPalette, filmmaker, who plays Madame Paoli, Italian emigrant; and
    Native American mother.
Astrid Grant who incarnates **Miss Mary Danaher,** firecracker and smoke spe-
    cialist, who plays Maria Vetsera, mistress of Rodolphe; Victoria, Empress
    and Queen; and Emelyne Jones, socialist and feminist.
Olivia Corsini who incarnates **Mademoiselle Marguerite,** waitress, who plays
    Marguerite's granddaughter, Rachel, a famous lyric singer; wife of Simon;
    and Sister Augustine, of the Salesian mission.
Paula Giusti who incarnates **Anita,** the acrobat (what today we'd call a tum-
    bler), who plays Amalia Paoli; and Herrera, delegate of the Argentine
    Republic.
Alice Milléquant who incarnates **Suzanne,** the other acrobat, who plays the
    port nurse; and Segarra, delegate of the Republic of Chile.

Dominique Jambert who incarnates **Mademoiselle Adèle**, who plays Anna, the schoolteacher; and Sister Magnanime, of the Salesian mission.

Pauline Poignand who incarnates **Mademoiselle Marthe**, the right-hand woman of Monsieur Félix Courage, who plays Marthe's granddaughter, Gervaise, worker in a mustard factory; Rodrigo, secretary-general of Patagonia; and Anju, young Native American woman.

Marjolaine Larranaga y Ausin who incarnates **Mademoiselle Flora**, the little washerwoman.

Ana Amelia Dosse who incarnates **Mademoiselle Rosalia**, waitress, who plays Louise Ceyrac, wife of Pierre Ceyrac.

Judit Jancsó who incarnates **Mademoiselle Eszther**, the Hungarian woman in charge of the cash register, who plays Rachel's nurse.

Aline Borsari who incarnates **Mademoiselle Fernanda**, waitress, who plays a sailor.

Frédérique Voruz who incarnates **Mademoiselle Victoire**, waitress.

and the voice of Miss Shaghayegh Beheshti.

For the reprise

Miss Delphine Cottu will be **the voice**.

Miss Julie Autissier will play **Mademoiselle Flora**.

And Sirs

Jean-Jacques Lemêtre who incarnates **Monsieur Camille Bérard**, the musician.

Maurice Durozier who incarnates **Monsieur Jean LaPalette**, filmmaker, who plays Émile Gautrain, banker and industrialist.

Duccio Bellugi-Vannuccini who incarnates **Monsieur Tommaso**, also a filmmaker, who plays Josef, coachman to Archduke Rodolphe of Habsburg-Lorraine; the ship's doctor; Sir Charles Darwin, famous English naturalist; and Marat Razine, galley slave, "Bolshevik tendency" ideologue.

Serge Nicolaï who incarnates **Monsieur Louis**, hawker at Felix's, who plays the Archduke Jean Salvatore of Habsburg-Tuscany, known as Jean Orth, known as the Kaw-djer (in Jules Verne); Lord Salisbury, Prime Minister of the British Empire; and the governor of Patagonia.

Sébastien Brottet-Michel who incarnates **Monsieur Ernest Choubert**, known as **Schubert**, actor, who plays an Austrian secret service agent; Simon Gautrain, banker and engineer; Armando Paoli, the mad son; and Octavio Mac Lennan, an Argentinian "bounty hunter."

Sylvain Jailloux who incarnates **Monsieur Alix Bellmans**, stage manager, who plays an Austrian secret service agent; Charles, Rachel's chauffeur; Professor John Jones, pastor, Christian socialist; Lieutenant Laurence, envoy of the British government; and Lusconi, an Argentinian "bounty hunter."

Andreas Simma who incarnates **Josef**, the Austrian waiter, who plays the Archduke Rodolphe of Habsburg-Lorraine; Father Matthew; a Sikh guard in the Indian Raj; and Lobo, an Argentinian "bounty hunter."

Seear Kohi who incarnates **Bonheur**, the Cambodian employee, who plays a young Austrian assassin; a young sailor; and Yuras, the young Native American.

Arman Sarybekian who incarnates **Monsieur Vassili**, the Russian painter, who plays Toni, joiner-carpenter; and Miss Blossom.

Vijayan Panikkaveettil who incarnates **Ravisharanarayanan**, known as **Ravi**, head of cabaret staff, who plays the Captain, commander of the ship; a Sikh guard of the Indian Raj; and Jenkins, sheep farmer.

Samir Abdul Jabbar Saed who incarnates **Farouk**, the Egyptian pastry cook, who plays a thug; Monsieur Paoli, Italian emigrant; the majordomo of Windsor Castle, and a galley slave.

Vincent Mangado who incarnates **Ulysses**, the Breton waiter, who plays Patrick O'Leary, sailor; and Pierre Ceyrac, geographer and Utopian socialist.

Sébastien Bonneau who incarnates **Jeannot**, little juggler and newsboy, who plays a young Austrian assassin; and Billy, the ship's boy.

Maixence Bauduin who incarnates **Jérôme**, the hunter, who plays a thug; and Manuel, the schoolteacher.

Jean-Sébastien Merle who incarnates **Monsieur Dauphin**, the hairdresser, who plays a groom on the ship; Winston Churchill; a young page to Queen Victoria; and a galley slave.

Seietsu Onochi who incarnates **Akira**, the regular client, who plays Huang Huang Hshing, Chinese laundry owner.

Jean-Jacques Lemêtre composed a great deal of the music in this play. He also invoked and convoked the souls of his great ancestors, composers from the nineteenth and twentieth centuries: Ludwig van Beethoven, Hector Berlioz, Johannes Brahms, Anton Bruckner, Emmanuel Chabrier, Dmitri Shostakovich, Vincent D'Indy, Claude Debussy, Anton Dvořák, Gabriel Fauré, César Franck, Edvard Grieg, Aram Khachaturian, Carl Orff, Sergei Prokofiev, Sergei Rachmaninov, Ottorino Respighi, Nikolai Rimsky-Korsakov, Franz Schubert, Jean Sibelius, Bedřich Smetana, Johann Strauss, Pyotr Ilyich Tchaikovsky, Giuseppe Verdi, Richard Wagner.

Ariane Mnouchkine dreamed up the stage space, which was brought into being by Everest Canto de Montserrat.

Charles-Henri Bradier assisted Ariane Mnouchkine in her direction with the help of Lucile Cocito.

Serge Nicolaï imagined and brought into being the sets with the help of Sébastien Brottet-Michel, Elena Antsiferova, Duccio Bellugi-Vannuccini, Andreas Simma, Maixence Bauduin, and everyone else.

Elsa Revol designed and executed the lighting with Hugo Mercier and Virginie Le Coënt.

Yann Lemêtre designed and set up the sound directed by Thérèse Spirli and Marie-Jasmine Cocito.

Nathalie Thomas, Marie-Hélène Bouvet, and Annie Tran made the costumes for the play with help from the actors and from Cécile Gacon, Adeline Boulé, Simona Grassano, Renaud Bélanger.

Danièle Heusslein-Gire painted all the painted canvases found in the performance. The "thousand Buddhas" on the walls of the theatre are also her handiwork, from an earlier play.

Erol Gülgonen and Marion Lefebvre covered the other walls with their Jules Vernian works and painted film posters for the Welcome Area with the help of Caroline Thibouville and Céline Schmitt.

Didier Martin created the vast fresco on the back wall of the Welcome Area, with the help of Virginie Drougard, and the writing on the outside of the theatre.

Tanguy Trotel and David Buizard worked wood with the help of Roland Zimmermann, and Iwan Lambert Kaveh Kishipour tamed metal with the help of Guillaume Parmentelas.

Adolfo Canto Sabido confronted all the material challenges.

Elena Antsiferova painted the bar, applied patina to the guardrails and flats, gave life to the fauna of Tierra del Fuego and crafted the revolutionary objects from the beginning of the twentieth century (phonograph horns, pedestrian street signs, props for special effects).

A thousand and one small details were scrutinized and solved by Sébastien Brottet-Michel and Serge Nicolaï.

Vincent Mangado and Dominique Jambert were and still are the forecastle team and riggers of our theatre of multiple takes.

Erhard Stiefel carved and eroded the glaciers and icebergs.

Paula Giusti reconstituted the cameras of cinematography's first steps.

Olivia Corsini, with Aline Borsari, Ana Amelia Dosse, Martha Kiss Perone, Andrea Marchant, and others, organized the crafting and maintenance of the great ice floe.

Sylvain Jailloux managed the comings and goings of all the flats and their counterweights. Andrea Marchant and Ebru Erdinc were assigned to chases and stage management.

The floor and some set elements were made at the workshop of our friend Dominique Lebourge (Artefact).

Major technical affairs and all sorts of other things: Everest Canto de Montserrat

Major computer and organization affairs, and all sorts of other things: Étienne Lemasson

Administrative affairs: Pierre Salesne and Claire Van Zande, with Judit Jancsó

And accounting affairs: Rolande Fontaine

Major public affairs and all sorts of other things: Liliana Andreone, Sylvie Papandréou, Élise Nerrant, Svetlana Dukovska

Humanitarian affairs, tours in France and abroad, and all sorts of other things: Elaine Méric

Editorial affairs: Franck Pendino

Ticket sales affairs: Maria Adroher Baus, Frédérique Mathieu, with the help of Luciana Velocci Silva, Charlotte Andrès, and Valérie Crouzet, Delphine Cottu, Caroline Panzéra

Kitchenmasters: Karim Gougam, Pascal Guarise, with the help of Charles Gonon

Posters, publicity leaflet, and programs: Thomas Félix-François, Catherine Schaub-Abkarian

Archivists: Claire Ruffin, Thémis Acrivopoulos, under the vigiliant eye of Liliana Andreone

Website: Frédéric Mastellari, Claire Ruffin, and Étienne Lemasson, with Gérard Bagot

Chief dispenser of care, and all sorts of other things: Marc Pujo

Trainer: Frédéric Roualen

Dance rehearsal leader: Nadejda Loujine

Typing of the text of the play: Annie-Joëlle Ripoll

Transcriptions of the improvisations: Marie Constant

Photography: Martine Franck, Michèle Laurent

Instrument-maker: Marcel Ladurelle

Night watch: Olivier Slimani, Azizullah Hamrah

Maintenance: Baudoin Bauchau (April 22, 1941 – May 20, 2010. Baudoin had been part of the Théâtre du Soleil troupe since 1962, in *Genghis Khan* at the Arènes de Lutèce.)

Shuttle: Fred Sharre

African juice merchant: Fanta Koïta

Interns and apprentices, priceless reinforcements, attentive and discreet observers from the world around: Beejan Olfat, Etsuko Tsuri, Mokonuiarangui Smith, Man Waï Fok, and Martha Kiss Perone, with Sofia Norlin, Celia Daniellou, Daniela De Stasio, Ngapaki Emery, Bea Gerzsenyi

Indispensable reinforcements:

For technical matters: Michel Fagon, Julie Kayser, Jean-Patrice Laîné, Yann Sanchez

For light and electricity: Vincent Lefèvre, Jean-Philippe Morin, and Rabah Benbahmeb, with Thomas Guedon*

For sewing: Cristina Aché, Marina Menzhulina, Franck Parravicini, Louise Watts

For painting: Rachel Albaut, Marine Dillard, Polina Komarova, Grégoire Martin, Solenne Musseau, Antonios Roussohadzakis, Camille Vallat

And Jean-François, Lydia, Claire, Florence ...

For everything: Hélène Cinque, who with Caroline Panzera and Harold Savary led **the brigade of "flying firemen"**: Olivia Algazi, Victor Arancio, Baharan Baniahmadi, David Baqué, Léo Bonnefont, Celia Chabut, Marie Chaufour, Guiti Doroudi, Farid Joya, Chiang Kai-Chun, Dan Kostenbaum, Quentin Lasherme, Véronique Laurens, Augustin Letelier, Julia Marin, Lynda Mebtouche, Nanor Petrosyan, Maylis Ripart, Amélie Rousseaux, Magali Rouvière, Ido Shaked, Valentin Simonet, Tseten and our Tibetan friends, and Anna, Audrey, Céline, Monica…

For the reprise, Miss Marion Lefebvre, Mr. David Baqué, and Mr. Thomas Guedon lent a hand to the valiant stage management team.

Thank you to our fellow travelers Erhard Stiefel, Françoise Berge, Guy-Claude François

Thank you to the child actors of *The Last Caravanserai* and *Ephemera* who followed many rehearsals patiently and passionately, and who accepted without bitterness having to wait for the next ship

For her help, a very great thanks to agnès b.

Thank you to Paul-Dominique Guidicelli, Jean-Pierre Mongarny (Crédit Coopératif), Liv Ullmann, the jury of the Ibsen prize; and the Norwegian Minister of Culture, Anne de Amézaga

Thank you to Gilles Corre and François Conan, the carpenter sailors from Douarnenez, indefatigable lifeguards

To Father Jaouen and Mr. and Mrs. Loiselet from the Jeudi-Dimanche Association, for the sails

Thank you to the Comédie Française, and more specifically to Stéphane Desmits, responsible for Wardrobes; Jean-François Chapelot, stagehand; and Jaafoura Raouf, upholsterer

To *L'Humanité*, and more specifically to Charles Sylvestre, journalist; Joël Lumien, photographer; and Lucien San-Biagio, archivist

To Patricia Ollivier (Hôpital de la Salpétrière) for the blankets

To Claude Cudon and Paulette Michel (from The Prisons of Montagny Inn) for the furniture

To Marie-Louise Crawley, for the English translations

To Michel Benjamin, for his expert advice on special effects

To Alain Rey, for his deep knowledge as linguist and lexicographer

To Madeleine Favre, for her permanent friendly and medical vigilance

To Anne Lacombe

To Stéphane Ricordel.

Thank you to our neighbors and partners:

The Atelier de Paris-Carolyn Carlson and the Théâtre du Chaudron for the loan of their rehearsal space

Jean-Claude Lallias and Gaëlle Bebin at CNDP (National Center for Pedagogical Documenation), for their brave pedagogical crusade and their loyalty

Thierry Maudet and Jean-Robert Filliard at INSEP (National Institute for Sports, Expertise and Performance), for their protective and amicable neighborly presence

And as always, for their concrete and faithful help, thank you to Françoise and Lorenzo Benedetti.

And thank you to all those who gave us a few hours of their time, or more, and who are not named here…

Macbeth

Tragedy by William Shakespeare
Translated by Ariane Mnouchkine, music by Jean-Jacques Lemêtre
Premiere: April 30, 2014, at the Cartoucherie.

DRAMATIS PERSONAE
First witch: Juliana Carneiro da Cunha
Second witch: Nirupama Nityanandan or Eve Doe Bruce
Third witch: Shaghayegh Beheshti or Eve Doe Bruce
Other witches: Dominique Jambert, Alice Milléquant, Astrid Grant, Judit
    Jancsó, Frédérique Voruz, Ana Amélia Dosse, Camille Grandville, Aline
    Borsari, Man Waï Fok, Andrea Marchant, Marie Chaufour
Duncan: Maurice Durozier
HIS SONS
Malcolm: Duccio Bellugi-Vannuccini
Donalbain: Martial Jacques
Captain: Arman Saribekyan
Lennox: Jean-Sébastien Merle
Angus: Sylvain Jailloux
Macbeth: Serge Nicolaï
Banquo: Vincent Mangado
His son, Fleance (alternating): Victor Bombaglia, Lucien Bradier, Blas Durozier,
    Joshua Halévi, Eraj Kohi, Dionisio Mangado
Chamberlain: Seietsu Onochi
Journalist: Shaghayegh Beheshti
Cameraman: Sébastien Brottet-Michel
Television crew: Ana Amélia Dosse, Judit Jancsó
Photographers: Eve Doe Bruce, Quentin Lashermes
Baroness Caithness: Dominique Jambert
Press attachée: Frédérique Voruz
Lady Macbeth: Nirupama Nityanandan

Lady Macbeth's steward: Camille Grandville
Gardener: Samir Abdul Jabbar Saed
A young lord: Seear Kohi
Seyton: Sylvain Jailloux
Duncan's guards: Sergio Canto, Vijayan Panikkaveettil
Old watchman: Seietsu Onochi
Porter: Eve Doe Bruce
Macduff: Sébastien Brottet-Michel
Ross: Maurice Durozier
"Bagpipe": Andrea Marchant
Assassins: Martial Jacques, Frédérique Voruz, alternating with Sergio Canto, Judit Jancsó
Banquet guests: Aline Borsari, Sergio Canto, Eve Doe Bruce, Ana Amélia Dosse, Man Waï Fok, Camille Grandville, Astrid Grant, Samir Abdul Jabbar Saed, Martial Jacques, Seear Kohi, Iwan Lambert, Andrea Marchant, Alice Milléquant, Seiestu Onochi, Vijayan Panikkaveettil, Luciana Velocci Silva
Maître d'hôtel: Duccio Bellugi-Vannuccini
Lady Macduff: Astrid Grant, alternating with Shaghayegh Beheshti
Her son: Dominique Jambert
Majordomo: Martial Jacques
A messenger: Camille Grandville
Malcolm's companions: Judit Jancsó, Iwan Lambert
Macduff's companions: Aline Borsari, Seear Kohi
Lady Macbeth's gentlewoman: Ana Amelia Dosse
Doctor: Juliana Carneiro da Cunha, alternating with Camille Grandville
Menteith: Vincent Mangado
A messenger: Quentin Lashermes
General Siward: Vincent Mangado
A messenger: Arman Saribekyan
Young Siward: Seear Kohi
AND
Households: Shaghayegh Beheshti, Aline Borsari, Marie Chaufour, Eve Doe Bruce, Ana Amélia Dosse, Man Waï Fok, Camille Grandville, Astrid Grant, Samir Abdul Jabbar Saed, Dominique Jambert, Judit Jancsó, Seear Kohi, Iwan Lambert, Quentin Lashermes, Agustin Letelier, Andrea Marchant, Alice Milléquant, Miguel Nogueira da Gama, Seietsu Onochi, Vijayan Panikkaveettil, Arman Saribekyan, Luciana Velocci Silva, Frédérique Voruz
Officers and soldiers: Man Waï Fok, Samir Abdul Jabbar Saed, Seear Kohi, Iwan Lambert, Quentin Lashermes, Agustin Letelier, Miguel Nogueira da Gama, Vijayan Panikkaveettil, Arman Saribekyan, Harold Savary
Servants: Marie Chaufour, Man Waï Fok, Samir Abdul Jabbar Saed, Judit Jancsó, Quentin Lashermes, Agustin Letelier, Miguel Nogueira da Gama, Vijayan Panikkaveettil, Arman Saribekyan
Militia members: Aline Borsari, Sergio Canto, Eve Doe Bruce, Samir Abdul Jabbar Saed, Sylvain Jailloux, Iwan Lambert, Agustin Letelier, Vincent Mangado, Seietsu Onochi, Vijayan Panikkaveettil, Arman Saribekyan, Harold Savary, Frédérique Voruz
Resistance fighters: Aline Borsari, Marie Chaufour, Samir Abdul Jabbar Saed, Iwan Lambert, Quentin Lashermes, Agustin Letelier, Andrea Marchant, Alice Milléquant
AND
Kokens, which is to say stage servants: all the actors, and Taher Baig, François Bombaglia, Saboor Dilawar, Camila de Freitas Viana de Moraes, Shafiq Kohi, Ghulam Reza Rajabi, Omed Rawendah, Wazhma Tota Khil, Luciana Velocci Silva

"Pilot fish," which is to say help for the young actors: Juliana Carneiro da Cunha, Nirupama Nityanandan, Duccio Bellugi-Vannuccini

The music for the play is the work of Jean-Jacques Lemêtre.

The lights for the play are the work of Elsa Revol with the help of Virginie Le Coënt.

The sounds governed by Thérèse Spirli and Marie-Jasmine Cocito were conceived by Yann Lemêtre with the help of Melchior Derouet.

The costumes of the play are the work of Marie-Hélène Bouvet, Nathalie Thomas, and Annie Tran, with Simona Grassano, Élodie Madebos and Élisabeth Jacques.

The Welcome Area is the work of the painters' workshop directed by Anne-Lise Galabielle, which includes Mathias Allemand, Fabrice Cany, Martin Claude, Camille Courier de Méré, Marine Dillard, Fanny Gautreau, and Marion Lefebvre, with Erol Gülgonen.

The great fresco is the work of Didier Martin with the help of Delphine Guichard.

The silks of the play are the work of Ysabel de Maisonneuve who dyed them, and Didier Martin who painted them.

The ground of the stage is the work of Elena Antsiferova.

The moors and heaths are the work of Sylvain Jailloux, Haroon Amani, Sayed Ahmad Hashimi, and Luciana Velocci Silva. Their dyes were done by Aline Borsari, Ana Amélia Dosse, Andrea Marchant, and Alice Milléquant.

The hills and bunkers are the work of Elena Antsiferova, David Buizard, Kaveh Kishipour, and Samuel Capdeville.

The mists, fogs, and clouds are the work of Astrid Grant and Harold Savary, assisted by Suzana Thomaz, with the help of Marie Chaufour and Man Waï Fok.

The gardens, greenhouses, and forests are the work of Shaghayegh Beheshti and Maurice Durozier, with the help of Theatre Studies students from Paris III University.

The guardrails are the work of Elena Antsiferova and Roland Zimmermann.

The paintings and patinas of the guardrails, sets, and props are the work of Elena Antsiferova, Mathias Allemand, Fanny Gautreau, and Anton Telegescu.

The constructions are the work of the technical workshop directed by David Buizard, Kaveh Kishipour, and Étienne Lemasson:

David Buizard, Roland Zimmermann, and Vivian Eon worked wood.

Kaveh Kishipour, Marie Antoniazza, and Benjamin Bottinelli Hahn tamed metal.

François Bombaglia and Samuel Capdeville affronted all materials.

Erhard Stiefel created certain mysterious and surprising props.

Overall stage management: Duccio Bellugi-Vannuccini, with Sébastien Brottet-Michel

Electricians: Ibrahima Sow, with Saboor Dilawar

Forecastle installation: Dominique Jambert, with Vincent Mangado

Upholsterer: Chloé Bucas

Bric-a-brac arrangers and set dressers: Sébastien Brottet-Michel, with Serge Nicolaï

Hair and wigs: Jean-Sébastien Merle

Daily filming of rehearsals: Lucile Cocito

Text helper and guardian angel of the children: Françoise Berge

The Assistants' Brigade:

Staging assistant: Lucile Cocito

Costume assistants: Clara Bourdais, Mélanie Dion, Mégane Martinez, Émilie Paquet, Sacha Pignon, Charlotte Walther

Paintings assistants: Saboor Dilawar, Wazhma Tota Khil, Laura da Silva, Alain Quercia, Xue Zhang

Dyeing assistant: Simona Grassano

Prop-making assistants: Ekaterina Antsiferova, Elena Diego Marina, Silvia Circu, Paula Giusti

Patinas assistants: Ekaterina Antsiferova, Majo Caporaletti, Alain Khouani, Maria Tavlariou

Construction assistants: Aref Bahunar, Ali-Reza Kishipour, Asif Mawdudi, Jérémie Quintin

Electricity assistants: David Baqué, Thierry Barbier, Kamel Beztout, Charles Goyard, Simon Jacquard

Child guidance assistant: Lucie Chenet

Of great help in managing the stage: Eugénie Agoudjian, Zoé Briau, Hédi Tarkani

All the major business affairs: Charles-Henri Bradier

Technical and organizational affairs: Étienne Lemasson

Administrative affairs: Astrid Renoux, with the help of Louise Champiré

Public affairs: Sylvie Papandréou, Svetlana Dukovska, Eddy Azzem, with the help of Sarah Sanchez and François Spirli, Ninon Argis, Margot Blanc

Editorial affairs: Franck Pendino

Ticket sales affairs: Maria Adroher Baus, with Ariane Bégoin, Flora Berger, Pedro Castro Neves, Olivia Corsini, Gérard Hardy, Lauren Hussein, Marjolaine Larranaga y Ausin, Nadia Reeb, Ido Shaked, Alexandre Zloto

National and international tours: Marie-Anne Bernard

Kitchenmasters: Karim Gougam and Virginie Collombet, with the help of Hamideh Ghadirzadeh, Asif Mawdudi

Chief steward: Hélène Cinque

The alternating bar brigades: Eugénie Agoudjian, Haroon Amani, Aref Bahunar, Taher Baig, Paul Balagué, Zoé Briau, Lucie Chenet, Cathy Couronne, José da Silva, Lucas Dardaigne, Camila de Freitas Viana de Moraes, Saboor Dilawar, Carla Gondrexon, Luis Guenel, Mutjaba Habibi, Mustafa Habibi, Sayed Ahmad Hashimi, Farid Ahmad Joya, Alain Khouani, Shafiq Kohi, Dan Kostenbaum, Valérie Pujol, Ghulam Reza Rajabi, Omid Rawendah, Nadia Reeb, Carole Renouf, Masoma Rezale, Shoreh Sabaghy, Kristina Skorikova, Hédi Tarkani, Wazhma Tota Khil, Artavasd Yusbashyan, Paloma Zapata

Posters, publicity leaflet, and program text: Thomas Félix-François

Our site on the web: Frédéric Mastellari

Chief dispenser of care: Marc Pujo

Dance teacher: Christophe Igor, assisted by Valérie Steiner

Photography: Michèle Laurent

Instrument-maker: Marcel Ladurelle

Night watch: Azizullah Hamrah

Maintenance: Janos Nemeth, Tsering Tsang, Sonam Chodon

Thank you to all those whom we desired to please and who returned the favor a hundredfold:

The interns and apprentices, attentive and discreet observers from the whole wide world: Marie Braun, Héloïsa Costa, Luis Guenel, Flavia Lopes Rodrigues, Lena Pitwell, Rosite Val;

The Theatre Studies students from the Sorbonne Nouvelle (Paris III university), priceless reinforcements, all members of young university theatre troupes: Paul Balagué, Raphaël Bocobza, Déborah Brian, Zoé Briau, Hanae Brossert, Jacqueline Chavanon, Silvia Circu, Nina Cottin, Lucas Dardaine, Elena Diego Marina, Magaly Dos Santos, Romane Finot, Paul Éloi Forget, Juliette Gazet, Véra Grunberg, Sarah Jamaleddin, Carmen Kautto, Morgane Lacaille, Pauline Lacaille, Laurent Lenoir, Anna Marionthiers, Judith Marx, Clara Normand, Laura Pardonnet, Lucile Perain, Ana Perez, Paolo Sclar, Raphaël Setty, Myriam Soignet, Irène Tchernooutsan, Baptiste Vareille, Arthur Viadieu, Clémentine Vignais;

The DTMS (technician in performing arts careers diploma) class of the Lycée des métiers du bois Léonard de Vinci, and their professeurs Anne Bottard and Thierry Decroix.

Thank you to Jean-Pierre Mongarny and the Crédit Coopératif foundation; to agnès b. for her patience; to Françoise and Lorenzo Benedetti, for their loyalty.

Thank you to Madeleine Favre, for her permanent friendly and medical vigilance,

Anne Lacombe, for her discreet and delicate gaze, and her work as an archivist of the creative arts,

Béatrice Picon-Vallin for her ceaseless, passionate, and immensely benevolent accompaniment,

Jean-Claude Lallias for his unceasing battle for artistic education,

Michèle Benjamin for her expert advice on special effects,

Marie Constant, Gérard Hardy, and our friend Thérèse Boareto, "Jeannette," for their friendly advice on costumes,

Fabrice Martolini (Tapis Sans Frontières),

Corinne Gibello-Bernette (BnF – National Library of France),

Edwige Capdeville and Francis Capdeville.

In Edinburgh, thank you to Dan Fearn (Walker Slater), Sylvie Slater, and Rod Slater.

Thank you to the Lorialets company (Matthieu Coblentz, Vincent Lefevre, Caroline Panzera), the Théâtre de la Tempête, the Théâtre de l'Épée de Bois, the Théâtre de l'Aquarium, the Parc floral de Paris, the museum of Reims, the museum of Amiens (Gauthier Gillmann, Olivia Voisin), The Acting Company (New York).

And thank you to all those who generously gave us a few hours of their time, or more, and who are not named here.

 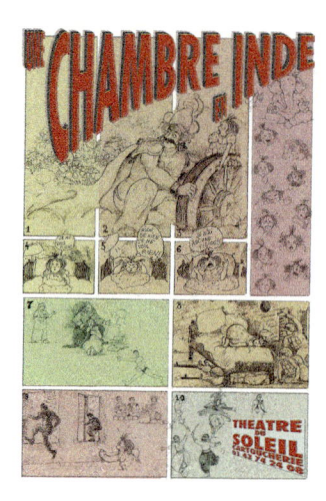 

Une chambre en Inde [*A Room in India*]

Théâtre du Soleil collective creation
In harmony with Hélène Cixous
And the exceptional participation of Kalaimamani Purisai Kannappa
  Sambandan Thambiran
Premiere: November 5, 2016, at the Cartoucherie.

With:
THE TROUPE
Cornelia, assistant: Hélène Cinque
Astrid, administrator: voice of Thérèse Spirli
Constantin Lear, director: voice of Vladimir Ant
Giuliano, an actor: Duccio Bellugi-Vannuccini
Cassandre, an actor: Shaghayegh Beheshti
Clara, an actor: Dominique Jambert
Jean-Paul, an actor: Martial Jacques
Saad, Iraqi actor: Samir Abdul Jabbar Saed
Etienne, an actor: Maurice Durozier
Yacine, intern participating in a rehabilitation program: Sébastien Brottet-Michel
Emese, Hungarian intern: Judit Jancsó
Rémy, an actor: Sylvain Jailloux
Amélie, an actor: Eve Doe Bruce
FRENCH OFFICIALS
Nicolas Carré, of the Alliance française: Sylvain Jailloux
Inspector Dallègre: Duccio Bellugi-Vannuccini
THE GUEST HOUSE AND ITS HOUSEHOLD
Madame Sita Murti, owner: Nirupama Nityanandan
Jayaraj, the Madman: Agustin Letelier
Gopal, night watchman: Taher Baig
Rani, servant: Wazhma Tota Khil
Rani's father: Vijayan Panikkaveettil
Servants: Farid Gul Ahmad, Andrea Marchant, Aref Bahunar
THE LITTLE CITY
Lieutenant Ganesh-Ganesh: Omid Rawendah

Kanaan, his second-in-command: Shafiq Kohi
Salim, Madame Murti's rickshaw-wallah: Omid Rawendah
S.S. Loganathan, a mafioso from the BJP, the Hindu nationalist party: Duccio
    Bellugi-Vannuccini
His henchmen: Sayed Ahmad Hashimi, Shafiq Kohi, Seear Kohi, Vijayan
    Panikkaveettil, Ghulam Reza Rajabi
Ravi Lookatmepur, maharajah and patron of the arts: Maurice Durozier
Ravi Lookatmepur's rickshaw-wallah: Sayed Ahmad Hashimi
Pimp: Omid Rawendah
His henchman: Ghulam Reza Rajabi
VISITATIONS
Lear and Cordelia: Seietsu Onochi, Man-Waï Fok
Monkeys: Seear Kohi, Arman Saribekyan
Bearer of News: Taher Baig
William Shakespeare: Maurice Durozier
His little page: Dominique Jambert
Faun: Martial Jacques
Seven Talibans: Duccio Bellugi-Vannuccini, Sébastien Brottet-Michel, Aref
    Bahunar, Samir Abdul Jabbar Saed, Shafiq Kohi, Ghulam Reza Rajabi,
    Vijayan Panikkaveettil
Cinema in the desert: Sébastien Brottet-Michel, Martial Jacques, Duccio
    Bellugi-Vannuccini, Samir Abdul Jabbar Saed, Judit Jancsó, Agustin
    Letelier, Shaghayegh Beheshsti, Shafiq Kohi, Aref Bahunar, Farid Gul
    Ahmad, Sylvain Jailloux, Ghulam Reza Rajabi, Eve Doe Bruce
The little white cow (alternating): Ghulam Reza Rajabi, Arman Saribekyan
Krishna (alternating): Naweed Kohi, Palani Murugan
Pakistan: Sébastien Brottet-Michel, Dominique Jambert, Shaghayegh Beheshti,
    Duccio Bellugi-Vannuccini, Maurice Durozier, Nirupama Nityanandan,
    Wazhma Tota Khil, Aref Bahunar, Farid Gul Ahmad, Shafiq Kohi,
    Vijayan Panikkaveettil
Demolition permit: Martial Jacques, Seear Kohi, Aref Bahunar
Mahatma Gandhi: Samir Abdul Jabbar Saed
A memory: Ravinder Singh, young lover of yesteryear: Seear Kohi
Madame Murti's brother: Aref Bahunar
Henchmen: Shafiq Kohi, Omid Rawendah, Sébastien Brottet-Michel
Two worlds: Martial Jacques, Samir Abdul Jabbar Saed, Duccio Bellugi-
    Vannuccini, Alice Milléquant, Arman Saribekyan
And: Sylvain Jailloux, Dominique Jambert, Judit Jancsó
A Syrian night's dream: Maurice Durozier, Sylvain Jailloux, Wazhma Tota
    Khil, Martial Jacques, Eve Doe Bruce, Samir Abdul Jabbar Saed, Ghulam
    Reza Rajabi
And: Sayed Ahmad Hashimi, Sébastien Brottet-Michel
Anton Chekhov: Arman Saribekyan
Irina, Masha, Olga: Dominique Jambert, Andrea Marchant, Alice Milléquant
Phantom: Duccio Bellugi-Vannuccini
His companions: Farid Gul Ahmad, Quentin Lashermes
AND, AT THE BEGINNING OF ALL THIS, THE MAHABHARATA:
Musicians and singers:
Thérèse Spirli: taal (cymbals), chorus leader
Marie-Jasmine Cocito: taal (cymbals), first voice
Aziz Hamrah: harmonium
Ya-Hui Liang: mridangam and dholak (percussion)
Andrea Marchant: mukavinai (Tamil oboe)
Quentin Lashermes: voice
Alice Milléquant: voice
Man-Waï Fok: voice
Chorus: the entire troupe

Katyakarans: Shafiq Kohi and Arman Saribekyan, alternating with Eve Doe Bruce and Dominique Jambert

THE RAPE OF DRAUPADI

Draupadi: Judit Jancsó, alternating with Shaghayegh Beheshti

King Duryodhana: Sébastien Brottet-Michel, alternating with Seear Kohi

Dushasana, his brother: Duccio Bellugi-Vannuccini, alternating with Omid Rawendah

Five Pandava brothers: Aref Bahunar, Taher Baig, Farid Gul Ahmad, Sayed Ahmad Hashimi, Ghulam Reza Rajabi

Krishna: Naweed Kohi

THE DEATH OF KARNA

Karna: Sébastien Brottet-Michel, alternating with Omid Rawendah

Ponnourouvi: Shaghayegh Beheshti, alternating with Judit Jancsó

Let us not forget, at the theatre entrance, **"The Grand Bazar Police Security Brigade,"** which includes, alternatingly: Farid Gul Ahmad, Mohd Haroon Amanullah, Aref Bahunar, Taher Baig, Man-Waï Fok, Aziz Hamrah, Sayed Ahmad Hashimi, Samir Abdul Jabbar Saed, Shafiq Kohi, Quentin Lashermes, Ghulam Reza Rajabi, Arman Saribekyan, Wazhma Tota Khil

Under the vigilant direction of: Vincent Lefèvre and Vincent Mangado, with Astrid Grant

With the precious counsel of: Yves Bernard

The music of the play is the work of Jean-Jacques Lemêtre who also performs it, with the help of Ya-Hui Liang and Marie-Jasmine Cocito.

Master and depositary of the art of Terukkuttu: Kalaimamani Purisai Kannappa Sambandan Thambiran

His assistant: Palani Murugan

Carnatic singing teacher: Emmanuelle Martin

Mridangam (percussion) teacher: Kesavan Narmapallam Arumuga Gowder

Mukavinai (Tamil oboe) teacher: Sri Thirugnanam

Ambassadors unto the Kingdom of Terrukkuttu, interpreters and translators of Tamil: Koumarane Valavane and Nirupama Nityanandan, who also acted as Tamil and dance rehearsal leader.

The lights of the play are the work of Virginie Le Coënt, Lila Meynard, and Geoffroy Adragna, under the expert and benevolent eye of Elsa Revol.

The sounds were conceived and harvested by Thérèse Spirli, Marie-Jasmine Cocito, and Jean-Jacques Lemêtre. They were governed by Thérèse Spirli.

The costumes of the play are the work of Marie-Hélène Bouvet, Nathalie Thomas, and Annie Tran, with the help of Élodie Madebos, Mohd Haroon Amanullah, Elisabeth Cerqueira, Simona Grassano, Sarah Bartesaghi-Gallo.

The paintings and patinas of the sets, furniture, and ground are the work of Elena Antsiferova.

David Buizard tamed all sorts of wood and materials, underground, on the ground, and in the air. The walls, doors, windows, bed and tables, blinds and sidewalks, among other things, are his work and that of his little armada made up of Aline Borsari, Maixence Bauduin, Samuel Capdeville, Ismaël Dahhan, Victor Langlare, Matthieu Le Breton, Clément Vernerey, Roland Zimmerman.

Kaveh Kishipour and Benjamin Bottinelli-Hahn tamed all sorts of metals, bamboos, and cements, underground, on the ground, and in the air. The entrance kiosk and all sorts of ties and tricks, visible or invisible, are their work, with the help of Martin Claude.

Kaveh Kishipour, Benjamin Bottinelli-Hahn, and David Buizard are also the conceivers and constructors of the new seats arranged in tiers in the main hall.

Chloé Bucas upholstered them and studded them, with the help of Vivian Guillermin, Cédric Lasne, Macarena Moreno Puig, Tristan Paoli.

The wall paintings of the Welcome Area are the work of Anne-Lise Galavielle and her little team made up of Céleste Gangolphe and Pauline Lebeau, helped and supported by many interns and so many friends, whose names will appear below.

The great luminous frescoes of the Welcome Area are the work of Anne-Lise Galavielle, and their crafting that of Virginie Le Coënt, Geoffroy Adragna, Lila Meynard, with the constant and patient aid of Ana Amelia Dosse, Mojtaba Habibi, Mostafa Habibi Shandiz, Saboor Sahak, Frédérique Voruz, and all the actors.

The hair and wigs are by Jean-Sébastien Merle.

The Terukkuttu headdresses and ornaments are the work of Elena Antsiferova and Xevi Ribas, powerfully assisted by the interns whose names will appear below.

The little white cow is the work of Erhard Stiefel, with the help of Simona Grassano.

The puppets are the work of Elena Antsiferova, Xevi Ribas, Pierre Bellivier, and Erhard Stiefel, with the help of Aran Ribas and Vern Ribas.

Certain props are the work of Xevi Ribas and François Bombaglia.

The glass lamps are the work of Simon Muller, artisan glassmaker from Nantes.

The ramps are the work of Sylouane Gafner, laboratory artisan from Meudon.

The hedges and plantings are the work of Maurice Durozier and Seietsu Onochi.

Étienne Lemasson made this all possible by being the Grand Quartermaster of all these flotillas, and ensuring that their supplies of munitions, correct information, and encouraging inspiration were topped up at all times.

Successive director's assistants, according to their availabilities: Hélène Cinque, Lucile Cocito, Suzana Thomaz, Nadia Reeb

Stage managers: Alice Milléquant, Quentin Lashermes

Daily filming of rehearsals: Suzana Thomaz, Lucile Cocito

Transcription of improvisations, and supertitling: Marie Constant, with Suzana Thomaz

Prompter and diction teacher: Françoise Berge

Original pilot fish: Juliana Carneiro da Cunha

The brigade of assistants, interns, and friends from the whole world, whose kindness and help were invaluable:

Wood: Xue Chao Huang, Mathias Vizcaino Lopez, Tanguy Wilnick

Costumes: Nathalie Alexdade, Marine Baney, Juliette D'Avout, Anna Friedhi, Joséphine Guin, Nadjes Hady, Maïté Ouceni, Sabine Tisseyre, Irma Viguier

Electricity: Annaëlle Marsille-Medun, Ouamourou Meïte, Louis Sady, Arto Yuzbashyan

Crafting: Diana Krasovska, Nora Sandholm-Azémar

Painting: Morgane Benyamina, Fabrice Cany, Vinciane Clémens, Marine Dillard, Dulan Haond, Sylvie Le Vessier, Clara Marchebout, Andressa Moretti Silva, Suganthi Natarajan, Nicolas Oriol, Lola Seiler, Marlène Soumboud, Georgia Tsipoura, Clothilde Valette, Morgan Valle, Eloi Weiss

And at all these stations, the precious, indispensable help of all the actors.

All the major affairs: Charles-Henri Bradier

Technical and organizational affairs: Étienne Lemasson

Administrative affairs: Astrid Renoux, with the help of Marie Constant

And accounting affairs: Rolande Fontaine

Public affairs: Liliana Andreone, Sylvie Papandréou, Svetlana Dukovska, Margot Blanc, Eugénie Agoudjian

International and humanitarian affairs: Elaine Méric, with Marie-Anne Bernard

Editorial affairs: Franck Pendino

Ticket sales affairs: Maria Adroher Baus, Luciana Velocci Silva, Caroline Panzera, with the alternating assistance of Charlotte Andres, Ariane Bégoin, Pedro Castro Neves, Olivia Corsini, Delphine Cottu, Yann

Dénécé, Gérard Hardy, Lauren Houda Hussein, Sheila Maeda, Ido Shaked, Frédérique Voruz

Kitchenmasters: Karim Gougam, Virginie Collombet, Mimlu Sen, Paban das Baul, Hamideh Ghadirzadeh, with the help of Asef Mawdoodi and Yvan Inofre

The alternating bar brigades: Aline Borsari, Ana Dosse, Mojtaba Habibi, Mostafa Habibi Shandiz, Alain Khouani, Naweed Kohi, Dan Kostenbaum, François Lepage, Justine Louvel, Jérôme Marchand, Valérie Pujol, Arun Rahimi, Nadia Reeb, Masoma Rezaie, Shohreh Sabaghy, Saboor Sahak, Nora Sandholm-Azémar, Harold Savary, Kristina Skorikova

Posters and publicity leaflet: Thomas Félix-François, with Catherine Schaub-Abkarian

Program: Catherine Schaub-Abkarian, with Thomas Félix-François

Our site on the web: Marine Quiniou, graphics by Thomas Félix-François, with drawings by Clémentine Yelnik and Catherine Schaub-Abkarian

Chief dispenser of care: Marc Pujo, with the alternating assistance of Fanny Pujo, Philippe Fargier, Anca Grosu

Photographers: Michèle Laurent, with Anne Lacombe

Instrument-maker: Marcel Ladurelle

Night watch (alternating): Nowrouz Soltan, Hakim Beg Rahmani

Housekeeping and maintenance: Dickey Khanchung, Janos Nemeth, Nora Sandholm-Azémar

Cartoucherie shuttle (alternating): Simon Lubin, Nadine Brunet, and Thomas Gaudin

Thank you to all those whom we desired to please by welcoming them and who returned the pleasure a hundredfold:

From Afghanistan: Naweed Kohi, Arun Rahimi

From Brazil: Vinicius Bustani Valente, Juan

From Chile: Pamela Lopez, Macarena Moreno Puig, Ivan Parra, Claudio Vega Lopez

From France: Alice Beroud, Alicia Gicquel, Rosalie Grand D'Esnon, Marie Lauricella, Olivier Nahmani, Mariam Soukouna, Ambre Stertzel, Charis Taplin, Joelle Varenne, Marie-Amandine Fredj, Hasmik Asatryan

From India: Tamilarasi Shanmugam, Thilagavathi Palani (Kattaikkuttu Sangam), Satish Thiagarajan

From Taiwan: Wen Yi-Chang (University of Taipei), Chang Han-Kung, Chen Yi-Chun

In India, thank you:

To our friend Rajeev Sethi

To the Théâtre Indianostrum: Koumarane Valavane, and Savee Sathishkumar, Banupriya Jagadeesan, Maneesh VM, Santhosh Kumar, Suganthi Natarajan, Subatra Robert, Shivanandan, Vasanth Selvam, Shilpa Mudbi, S. Avinash, Vetri VM, Living Smile Vidhya, Kalieaswari Srinivasan, Siddanth Sundar, Cordis Paldano, Bhakyam

To the Kattaikkuttu Sangam School: Hanne M. de Buin, P. Rajagopal

To the Théâtre Sri Mariyamman Therukoothu Nadaga Saba: Kalaimamani V. Dhasnamoorthy

To our donors: Venu Srinavasan, Claude Marius, Olivier Litvine, Anne Falcone, with Nicolas Deleau

To the French Consulate in Pondicherry: Philippe Janvier-Kamiyama, Consul general; Isabelle de Marguerye, deputy consul in charge of social affairs; Hélène Charpin, deputy consul and head of chancellery; Gauri Shankar Pattanaik, Christine Nerrière, visa services

To the Institut français in Delhi: François Vandeville, cultural counselor; Jean-Yves Coquelin, deputy cultural counselor; Estelle Berruyer, cultural attachée

To the Pondicherry Alliance française: Olivier Litvine, director; Lalit Varma, president; Alexandre Legay, intern

To the Pondicherry Lycée français

To the Union Territory of Pondicherry: Mihir Vardan, I. A. S., tourism secretary

To our hosts in Pondicherry: Olivier Litvine and his family, Isabelle de Marguerye and her family, Alberto and Françoise Crespo, Cécile and Nathanaël Hoorelbeke, Cécile and Philippe Dariel, Christine Pozzobon, Maren Sell, Marie and Albert Desjardins, Frédéric Vidal, Roselyne Weill, Muriel Bertille, Nathalie Blondeau, Anne Falcone and Nicolas Deleau, Virginie Malé, Zoé Headley, Pierre Grard (director of the Pondicherry Institut Français)

To our guides and friends: Tapas Bhatt, V.R. Devika, Nissar Allana, Vinay Kumar (Théâtre Adi Shakti, Pondicherry)

To our "sherpas": Thierry, Valou, Maïa and Titouan Adam-Delaplace, Catherine and Philippe Bernard, Thierry Lepreux, Isabelle de Marguerye, Philippe and Lisiane Duval, Anne Falcone and Nicolas Deleau

And to the Hôtel de Pondichéry in the persons of Christie and Jayaraj.

Thank you to: Wes Williams, Fiona Macintosh, Olivier Taplin (Archives of Performances of Greek and Roman Theatre, Oxford University), Louise Chantal (Oxford Playhouse), Lucy Maycock (North Wall), Anne Simonin (Oxford Maison française)

Dounia Bouzar, Smaïn Laacher, Emmanuel Wallon

Pascal Brice, Christophe Musitelli, Catherine Baratti-Elbaz, mayor of the twelfth district in Paris

Milena Salvini, Eliane Béranger (Centre Mandapa)

Gilles Brion, Ombeline Merel (Cabinet Brion)

Nathalie Hance, Marc Audouin (Crédit Coopératif), Blandine Vulin (PIE), Judith Laure Mamou-Mani (France Active), Guillaume de Vauxmoret (Ecofi Investissements)

Dominique Mahé, Christian Cortes, Annick Valette, Olivier Ruthardt, Fabrice Badreau (MAIF),

Our friends: Myriam Azencot, Eugenio Barba, Thérèse Boaretto, Madeleine Favre, Louis Joinet, Yann Lemêtre, Elaine Méric, Gaëlle Méric, Béatrice Picon-Vallin, Françoise Robin, Bernard Sobel, Bruno Tackels

For the loan of spaces and/or equipment: Dominique Fortin (Théâtre de l'Aquarium), Lucia Bensasson, Jean-François Dusigne, Federica Buffoli (ARTA), Antonio Diaz-Florian, Miguel Meireles (Théâtre de l'Épée de Bois), le Théâtre de la Tempête, the CDC Atelier de Paris-Carolyn Carlson

For their presence at the reception of rehearsal rooms: Nicolas Roy, Christian Dupont, Patrice Riera, Arthur Viadieu, with Clara Drzewuski, Vincent Lenfant

For her Sunday watch over the bookstore: Sylvie Hudelot

For their precious sewing assistance: Ysabel de Maisonneuve, Claire-Marie Guillemot, Sheila Maeda, Paulette Michel

For their brave pedagogical crusade and their loyalty: Jean-Claude Lallias, Marie-Laure Basuyaux, Cécile Roy (Pièce (dé)montée, Canopé)

For his kind accompaniment: Michel Janin (Generale Décors)

For their patient loyalty and kind accompaniment during our masonry work: Nicolas Monniot, Julio Rodrigues (Plamon et Cie)

The students in the theatre class at the Collège Chateaubriand de Villeneuve-sur-Yonne:

Tom Bendler, Agathe Brayotel, Lisa Chauvineau, Iris Cherel, Enzo Crochet, Cassy Denis, Romain Gautier, Morgane Grimaux, Mayliss Guerin, Emilie Lasson, Maxime Lefort, Lucas Lemaître, Damien Maas, Yanis Madaoui, Océane Mazars, Emilien Michaud, Bastien Michel, Simon Orechowa, Océane Pinard, Amaryllis Plait, Aurélia Ponce, Mathilde Rostykus, Sofiane Sefrioun, Elodie Sesena, Cyliann Tournier, Adrien Vermeulen, Angel Wierczynski, Guélan Zaour

And their teachers: Stéphane Mahdi, principal education counselor; Sylvie Mortier, physical education teacher; Charlotte Rafaéli, physical sciences teacher; Sylvestre Thibert, mathematics teacher, Camille Puech, English teacher; Jenifer Jaffeux, English teacher; Séverine Torres, French teacher; Jérôme Rouillon, French teacher

The young *troisième* students who chose to do their internship with us: Bettina Lobel, Justine Bergogne, Raphaëlle Cornevin, Zoïa Mossour

The DTMS (technician in performing arts careers diploma) class of the Lycée des métiers du bois Léonard de Vinci, who repaired our garden tables.

Finally, thank you:

To Martine Franck, who, even from beyond, continues, with her photographs of India, to send us signs of affection;

And in the same way, to Guy-Claude François.

And thank you to all those who generously gave us a few hours of their time, or more, and who are not named here.

Kanata, Épisode 1: La Controverse [*Kanata, Episode 1: The Controversy*]

Directed by Robert Lepage
Premiere: December 15, 2018, at the Cartoucherie.

With the actors of the Théâtre du Soleil, namely, in order of appearance:
Leyla Farrozhad, restorer at the National Gallery of Canada: Shaghayegh Beheshti
Jacques Pelletier, curator: Vincent Mangado
Tobie, a documentary film maker: Martial Jacques
Landlady: Man Waï Fok
Miranda, artist and painter: Dominique Jambert
Ferdinand, an actor: Sébastien Brottet-Michel
Rosa, a social worker at the safe injection center: Eve Doe Bruce
Tanya Farrozhad: Frédérique Voruz
Accent coach; nurse at safe injection center: Sylvain Jailloux

Newman, police commissioner; director of safe injection center: Astrid Grant
Marcello, a police officer: Duccio Bellugi-Vannuccini
Other police officers: Omid Rawendah, Taher Baig, Aref Bahunar, Jean-Sébastien Merle, Shafiq Kohi, Saboor Dilawar
Robert Pickton: Maurice Durozier
Restaurant staff: Shafiq Kohi and Sayed Ahmad Hashimi
Acting coach: Seear Kohi
Student actors: Miguel Nogueira, Omid Rawendah, Ghulam Reza Rajabi, Shafiq Kohi, Sayed Ahmad Hashimi
Sarah, Tanya's friend: Alice Milléquant
Ariel, the pharmacist of Hastings Street; Oblate missionary: Arman Saribekyan
Ken, Sarah's friend: Ghulam Reza Rajabi
Dealer on Hastings Street: Shafiq Kohi
Louise: Nirupama Nityanandan
Morgue employees: Andrea Marchant and Agustin Letelier
An actress; a nurse at the safe injection center: Camille Grandville
Producer: Ana Amelia Dosse
And in Hastings Street: Aline Borsari, Ana Amelia Dosse, Camille Grandville, Andrea Marchant, Wazhma Tota Khil, Omid Rawendah, Taher Baig, Aref Bahunar, Sayed Ahmad Hashimi, Miguel Nogueira, Saboor Dilawar, Agustin Letelier, Samir Abdul Jabbar Saed

Dramaturg: Michel Nadeau
Art director: Steve Blanchet
Set design and props: Ariane Sauvé, with Benjamin Bottinelli, David Buizard, Martin Claude, Pascal Gallepe, Kaveh Kishipour, Étienne Lemasson, and the help of Judit Jancsò, Naweed Kohi, Thomas Verhaag, Clément Vernerey, Roland Zimmermann
Paintings and patinas: Elena Antsiferova, Xevi Ribas, with the help of Sylvie Le Vessier, Lola Seiler, Mylène Meignier
Lights: Lucie Bazzo, with Geoffroy Adragna, Lila Meynard
Music: Ludovic Bonnier
Sound: Yann Lemêtre, Thérèse Spirli, Marie-Jasmine Cocito
Images and projection: Pedro Pires, with Étienne Frayssinet, Antoine J. Chami, Vincent Sanjivy, Thomas Lampis, Gilles Quatreboeuf
Supertitles: Suzana Thomaz
Costumes: Marie-Hélène Bouvet, Nathalie Thomas, Annie Tran
Hair and wigs: Jean-Sébastien Merle
Prompter and diction teacher: Françoise Berge
Director's assistant: Lucile Cocito
Thank you to the fourth- and fifth-year students at the ENSAD (National School of Decorative Arts) and their teachers Elise Capdenat and Annabel Vergne, as well as to the students and graduates of the DTMS (technician in performing arts careers diploma) of the Lycée Léonard de Vinci (Paris): Louise Morizot, Alexis Delair, Mathilde Apert, Noémie Notseck, Emeline Jenger, Gaëlle Lebris, Mathilde Coursault, Théophile Carrot, and Caroline Siau, and their professors Anne Bottard, Thierry Decroix, Julie Strauss, and Franck Vallet.
Thank you to: Marie Germain, Clément Laillet, Saphir Reid, Faustine Roux, Joséphine Guin, Esther Genoux, Emeline Antiopermo, Adèle Billot-Morel, Salomé Vanderdriessche, Ming Liang, Melissa Nibbio, Noémie Jarry, Emma Chapon, Baptiste Di Nicolo, Alice Jeannerat (sewing reinforcements),
Martine Loit (props reinforcement),
Mordjane Djaouchi (acrobatics counselor),
Rea Nolan (English dialects consultant),
Catherine Schaub,

Erhard Stiefel.

The development of the project benefited from Ex Machina's asssistance. In this sense, the following people also participated in the production: David Leclerc (video), Olivier Bourque and Mateo Thébaudeau (technical direction), Benoît Brunet-Poirier (video management), Gabrielle Doucet (creating the painting), Virginie Leclerc (props), Rick Miller (voice of Robert Pickton), Marie-Soleil Bélaner (musician – erhu), Tommy Gauthier (musician – violin), Viviane Paradis (production).

With the support of the Banff Centre for Arts and Creativity in Alberta (Canada) and Simon Fraser University Woodward's Cultural Programs in Vancouver, British Columbia (Canada).

All the major affairs: Charles-Henri Bradier

Technical and organizational affairs: Étienne Lemasson, with the help of Pascal Gallepe

Administrative affairs: Astrid Renoux, with the help of Joséphine Supe

And accounting affairs: Rolande Fontaine

Public affairs: Liliana Andreone, Sylvie Papandréou, Svetlana Dukovska, Margot Blanc

International affairs: Elaine Méric

Editorial affairs: Franck Pendino

Ticket sales affairs: Maria Adroher Baus, Eugénie Agoudjian, Pedro Castro Neves

Barmasters and kitchenmasters: Karim Gougam, Paban das Baul, Mimlu Sen, Hélène Cinque

Poster and publicity leaflet: Thomas Félix-François

Chief dispenser of care: Marc Pujo

Photographer: Michèle Laurent

Alternating bar brigades: Maixence Bauduin, Lucas Dardaine, Magdalena Galindo, Farid Gul-Ahmad, Azizulah Hamrah, Alain Khouani, Naweed Kohi, François Lepage, Quentin Lashermes, Ya-Hui Liang, Justine Louvel, Vijayan Pannikkaveettil, Valérie Pujol, Masoma Rezaie, Shohreh Sabaghy, Kristina Skorikova, Martin Van Eeckhoudt

Housekeeping and maintenance: Dickey Khanchung, Janos Nemeth, Nora Sandholm-Azémar

Night watch (alternating): Nowrouz Soltan, Hakim Beg Rahmani, Mohd Haroon Amanullah

Macbeth (rehearsal). On the moor, the first "trees" of Birnam Wood slowly emerge from the midst, heading in the direction of Dunsinane. The invitation to resist Evil actively is summed up in the finale by the line: "Thanks to all at once and to each one." Photo by Michèle Laurent.

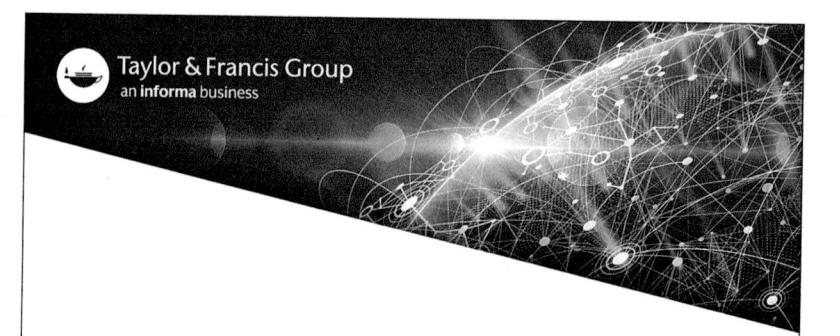